Performing Music
in the Age of Recording

Robert Philip

YALE UNIVERSITY PRESS

NEW HAVEN AND LONDON

Copyright © 2004 Robert Philip

2 4 6 8 10 9 7 5 3 1

For information about this and other Yale University Press publications, please contact
U.S. Office: sales.press@yale.edu   yalebooks.com
Europe Office: sales@yaleup.co.uk   www.yaleup.co.uk

Set in Bembo by Northern Phototypesetting Co. Ltd, Bolton
Printed in Great Britain by St Edmundsbury Press Ltd, Bury St Edmunds

Library of Congress Control Number 2004100136

ISBN 0–300–10246–1

A catalogue record for this book is available from the British Library

Contents

Acknowledgments   vii

Introduction   1

1 Life before Recordings   4

2 The Experience of Recording   26

3 Ensemble and Freedom: Orchestras   63

4 Ensemble and Freedom: Chamber Groups and Pianists   104

5 Questions of Authority: the Composer   140

6 Questions of Authority: Schools of Playing   183

7 Questions of Authority: the Archaeological Approach   204

8 Listening Back: Lessons from the Twentieth Century   231

Notes   253

Index   266

Acknowledgments

My first thanks should go to Malcolm Gerratt and Robert Baldock at Yale University Press. They originally proposed quite a different book, but when I said that I wanted to write this one they accepted it enthusiastically, and waited patiently for it. My colleagues at the Open University have been most supportive throughout the project. Timothy Day at the National Sound Archive gave me an important platform for my ideas by inviting me to inaugurate the Saul Seminars at the British Library. Peter Hill, Erich Höbarth, Stephen Hough, Steven Isserlis, Bill Lloyd and John McCabe allowed me to quote from private conversations and correspondence. Paula James gave me the interview that she recorded with her violinist father, Alfred Deahl. Edward Johnson sent me letters from Leopold Stokowski and Adrian Boult. Andrew Keener, whom I interviewed, allowed me to include an example of his editing notes (a glimpse into a generally secret world). Stephen Ferre, of New Notations Computer Services, set the music examples.

This book would not have been possible without the help of my partner, Susan Tomes, a musician and writer of unique insights. She and her colleagues in the Florestan Trio, Anthony Marwood and Richard Lester, have given me privileged access to music-making at the highest level, and to all the preparation that goes into it. Susan herself has not only read my drafts, made suggestions, and allowed me to quote from her own writings, but, more importantly, has kept up a constant dialogue about music and life. She has made me aware that many more aspects of the subtle art of performance are expressible in words than I had previously thought. And through her inspiration the book has acquired a scope that I could not have imagined when I started.

Introduction

If you walk into any large music shop in the early twenty-first century you find the racks full of historical recordings. They have become so commonplace that they are no longer in a separate section of their own, but side by side with the latest digital recordings. The popular cheap label Naxos has a growing catalogue of historical recordings by great pianists, violinists, conductors and singers. In the modern marketing world this can mean only one thing: that people are buying historical recordings in large numbers.

When I first became interested in historical recordings in the late 1960s, and began to broadcast about them, very few were available in the shops. HMV's Great Recordings of the Century included Schnabel's Beethoven, Casals's Bach, and Lieder sung by Elisabeth Schumann. Menuhin and Elgar's recording of his Violin Concerto was available, and there were some early recordings of opera singers – Caruso, Gigli, Melba, et al. The British Institute of Recorded Sound, a pioneering enterprise which later became the National Sound Archive at the British Library, had opened in 1955. But the great majority of recordings from the first half of the twentieth century were generally forgotten, left in dusty piles in attics.

In 1968 I began work on a Ph.D. dissertation at Cambridge, on changing orchestral style from 1920 to 1950.[1] I was the first research student to have tackled historical recordings at any university (so far as I am aware). I frequently met people in the academic world who did not regard what I was doing as proper academic research at all. When I wrote to the professor of music at Oxford, Sir Jack Westrup, to ask whether I might be able to do this research at Oxford, he replied, 'I feel bound to tell you that I could not recommend this topic to the Faculty as appropriate for research.'

'Performance Practice' had become a respectable academic field, but it was restricted to the study of traditional sources of historical evidence: printed texts, manuscripts, scores, treatises and, increasingly, instruments. My research was suspect for two reasons. In the first place it involved listening to records, which was something to be done in one's spare time for relaxation, and was not regarded as a serious occupation. Secondly, the period of performance I was studying was very recent. The idea that the playing of one's grandparents might be of historical interest was dismissed by many academics. Even those who were interested were often no more than amused by the sounds of unfashionable swooping and scampering. How could the old-fashioned and quaint have anything useful to teach us about the history of performance practice?

But this was precisely the point – and, to be fair, it was not lost on the most intelligent and open-minded academics. It seemed to me that there was a gaping hole between the sort of research that resulted in neat, tidy, modern-sounding playing of Bach and Handel, which was then confidently asserted to be true to the style of the distant past, and the actual performance of the recent past, which was dismissed as 'sloppy' and 'old-fashioned'. At what point in history did the 'historical' end and the 'old-fashioned' begin? The question revealed an absurdity: that researchers were confident in recreating the unknowable sound of an early performance of *Messiah*, and yet dismissed the actual sounds of Elgar's own performances as irrelevant (if they even knew of their existence).

Now, at the beginning of the twenty-first century, both halves of that equation have changed dramatically. Historical recordings are increasingly the subject of academic study at universities across the world and are beginning to have an impact on practising musicians. And, partly as a result of this, scholars and musicians are less inclined than they were to claim 'authenticity' in reconstructing more distant performance practices. You only have to play a recording from the 1920s or earlier to realise that the past remains 'another country' where things were done differently from today. This was the subject of my book, *Early Recordings and Musical Style: Changing Tastes in Instrumental Performance, 1900–1950* (Cambridge, 1992). In it I described some of the most striking features of early twentieth-century performing styles, and suggested that they provided important evidence for the ways in which practices change over time. On the one hand, early recordings strongly suggest what nineteenth-century playing must have been like. On the other hand, recordings show how our modern styles and approaches have developed. One of the conclusions of this study was the realisation that it is futile to suppose that musicians can actually transport themselves back to the thinking and practices of earlier centuries. Much of the strangeness of early recordings is undocumented in other sources, and therefore the documents of earlier periods, before the existence of recordings, can give us only fragmentary evidence. The ways in which we piece together this evidence are bound to be heavily influenced by the taste of our own time, and there is no escape from that. This obvious truth, which was then striking enough to provoke a leading article in *The Times*, is now much more widely understood than it was ten years ago.

This second book is in some ways a sequel to the first, but is in other ways quite different. It looks at the broader picture of twentieth-century recorded performance, and discusses the trends across those hundred years. As before, the main emphasis is on the strangeness, from our perspective, of the styles and practices of the early decades of the century. And, as before, the main concentration is on instrumental playing. But I also consider areas of the subject that were barely touched on in the earlier book: the changing lives of musicians, the experience of making records, the increasing impact of recordings on musicians and audiences, and the state of music-making that we have reached at the beginning of the twenty-first century. I also look at the ways in which recordings shed light on the different sources of authority for playing styles and interpretation: the authority of the composer (either as performer or as approver of other musicians' performances), the schools of playing that were so much a feature of early twentieth-century playing, and the appeal to the authority of historical evidence, which erupted in the 'Early Music' movement in the second half of the century.

One of the reasons for writing this book is a feeling that a lot of important questions about the performance of classical music are simply not receiving enough thought. In the age of globalisation and mass marketing it is easy just to sit back uncritically and accept the perfectly edited and beautifully packaged products we are given. We are privileged above all previous generations in having access to whatever music we want, whenever we want it. More than a century of recordings has been preserved, and we can listen to the playing of Rachmaninoff and orchestras conducted by Elgar or Richard Strauss, recorded a lifetime ago. No previous generation has had such easy access to music, or such an ability to leap across space and time to find it. And yet the evidence that recordings present is like all other historical evidence. It needs to be examined critically, its context needs to be understood. Only then can we come to see what recordings are, what they have done to us, and where we now stand in relation to them. The questions that are raised by more than a century of recordings are complex and profound, and this book is an attempt to think about some of them.

CHAPTER ONE

Life before Recordings

Finding music

During the course of the twentieth century the world of music underwent great change. For performers of music, and those who listen to them, the change that had a more profound effect than any other was the development of recording. Invented twenty-three years before the start of the twentieth century, it was at first an expensive and insignificant part of a small minority's musical experience. As the record industry became more successful, and recordings became better (particularly with the advent of electrical recording in 1925), playing music on the gramophone became a widespread and popular pursuit. With the coming of the LP around 1950, and then the CD in the 1980s, listening to recordings became, in the prosperous countries of the world, so general and so cheap that it came to replace live music-making as the main source of music for the majority of listeners.

The history of recording is complex and fascinating, and has been well told elsewhere.[1] Together with its sister, broadcasting, recording is all around us in the twenty-first century, and affects all aspects of musicians' and audiences' lives. Perhaps there are music-lovers living in the West who never buy or listen to a CD, and never turn on the radio to hear music, gaining all their music from playing with friends and going to concerts. But such a person must now be regarded as a rare eccentric. For the vast majority of us, most of the music we hear comes out of black boxes, with no musicians in sight. Going to a concert, or performing music themselves, is, for most people, a secondary activity, if they do it at all.

It is impossible to overemphasise the extent to which the growing availability of recordings over the last hundred years has changed the ways in which musicians and audiences experience music. If we could transport ourselves back to the late nineteenth century, before the existence of recordings, we would find ourselves in a deeply unfamiliar world. Brahms and his contemporaries never heard a note of music unless they were in the presence of someone performing it. One of the consequences of this fact – which had remained true, apart from mechanical instruments and musical boxes, since the dawn of time – was that music-lovers had to seek out music, or make it for themselves. It did not come to them with the press of a button. Music was therefore not just an aural experience, as it has largely become. It was also a matter of physical presence, social interaction, and direct communication between musicians and audience.

People looked for music with a determination that is much rarer in the modern world. This was particularly true in central Europe. Max Graf described the Viennese musical culture in which he was brought up before World War I: 'We became musicians without knowing why or how. Everywhere we went we encountered music. We sang and fiddled. As a student in high school, I took my violin every evening and went to other houses and played classical string-quartets with minor officials, teachers, or business people, just as if that were self-understood. On Sundays, I played Haydn's or Mozart's masses in church choirs. On excursions we all sang choruses and canons. Or we stood, evenings, in front of restaurant gardens or in the parks and listened to band concerts.'[2]

Artur Schnabel, who studied in Vienna in the 1890s, preferred German audiences to the Viennese, too many of whom exhibited a 'lazy superiority complex'. In the medium-sized German towns where he had his first engage-ments, audiences were 'composed of people who loved music unselfishly. They knew most of the music they went to hear at concerts. They knew it very well. There was probably not one in these audiences who was not involved, actively or passively, in home music-making – and without any fuss made about it. It was part of family life, old and young co-operating.' And he spoke enthusiastically of evenings in which amateurs and professionals joined together: 'I think house-music is at its highest conceivable level when amateurs mix with professionals, all doing it for love.'[3]

The composer Ethel Smyth lived for a time as a student in Leipzig in the 1870s. She describes the family of Engelbert Röntgen, concert-master of the Gewandhaus Orchestra. He was 'as great a gentleman and as true a musician as I have known. She was of the old Leipzig musical stock Klengel, a family that could raise a piano quintet among themselves, and together with their Röntgen cousins a small orchestra. Every violin sonata, every piano trio or quartet printed, would Frau Röntgen or her daughter tackle – the mother's performance unplaned perhaps, but of a fire and musicality that carried all before it.'[4]

The head of the Röntgen family was a professional musician. But professional and amateur musicians in Germany were intimately bound up together. Here is what Smyth has to say about the family of Consul Limburger, a prosperous wool merchant, and president of the Gewandhaus Concert Committee: 'The

Limburgers were typically German in that, with the exception of the mother and the one daughter, every member of the family was as much at home in music as ducks in water. They danced, shot, rode, skated, besides being assiduous young men of business, but all played the piano or some other instrument, and a new work played at the Gewandhaus was as much an event for them as the Herzogenbergs [Heinrich and Elisabet von Herzogenberg, friends of Brahms]. Their criticisms may have been less technical but I discussed music as gladly with them as with many an expert; and this is the supreme claim of a musical civilization – that amateurs are in it and of it as well as professionals.'[5]

It would be a mistake to create too generalised a picture of an ideal musical culture in the late nineteenth century. Amateur music-making came at all levels, from the virtually professional to the tentative and the stumblingly incompetent, and the same applied to musical appreciation. Britain was, in this repect, less 'civilised' than middle Europe. Smyth several times contrasts the highly musical world of Germany with the much more casual and indifferent culture of England in her day.

The conductor Dan Godfrey remembered visiting Germany in the 1880s, where he was greatly impressed by the value placed on good music there compared with England, and remarked on the concerts and the light and grand opera performed in municipal theatres across the whole of Germany. Writing in the 1920s, he detected 'signs of an awakening to a deeper appreciation of the value of good music' in Britain, but little by way of serious progress since the nineteenth century.[6]

The comparative backwardness of British musical culture is a recurring theme of writers through to the early decades of the twentieth century. And any nostalgic yearning for the days before recording and broadcasting, when everyone in Britain, as elsewhere, had to rely on their own amateur musical resources, is put firmly in its place by Charlotte Haldane, writing in 1936:

Amateurism in art is the capital crime, it is the sin against the Holy Ghost. Thank goodness the modern parent is socially more honest than the old-fashioned one. Thank heaven 'accomplishments' are going out. It is no longer an asset in the matrimonial market to be able to grind out 'The Maiden's Prayer' on the cottage pianoforte .... I consider mechanical reproduction of great music a boon and a blessing to mankind. I whole-heartedly approve of the B.B.C. I admit at once that the present system of gramophone recording is highly unsatisfactory .... There is no question but that even with the best radio receiving set the average person can afford there is always a good deal of distortion and falsification of tone. BUT those are minor evils compared to the drawing-room massacres which sensitive ears had to endure in the days of parties, the invitations to which included the ominous little line 'Please bring your music'.[7]

Haldane echoes a moment in Jane Austen's *Pride and Prejudice*, when Mr Bennet interrupts his daughter Mary at the piano with the words 'You have delighted us long enough'. Austen was writing in 1797, and no doubt much was endured in drawing-rooms throughout the following century. Amateur music-making was not always good music-making. But the role of the amateur musician was central in musical culture in the nineteenth century in a way that it is not now. There is still a lot of amateur music-making about, often of a very high standard, but it no longer occupies the place it did before recordings replaced it as the main source of domestic music. One indication of this is the change in the relationship between composers and amateur performers. From the late eighteenth century through the whole of the nineteenth century, major composers supplied both the professional and the amateur market. As well as songs, which were published by their thousands and avidly bought by households across the Western world, composers wrote for those who, increasingly, owned pianos, as they became cheaper and more reliable. Haydn wrote piano trios for the domestic market. Schumann wrote not only virtuoso works but also albums of pieces 'For the Young'. Chopin's piano music ranged from the frighteningly virtuoso to the relatively simple that amateurs could play at home. Brahms published his Waltzes in two editions, one simplified for the less accomplished performer.

Brahms, indeed, was one of many major composers who took the amateur performer seriously. In the late nineteenth century, orchestral works were published in piano-duet arrangements, and it was primarily in that form that they were learned by audiences. Brahms himself understood the importance of this market as a way of enabling his public to get to know his works. He wrote more than twenty piano-duet arrangements of orchestral and chamber works, and also arranged the third and fourth symphonies for two pianos. These were aimed at the amateur music-lover, but at the level of serious accomplishment. The arrangements are not at all easy, and Brahms was not interested in simplified arrangements of orchestral works for a solo pianist. When Robert Keller, editor at Brahms's publisher Simrock, arranged Brahms's first two symphonies for solo piano, the composer's comment was, 'You must know better than I whether such an arrangement for girls' boarding school is necessary! I would have considered a two-hand arrangement interesting only if an extraordinary virtuoso did it. Somewhat like the way Liszt did the Beethoven symphonies.'[8]

The link between major composers and the amateur performer continued fitfully into the first half of the twentieth century. Some composers, notably Bartók and Kodály, took a keen interest in music education. Stravinsky wrote easy pieces for piano duet. To open the first Aldeburgh Festival in 1948, Britten wrote *Saint Nicolas*, a cantata for professional instrumentalists, school choirs, and audience participation. As Philip Brett has written, this 'would have appeared ludicrous to the postwar avante garde', but 'it seems now as courageous and adventurous as the experimental music of the time'.[9] For the fact is that few major composers were by then paying any attention to the mass of amateur music-lovers. This severing of an ancient connection has persisted to our own day. Do any of the best-known 'classical' composers of the early twenty-first century write for the amateur performer? In music shops are to be found plenty of simple editions of pop songs, jazz tunes, numbers from shows and classics of the past. Dedicated composers write specific teaching material, some of it of very high quality. But the routine relationship between the professional composer and the amateur performer has gone. Little or nothing is written by major classical composers of the present day for ordinary people to play themselves. The professionalisation of music-making and the growth of recording and broadcasting has divided people into performers or listeners. The bulk of music-lovers now listen passively to CDs, without needing any skill. Many composers, supported by grants from bodies promoting contemporary arts, write only music that musicians of a high level of specialisation can play, and are free to treat the ordinary amateur musician with disdain.

In the late nineteenth century, people either made music themselves or sought out places where they could hear musicians playing. But opportunities to hear orchestral works professionally played were infrequent, unless you were lucky enough to live in a major musical centre. With the pioneering exception of Hans von Bülow's Meiningen Orchestra, orchestras did not tour regularly. So there were none of those series by 'Great Orchestras of the World' that could be heard in all major cities a century later. In the 1880s the Vienna Philharmonic Orchestra, whose members were drawn from the Opera orchestra, gave a series of eight concerts a year. The semi-professional Gesellschaft der Musikfreunde gave half a dozen more in Vienna. Orchestral concerts in Berlin were more frequent: the recently founded Berlin Philharmonic gave twenty a year, the Berlin Opera orchestra a further twelve. In Leipzig, the Gewandhaus Orchestra gave twenty-two concerts a season. But as Ethel Smyth relates, most of the seats in the Gewandhaus were owned by subscribers, and it was very difficult for others to obtain a ticket: '. . . only by intrigue or charity could you get one. But the rehearsals the day before were supposed to be the real thing, especially as they only cost two shillings and to us Conservatorists nothing at all.'[10]

In London in the late nineteenth century there were concert series rather than regular orchestras: the Crystal Palace Concerts, conducted by Augustus Manns, the Philharmonic Society Concerts, the (Hans) Richter Concerts, the (Sir George) Henschel Concerts. Until the Queen's Hall Orchestra was established in 1895, the most regular orchestra with a permanent conductor in England was the Hallé Orchestra in Manchester, still under its founder Sir Charles Hallé (until his death in 1895). The biggest musical events of the year were the choral festivals lasting several days, at Leeds, Sheffield and Birmingham, and the Handel Festival at Crystal Palace.

The major centres of America were well ahead of Britain in the development of symphony orchestras. By the year 1900, regular symphony orchestras had already been established in the following centres: New York (the Philharmonic in 1841 and the Symphony Orchestra in 1878), Boston (1881), Chicago (1891), Cincinnati (1895) and Philadelphia (1900). They were modelled on German orchestras, and heavily dependent on German conductors. But, whereas most orchestras in continental Europe were basically opera orchestras that gave series of symphony concerts, the new American orchestras were independent bodies. As the *Boston Musical Herald* proudly declared when the city's orchestra was founded in 1881, 'A symphony orchestra pure and simple does not exist in all Europe. That is to say, that in no city in Germany, Italy, France or Russia is there an orchestra which is made up of players whose *only* business it is to perform such music as is to be found on programmes of symphony concerts.'[11] This was a slight exaggeration (the Meiningen Orchestra was a notable exception), but it was broadly true. The development of the great American symphony orchestra was under way – though, as in Europe, the orchestras played only for a season of concerts, and not throughout the year.

The availability of music today can be taken for granted in the prosperous parts of the world, because it is all accessible on CD. In the days when music was less easily available, and required more effort, the attitudes of performers and audiences to concerts was rather different. An extreme example is the importance that music took on during wartime. By World War II, recordings were much more widely available than they had been, but still they were expensive, they were on cumbersome 78 rpm discs lasting less than five minute a side, and they were not a serious substitute for hearing music played without interruption in the concert hall. E. M. Forster was a regular member of the audience at the famous concerts of chamber music at the National Gallery, London, which were run by the pianist Myra Hess and the composer and pianist Howard Ferguson, and took place every weekday throughout World War II. For a commemorative booklet on the fifth anniversary of the concerts in 1944, Forster, who was not himself a musician, contributed an essay on what it was like to be in the audience, and what effect the music had on someone like himself. He encapsulates in this short essay the importance of live concerts in a world less dominated by recordings and background music than our own:

> . . . if the soul of an audience could be photographed it would resemble a flight of scattering dipping birds, who belong neither to the air nor the water nor the earth. In theory the audience is a solid slab, provided with a single pair of enormous ears, which listen, and with a pair of hands, which clap. Actually it is that elusive scattering flight of winged creatures, darting

around, and spending much of its time where it shouldn't, thinking now 'how lovely!', now 'my foot's gone to sleep', and passing in the beat of a bar from 'there's Beethoven back in C minor again!' to 'did I turn the gas off?' or 'I do think he might have shaved'. Meanwhile Beethoven persists, Beethoven does not flicker, Beethoven plays himself through. Applause. The piano is closed, the instruments re-enter their cases, the audience disperses more widely, the concert is over.

Over? But is the concert over? Here was the end, had anything an end, but experience proves that strange filaments cling to us after we have been with music, that the feet of the birds have, as it were, become entangled in snares of heaven, that while we swooped hither and thither so aimlessly we were gathering something, and carrying it away for future use. Schumann – or was it Brahms? – sings against the gas and obliterates the squalor, or, sinking deeper till he reaches the soundless, promotes that enlargement of the spirit which is our birthright. The concert is not over when the sweet voices die. It vibrates elsewhere. It discovers treasures which would have remained hidden, and they are the chief part of the human heritage.[12]

Audiences and performers

Before recordings and broadcasting became widespread, the experience of concert-going was very important for the music-lover, even in less extreme circumstances than wartime. The members of the audience knew that it might be a long time before they heard that piece of music again. One of the conseqences of this was that audiences often demanded, and received, encores, something which is now rare in concerts of classical music except at the end. This was common even in the middle of symphonies and concertos. At early performances of Brahms's symphonies, the third movements were regularly repeated before continuing to the finale. The scherzo of the Second Symphony was encored at its première in Vienna under Richter in December 1877. When Joachim conducted it at the Festival of the Lower Rhine in 1878, 'The audience was jubilant after each movement, and would not be satisfied till the third was repeated.'[13]

There are frequent reports of encored movements in London. The third movement of Brahms's Second Symphony was again repeated when Richter conducted it in London in June 1880. When Debussy conducted the British première of *Nocturnes* in 1909, the performance started to come apart in the middle of 'Fêtes': 'Disaster seemed imminent, and M. Debussy was disposed to stop, but the band went on resolutely and happily recovered. The audience, whether for sympathy or satisfaction, encored the movement, and it was performed for the second time with great success.'[14] When Henry Wood conducted the London première of Mahler's *Das Lied von der Erde* in 1914, the third movement, 'Von der Jugend', was encored.[15]

Joachim described his impressions of Pasdeloup's 'Concerts populaires' at the Grand Cirque in Paris, 'with about 5000 people, from academicians to labourers, sitting crowded together, listening, judging, believing and enjoying. And what an outburst of sympathy there is after a movement of Haydn's or Mendelssohn's, which they insist on hearing twice over, as they did last Sunday, because they refuse to move until they do.'[16]

Even when they were not demanding encores, audiences a hundred years ago almost always applauded between movements. If they did not, it meant that they were expressing their disapproval of the music or the performance. If an audience were really enthusiastic, they would applaud not only between movements but sometimes even during them. Hans von Bülow said about the opening bars of Beethoven's 'Emperor' Concerto, 'I have always had applause after the cadenza.'[17] And Brahms wrote about an early performance of his Violin Concerto, with Joachim playing the solo part, 'the Cadenza sounded so beautiful at the actual concert that the public applauded it into the start of the Coda'.[18] There is no hint in this that Brahms disapproved, but it would be unthinkable for a modern audience to clap during a movement. That is now the behaviour of jazz fans.

Before the ubiquity of recordings musicians were aware that audiences had few opportunities to hear works, and that at a concert this might be the first time they had heard the music being played – particularly if it was a new work. This undoubtedly had an effect on the manner in which musicians performed. Adrian Boult wrote about his experience of rehearsing Ethel Smyth's Mass in D in Birmingham in 1924: 'She was very keen about "iron rhythm", no *rubato* (although her mind changed several times over what the pace should actually be in places). This is *most* inadvisable because it makes it impossible to underline certain things which a first-performance audience should have underlined . . . .'[19] Boult was not noted for exaggerated 'underlining' at any stage of his career, so this testimony from him is particularly striking.

Hans von Bülow, on the other hand, was well known for a highly personal style of rubato and flexibility of tempo, which some writers loved and others loathed. But according to Max Kalbeck, Bülow particularly exaggerated these touches when a work was unfamiliar: 'Both as a pianist and as a conductor, Bülow used these brilliant and distinctive nuances in his interpretations only until he himself, the orchestra and the audience were assured. His exaggerations seemed to him a necessary persuasive measure. Once he felt that he was understood, and that the situation was fully under control, he restrained his personal interpretation, and ever thereafter let the work speak for itself.'[20]

This report suggests that Bülow thought that orchestras, as well as audiences, needed help with extra 'underlinings' in unfamiliar music. Brahms made the

same point in a letter to Joachim. Joachim was to conduct an early performance of Brahms's Fourth Symphony in Berlin in 1886, and he had written to
the composer asking for more guidance about tempi. Brahms then sent
Joachim a marked-up score of the symphony with a letter: 'I have marked a
few tempo modifications in the score with pencil. They may be useful, even
necessary, for the first performance . . . . Such exaggerations are only necessary
where a composition is unfamiliar to an orchestra or a soloist. In such a case I
often cannot do enough pushing or slowing down to produce even approxi-
mately the passionate or serene effect I want. Once a work has become part of
flesh and blood, then in my opinion nothing of that sort is justifiable any
more.'[21] The view of Brahms, Boult and Bülow, that audiences and performers
need more underlining of changes of mood in a new work than they do in later
performances, is an idea that would be unlikely to occur to a modern musician.

Quite apart from the performance of new works, there is a more general
point to be made about the approach to performing in concert. In the days
when music was not accessible on CD and audiences had fewer opportunities
to hear a work, the most important task for the musician was to put the music
over, and to make clear what was happening in the piece. Each performance
was unique. Once it had started, it continued inexorably through to the end,
with or without mistakes, bad tuning, moments of confusion. It was an attempt
to put over a narrative in a way which would make sense to the audience at a
single hearing. It was not primarily an exercise in giving a perfect rendering of
the score. Many of the old-fashioned habits, which have now died out, can be
seen in the light of this need to put over the narrative thrust of the music to
an audience. This applies particularly to the old-fashioned ways of creating
points of emphasis: portamento, tempo rubato, changes of the tempo itself.
Good modern musicians have their ways of rendering the narrative clear too,
but by comparison their playing tends to be more even in pace, and less highly
characterised in detail (more of this in later chapters). There are no doubt many
reasons for this development, but one of them must be that there is less sense
that audiences have only one opportunity to understand what is going on.
Today, most music is available on CD, and a member of the audience can
always acquire it after the concert. At a concert a hundred years ago, it was
'now or never', and this was reflected in the manner of performance.

Standards and expectations

The fact that musicians and audiences experienced a performance only once,
and were never able to repeat it by means of a recording, meant that mistakes
and roughnesses were soon forgotten. In principle the same might be expected
to apply in concert performance even today. But, by the beginning of the

twenty-first century, musicians and audiences have become so used to hearing perfect performances created by editing that the general standards in the concert hall are also much higher than they used to be. Early recordings make it clear that standards of accuracy, tuning, clarity and precision were generally lower in the early twentieth century than they are today, and there is no reason to suppose that they were higher through the nineteenth century. There is much to discuss about this change, including the question whether it has been entirely for the better.

In Britain in the early years of the twentieth century, orchestral standards were kept down by the generally casual employment of musicians, and the limited amount of rehearsal time. In Germany there was much more regular employment to be had in the many opera houses. In Britain almost all orchestral musicians earned a living by playing a great range of music, from the popular songs and dance music of the day to symphonies and grand opera. A wide range of institutions employed musicians: theatres, hotels with their 'palm courts', restaurants, ships and, from around 1910 onwards, the new cinemas. Until the late 1920s all cinemas employed musicians, ranging from a single pianist or trio in small houses to a substantial orchestra in large cinemas in city centres. The number of musicians employed in the cinema was huge, and its impact on musicians' lives extended across many countries of the world. As Cyril Ehrlich has expressed it, 'Silent films functioned as if they had been designed to create jobs for musicians.' Around 20,000 musicians were employed in cinemas in Britain by the late twenties, 4,000 of them in London alone (a situation that changed rapidly and dramatically when the 'talkies' were introduced from around 1929 onwards).[22]

Sir Dan Godfrey deplored the lure of the cinema to young musicians, which encouraged music students to give up their studies for the sake of a regular salary: 'Spoiled by the adulation of the emotional crowd, they lapse into a state of mediocrity, which, considering their glowing prospects when they entered college, is deplorable.' Many restaurants employed musicians, good, bad and indifferent, according to Godfrey: 'The most enterprising people in this connection are Messrs. Lyons, who spend as much as £150,000 a year on orchestras and artistes in their different establishments. Such an astute firm would not do this if it were not a business proposition . . . . Their latest experiment in providing miniature operas at the Corner House is being watched with interest.'[23] Sir Thomas Beecham famously discovered Albert Sammons, who was to become the leader of his orchestra, playing at the Waldorf Hotel in London in 1909. At Beecham's request, Sammons played the last movement of the Mendelssohn Concerto – popular classics were regularly played everywhere, among the lighter music.

Alfred Deahl was a violinist in Southampton, playing in theatres and cinemas and on cruise ships in the 1920s.[24] His father was leader of the orchestra at the old Grand Theatre in Southampton for many years, and it was there that Alfred did much of his playing. The theatre staged a great variety of shows – grand opera, Gilbert and Sullivan, Viennese operetta, musical comedies, Shakespeare, melodrama – and the same audience used to come to everything. The D'Oyly Carte company visited regularly, performing Gilbert and Sullivan with a reduced orchestration of half a dozen strings, two or three wind and timpani. Deahl's reminiscences give a vivid flavour of the musician's life in the provinces:

> In the old orchestras in those days nearly all the music was manuscript copies. You had to be a damn good sight-reader to read the stuff, and sometimes you had to guess it. But they used to rush through the Monday morning rehearsal – and with the Gilbert and Sullivan we used to go through not one but more than one operetta. And we were all good sight-readers, real professionals. Sometimes for some of the shows they used to bring their own leader, and a viola player sometimes, but otherwise we were on our own. But the manuscripts, they were hurriedly written copies, you see, and sometimes if you had a speck of dirt on the copy it looked like a bloody note, and you had to be very careful. And turning over: at the bottom of the page you used to have 'v.s.', volti subito, turn over quickly. And where they'd been turning over so much the copies were in a terrible state sometimes. Half the bloody bar the music was missing, you had to more or less guess what was coming. But it was a scream really.
>
> I always remember at the old Grand Theatre it used to be so bloody cold in winter. And I always remember when the grand opera came. Their conductor was generally a German, foreigner. And we were rehearsing *Lohengrin*. And it starts off with the strings playing all harmonics . . . and it was cold, and you never heard such a bloody noise in all your life. And this conductor, he throws his arms up, helpless: 'Gentlemen! Again!' And eventually we used to manage it.

Deahl played for the silent films until the talkies came in:

> In the cinemas you always had a trio – piano, cello and violin – you usually had that. There was a relief piano who'd come on for the light comedy, and the main film you had the trio. I played for years. Just piano and violin where I finished up, just me and a piano. I've had some very nice times playing in the cinema. It'd be a good old slog. But it was nice, you used to feel satisfied when you'd finished. When *Ben Hur* came, I was engaged as leader of the orchestra at the Palladium. They had their own music for that, of course. But we changed it – instead of the music for the chariot race we played *Rienzi*. That was very effective.
>
> I did about three and a half years cruising, playing the violin all over the world – all the capitals, fjords, West Indies, New York in the early twenties.

I used to play for the dances [on ship] – hated it. I detested dancing. But we also used to play overtures, and we used to play concert pieces, we used to play some good stuff, very good stuff. There were two violins, cello, double bass, piano and drums.

In London, the supply of lucrative work for musicians meant that the principal players of the symphony orchestras frequently sent deputies to rehearsals or concerts. Sir Henry Wood put a stop to this system in his Queen's Hall Orchestra in 1904, offering a basic salary to players who were prepared to attend regularly. Those who were unwilling to accept the new regime left to form the London Symphony Orchestra. The composer William Alwyn, who began his career as a flautist in London in the 1920s, frequently played as a deputy:

Each of these experts [the principal players] for any one day would have half a dozen engagements he had accepted, and he would attend any one according to his whim. In fairness I should say that the bona fide members of, say the LSO, were fundamentally loyal to the orchestra and would put in sufficient appearances to justify their posts; but a week's engagement as first flute at Covent Garden Opera was more remunerative than one concert with the LSO at Queen's Hall, so on the whole, who could blame them? . . .

. . . I remember one occasion when Murchie asked me to do a Queen's Hall concert for him; he of course was appearing at the morning rehearsal (incidentally no concert had more than one rehearsal). I asked him what was the programme. 'Oh, nothing to worry about. I forget what the symphony is, but look out for the Ravel *Daphnis and Chloe*; that scale that begins on the piccolo, and then by way of first flute and second flute ends with a solo scale on the third flute. If you miss it, it leaves an awful gap! But nothing to worry about, old chap, it'll be all right!' This was a hard school to be brought up in, and no profession for the constitutionally nervous. But it was the foundation of the British orchestral player's abnormal talent for sight-reading, the envy of the world, and traditionally still existent.[25]

Things had changed little since the 1890s, when a critic reported of the final concerts of the Promenade season, 'Although the Leeds Festival called away many members of Mr. Henry Wood's orchestra, the excellence of the performances was well maintained . . . .'[26]

It would be a mistake to suppose that, a century later, orchestral life in London at the start of the twenty-first century consists of a diet only of thoroughly rehearsed concerts given by regular bodies of musicians. There are still plenty of occasions when concerts and recordings are performed by more or less ad hoc orchestras, and when rehearsal is minimal. But the general standard expected and achieved is much higher than it was a century ago.

Browsing through the concert reviews of the *Musical Times* for the last two decades of the nineteenth century reveals a world in which much of the music-making in England was, by modern standards, casual and slapdash.

New and unfamiliar works were not even expected to receive a really good performance at their première. Tchaikovsky's 'Pathétique' Symphony was first played at Queen's Hall in February 1894, and then repeated three weeks later: 'Dr. Mackenzie conducted the fine work with obvious sympathy, and both performances were really triumphs of interpretation, on which let all concerned be heartily congratulated. We make no reflection upon conductor or orchestra when we say that the second performance was much better than the first. Music so elaborate, and, in some respects, so new, cannot be conquered in the short time ordinarily devoted to rehearsal for a single occasion.'[27] If the first of these concerts received the Philharmonic Society's usual allocation of two rehearsals, it is hardly surprising that the performance was somewhat rough. Similarly, when Wood first conducted Brahms's Third Symphony in 1899, a critic reported, 'Though the orchestra was evidently not too well acquainted with it, the performance was worthy of the work on the whole.'[28] Hasty though modern preparations can be, it is inconceivable that a performance could nowadays be reported as 'worthy' even though the orchestra was 'not too well acquainted' with the work.

Series of opera performances were often said to have improved after a shaky opening night. That can happen today, but it is clear that the level of shakiness was of a different order a century ago. In 1900 a new production of Wagner's *Ring* opened at Covent Garden, conducted by Felix Mottl. 'There were times when the orchestra played very finely. But still the faults of slowness and lack of grip were very marked. How far this is due to want of rehearsal – which can be remedied in the interval between the first and second Cycles – will be known before these lines are in print.'[29] Sure enough, during the second cycle, 'the orchestra played with much more grip and vigour throughout'.[30]

As it happens, the conductor who, more than any other, was to put his stamp on the twentieth-century orchestra was present at one of those performances. Arturo Toscanini wrote in 1905 explaining why he was reluctant to conduct in London: '. . . I especially fear London because I remember a performance of *Götterdämmerung* in which the orchestra, under the direction of Felix Mottl, was sight-reading the final scene before an audience. The audience noticed nothing, and the press found the performance superb. Of course! An eminent maestro was conducting, and he was German to boot.'[31]

Comparisons between conditions in Britain, where rehearsal was often inadequate, and the continent, where conditions were usually better, were often made in British reviews of the time. When the London première of Verdi's *Falstaff* took place at Covent Garden in 1894, the reviewer in the *Musical Times* wrote, 'To those who did not witness the original production at

Milan, the Covent Garden performance must seem fairly satisfying, though of course it was given without the many rehearsals which are regarded abroad as essential.' But this did not stop him adding, 'The orchestra and chorus this season are of unusually fine quality.'[32] This is a sentiment often repeated in the press of the time: that British musicians are as fine as anywhere, and do a remarkably good job in trying circumstances.

It was not uncommon in Britain for concerts to be given with no rehearsal at all. During the 1890s, Alberto Randegger conducted a long series of Sunday concerts at Queen's Hall 'and skilfully steered, clear of disaster, the performance of about 180 symphonic works, concertos, &c., without their having had any rehearsal whatever'.[33] The Leeds Festival in 1895 began, as usual, with a performance of Handel's *Messiah*. The conductor, Sir Arthur Sullivan, caused 'the greatest astonishment and some rumbling' by calling a general rehearsal of the work. Because it was assumed that all the participants knew the work backwards, conductors in previous years had thought this unnecessary.[34]

Sir Dan Godfrey recounts various unrehearsed public performances with his Bournemouth Municipal Orchestra (the first municipally funded orchestra in Britain). On one occasion around 1900, 'we were trying the Venusberg music, which we had not previously rehearsed. It was one of our "off" days. Nothing seemed to go right. Finally we got into such a hopeless tangle that I began to wonder what on earth would be the end. Byrne [the timpanist] . . . saw the look of consternation on my face and commenced a drum roll, increasing to *fortissimo*, then falling back to *pianissimo*. Realising his intention, I brought the band down and concluded the piece. After the performance, a lady came up to me and said, "What an effective finish[!]" Had it been anyone else I would have thought my leg was being pulled.'[35]

Reading reviews of the period, one gets the impression that, in Britain, freedom from disaster was the standard for a good concert. The young Henry Wood rapidly made a name for himself as a conductor who could be relied upon to keep the orchestra under control, even though much of the repertoire that he conducted at early Promenade Concerts from 1895 onwards received little or no rehearsal. The Queen's Hall Orchestra, which he conducted, received much praise in the press, often being described as 'magnificent', even by visiting composers. But Wood, though the first English conductor to make a successful full-time career, was essentially a man who succeeded through discipline and efficiency rather than through the power of his interpretations. Few of his recordings suggest that he would impress as an interpretative conductor today (Vaughan Williams's *London Symphony*, recorded in 1936, is perhaps the best of them). He was in the school of Sir Michael Costa, conductor at Covent Garden for many years, who conducted the Handel Festival for twenty-six years until 1882. Sir George Grove wrote of Costa, 'He was a splendid drill-sergeant; he brought the London orchestras into an order unknown before. He acted up to his lights, was thoroughly efficient as far as he went, and was eminently safe.'[36]

That could be a description of Henry Wood. But it could equally describe Charles Lamoureux, who founded the Concerts Lamoureux in Paris in 1881, and who brought his orchestra to London for extended visits in the 1890s. On their first visit in 1896, the critic of the *Musical Times* wrote, '. . . these artists, by constantly practising together under the same chief and by means of rehearsals, numerous and sectional to a degree that English musicians would regard as ridiculously in excess of actual needs, have so learnt to play together that, in execution, phrasing, balance of tone, and relationship of parts to the whole, something very near perfection has been attained. Without being exactly a "great" conductor as regards sympathy, insight, and inspiration, M. Lamoureux is master of that "art of taking pains" which has been spoken of as identical with "genius".'[37]

Lamoureux and Wood collaborated during these visits, swapping and combining orchestras. Lamoureux's command of orchestral discipline, previously unknown in England, was undoubtedly an inspiration to Wood. But Lamoureux's orchestra could afford much more rehearsal than the London orchestras at this period. Carl Flesch, the great violin teacher, joined the Lamoureux Orchestra in the 1890s. There were three or four rehearsals for each concert (exceptional in Paris, as in London), and Lamoureux 'did not mind taking the trouble of hearing each of his 120 orchestra members pass by him one by one before each concert, in order to check, with a violin in his hand, the tuning of every instrument most carefully'. (Henry Wood later adopted a similar routine with his Queen's Hall Orchestra.) Lamoureux's players were required to take their parts home and learn the difficult passages. Such thoroughness contrasted with the general standard in France: 'he tried to counteract the slovenliness of French orchestras of the day by a meticulous, in fact pedantic, orchestral discipline'.[38]

In continental Europe, the amount of rehearsal varied greatly. At the Bayreuth Festival rehearsals went on for months. So did rehearsals for the Paris première of *Die Meistersinger* under Paul Taffanel in 1897, 'with the utmost regard for every detail'.[39] But performance of operas already in the repertoire received scant rehearsal at most opera houses. When Mahler first conducted at the Vienna Opera, he had to conduct Wagner's *Ring* with no orchestral rehearsals, because it was already in the repertoire.[40] Puccini wrote, in 1922, 'All too long have we in Italy fallen into the habit of giving the so-called repertory operas, those which resist time and sloppy performances, in an indecent way: one rehearsal for the orchestra, none for the stage, and away we go, carrying all the foul rubbish with which little by little the abuses and the bad habits of conductors and singers have encrusted the work.' This was in reply to a critic who, after hearing a performance of *Manon Lescaut* conducted by Toscanini, had assumed that Puccini had retouched the scoring, which he had not. Toscanini had taken the trouble to rehearse it so that previously unnoticed details were revealed: 'Arturo Toscanini, with the faith and love which inflame him, grasps the chisel and chips away until the work is revealed to the public with the true intention of the author.'[41]

Of orchestras in Germany in the late nineteenth century, the one that had the highest reputation for care of rehearsal was the Meiningen Court Orchestra, conducted by Hans von Bülow. Brahms commented on 'how outstandingly his people have been rehearsed'.[42] Weingartner (not a great admirer of Bülow himself) wrote, 'The precision of the small orchestra was astonishing – it gave the impression of a single instrument played by a master hand',[43] and Hanslick wrote that 'Bülow conducts the orchestra as if it were a little bell in his hand. The most admirable discipline has transformed it into an instrument on which he plays with utter freedom and from which he produces nuances possible only with a discipline to which larger orchestras would not ordinarily submit.'[44]

These testimonies suggest an orchestra of exceptional discipline. But this did not stop Bülow handing a performance of Richard Strauss's Suite Opus 4 for thirteen wind instruments to the composer with no rehearsal whatsoever. Strauss had never conducted before, and Bülow assured him that the players would have looked at the parts. 'I conducted my piece through something of a haze', Strauss reported; 'all I can remember now is that I didn't make a complete mess of it, but I simply couldn't say what it was actually like otherwise.'[45] Handing a performance to a totally inexperienced young composer without rehearsal would be unthinkable in the modern concert hall. Occasionally reviews indicate that, even under Bülow himself, the orchestra was not infallible: '. . . nor could the occasional inability of the orchestra to follow their conductor's swift transitions of *tempo* seriously mar the effect'.[46]

The point of this is not to pour cold water on the achievements of Bülow and his orchestra, but to suggest that even the most emphatic use of a word like 'excellent' or 'outstanding' is always relative. What is undoubtedly true is that the Meiningen Orchestra had unrivalled opportunities for lengthy rehearsal, because it was privately owned and funded. State funding of orchestras and opera houses in Berlin and Vienna similarly resulted in a stability of attendance and a level of rehearsal that was unknown in Britain, even though Mahler and others were continually fighting to improve standards.

In America, it was the patronage of wealthy individuals which made possible the development of symphony orchestras in the late nineteenth and early twentieth centuries. A Boston financier, Henry L. Higginson, provided one million dollars to found the city's Symphony Orchestra in 1881. Musicians and conductor were paid a salary for the season of weekly concerts, and it was the first orchestra in America to be made permanent in this way, setting a pattern that was soon followed in other cities. An oil magnate, Henry Harkness Flagler, did the same for Walter Damrosch's New York Symphony Orchestra in 1907. Flagler guaranteed the New York SO to a maximum of $100,000 per annum, and paid $250,000 to cover the costs of its tour of Europe in 1920. This was the first ever European tour by an American orchestra, and the standard of ensemble was greatly admired, particularly in London with its haphazard orchestral life. Damrosch was also envied by Europeans for this, to them, unimaginable level of private support.[47]

The virtuoso conductor

One of the factors that encouraged the development of the modern orchestra was the evolution in the late nineteenth century of a new type of powerful figure, capable of bending an orchestra to its will: the virtuoso conductor.

Costa, Lamoureux and to a large extent Wood were essentially orchestral technicians, men of discipline rather than interpretation. The new breed – Nikisch, Richter, Bülow, Mahler and, a little later, Toscanini, Furtwängler and Mengelberg – were in quite a different mould. Carl Flesch, who admired Lamoureux for his attention to detail, admired Nikisch for quite different qualities: 'To me he was a revelation. From the time of my work under Lamoureux, I was still used to the type of unimaginative stick-wagger who, strictly according to the compass, beat $\frac{4}{4}$ time in the four cardinal points. Now for the first time I saw a musician who, impressionistically, described in the air not simply the metrical structure, but above all the dynamic and agogical nuances as well as the indefinable mysterious feeling that lies between the notes; his beat was utterly personal and original. With Nikisch began a new era of the art of the conductor.'[48]

Tchaikovsky wrote of Nikisch, 'He does not seem to conduct, but rather to exercise some mysterious spell; he hardly makes a sign, and never tries to call attention to himself, yet we feel that the great orchestra, like an instrument in the hands of a wonderful master, is completely under the control of its chief.'[49]

The new breed of conductor made a great impression. But some writers regretted this new emphasis on the conductor rather than the orchestra and composer: 'The performer can only play with enthusiasm and freedom when he feels himself an individual. With the countless, uninterrupted variations of *tempi* of the rubato conductors, with the capricious gestures they make which are supposed not to indicate the beat, but the "melos", all individuality is lost, and the player is a mere slave.'[50]

These criticisms of the new style of conductor recurred from time to time, though the accusation of 'rubato conductor' was applied only to some of them (and particularly to Bülow). What is clear is that these powerful figures transformed the effect of the orchestra, for good or ill, and set in train the development of the orchestra in the twentieth century. Recordings at first made little impact on the orchestra or its audiences, because of the impossibility of recording a complete orchestra in realistic sound quality. But with the coming of electrical recording in 1925, orchestral recordings became bestsellers. Tours by Toscanini with La Scala and the New York Philharmonic, and Furtwängler with the Berlin Philharmonic, made a great impact, and in particular made the London orchestras look to their laurels. But in the long term, it was recordings that spread the knowledge of what was best in orchestral performance. Increasingly, the great conductors were promoted by their recordings, and the orchestras became 'theirs': Toscanini's New York Philharmonic, Mengelberg's Concertgebouw, Stokowski's Philadelphia. Following the supremacy of Karajan and his Berlin Philharmonic, at the end of the twentieth century conductors were being chosen by orchestras as much for their ability to bring in recording contracts as for any more purely musical reasons.

Soloists and chamber musicians

The difficulty of getting enough rehearsal for orchestral concerts and operas has always been, and will always be, one of the obstacles to fine music-making. With solo and chamber music the situation is different. There are no restrictions on the amount or intensity of rehearsal beyond what individuals are prepared to put themselves through. One might think, therefore, that nothing much has changed over the last hundred years, and that the supreme instrumentalists of the late nineteenth century were much like the supreme instrumentalists of today. Early recordings suggest that much was very different, in style, in ensemble, and in expression.

The string quartet acknowledged as the first modern 'ensemble of equals', the Bohemian Quartet, played with what now seems a strange mixture of homogeneity and looseness, and with none of the modern ideas of control or precision. The Joachim Quartet, who were considered supreme in the late nineteenth century, would surely have seemed stranger still if modern ears could have heard them (they did not make any records). Writers of the time referred to Joachim's extraordinary fire, freedom and spontaneity in the company of his colleagues. It seems as if it must have been an ensemble in which the other three players spent their time guessing at what the great man would do next.

In 1899 there was a concert in Berlin to mark the sixtieth anniversary of Joachim's first public appearance. The crowning event of the evening 'was when Dr. Joachim, at the unexpected invitation of some members of the orchestra, was asked to play Beethoven's Violin Concerto, which, although, as he stated publicly, quite unprepared, he performed superbly'.[51] Modern soloists often have to cope with inadequate rehearsal for concertos; but is such a 'spontaneous', unprepared performance of the Beethoven Concerto something that any modern violinist would like to undertake in public?

Audiences expected not only under-rehearsal and roughness, but also that musicians would take time to warm to their task during the concert. To an extent this is still true. In many modern concerts one can hear the musicians settling down during the first piece, particularly if, as is often the case, the acoustics of the hall have changed significantly since the rehearsal because of the presence of the audience. Kreisler used to take this to extremes. On principle, he did not practise the music he was to play on the day of the concert: 'I never practise before a concert. The reason is that practice benumbs the brain, renders the imagination less acute, and deadens the sense of alertness that every artist must possess . . . . The secret of my method, if I may say so, consists of my having to concentrate and exert myself, when on the platform, much more than if I had previously practised the music for many hours. The extra alertness required to master any uncertainties that may exist enables me to play all the better.'[52] His duo-partner in the 1930s, Franz Rupp, confirmed that Kreisler disliked rehearsing in too much detail: 'He told me that he always wanted to be fresh, so we didn't work things out as much as I would have liked.'[53] This combination of limited practice and limited rehearsal often meant that the audience had to sit through a somewhat exploratory opening to the recital, as Kreisler 'mastered any uncertainties' and got into his stride. Would a violinist be able to pursue this relaxed approach to public performance in these days of the 'perfect' CD? One of the delights of early recordings is to find oneself transported at least halfway back to such days, with the occasional slip or uncertainty, and then the sense of the musician regaining mastery over the situation.

Diversity

That this informality was acceptable, even welcomed, a hundred years ago is due partly to the fact people did not have the perfection of edited recordings as a yardstick. But it was also the case that each concert was a unique and unrepeatable event. Every one was different, each artist was different, they looked different, they walked differently to the platform, turned to the audience differently – Kreisler greeting them like their favourite uncle, Rachmaninoff scowling as if the last thing he wanted to do was to play the piano. Concerts and musicians were extremely diverse, and on early recordings we can hear something of how diverse they were in the days before the globalisation and homogenisation of styles.

This diversity was ensured by the relative isolation of musicians and audiences compared with today. The range of musicians they heard, and were influenced by, was much narrower than in the modern world. There were touring soloists, such as Joachim, who were accustomed to playing with orchestras in different countries. But most members of, for example, the Vienna Philharmonic Orchestra spent almost all of their musical lives listening to musicians of middle Europe. Because of this comparative isolation, styles in different countries were quite distinct, and we can still hear those differences in recordings of, for instance, the orchestras of France, Germany, Holland and England from the 1920s and 1930s. Today, when recordings are available across the world, and musicians of all nationalities sit in orchestras far from where they were born, styles and approaches have become, to a large extent, globalised, and this makes the musical world a very different place.

This is not to say that all musicians play the same as each other in the twenty-first century. But the differences between them are much narrower than a hundred years ago. And musicians who play together are now expected to reach agreement. In early twentieth-century recordings we hear musicians of quite different styles playing together without any attempt to 'marry' their approaches: Kreisler and Rachmaninoff in Grieg and Schubert, Kreisler and Zimbalist in a famous early recording of J. S. Bach's Double Concerto. Jelly d'Aranyi and Adela Fachiri played that work together at a concert in September 1925, and the performance was praised in *The Times* precisely because of the difference in character between the two soloists: 'The whole effect is finely satisfying, the solo parts stand out the more clearly for this difference in style [i.e., Fachiri's Classical restraint versus d'Aranyi's Romantic warmth] while the pull, first one way and then the other, seems to give the whole interpretation great vitality and interest.'[54] Such coming together of opposites must have been commonplace before the twentieth-century trend towards uniformity of style got under way.

By the beginning of the twenty-first century, we have reached the point where it is difficult to tell the difference between instrumentalists and orchestras which used to be so distinct from each other. At the beginning of the twentieth century, for example, Joachim, Ysaÿe and Sarasate sounded quite distinct from each other, and still do through the dim recordings of the period. The same is true of the 1920s and 1930s: Kreisler, Huberman, Heifetz, Rosé. But the diversity becomes much less once one gets into the second half of the twentieth century, and is now very narrow indeed except among outstandingly individual players.

The sort of homogenised and globalised sound of the modern orchestra is a synthesis of what used to be different styles. The beginnings of this trend towards compromise can already be heard in recordings of American orchestras in the 1920s and 1930s, in which European immigrants from different countries sat side by side adapting to each other and to the big orchestras and big halls in which they found themselves playing. Wilhelm Furtwängler, writing in the

1920s, was already somewhat critical of these American 'luxury' orchestras, which 'have something of the beauty contest about them .... American orchestras have the best components – French woodwinds, German brass, etc. – but the result is like a statue or painting of Venus compounded of the most beautiful nose, arms and legs borrowed from different models, and not to be compared with the homogeneous and distinct tone quality of the Vienna Philharmonic Orchestra.'[55] Even the Vienna Philharmonic Orchestra has now, in the twenty-first century, lost something of its old distinctness, and, when playing Stravinsky or Debussy, can be mistaken for an American orchestra.

The loss of diversity has been hastened by the availability of recordings of the best players from around the world. Naturally, when everyone hears everyone else all the time, there is a steady drip of mutual influence.

Self-consciousness

Finally, there is another effect of the growing dominance of recordings. It is that musicians are now aware of their own sound and style as they never were a hundred years ago.

Before the existence of recordings, musicians never heard themselves except when they were actually performing. Nowadays professional musicians are used to listening to their own performances, and examining them in detail. One does not have to be a musician to realise what a profound impact this change must have made. Anyone who has ever heard a recording of their own voice will know what is involved. When the telephone answering machine was invented, a few decades ago, many people heard the sound of their own voice for the first time. Almost all of them disliked the experience, and asked, 'Do I really sound like that?' It did not matter whether their voice was ugly or beautiful. People with the most attractive voices could not bear the sound of themselves at first hearing.

P. G. Wodehouse described this experience in the preface to his first full-length Bertie Wooster novel, *Thank you, Jeeves*, published in 1934. Before writing it, he acquired

> one of those machines where you talk into a mouthpiece and have your observations recorded on wax, and I started *Thank you, Jeeves* on it. And after the first few paragraphs I thought I would turn back, and play the stuff over to hear how it sounded.
>
> It sounded too awful for human consumption. Until that moment I had never realized that I had a voice like that of a very pompous school-master addressing the young scholars in his charge from the pulpit in the school chapel. There was a kind of foggy dreariness about it that chilled the spirits

. . . . I sold the machine next day and felt like the Ancient Mariner when he got rid of the albatross.[56]

Musicians who first heard their own recordings in the early years of the twentieth century were often taken aback by what they heard, suddenly being made aware of inaccuracies and mannerisms they had not suspected. When recording equipment became cheap and portable in the late twentieth century, it was a common experience of amateur musicians to make a recording of one of their concerts, and to be deeply depressed by what they heard: the patches of poor tuning, passages which were not together, or which sounded clumsy. The audience may or may not have been aware of these imperfections, but they certainly did not care about them as the performer does when 'listening back'.

The most obvious effect of getting used to hearing one's own recordings, as professional musicians do today, is to become highly self-critical about details. Any tiny blemish or inaccuracy takes on hideously exaggerated proportions. Making a recording becomes a process of detailed self-examination which would have been impossible a century ago. Seeking after precision and clarity becomes a habit, so that, in the concert hall too, musicians aim for technical perfection – often, it seems, above everything else.

There are also more subtle forces at work. If you hear the sound of your own voice, you are made aware that you cannot hear yourself as others hear you. You have to learn to hear what others hear. And that is a basic fact for musicians too. If you listen to your own performance, and do not like what you hear, you then start adjusting it to something which sounds more like what you thought you were doing.

Musicians have, since the late twentieth century, become so used to hearing themselves in recordings, and analysing what they hear, that they are self-conscious to an extent that was not possible in any earlier period in musical history. This self-consciousness can be helpful or destructive, but now the genie is out of the bottle it cannot be put back. Once a musician has had the experience of listening to playbacks and adjusting to them, it is not possible to go back to a state of innocence.

Thomas Alva Edison could never have imagined any of this when he first heard himself reciting 'Mary had a little lamb' on his tin-foil machine in 1877. But the evolution of recording over the twentieth century has wrought profound change in the way musicians make music, and in the ways that audiences listen to it. How the recording process has impinged on musicians, and how they have adapted to its evolution, is the subject of chapter 2.

CHAPTER TWO

The Experience of Recording

The 'Classical' sections of large music shops are now full of CDs spanning a hundred years of recording, from opera arias recorded at the very beginning of the twentieth century to the latest digital releases. These recordings were made to be enjoyed by those who buy them, and to give them the illusion in their own home that the musicians are actually there, performing just the other side of those mysterious black boxes. The illusion has become more complete as sound-reproduction has improved, but illusion was always the point, even in the most primitive recordings.

Perhaps it is not necessary for the music-lover to know anything about how the music got onto the disc. But anyone who is interested in the history of performance on record needs to keep in mind what sorts of documents these discs actually are: how they were made, what their limitations are, how musicians have approached the recording, the conditions in which they have performed, and ways in which those conditions may have affected the manner of performance. Recordings can be judged without taking all this into consideration (and often are), but anyone who does not know something of the history of recordings as a technology and as a musical and social phenomenon, and who is unaware of the ways in which the sounds that issue from loudspeakers are likely to have got onto the disc, is easily misled when making musical judgements about the performances on them.

This chapter is about some of those issues. It is not a history of recording techniques, but a collection of thoughts about that history, and how it has affected, and continues to affect, musicians and listeners.

The early recording studio

The early recording studio was a very different place from the modern studio, and musicians had to play in conditions quite unlike those of the concert hall.

Before electrical amplification became available in 1925, music was recorded mechanically, with the sound being gathered by one or more large horns. From there the sound was transmitted to a machine which cut the wave-form into soft wax on a cylinder or disc. Because there was no electrical amplification, all the musicians had to be contained in a small room and within close range of the recording horn in order to be audible.

The most successful early recordings were of singers. The operatic voices of the early twentieth century were transmitted through the limited machinery with remarkable impact and quality (and still are in sensitively transferred CD reissues). But the accompanying instruments, whether orchestra or piano, had largely to fend for themselves. Pianists in the early days had to play on an upright piano on a platform at the level of the singer's head, so that the recording horn had a chance of capturing some of its sound. Raoul Pugno, one of the first major pianists to go into the recording studio, made solo recordings under these conditions in 1903.[1] When Paderewski made his first recordings, in 1911, Fred Gaisberg took the recording equipment to the great man's home, and recorded him on his own grand piano. From then on, solo piano recording soon became well established, and grand pianos were routinely used in the studio.

But the pre-electric recording still had limitations. The range of frequency and dynamics was still very restricted, and the peculiar response of the recording equipment meant that musicians could not just play as they normally did. Busoni left a vivid description of his first experience of recording Liszt's arrangement of the waltz from Gounod's *Faust* in 1919. It involved 'watching the pedal (because it sounds so bad); thinking of certain notes which had to be stronger or weaker in order to please this devilish machine; not letting oneself go for fear of inaccuracies and being conscious the whole time that every note was going to be there for eternity; how can there be any question of inspiration, freedom, swing, or poetry?'[2] Restrained pedalling, which Busoni mentions, is a feature of many pre-electric piano recordings. The only disc published from Busoni's first session in 1919, Chopin's Etude in G flat major Opus 10 No. 5 ('Black Keys'), is clear and delicate, with very little pedalling. Similarly, Paderewski's earliest recordings from 1911, which include Chopin's Nocturnes in F major and F sharp major Opus 15, are much more lightly pedalled than his later, electrical recordings.

In the pre-electric studio, orchestras were drastically reduced in size, to a maximum of perhaps thirty, in order to fit into the room and to be close enough to the horn. In recordings of operatic arias the best position was occupied by the singer, so the orchestra was at a disadvantage. To compensate for this, string sections were often adapted into a strange hybrid creation which would have sounded dreadful in the concert hall (and frequently does on record) but could at least be heard. This included the 'Stroh Violin', a specially devised instrument amplified by a horn. An article in the *Gramophone* in December 1928 looks back at the days of acoustic recording, and lists a typical string section of a recording orchestra as follows: 4 first violins, 2 Stroh second violins, 1 or 2 Stroh violas plus 1 clarinet, 1 cello plus 1 bassoon, 1 contra-bassoon plus 1 tuba. It is the tuba replacing the double-basses which gives the 'oom-pah' character to many early recordings of opera arias, providing a sad contrast between the vividness of the voice and the dullness of the group accompanying it. But the quality of the playing on such recordings is also very variable. Even if the best orchestral players were engaged (which, to judge by the results, was not always the case), much depended on the skill of the conductor. Experienced opera conductors, such as Landon Ronald and Percy Pitt, could achieve reasonable precision and point even under such conditions. The anonymous conductors who directed many of the early opera recordings presided over lamentable performances, ill-tuned and rhythmically leaden.

Clearly, therefore, the performances on pre-electric recordings have to be taken for what they are: a partial representation of what the musicians would have achieved in concert performance, adapted to suit the limitations of the recording machinery of the day.

There were much more sophisticated attempts at early recording of orchestras without resort to such drastic rescorings. Nikisch's 1913 recording of Beethoven's Fifth Symphony is perhaps the most famous pre-electric orchestral recording, one of the earliest complete recordings of a symphony, and the first to be conducted by an internationally famous conductor. But the quality of the result is much less than its fame would suggest. Little of the power of the (reduced) Berlin Philharmonic comes through, and without it one gets little impression of Nikisch's greatness as a conductor (both Boult and Toscanini said that this recording was not at all like Nikisch's concert performances). What could be achieved in the pre-electric studio is more clearly demonstrated by one of the first recordings made by the Boston Symphony Orchestra, conducted by Karl Muck in 1917, in which they play the Prelude to Act 3 of Wagner's *Lohengrin*. Subsidiary recording horns were set up for the front desks of the strings, and wind soloists ran over and played into them at important solos.[3] The result is impressive for its day, though the strings inevitably sound rather thin.

Considering the problems of recording an orchestra, a remarkable amount of orchestral repertoire was recorded in pre-electric days, and there were some substantial achievements.[4] The first recording of a Mahler symphony, No. 2, was made in 1923/4 by the Orchestra of the Berlin State Opera under Oskar Fried. Despite the small orchestra and the cramped conditions, much of the symphony is rhythmically well disciplined and remarkably successful – though the choral ending, sung by a small choir, is quite beyond the technology of the time. The first recording of Stravinsky's *Petrushka*, issued early in 1924, is also impressive for its day. It was played by the Royal Albert Hall Orchestra under Eugene Goossens. Stravinsky had already worked with Goossens in London, and praised him as 'a master of orchestral technique'. The rhythmic control is better than in Stravinsky's own early (electrical) recordings of a few years later: 'Dance of the Coachmen', for example, though it starts messily, develops into an incisive performance.

As with the thousands of recordings of opera arias, the best orchestral recordings are the result of a combination of things: clever and sensitive use of the technology, care in the arrangement of players in relation to the recording horns, skill in reducing the forces to what could be accommodated, players of the highest quality, and a conductor able to adapt to the circumstances and to maintain complete control in uncomfortable conditions. Although Toscanini always disliked recording and particularly hated the pre-electric recording studio, declaring the results a failure, the few recordings that he made with the orchestra of La Scala in 1920 and 1921 are remarkably successful. As a member of the orchestra's staff remembered, for these sessions 'The orchestra, reduced to its bare essentials, was stuffed and squashed into an enormous wooden niche, from which four or five shiny megaphone-shaped phonograph horns stuck out. The double basses were partly reinforced by the tuba.'[5] Despite these conditions, the Overture to Donizetti's *Don Pasquale* has marvellously subtle flexibility and witty rhythmic point.

Of major composers working in the early days of recordings, Elgar, Richard Strauss and Rachmaninoff were the first to take recordings seriously, conducting and playing pre-electric records of a number of their works. Elgar went to great efforts to rescore his music for the limited technology. One result was his first recording of the Violin Concerto with Marie Hall as soloist (1916), for which he wrote a new harp part to fill in the quiet textures. But this recording also illustrates the savagery with which pre-electric recordings of major works were often cut. Elgar reduced each movement of the Concerto to a fraction of its original length to fit on one side.[6] It becomes clear just how drastic these cuts are if one compares this recording with Elgar's later, complete, recording with the young Yehudi Menuhin (1932). Menuhin's performance of the slow movement lasts just over thirteen minutes, divided into three sides; Hall's cut version lasts just over four minutes. The recording amounts to little more than a 'selection of themes' from the Concerto.

In 1916, when Elgar made that recording, cutting of long movements was routine. When Busoni first recorded in 1919, 'They wanted the Faust waltz (which lasts a good ten minutes) *but it was only to take four minutes*! That meant quickly cutting, patching and improvising, so that there should still be some sense left in it.'[7] Gramophone records were very expensive, and it was rare for a record company to take the commercial risk of issuing a major work complete. By the 1920s, however, the practice of cutting was being regularly deplored in the pages of the new *Gramophone* magazine (established in 1923). In February 1924 a review of a disc by the Léner Quartet, containing a movement of Brahms's A minor Quartet with most of the middle section removed, concluded, 'apart from the pleasure the melody gives *per se* the record is worthless from the musical point of view'. On the same page the reviewer of a cut recording of Beethoven's Rondino for wind instruments wrote 'any cutting of reputable works is strongly to be deprecated'.[8] However, it would be a mistake to judge this practice of cutting by the standards of the twenty-first century. Cuts were also common in the concert hall in the 1920s and earlier, particularly in the orchestral tuttis of concertos. The modern reverence for composer's texts was not fully developed in the early twentieth century, and what was done on record was an exaggeration, for commercial reasons, of what was normal practice in the concert hall.

Piano rolls

Sound recording was incapable of reproducing anything like the full frequency-range or dynamic range of a piano or orchestra until the mid-1920s. The orchestra had to wait for the arrival of electrical recording. For the piano, there was in the early decades of the twentieth century an alternative to sound recording, which avoided the limitations of the gramophone but imposed limitations of its own. This was the 'reproducing piano', a highly sophisticated development of the pianola. The pianola was an automatic piano, which incorporated a pneumatic mechanism to operate the hammers. Holes cut into a paper roll instructed the machine when to play each note. A treadle was operated to fill the bellows and to turn the roll, and there were levers which could be used as crude volume-controls for the bass and treble sections of the piano. It was first manufactured in the last years of the nineteenth century, and over the following three decades developed into a huge market. A wide range of music was available on piano rolls, and a number of composers, including Stravinsky, wrote original works for pianola, taking advantage of the machine's ability to transcend the limitations of human hands. For a few years, sales of pianolas surpassed those of conventional pianos, until the combination of economic depression, electrically recorded gramophone records, and radio led to the collapse of the pianola market in the late 1920s.[9]

The pianola, despite extravagant advertising claims, was never able to reproduce the subtleties of a real pianist's performance. The reproducing piano, the Rolls Royce of pianolas, was another matter. Its recording machinery was built into high-quality grand pianos, and, as a pianist played, it recorded onto a roll of paper not only the timing of each note, but also the speed of the hammers and the use of the pedals. Holes were then cut in the roll, corresponding to the recorded marks, so that when it was played back the pneumatic mechanism operating the hammers reproduced the original performance as accurately as possible. Most of the prominent pianists in the first three decades of the twentieth century made piano-roll recordings for one or more of three makes of reproducing piano: Welte-Mignon, Duo-Art and Ampico. Of these, Welte-Mignon was the first in the field, and Ampico was the most sophisticated.

Because reproducing pianos were very expensive, they never developed the mass market of the cruder pianola. But they did achieve a far higher level of musical respectability. Famous pianists gave their public stamp of approval to their rolls, though some, notably Schnabel, refused to record for the reproducing piano. There has been a revival of interest in piano rolls in recent years, and painstaking restoration of the original machinery, sometimes aided by computerised controls, has produced some remarkable results. However, the musical value of piano rolls and their accuracy as documents of a performance remain controversial. If sound recordings do not give the whole picture of a pianist, they do at least reproduce, within their limitations, the actual sound of a musician playing. The reproducing piano does not reproduce the sound, but the action of a pianist. The question is whether such a machine, however accurate, could ever end up sounding like the real thing.

The accuracy of the reproducing piano certainly had its limitations. Though all three of the principal makes of machine could make a clear distinction between the dynamic levels of melody and accompaniment, none of them could record and reproduce the precise volume of each note in a complicated texture. As a result, their rolls often sound rhythmically clumsy, particularly in the relationship between melody and bass. The most sophisticated system, Ampico, though capable of more subtlety than the others, has been criticised for the extent to which the technicians were in the habit of tidying up the performances by ironing out rhythmic irregularities in rapid passages. And the available evidence suggests that, with all three makes of machine, much of the 'expressive' content was added by technicians after the performance, rather than recorded accurately at the time.

This is a field in which balanced judgement and good scholarship are in short supply. Extravagant claims for the accuracy of piano rolls are often made, particularly by enthusiasts involved in their reproduction or promotion. Reproducing pianos are undoubtedly remarkable and exciting machines, and it is easy to be carried away by the sheer cleverness of them. Actually being in the room while one is playing is like being in the passenger seat of a very expensive sports car: one cannot help but admire the technology. It is understandable that, in the days when sound-recordings of the piano were so unsatisfactory, pianists and others were extremely impressed by what the reproducing piano could do. Cool appraisal of them is hampered by the fact that the makers of the reproducing pianos guarded the secrets of their mechanisms jealously, so it is difficult to find accurate information about their workings and, especially, their mechanical (and therefore musical) limitations.

One point which applies to all three types is that it can never be wholly satisfactory to record the actions of a pianist on one piano, and then transfer this information to a different piano with different acoustical properties, and with hammers in a different condition. Anyone who has ever witnessed a concert pianist trying out an unfamiliar piano will know what an absurd suggestion this is. Delicate adjustment of the playback mechanism of a reproducing piano is needed to achieve even a plausible result, and it can never be known how close the reproduction is to the original performance on the original instrument.

The pianist David Wilde convincingly demonstrated this point in a programme on BBC Radio 3 in 1979.[10] He described attending a rehearsal for a performance of piano rolls at the Purcell Room on London's South Bank, given by the Player Piano Group. 'Throughout the rehearsal I was aware of a rather subdued quality in the performances we were hearing. Afterwards I asked for, and was kindly permitted, an opportunity to play the piano that was being used for the playbacks myself. I found that it was a little-known make which was very subdued in sound. Had I been giving a recital on it, I would have had to rebalance the harmonies accordingly, making a great deal of the top of the instrument, and probably playing with more arm-weight than I would normally use. Of course, the opportunity for such readjustment was not available to the shades of the pianists whose rolls were being played back on it. And I suspect that some of them would have declined to record on it in the first place.'

To show how he himself responded to the characteristics of different pianos, Wilde played two recordings he had made of a Consolation by Liszt. The first was recorded in 1961 on a Steinway, the second in 1974 on a Bösendorfer. The 1974 performance was much slower than the first, barely half the speed. Wilde attributed this mostly to the different sustaining characteristics of the two pianos, because the timing of the repeated notes in the slow melody depended on playing the repetition at just the right point in the decay of the preceding note. As he pointed out, 'If a piano roll of the second performance had been played, recorded and issued on an instrument for which I would normally have chosen the tempo of the first, the result wouldn't have been a slight difference but a total travesty . . . . Differences in the sound of the piano can make quite remarkable differences to rubato and tempo. And some rubati which sound grotesque on piano rolls would, I suggest, sound perfectly acceptable if the recording permitted us to hear the tonal subtleties that gave rise to them.'

Putting side by side a sound recording and even the most sophisticated piano-roll recording of the same pianist playing the same piece invariably reveals small but important differences, in the form of tiny dynamic nuances and subtleties of balance which are missed by the piano roll. And it is precisely in these tiny details that the character of a great pianist resides.

An example is Sergei Rachmaninoff playing his own piece 'Lilacs', a transcription of a song Opus 21 No. 5. Rachmaninoff made three recordings of it: an Ampico piano roll in 1922, an acoustic recording in 1923, and an electrical recording in 1942. The dynamic range and sound quality of the 1923 recording is very limited, so the 1922 Ampico roll is best compared with the 1942 sound-recording despite the twenty-year gap between them. Rachmaninoff's interpretation of the piece is very similar in these two recordings. But there are noticeable differences between them, of a kind that are usual in comparisons between sound-recordings and piano rolls. The 1942 gramophone recording is absolutely characteristic of Rachmaninoff. The way the lines sing out, the way the different strands of the texture are subtly layered, so that the prominence of each line comes and goes, the way in which he separates a melodic line from its accompaniment by subtly dislocating it rhythmically, particularly by playing melody notes fractionally late: these are all vintage Rachmaninoff. The 1922 Ampico roll sounds like someone who is having a go at imitating Rachmaninoff and making quite a good job of it. Although the timing is remarkably accurate the performance does not quite hang together, because the melodic fragments do not sing out as in the sound recording, and they therefore fail to achieve the right balance with the accompanying texture. One of the results of this is that the subtle rhythmic dislocations sound messy, like failures to co-ordinate rather than purposeful expressive devices. This is no doubt partly the result of insensitive recording of detailed dynamics on the roll (which no mechanism was capable of reproducing exactly), and partly what David Wilde illustrates: that a performance recorded on one piano cannot be played back accurately on another.

'Lilacs' is a simple example. Comparison between roll and sound-recording in virtuoso works often shows that the roll evens out rapid passages, making them sound superhuman. A good example is Josef Lhévinne playing Schulz-Evler's transcription of Johann Strauss's *Blue Danube*. His Ampico roll performance attracted enthusiastic attention when it was featured in a BBC Radio 3 programme about Ampico reproducing pianos in the 1960s, and then issued with other, equally spectacular performances, in a series of LPs (Great Virtuosi of the Golden Age on the Argo label). The feathery lightness of the quiet playing is incredible, and runs are extraordinarily even and secure. It gives the impression of a player for whom technical difficulties simply do not exist. Lhévinne's sound-recording of *The Blue Danube* (1928) is not like that at all. It is very impressive playing, but it lacks the machine-like regularity and effortlessness of the roll. Comparison with the sound-recording proves that the playing on the roll is literally incredible, and that not only were runs made more even than Lhévinne could actually play them, but that the machinery of the piano on which the rolls were played back for those reissues in the 1960s was set to produce a super-pianissimo that was not actually in Lhévinne's habitual catalogue of effects (this was particularly impressive in his roll of Liszt's *La campanella*).

Any comparison between piano rolls and sound-recordings reveals differences of these kinds. Welte-Mignon and Duo-Art often sound clumsier than Ampico, because their mechanisms are less sophisticated. As David Wilde said, one simply cannot judge what these clumsinesses would have sounded like if the dynamics had been accurately reproduced. Rolls of, for example, Debussy and Leschetizky fall so far short of descriptions of their playing by contemporaries that it is impossible to know from the rolls what they really sounded like. And yet one can hear and read an increasing number of enthusiasts and academics describing such material as if it can be relied upon: stating, for example, that Leschetizky's use of arpeggiation was less subtle than that of his pupils. The truth is that the few Welte-Mignon rolls of Leschetizky are dismally inadequate. The arpeggiation certainly sounds clumsy, but what would it sound like if one could hear all the subtleties of balance and nuance?

The undoubted value of piano rolls is to increase our knowledge of pianists who did not survive into the period of electrical gramophone recordings. Busoni is perhaps the most important example. According to Ferruccio Bonavia, he 'commanded a wider range of tone than any other living pianist',[11] so the short pieces which he recorded for the pre-electric gramophone in 1919 and 1922 could hardly be expected to give an adequate picture. Again, extravagant claims are made for the accuracy of his piano rolls, most recently in Nimbus's Grand Piano series, but any idea that they convey the full range and subtlety of Busoni's piano-playing does not stand up to close scrutiny. Nevertheless, some of his piano rolls do convey considerable power, and they help us to gain a more complete impression of what his playing must have been like.

The place of piano rolls could be summed up by saying that they are important, but limited, historical documents, and what they contain and do not contain needs to be considered carefully if they are to be evaluated properly. This is really no more than is true of any other kind of recording, and for that matter any other kind of historical evidence. But piano rolls in particular have a way of provoking blind (or rather deaf) faith from the enthusiasts, answered by a dismissive snort from the sceptical camp. The truth is much more complex than these responses suggest, and can be arrived at only by careful listening and accurate gathering of evidence.

Time-limits and side-joins

With the coming of electrical recording in 1925, many of the limitations of the acoustic process disappeared. There were to be refinements over the next twenty-five years, but straight away in the late 1920s recordings were being issued on which a grand piano sounded like a grand piano, and a full orchestra sounded like a full orchestra. It was certainly not High Fidelity, but it was much more like the real thing than anything achieved in earlier years. This helped to accelerate the decline of the reproducing piano, as more and more of the great pianists recorded substantial works for the gramophone in good-quality sound.

As for orchestral recordings, they suddenly came into their own. One indication of their new success is the change in public attitudes to them. When, at the end of the period of acoustic recording, the *Gramophone* in October 1925 published a list of the most popular records as voted for by their readers, very few orchestral recordings were included. This was despite the fact that many orchestral works were by then available, including all of Beethoven's symphonies. When a similar survey of the most popular electrical recordings was published after only three years of electrical recording, in April 1928, two thirds of them were orchestral, including seven of the ten most popular.

The most serious remaining limitation of the gramophone record was its length. Until the development of the Long-Playing Record in the late 1940s, a long movement usually had to be recorded, and always had to be played back, in short sections. A 12-inch 78 rpm record had a time-limit of under five minutes per side (though occasionally longer), nearer four minutes in the early days. If the music did not fit conveniently on a side, it could be split between two or more sides, or shortened by cutting, or played faster than usual. For long movements, difficult decisions sometimes had to be made. A movement lasting twelve minutes would have to be split between three sides. A movement lasting nine and a half minutes might just be accommodated on two sides, but only if a convenient stopping point could be found halfway, and only if the performers were careful not to relax the pace and overrun the time-limit. Performers might well decide to take a movement slightly faster than usual in order to fit it onto the side. This was common practice in the days of pre-electric recordings, and probably more common than was publicly acknowledged after that.

The need to stop in the middle of long movements also meant that the train of thought was broken. A side might be recorded two or three times before going on to the next. The side eventually chosen as the 'master' might have been recorded hours apart from that chosen as the preceding master. If there was a fault, an individual side might be re-recorded days or weeks later. Now that editors using modern computer techniques are so skilful at joining the sides together for CD reissues, we get the impression that the whole thing was continuous. But it was not, except when two recording machines were used to cover continuous recording, as was sometimes done in order to record a live concert (some of Toscanini's recordings were made like this, as were the famous recordings of Mahler's Ninth Symphony and *Das Lied von der Erde* conducted by Bruno Walter in Vienna in the late 1930s). So when analysing tempo, and the relationships between tempi over the course of a long movement, one has to bear in mind that what was done on the sides of the issued recording may be only an approximation to what might have happened in continuous performance, and particularly in live concert conditions, when there was no clock to watch and no interruption between one part of the movement and the next.

What went on at recording sessions seventy or eighty years ago was not generally documented in detail, any more than it is now, and facts are hard to establish. Jerrold Northrop Moore gives two very clear examples in his *Elgar on Record*. The first is Elgar's acoustic recording of *Sea Pictures* (1922–3) with the contralto Leila Megane: 'The big songs were not cut, but were taken at rapid speed – especially 'The Swimmer', which proved a gruelling test for the singer.'[12] It is not clear whether Moore deduced this from the result, or whether there is documentary evidence for it. Certainly there are many pre-electric recordings of songs and single movements which sound as if they were taken at an uncomfortable pace to fit them on the side.

There are more details for Elgar's recording of the *Nursery Suite* on 23 May 1931. All went well until the recording of the last side, which overran the limit for the length of the side. There was not time to repeat it at that session, so another was arranged. Fred Gaisberg wrote to Elgar on 26 May 1931: 'We are trying to arrange a session to complete the "Nursery Suite" on June 4th. You will recollect that the last record was about 10 seconds too long, and Willie Reed [the leader], with whom I was speaking after the session, said that he thought it would be quite easy to make up this difference in time so as to get the record on one side instead of making two records of it, which would be uncommercial.'[13]

Evidence for the speeding up of a side occasionally comes to light years after the event. Bruno Walter conducted a studio recording of Mahler's Symphony No. 4 in 1946. The biographer Henry-Louis de la Grange describes Walter's tempo for the finale as 'surprisingly rapid', and reveals that 'The soloist, Desi Halban, informed me that he was following the instructions from the recording engineers, who had to keep in mind the duration of the 78-rpm side.'[14] Albert Sammons made a famous recording of Elgar's Violin Concerto with Henry Wood and the New Queen's Hall Orchestra in 1929. Sammons had often played the work under Elgar, and yet some of his tempi are faster than the metronome markings, and substantially faster than those in Elgar's own recording with Menuhin (1932, a recording that is discussed in chapter 5). The last movement in particular is taken at a breakneck pace. Sammons told his students that tempi in the finale, and the first movement, were faster than those he usually adopted in concert performance, so as to fit the music on the sides – 'considerably faster' in the finale, according to Sammons's biographer Eric

Wetherell.[15] This is interesting as far as it goes, but it does not tell us exactly what Sammons and Wood did. Both the first and last movements have various tempi within them, and the finale includes the long unaccompanied cadenza. How much was taken at a faster tempo than usual – entire movements, or just the fast sections? None of the twelve sides of the set lasts longer than four minutes, so any one of them could have been taken at a slightly slower pace without overrunning. The subject is a good deal more complicated than it seems at first.

Slight speeding up of a tempo must have been very common, where a movement or section almost fitted within the time-limit. Quite apart from the commercial considerations, to which Fred Gaisberg referred, in many cases it was musically more satisfactory to compromise in this way rather than to have to break the music at an inappropriate moment. But identifying which sides were treated like this is, in most cases, impossible. Many performances on 78 rpm records give the impression of haste compared with modern performances, and it is difficult to disentangle anxiety about the side-lengths from the general style of the time. One certainly cannot assume that all the tempi on 78 rpm records are the tempi of concert performance. Whenever a 78 rpm side is tightly filled, it is right to suspect that the performers might have had their eyes on the clock, and that without the restraint of the side-length they might have taken the music a little more slowly. On the other hand, there are plenty of performances which sound hasty even when there was room to spare at the end of the side. From a modern perspective, haste was part of the style of the time.

There is, for example, a 1923 recording of Ravel's Introduction and Allegro, played by British musicians and conducted by Ravel. It lasts nine and a half minutes, substantially less than most later recordings, and the Allegro sounds very fast to modern listeners (by comparison, a 1938 recording by Lily Laskine and the Calvet Quartet, for example, lasts just under eleven minutes). Surely, one might suppose, the music was a tight fit on the records, and Ravel compromised by taking a faster tempo than he would have in the concert hall. But the recording occupied four sides, two 12-inch Columbia discs, with plenty of room at the end of each side if Ravel had wanted to take slower tempi. A reviewer in the *Gramophone* in February 1924 complained, 'surely it was not necessary to leave such large unused spaces on the records – why not have had two 10in. discs? This is a very flagrant instance of waste.'[16] The two discs cost 7s.6d. each, a substantial amount of money in the 1920s. Indeed, later recordings of the work were either fitted on three sides, with another piece of music occupying the fourth side, or recorded on 10-inch discs. The 1938 Calvet Quartet recording occupies four 10-inch sides, and yet is much slower than Ravel's performance on four 12-inch sides.

Despite this cautionary example, even when there was a comfortable amount of room on the disc musicians would have been aware that the limit was there. In 1971 Adrian Boult was asked by Edward Johnson whether, in the days of 78 rpm recording, he had ever speeded the music up to fit it on a record. Boult replied, 'You have raised a very interesting point and one which I am afraid I cannot answer really successfully. You see when you have it in mind that you have got to get to a certain point in 4¼ minutes, or whatever it is, you are inclined to hurry even though you know it is really all right, and I think there is no doubt that the recording managers were very nervous about it and we all had it a bit on our minds . . . .'[17] On the other hand, one cannot assume that, even when there is a tight fit on the record, the tempo was necessarily speeded up. Writers and critics are sometimes too ready to assume that any exceptionally fast tempo on a 78 rpm record must have been influenced by the side-limit. One example was a claim by Joseph Cooper, in a review of Rachmaninoff's recording of his Second Piano Concerto, that he 'rushed' the ending of the finale to keep it within the time-limit. Rachmaninoff's tempo for much of the finale is, indeed, substantially faster than his metronome markings in the score.[18] Edward Johnson (who has taken an interest in these matters) observed that the timing for the final side of the set was a mere 3 mins 25 secs, well under the limit. So he wrote to Stokowski, who conducted the Philadelphia Orchestra for that recording, and asked him whether he had indeed rushed the ending. Stokowski replied laconically, 'We did not take the ending faster for any reason other than that the composer wished.'[19]

The Adagietto from Mahler's Fifth Symphony is a movement that was taken much faster on 78 rpm recordings than in most later performances. De la Grange lists the timings for several recordings, from Mengelberg in 1926 through to modern times. The performances recorded on 78s by Mengelberg (1926) and Walter (1938) are under eight minutes, neatly fitting two 78 rpm sides. All the recordings from later years are substantially longer, ranging from Solti at 9 mins 40 secs to Haitink at 13 mins 55 secs. But suspicions that Walter and Mengelberg might have speeded up their performances have to be put against timings of Mahler's concert performances: 7½ minutes at Hamburg in 1905 (in Walter's copy of the score) and 7 minutes at St Petersburg in 1907.[20] Both Mengelberg and Walter were closely associated with Mahler, and heard Mahler conduct this work. This does not prove that Mengelberg and Walter took the music at the pace they wanted to in the recording studio, but it makes it far more likely than if Mahler had habitually taken the movement much more slowly in concert.

Take numbers

Until the introduction of tape-recording around 1950, musicians recorded onto a wax disc one side at a time. Recordings could not be edited, and they could not even be played back at the time without damaging the wax master. After electrical recordings were introduced in 1925, it became possible to record onto two or more machines at once. Sometimes the extra copy was played back at the time, but more often it was kept as a back-up in case the master was damaged. Sometimes two machines were set at different recording levels, so that the one with the better dynamic level could be chosen as the master.

In the vast majority of 78 rpm recordings there was absolutely no editing (though a technique of 'overdubbing' to correct faulty sections was occasionally used). Nevertheless, there were choices. For each side, a choice had to be made between the different takes. A particular take could be chosen for a number of reasons. The most obvious was musical: the master take was often the one which worked best as a performance, either in spirit, or because it was the most accurate in ensemble, or because it contained the fewest number of mistakes – or, most often, a combination of these factors. But there were technical reasons why the musically best take could not always be used. The recording machinery could malfunction in various ways. The wax recording might be damaged, or the master derived from it might fail the tests for technical quality. One particular hazard was 'blasting', the overloading of the disc in loud passages, causing distortion or the jumping of the needle. Too high a dynamic level would also cause the disc to fail the 'Wear Test'.

The matrix numbers of 78 rpm records, stamped in the shellac, often include the take number at the end, either as a Roman numeral (in the case of many HMV discs) or as a number after a dash. Some examples are given in Table 1. It is striking how first and second takes are in the overwhelming majority. Rachmaninoff provides an exception. His electrical concerto recordings were all achieved with a maximum of three takes for each side (the pre-electric recording of the second concerto has take 4 for two sides). The expense of orchestral sessions must always, throughout recording history, have limited the number of retakes. Rachmaninoff's solo recordings are extremely variable: Chopin's Sonata in B flat minor has only first and second takes, but a few solo pieces were taken many times (twenty-three times in the case of Mendelssohn's 'Spinning Song'). Rachmaninoff's attitude to recording was the antithesis of Kreisler's, as Geraldine Farrar reported to Kreisler's biographer Louis Lochner when reminiscing about their recording sessions for Schubert and Grieg sonatas: 'Kreisler would come out of the studio in high glee, still aglow with the beautiful music which he had helped to create. Rachmaninoff, on the other hand, emerged with his sad face, worried about this or that phrase which he thought had not quite come out as it should. He would continue to brood over the situation for days and finally decide that another recording ought to be made.' Kreisler 'artfully dodged the issue of doing the whole thing over again'.[21]

To judge by her recording of Schumann's Carnaval, Myra Hess, a pianist who loathed recording even more than Rachmaninoff did, needed more takes

Table 1: Take numbers of a selection of 78 rpm recordings, 1919–1938

Schumann, Piano Concerto. Myra Hess, Orchestra, Walter Goehr (1937)
1, 3, 2, 1 (replaced by take 3 in 1949), 1, 2, 1, 1

Schumann, *Carnaval.* Myra Hess (1938)
3, 3, 5, 2, 4, 3

Berlioz, *Symphonie fantastique.* Paris SO, Monteux (1931)
1, 3, 2, 2, 1, 1, 2, 2, 3, 2, 2, 3

Brahms, Violin Concerto. Kreisler, LPO, Barbirolli (1936)
1, 2, 2, 1, 1, 1, 1, 4, 4

Dvořák, Cello Concerto. Casals, Czech PO, Szell (1937)
2, 2, 2, 2, 2, 2, 1, 2, 3, 1

Dvořák, Symphony No. 8. Czech PO, Talich (1935)
2, 1, 1, 1, 1, 1, 1, 1, 2, 1

Beethoven, Symphony No. 6. BBC SO, Toscanini (1937)
1, 1, 1, 2, 2, 1, 2, 1, 2, 1

Mozart, Symphony No. 41. Vienna PO, Walter (1938)
1, 1, 1, 1, 1, 1, 2

Brahms, Clarinet Quintet. Kell, Busch Quartet (1937)
1, 1, 1, 1, 2, 1, 1, 1

Beethoven, String Quartet in A minor Op. 132. Busch Quartet (1937)
1, 1, 1, 1, 1, 1, 1, 1, 1, 1, 1

Brahms, String Quartet in B flat. Budapest Quartet (1932)
1, 1, 1, 1, 1, 1, 1, 1

Schubert, Piano Trio in B flat. Cortot, Thibaud and Casals (1926)
1, 1, 1, 1, 1, 1, 1, 1

Beethoven, Piano Sonata in B flat Op. 106 ('Hammerklavier'). Schnabel (1935)
1, 2, 3, 2, 2, 1, 2, 1, 2, 5, 2, 4

Beethoven, Piano Sonata in E flat Op. 7. Schnabel (1935)
1, 5, 1, 1, 1, 1, 1

Chopin, Ballades. Cortot (1929)
No. 1: 2, 1
No. 2: 2, 1
No. 3: 1, 1
No. 4: 1, 3

Stravinsky, *Petrushka.* London Symphony Orchestra, Coates (c.1928)
2, 3, 1, 4, 2, 1, 2

Stravinsky, *The Rite of Spring.* Straram Orchestra, Stravinsky (1929)
1, 1, 1, 2, 2, 1, 2, 2, 1, 2

Stravinsky, *Petrushka* Suite. 'Symphony Orchestra', Stravinsky (1928)
3, 3, 1, 1, 1, 2

Rachmaninoff, Piano Concerto No. 2. Rachmaninoff, Philadelphia Orchestra, Stokowski
(second recording 1929)
2, 2, 2, 1, 1, 3, 2, 1, 3, 3

Rachmaninoff, Rhapsody on a Theme of Paganini. Rachmaninoff, Philadelphia Orchestra, Stokowski (1934)
1, 1, 1, 1, 1, 1

Rachmaninoff, *Isle of the Dead*. Philadelphia Orchestra, Rachmaninoff (1929)
5, 4, 4, 5, 4

Rachmaninoff, Prelude in C sharp minor Op. 3 No. 2. Rachmaninoff
(first recording 1919) 3
(second recording 1921) 3
(third recording 1928) 23 (*sic*)

Chopin, Sonata in B flat minor. Rachmaninoff (1930)
2, 2, 2, 2, 2, 1, 2

Mendelssohn, Spinning Song. Rachmaninoff
(first recording 1920) 2
(second recording 1928) 21 (*sic*)

Schubert, Sonata in A for Violin and Piano. Kreisler and Rachmaninoff (1928)
5, 5, 2, 4, 3, 4

than most pianists to achieve masters that satisfied her. But, as with Rachmaninoff, an orchestral session, the Schumann Concerto, resulted in a predominance of first and second takes for masters.

Of course a 'first take' is only the first take that was deemed to be usable, and was therefore kept. Before reaching that stage, musicians would, then as now, spend some time playing trial takes, to establish the best microphone positions, the best balance, the most natural quality of sound, the best sense of immediacy. They could listen to such trials, but playing them damaged the impression in the wax, so they were not generally used for the issued discs. Once the musicians and technicians were satisfied with the trials, subsequent takes would be preserved without being played back.

The numbers of the issued takes give no idea of these preliminary trials. At modern recording sessions it is not unusual for most of the first session to be spent trying to achieve a balance and quality of sound that satisfies everyone. Things were simpler in the days of mono recording in the 78 rpm studio, but it could nevertheless take some time to get a satisfactory result, even before starting to record a 'real' take. Adolf Busch described a particularly difficult day in 1937, when his quartet recorded Brahms's Clarinet Quintet with Reginald Kell:

> This was one of the most interesting recording sessions I ever had. When we started at ten o'clock in the morning, I thought we would get nowhere that day. Everything seemed to go wrong. The first playbacks were completely unsatisfactory. 'I want more warmth of tone', I told the recording engineer. He understood, and accordingly arranged the microphones to better advantage. It is a pleasure to work with the people in His Master's Voice Studios – they are always so patient and understanding. We

got the warmth of tone in the recording, but the work formed itself slowly. I feel, however, that we gave one of our best performances in this composition. After playing for six hours, you might think we were tired, but this was not the case. As a matter of fact, we were playing better at the end of six hours and with more enthusiasm than when we started in the morning.[22]

The take numbers on the published recording give no indication of these difficulties: all the sides chosen as masters are first takes, apart from one second take for the end of the second movement. Busch does not describe exactly what happened, but if 'the work formed itself slowly' presumably they must have made several attempts at the early sides but abandoned them at the time, perhaps not even completing them. Such 'false starts' do not show up in the take numbers.

Jerrold Northrop Moore in *Elgar on Record* gives the number of takes recorded, and the decisions about which take of each side was chosen as the master, for each of Elgar's recording sessions. Elgar's first electrical recording, of the 'Enigma' Variations, was recorded on 28 April 1926, using two recording lathes working in parallel (this had not been possible with acoustic recording).[23] The Theme and Variations 1–7, 10 and 11 were recorded in single takes (apart from any trial takes for playback at the time). Variations 8–9 and 12–14 had two takes each. Of the discs recorded on the first machine, five were later rejected after technical tests, most of them failing the 'Wear Test'. Those recorded on the second machine were more successful, presumably because the dynamic level was set a little lower for safety. Only one of these duplicate sides failed the technical tests (Variations 5–7), but unfortunately this was a take which also failed on the first machine. So that side had to be re-recorded at Elgar's next session four months later.

For Elgar's recording of the First Symphony, recorded over three sessions on 20–21 November 1930, one recording machine was used, but two takes were recorded of each side. Only one side (the second take of side 1) failed for technical reasons, so the remaining masters were presumably chosen for musical rather than technical reasons. The takes chosen were as follows: 1, 1, 2, 2, 2, 2, 2, 2, 1, 2, 1.

Recording and editing for LP and CD

The experience of the modern recording session is similar in some ways to the days of 78 rpm records but very different in others. Attitudes to accuracy have changed greatly. Recordings reveal that the expectations of precise accuracy were far lower in the 1920s–1930s than they are today. Over the last fifty years it has gradually become less and less acceptable for mistakes and bad tuning to find their way onto the finished disc. Since the advent of digital recording and modern computerised editing techniques, most of the CDs issued for sale have been, in terms of musical technique, virtually perfect. This level of expected perfection is quite a recent development. One only has to listen to some of the best-known recordings from the 1960s to realise that expectations were not set so high then, even though tape-editing was already well established (listen, for example, to the wind tuning in Solti's famous set of Wagner's *Ring* with the Vienna Philharmonic Orchestra, or in the recordings of the Suisse Romande Orchestra under Ansermet).

Modern musicians, therefore, have to contend with unprecedentedly high expectations. But they also know that editing is now extremely sophisticated. In the studio they have to play every note of the music perfectly at least once, but the illusion that they have done so continuously can be created by editing afterwards. Does this put them in a better or worse situation than the musicians entering the studio seventy years ago to make a set of 78 rpm discs? How does one balance the lower requirement for accuracy in those days against the absence of editing?

There was no safety net in the days before tape-editing. What you hear on the disc is what was actually achieved in the 4–5 minutes. This therefore imposed on the musicians the pressure of live performance, plus the additional anxiety caused by the need to be as accurate as possible. For many musicians, making records remained a very unnerving experience right through the era of 78 rpm recordings, until the advent of tape-editing. Rachmaninoff's view was widespread: 'When the test records are made, I know that I can hear them played back at me, and then everything is all right. But when the stage is set for the final recording, and I realise that this will remain for good, I get nervous and my hands get tense.'[24] It would be reasonable to deduce that many of the performances issued on 78 rpm records are more cautious than a concert performance would have been. On the other hand, it is difficult to imagine greater dare-devilry than Percy Grainger's studio recording of the finale of Chopin's B minor Sonata (1925), or Schnabel's of the 'Hammerklavier' Sonata (1935).

Most modern musicians are, on the whole, grateful for the existence of editing. But many regret that the quest for perfection has gone so far. Asked to name their favourite records, many musicians will name recordings of the distant past, made when there was no editing, and when the performance of each side was reproduced warts and all. Yet those same musicians would be horrified if some of the inaccuracies heard in those famous old recordings were ever to appear in their own CDs. Musicians today live with something of a conflict between the need to be perfect and the desire to be real. And this conflict is seen in the history of recording methods and approaches since the end of the relatively straightforward days of 78s, and the development of highly sophisticated recording and editing techniques.

Modern studio recordings (in the broad sense of performances recorded specially for issue on disc, whether in an actual studio or some other hall or church) cover a wide range of practices, and have changed over the years. In the half-century since the introduction of tape-editing and, a little later, stereophonic recording, different recording companies have developed different policies with editing and microphone techniques. Some of the most successful orchestral recordings from the early days of LP were recorded very simply. The American company Mercury, with their famous slogan 'Living Presence', made extremely vivid mono recordings in the 1950s using a single microphone. Their early stereo recordings, from 1956 onwards, were recorded on three channels, using three microphones only. Mixing the result to two channels for conventional stereo was a compromise, but the results were still very clear and colourful. By contrast, an alternative approach was to place many microphones at different points in the orchestra, to record onto several tracks, and to mix the result in the studio. Over the years, schools of recording became somewhat polarised between two schools, the simple and the complex. The idea of simplicity was also applied to editing. Some companies aimed to create a recording with the minimum of editing or rebalancing, with the intention of simulating the effect of live performance. The best-known of these was Nimbus, who used little editing, and recorded from a single microphone position. In their recordings there is therefore no mixing of the sounds from several microphones. The balance is what is heard from one point, even when recording a symphony orchestra or a large choral work.

The two extremes of simplicity and complexity can produce quite different results, in balance, clarity, and blend of sonorities. Proponents of one or other of these extremes tend to talk as if their approach were a matter of philosophy or morality – particularly those who advocate the simple approach. But neither of these two extremes is 'right' or 'wrong'. They are different approaches which produce different results. They also make the experience of recording different for the musicians. One might think that a single microphone position would be most 'natural' for musicians, and would therefore make them most comfortable. Some do respond well to these conditions, but others find them difficult. The need to make the balance and blend of sound satisfactory with a single microphone position means that musicians sometimes find themselves having to sit in unusual formations so that the balance of sonorities is right – far apart from each other, or with a trumpet soloist at the back of the orchestra instead of the front, for example. By contrast, the multi-microphone, multi-tracking technique means that much trust has to be placed in the recording engineer and producer, who have to mix the tracks to produce a realistic balance. But use of many microphones does mean that a large orchestra can come in and sit in their normal places, and record quickly without hours of setting up. Cost is a large factor in these artistic and technical decisions.

In practice, the two traditions have tended to encourage (or perhaps have been led by) different ideas of what the result should sound like. In the single-microphone-position tradition, the emphasis is on a natural-sounding blend and ambience, often in a rather resonant hall. In the multi-microphone tradition, clarity has tended to be the first priority, often with the result that everything can be heard very well. But the effect can be rather clinical, with little sense of being in the audience in a concert hall. This was particularly true of many American recordings of the 1960s and 1970s. The extraordinarily beautiful blend of sound which George Szell and the Cleveland Orchestra achieved in the concert hall, for example when they visited the Edinburgh Festival in the early 1960s, was simply not reproduced on the CBS recordings. The playing was just as good, but the blend had been replaced by what sounded more like a clinical dissection of the sound (an effect that has been somewhat modified in subsequent reissues on CD).

Modern recordings of classical music usually fall between these extremes. One can usually hear the detail very well – often better than in the concert hall – but even with multi-microphone, multi-track recording, the dry, clinical approach has mercifully gone out of fashion, and the result when all the tracks are skilfully combined is something not unlike the sound from the best possible position in the ideal concert hall. Whether such a position in such a concert hall could ever really exist is another matter. Modern recordings have an impact and clarity that is often an exaggeration of what one hears when sitting in a real hall.

The question of editing is, similarly, often debated from a moral and philosophical standpoint. Again, one might assume that musicians would be happier with less editing, so that what is heard on the CD is what they really did. Those with a minimalist approach to editing regard this as the most 'honest' approach. But the modern expectation of accuracy in every detail, particularly on a CD, puts great pressure on musicians and record producers not to let a single blemish be heard on the finished recording. Some musicians like the idea of having no editing, and, in the days of LPs, made 'direct cut' recordings straight onto disc, so that no editing was possible. But being required to play with minimal editing can make musicians nervous and cautious, and unwilling to take risks if mistakes cannot be corrected afterwards. For some musicians, this presents them with the worst of both worlds: the old world of 78 rpm recording, when there was no editing, and the new world in which everyone expects accuracy.

It is not surprising, therefore, that musicians themselves sometimes press for editing that the producer does not think necessary. The correspondence of Nimbus Records, who prided themselves on minimal editing, contains letters with musicians arguing about how much editing is needed.[25] Some of the musicians who recorded for them relished the opportunity to play as in a concert with no thought of editing, among them Bernard Roberts, Shura Cherkassky and Martin Best. Bernard Roberts recorded the complete Beethoven Piano Sonatas direct to disc in the early 1980s, with no editing at all, and then, some years later, repeated the cycle for CD. He admits that though he enjoyed making both recordings, his playing was to some extent restrained in the first 'direct cut' recording: 'When we went to CD I thought it would be a good idea to do the Beethovens again because I'd not only developed but the constraints were a little less as you can stop if you make the most terrible mistake and you don't have to play the whole twenty-five minutes again to cope with one error near the end. I hope the second set are a bit more urgent and expressive as I think the direct-to-disc were rather careful because of my awareness of the consequences of making a mistake.'[26]

Other musicians were less happy with the whole philosophy of minimal editing, and there were sometimes heated exchanges between producer and musician. The relationship between Nimbus and the violinist Oscar Shumsky started well and then went extremely sour.[27] Plans for a recording of Brahms's Violin Concerto in 1983 came to nothing, because Shumsky feared that Nimbus's principle of recording from a single microphone position might allow the orchestra to swamp him. Then the following year, he was unhappy with the unedited tapes of Brahms's Hungarian Dances, arguing (as many people do) that mistakes which pass almost unnoticed at a concert would become irritating on repeated listenings. He also stated that his recordings with other companies, in which the performance had been extensively edited, were 'none the worse for that'.

The Nimbus principle, however, was that anything more than minimal editing destroys the spirit of the performance. Nimbus's producer Adrian Farmer wrote to Shumsky about a Bach concerto recording: 'I will not, repeat not, for any artist, bend the rules on this subject, nor do I take well the suggestion that since you got away with it on your (other) recordings you will get away with it on your Nimbus recordings.'[28] That was the end of Shumsky's relationship with Nimbus.

To the Hanover Band, about one of their Beethoven series, Farmer wrote: 'To be blunt – the few corrections I made (and was happy to do so) have already made the Band sound better than they were, even in its present modestly corrected state it is of a total quality which is actually beyond the competence of the Band to reproduce in a live concert. . . . I know that none of you believe it but it is true and must be said again and again until it becomes part of everyone's soul – editing only improves the notes, the more important quality of communication is absolute and cannot be improved by cutting it up.'[29] For the time being, the Hanover Band accepted the Nimbus approach.

No doubt there have been many such arguments over the years, most of them undocumented. The argument about editing always comes down to two basic questions: Do recordings need to be perfect? And, is a recording that has been edited as 'real' as one without edits? To someone whose view is that unedited is best, and that a few mistakes do not matter, the logical conclusion would be simply to make recordings of concerts, and issue them on CD unedited. Many such 'live' recordings have been made over the last hundred years, and the best of them are exceptionally vivid. But how does the modern world reconcile the desire for vivid performance with the need for perfection?

Live and studio performance

The balance between live music-making and recording has changed radically over the last century, both for musicians and for audiences. In the prosperous parts of the world, most people today obtain most of their experience of music from recordings. By the same token, professional musicians are accustomed to making CDs, and the reputations of the most famous of them rest heavily on their recordings. Their concerts are secondary, in the public's awareness of them, and in the case of the most high-profile recording artists, in income. This is very different from the situation seventy or eighty years ago, and from the experience of people elsewhere in the world today without regular access to CD-playing or recording equipment.

Live music-making is a different activity from making recordings in a number of ways, some obvious, some less so. In the days before recording existed, any performance of music took place in 'real time', and when it reached the end it was over. The piece could be played again, but the performance which had just taken place was unrepeatable. Fundamental things flow from this, both for audiences and for musicians, and some of the consequences have been discussed in chapter 1. What happens in a live performance is not wholly controllable by musicians, and not wholly predictable by audiences. A live performance can get off to a shaky start and settle down. A tempo may at first be too slow or too fast, and need adjustment. Risks can be taken, and they may come off or not. The experience of hearing a performer taking risks in a live concert is very different from hearing it on a recording afterwards – and it is different for the performer too. In the concert, the performer 'goes for it', in the hope that it will come off. When the recording is played, the performer is absent, quite possibly even dead. Risks were taken at the concert, but now the consequences remain the same at every replaying.

Comparison between genuine live recordings and edited studio performances reveal that much can be lost by removing every trace of 'poor' ensemble. Part of the essence of performance is the awareness that human beings are performing, and that when they are performing together in an ensemble there is a continuous process of negotiation between players. The more thoroughly the moments of imperfection are removed, the less the listener is aware of this human process.

In 1961, Karel Ančerl and the Czech Philharmonic Orchestra recorded Dvořák's 'New World' Symphony. The scherzo has marvellous rhythmic point and bite, with the pairs of quavers (eighth notes) sharply articulated throughout. The tempo, once the rhythm becomes continuous at bar 12, is ♩. = 88. There is also a live recording of the symphony played by the same performers in 1958. In the live concert the scherzo sets off slightly too fast for the quavers (eighth notes) to be articulated clearly, at ♩. = 92. Gradually, over the first few bars, the pace settles to 88, and the articulation becomes sharper. By the time they reach the first repeat, the orchestra and conductor have found the same precision and crispness as in the studio recording. Listening to the live recording, one hears the process of achieving this over the opening bars. If this had occurred in the studio, the slightly uncertain start would have been replaced, so that the rhythm was perfect from the first bar. But what we hear in the live performance is a process of evolution, of finding the focus. It is a satisfying thing to hear, and it is denied us in edited recordings.

In 1957, Klemperer with the Philharmonia Chorus and Orchestra made a famous recording of Beethoven's Ninth Symphony. There is also a recording of the live performance which preceded the studio recording, and the two make a fascinating comparison. The concert took place at the Royal Festival Hall in London on 15 November 1957. The Philharmonia Chorus had been founded specifically to perform this work with Klemperer and the Philharmonia Orchestra, and this was their first concert. The studio recording was made on 21 and 25 November, soon after the concert, and it is very fine. Most of it is very similar to the concert performance, but there are one or two moments where it is different. One is in the finale, at the end of the 'Turkish March' (bars 431ff., letter K). The tenor and chorus finish, and the orchestra sets off into a *fugato* passage. Both the studio and the concert recording begin this passage at ♩. = 116. In the studio at this point, the rhythm is rock-solid, typical of Klemperer at his best. There is a very slight acceleration to about 124 by letter L, but there is no sense of the passage losing control. In the concert, the *fugato* begins with a moment of uncertainty. Some players begin to accelerate, and pull the rest of the orchestra with them. It is impossible to know whether Klemperer was pushing them forward, or whether they were doing it spontaneously. But over the whole of the passage to the next chorus entry the pace gradually accelerates to 132, and one can hear the musicians urging each other on. It is, by comparison with the studio recording, slightly ragged. But it is far more exciting and dynamic; and part of the reason is that one can hear the musicians grappling with the music and struggling to achieve perfect ensemble. Again, if this had happened in the studio (perhaps it did) there would have been a retake so as to achieve greater unanimity and control. What we have in the studio recording is more perfect, but less vivid. Many of Toscanini's NBC performances are like that: detailed examination reveals that the precision is not quite as immaculate as the orchestra's formidable reputation might lead one to suppose. But the force of collective music-making is so powerful that they sound more 'together' than modern, perfectly co-ordinated performances.

Many of the most impressive recordings of the last seventy years are taken from concerts, but they are not always quite what they seem. Most of the older recordings of concerts to have been issued on CD are unedited – Toscanini with the BBC Symphony Orchestra and the New York Philharmonic in the 1930s, Walter and the Vienna Philharmonic before the outbreak of World War II. The earlier the date, the less likely concert recordings are to have been edited. But since the 1950s, when tape-recording and editing became available, it has become increasingly common to record retakes and edit them into the concert recording to cover unsatisfactory passages. 'Live' concert performances by Vladimir Horowitz in some cases include many passages which were replaced at a later session. Toscanini and the NBC Symphony Orchestra in the 1950s sometimes returned to the studio after a live opera broadcast to re-record unsatisfactory sections before they were issued on disc.

Today there is a widespread feeling that many highly edited modern studio recordings of orchestral works are somewhat bland. Partly for this reason, and partly because of economic pressures, there has been in recent years an increasing number of newly issued orchestral recordings carrying the label 'live recording'. But it is rare to find any mistakes or significant audience noise in such recordings. This is not just the result of higher standards and well-behaved audiences, but because the practice of editing live performances has reached new levels of sophistication. Modern editing techniques (of which more later) make it possible to correct tiny blemishes by inserting single phrases or even individual notes taken from other sessions or from elsewhere in the performance. The label 'live' on a recording cannot be taken at face value.

The role of the producer

Even the recording of a live event with the simplest machinery needs someone to be in charge of the recording. From the earliest days, recording music involved skilled judgement. If there are retakes and, in later years, editing, someone needs to be making, or co-ordinating, decisions. As recording has grown increasingly complex, the more crucial the role of such a figure has become. For the last fifty years this figure has been known as the 'record producer'.

In the days of 78 rpm recording, the nearest approach to a producer was Fred Gaisberg. Employed by the Gramophone Company for many years, he had a role that was in some ways much more, in some ways much less, than that of the modern record producer. He supervised the establishment of early recording studios in America and Britain. For three decades he played a crucial part in persuading the finest musicians to enter the recording studio, notably Caruso in 1902. He looked after musicians, in many cases becoming their friend, and made sure that the process of recording was as successful and as artistically satisfying as possible. It was he who supervised the many recordings that Elgar made between 1914 and 1934, coaxing the great man to give of his best through periods of intense depression.

Gaisberg was a great expert on the art of recording, and many of the records that he supervised were wonderfully successful, within the limitations of the technology. But he was not what we would now call a producer. The era of the record producer began in earnest with Walter Legge. He started his recording career as Fred Gaisberg's assistant in the early 1930s. But he rose to prominence around the time that tape-editing was becoming available, and he went on to exploit the new possibilities to the full. A formidable and demanding character, he was insistent that a recording should be both accurate and intense, and he had no qualms about using the new possibilities of editing to create it. He was the first of the 'interventionist' school of producers. John Culshaw was the best-known of the next generation, adding to Legge's perfectionism a highly imaginative use of stereophonic sound, pioneering in his famous Decca recording of Wagner's *Ring* a style of opera recording far beyond what was sonically possible in a theatre.

Much can be learned about Legge's approach from the book written by his wife Elisabeth Schwarzkopf, most of whose recordings he produced. Culshaw was not only a brilliant producer but also a brilliant self-publicist, so his methods also became well known.[30] But the general CD-buying public today knows very little of how modern producers and musicians work together at and after recording sessions.

Producer and musician: Andrew Keener and Susan Tomes

A producer who is anxious to educate the public about his work is Andrew Keener, one of the best-known freelance producers currently based in the UK. One of the musicians with whom he has worked regularly is Susan Tomes, who has written and broadcast about her experience of recording. She made recordings as pianist of the group Domus over a period of ten years from 1985. Since 1995 she has recorded with violinist Anthony Marwood and cellist Richard Lester as the Florestan Trio. With these two groups she has made a total of more than forty recordings for Hyperion, and most of them have been produced by Andrew Keener. They have worked together over nearly twenty years, and their collaboration has been extremely successful and harmonious, with their recordings winning Gramophone Awards and the highest critical ratings. But the musician and the producer have very different perspectives on the methods by which this is achieved.

Susan Tomes has written about her first experience of making a commercial recording, the 1985 Hyperion recording of Fauré's two piano quartets, with Domus.[31] Musicians rarely reveal the struggles of recording in such detail, so her essay is worth quoting at length. Domus had given concert performances of this music over several years, and had a fully developed interpretation that they expected to record with few problems. But as soon as they started listening to playbacks, they found that their performance sounded different from what they expected, even though they had played the work many times in concert.

The tempo that you felt was moving and stately suddenly seems lethargic; the attention to detail seems pedantic and overdone. The ideal balance that you heard in the church seems to have vanished too: why is the cello line submerged? Why is the violin louder? Why does the piano seem to be in another room?

Painful discussions with the sound engineer ensue. His dignity is wounded by the suggestion that his judgement is at fault. He may parry your suggestion of 'a change to the microphone' with a counter-suggestion that his recorded sound is 'an accurate picture of the way you play'. Inner security begins to crumble within the group. The producer and engineer begin to indulge in techno-speak, hinting that perhaps they should 'artificially enhance' one of the players by electronic manipulation at the recording unit. The pianist wants to be 'brought forward' in the sound. A microphone is placed at the end of the piano to pick up more direct resonance. Now the pianist is happy, but the string players feel that *their* sound is indirect in comparison. Now the cellist is put on a small podium to raise him up towards the mike. Another take is done, and this time the violinist feels that he is hearing more cello sound than he's used to, and the sound picture is 'distorted'. The engineer retorts that he can do anything *artificially*, but didn't we 'want to sound natural' on the disc? Finally an acceptable balance is achieved, but usually with at least one person unconvinced that the best result *for them* has been found.

So, on to recording 'our interpretation' of the music. After listening to some of the takes, we decide that the tempo really is too slow. However, we may never have rehearsed it at a faster tempo, so some lightning adjustment is needed. When we next come down to listen, it seems to us that the opening theme is too glibly presented, not 'special' enough; the whole opening section sounds like a 'received idea', not fresh and inspired. Back to the platform we go, to re-think our way of playing it. Next, a transition which seemed delicate and subtle in our rehearsals now seems shallow when we listen back to it. How could we not have heard this? Or does it seem different because we just changed the opening?

Because the tempo is now faster, and the transition now more emphatic, we have to play the movement several times to get used to the new feeling, and during these several times, someone starts to get tired. We realise this when they start making mistakes. We have not yet got a single bar that we could release on a disc. Should we go back to the original conception, as time is short? Should we record alternative versions, and then go downstairs and compare them? Do we need to lie on the floor and rest for twenty minutes?

That the finished, and much-acclaimed, result of those first recording sessions is different from the way Domus previously played the works in concert is borne out by comparing that 1985 Hyperion recording of Fauré's Piano Quartet No. 1 in C minor with a BBC studio tape made by the same players two years earlier.[32] The BBC recording was recorded more or less 'as live', with, as far as Susan Tomes remembers, repetition only of a few sections. Most of the tempi of the BBC recording are a little slower than those of the Hyperion recording, apart from the first movement in which the BBC tempi are faster. The difference is most striking in the second movement, a scherzo. The players found, when they listened to the playback at the Hyperion sessions, that their tempo, which they had thought fast and exciting, seemed dull. In response to this discovery, they played it faster than they had been accustomed to (see Table 2).

Table 2

Fauré, Piano Quartet No. 1 in C minor: comparison between BBC recording (11 Dec. 1983) and Hyperion recording (1985)

	BBC (1983)	Hyperion (1985)	Fauré's mm
First movement, start ♩ =	88	80	84
Second subject (bar 38)	80	76	
Second movement ♩. =	172–176	192	160
Third movement, start ♪ =	52	54	72
Bars 40ff.	68	66	
Fourth movement, start ♩ =	174	186	176
Recap. Fig. K	186	186	

The experience of Domus and the Florestan Trio (two of whose members, Susan Tomes and Richard Lester, were members of Domus) confirms that self-awareness tends to lead not only to greater accuracy but also to greater consistency. Comparisons between 'live' and studio recordings of the Florestan Trio tend to show only slight differences in tempo (see Tables 3 and 4).

Table 3

Schumann, Piano Trio No. 1 in D minor: comparison between BBC recording of concert in Manchester (29 March 1996) and Hyperion recording (1998)

	BBC (1996)	Hyperion (1998)
First movement ♩ =	116 (112 at repeat)	108
Second movement ♩. =	66	68
Third movement ♪=	64	64
Fourth movement ♩ =	112	112

Table 4

Schubert, Piano Trio No. 2 in E flat: comparison between BBC recording from Cheltenham Festival (23 July 1998) and Hyperion recording (2001)

	BBC (1998)	Hyperion (2001)
First movement (from bar 12) ♩ =	156	164
Second subject (bars 50ff.)	156	156
Second movement ♪=	96	96
First forte (bars 67ff.)	116	112
Third movement, start ♩. =	68	69
Trio	64	66
Fourth movement, start ♩. =	112	116
Bars 73ff.	126	126
Bars 121ff.	118	118

As her description of the recording process reveals, Susan Tomes resents the emphasis on technical perfection that recording sessions tend to create. She much prefers playing concerts, and somewhat dreads recording sessions. But she admits that there are positive aspects to the recording experience. Over the years, she and her colleagues have learned to take advantage of the opportunities that recording sessions offer, painful though the process can be. Seventeen years after Domus's first recording, she wrote about the Florestan Trio's recording of Schubert's Piano Trio in E flat, which took place in December 2001. This is a massive work which is always exhausting to play in concert, particularly for the pianist:

We find ourselves recording the last pages at the end of a very strenuous day. Each time we play them, our accuracy rate seems to decline, and finally Andrew suggests that we should all go home, have a rest and return the next morning to 'have another go at it'. So we adjourn for the night. The following morning we listen to what we've done. It's clear that, because the last movement is so long and so physically tiring, the climax of the movement is underdone in our performance . . . . Approaching it freshly the next morning allows us to tackle the last pages on their own unaffected by performance fatigue. Here is one instance of the recording process actually helping our artistic vision. Recording can create an opportunity one would never have in the concert hall. Some might think that it's a false opportunity, an illusion. Yet one might also think that the composer didn't intend physical fatigue to ruin one of his greatest emotional expressions in the piece. In a concert performance the sense of being at the extreme of physical possibilities can be very powerful, and some loss of accuracy can even add to that effect. It might also work on disc as a recording of a live perfor-mance, but even then the 'wobbliness' might pall after a couple of hearings. Our record of the E flat Trio will have an accuracy and freshness it doesn't have in concerts, and as a recorded performance will be more enduring as a result – though it won't be more human.[33]

For Susan Tomes, therefore, recording can offer the opportunity to achieve something that is impossible in the concert hall, but she wishes that the perfec-tionism of the modern recording studio were not necessary. She feels much more at ease in concerts, where there are no retakes, any mistakes are soon forgotten, and musicians are communicating directly to the audience without the intervention of producer or engineer.

Andrew Keener's perspective on the recording process is very different.[34] He has a very clear idea of why musicians need the modern, 'interventionist' producer in the recording studio:

Well, I think a good analogy might be the comparison between cinema and theatre. As a pianist friend of mine says, nobody berates Meryl Streep for wanting to do twenty takes of a single twenty-second shot. Each time she will bring another nuance, another eyebrow-raise, another eyelid-flash to a different part of the take. Not every musician works like that, but I think the analogy can work very well in recording. There's the obvious point that the second time you listen to a recording it's exactly the same performance as the first time you heard it . . . . Nowadays in film, in television, in all sorts of 'entertainment' (for want of a less ghastly word), the clarity offered by technology encourages us – sometimes over-encourages us – to expect a certain repeatability, a certain polish on the finished article, and we acknowledge that the performance of music may come over very differently with that repetition at home, and without the benefit of the eyes to see the musicians working away, and without the benefit of the occasion. We've all been at wonderful concerts where we've been swept off our feet, and we've heard the relay on the radio a couple of days later in very good sound, and we've thought, 'That's a pale reflection of what I experienced in the hall, with people around me getting excited, and seeing musicians in animated mode.'

Ex.2.1 Mendelssohn, Violin Concerto, first movement, cadenza (bars 299–334). Editing notes from a CD recording. The figures are take numbers (which ran consecutively throughout the sessions). Reverse ticks indicate that the edit was successfully carried out. (Courtesy of Andrew Keener)

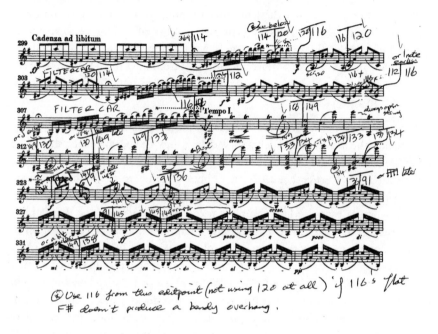

Recordings produced by Andrew Keener, like most of the best modern recordings of the finest musicians, involve a great deal of retaking and detailed editing. Quite how detailed the editing can be is shown by music example 2.1, which is a page of Keener's editing notes from a recording of Mendelssohn's Violin Concerto. In this little cadenza from the first movement, there are 22 edits within a passage of 35 bars. What are all these edits for?

> Well first the artist involved here – a superb player and musician – insists on that density of editing, and, in tune with Meryl Streep's philosophy, I support him. Not all artists follow this way of thinking to such an extent, and one supports them too. This is part of what a producer is all about. But what Walter Legge always used to say was that one of the roles of a producer is to collect all the jewels. I firmly believe this. It's one of the reasons for making a record, as distinct from holding a microphone up in front of a concert – which can also work wonderfully. We never know whether it will or not: a concert can be electrifying, a recording boring, or vice versa. But one of the reasons for making a record in the studio is indeed to collect all the jewels, as far as I'm concerned. And even in the very first take, where the musician hasn't settled quite, there may be a nuance, there may be a

group of notes which are most beautiful, which that person didn't play in quite that most beautiful, spontaneous, coloured way in any subsequent takes, when he or she was going after accuracy. And you owe it to the artist to mine the early takes as comprehensively as the later takes for that kind of thing. And when you do that amount of mining you're bound to end up, if you're doing your job properly, with that amount of editing, because you're searching for details as well as a span, details which are beautiful and will still captivate on second and third and fourth listening. I'm not talking about mannerism, which doesn't wear well on recording, I'm talking about invention and spontaneity.

It sounds from this description as if it is the producer rather than the musicians who makes the artistic judgements in deciding how the performance should be edited together. It really is like assembling a film, or even punching holes in the old piano rolls. Keener concedes that there is some truth in that. But the starting-point is a genuine performance. Always the musicians begin work on each movement by recording complete takes, until they have one that satisfies them and can be used as the master. They then record takes of each section of the movement, in order to cover any problems without losing the flow. Only then do they record small patches to correct any details that have not already been covered. When it comes to the editing, all the detailed patches are chosen to fit with the master takes, so that the finished result is a tidied-up version of what the musicians did actually play when they performed the complete movement. Keener does not make decisions in a vacuum. He works very closely with musicians, and gets to know how they think. In an orchestral session there are always severe time-constraints, but with soloists and chamber groups there is a great deal of communication about what works and what doesn't:

> With an artist I know well I take copious notes down on the score of what the artist approves bar by bar, at any given time. You've seen in the Florestan Trio recordings, and you'd also see in an orchestral situation, with artists whom I work with all the time, there's constant unspoken eye contact in the playbacks, and I write down notes as a result of that. So I will, in the best scenario, go away from a recording with a blueprint which is a combination of knowing what these artists want through experience of working with them, knowing what pleases them, knowing what displeases them in a particular way, and a concrete writing down of things that have been said at the session, eye contact during takes which have been played during playback. And one can build up a very good picture, when one knows an artist, having made lots of recordings with an artist, one can actually be quite confident in producing what he or she wants.

Keener admits that the search for perfection can become obsessional, and he also admires many old recordings, made before the days of modern editing. But it is impossible to go back to those days, and it is often the musicians themselves who insist on perfection. There are many stories, told by producers and others, about musicians who have become obsessional in the recording studio. One of the top international pianists recently recorded the last three Schubert sonatas. It took twelve days, of which the first two were spent creating a piano sound which satisfied him. By the end of the ninth day he had recorded wonderful performances of all three sonatas. But he nevertheless spent the remaining three days playing yet more takes, in case he could achieve something even better. Film-makers talk about 'shooting ratios' – the ratio of the footage that was shot to the amount that was used in the final film. The ratio for that Schubert recording must have been something like 50:1.

The general public is unaware of this process, or at least is unaware of the lengths to which it goes. In the world of pop music, a recording has become quite a different art-form from a concert performance, and elaborate construction of effects is accepted as the norm. Recordings are built up layer by layer, and any ingredient can be manipulated at will. Not only are there electronic effects, sampling, and all manner of manipulations of the sounds, but the performance of musicians can be changed at will – the pitch can be adjusted so that all singers sing in tune, for example. Such extremes are rare in the world of classical music CDs, but there are nevertheless occasions when musicians and producers do take advantage of these modern methods. It used to be inevitable that, if you changed the speed of a tape or disc, the pitch would change. Modern software makes it possible to change the speed without altering the pitch. A technically difficult passage or movement can therefore be taken at a steady pace by the musicians, for the sake of accuracy, and then speeded up afterwards to whatever pace they wanted to play it at. One producer gave an example of a pianist who, after the recording, asked him if he could change the shape of a particular phrase, by speeding up some notes and slowing down others. The result was what the pianist wanted, but had never in fact played.

Andrew Keener resists such adjustments as much as possible, but he does make the fullest use of editing. What emerges at the end is a true picture of the musicians' interpretation on the day, but with all the imperfections removed, and the best available option chosen for each part of the work. That, at least, is the case with most of the musicians with whom he works – musicians of the highest rank, who have the ability to perform in the studio much as they perform in concert. But there are also musicians whose published recordings are far better than anything they can achieve in live concert. Keener, like other producers, from time to time finds himself recording musicians who are ill-prepared, inexperienced, or not as good as their promotional material might suggest. Inevitably he ends up rescuing them by editing, and then it really does become like a jigsaw:

In the worst scenario of that kind one is just 'note-bashing', and stops often. One really has to take charge, and one has to keep in mind tempi, because very often things won't match from take to take because the tempi are all different. And there is sometimes the extra difficulty that the ego is out of all proportion to the actual talent, so one has to be so flattering and still take command to an inordinate and insulting extent.

During the session itself one sometimes feels indignant enough to think that the public should know about it. And now and again you'll get a producer or an engineer who does name names. I don't think this does any good, because on a human as well as a professional level one has been trusted to do something and one has to do one's job well, and with a certain amount of discretion . . . . It doesn't matter if I record a violin concerto with a guy who has not prepared it, and has come into the studio with millions of mis-readings. It's god-awful at the time, but in world terms it doesn't matter. Sometimes the record has been praised to the skies. And it's very annoying. One's ego does emerge screaming inside, 'My name should be on the record bigger than this guy's'. And he actually may say at the end of the session, 'You know, your name should be on the record bigger than mine'. And you know damn well what his reaction would be if you said 'All right, then'! If I had too much of this type of recording I'd go crazy and I'd want to do something else for a living. It would be awful. One comes across perhaps one example of this in twenty or thirty records. Of course it's quite different when an artist comes into the studio whom you love and admire, and who is having an off day. The work has got to get recorded then, there's an expensive orchestra, or his diary won't allow another time in the foreseeable future, the company wants to get the record out, and the company is not going to bend and say 'Oh, we'll do it in a year's time'. Then you move heaven and earth, because you know that this is not normally the case with this artist; you want to do your best for him or her, and this is your job and you have to do it.

Keener's view, that he must use as much editing as it takes to get the best possible results, contrasts with Adrian Farmer's refusal to 'bend the rules' of minimal editing. The implication of Farmer's view is that there is something inherently dishonest about editing, and this is a view that has been expressed in different ways ever since editing began. But if one wants to take such a moral stand, what are the consequences? If, in the days of 78 rpm records, take 3 was chosen for the master, that was to deny listeners the knowledge that take 1 was ragged, and take 2 was out of tune. Choice of take was, in effect, 'editing' the set of 78s, even though the pieces were not joined together. Come to that, recording itself creates an illusion: the musicians are not actually there in the room. Once one starts down the path of seeing editing as deception, the logical conclusion is that only live music-making is true, and that any recording is fundamentally dishonest.

On the other hand, Keener's analogy with film can only be taken so far. Most films are new works and are not claiming to be records of something else. If Meryl Streep gives twenty different performances of a shot, and the director chooses one, this is to create a structure in the edited result that is satisfying, and works in the context of the scene and the film as a whole. It is the film that is being created, and it can go in any direction. By contrast, a recording of a piece of classical music is not just a creation but a re-creation. The whole purpose is to give the impression that musicians are performing the work in one's own room, as if they were giving a concert. There is something fundamentally uncomfortable about the fact that, in order to create the illusion that musicians are doing what they do in concert, they have to spend three days or more in the studio taking and retaking, and producer and editor (sometimes the same person) have to spend weeks piecing together 'the jewels' before a satisfactory result can be achieved. What sort of a musical world is it in which this has become necessary?

The balance between producer and musicians varies, depending on circumstances and the personalities. Some musicians insist on much more control over editing than others. But are the musicians themselves the best judges of their own playing? Until the existence of recordings musicians never heard themselves except when they were actually engaged in the activity of playing. Performing was a process of communicating with an audience, and it was the audiences who judged the results. Can musicians ever be a satisfactory substitute for their own audience? Can they learn to hear themselves the way audiences do? Some of the obsessions that develop in the recording studio suggest that, far from having the ears of a real audience, some musicians just develop an insatiable ambition to build a bigger and better musician.

Now that the expectations of the public, the critics, and the musicians themselves are so high, and everyone has spent the last decade or more listening to perfect playing on CDs all the time, Keener's argument that he has to do everything he can to create the best possible result, from whatever material presents itself, is very strong. But most of the people who buy the CDs know little about what goes on in the recording studio and the editing room. Audiences are, on the whole, much less aware of the conventions of recording than they are about the conventions of film. Even music critics can be extraordinarily ignorant and naïve about what is involved. For example, some of them still claim that patching over mistakes 'never works' because it is impossible for musicians to match the flow and intensity of a main take in a short retake. There are plenty of examples from the past to back up this assertion: blundering mismatches of tempo, dynamic level and acoustics can be found in some of the most famous recordings of Horowitz and Beecham, for example. But a critic who makes such an assertion today has clearly never set foot in the modern recording studio. If it were really true that patching cannot work, then most of the recordings to have won awards in the last ten years would have been dismal failures. The fact is that the best modern musicians, or at least those who make successful recordings, have developed an extraordinary ability to retain accuracy and consistency in the recording studio, while keeping up a level of expressive intensity close to what they achieve in concert. It is a different world from half a century ago, and the finest musicians, not just the mediocre, have learned to live in it.

But learning to live in it is not the same as wanting it to be like that. Many musicians, probably the majority of classical musicians, regard making records as not quite the real thing. Concerts in front of an audience are still what counts, and are the events that most musicians measure their lives by. Admittedly, there have always been some musicians who feel most at home in the recording studio, and who actually prefer recording to giving concerts. The most famous example was Glenn Gould, who gave up playing concerts altogether. And there are many musicians who actually enjoy recording. But musicians who regard recordings as preferable to concerts are in a tiny minority.

Consequently, when musicians do make recordings, many of them would like the experience to be as much like giving a concert as possible. They often do this by recording soon after performing works in concert, and they generally prefer to record in complete movements. How much they then retake and patch is another matter, but the preference for long takes as a starting point applies to both the 'minimalist' school of Nimbus and the highly 'interventionist' school of producers like Andrew Keener. In this respect the preferences of musicians have not really changed very much since the 1960s and 1970s, when editing was already available, but not nearly as sophisticated as it is now. George Szell found that, of all his recordings, those that he made in Cleveland gave the most gratifying results, 'because we usually record a work the day after we have given it in concert so that it is already thoroughly rehearsed. After a brief warm-up, mostly for balancing purposes, we run straight through the piece, and we use second "takes" only for correcting the odd spot, as a rule. We did Beethoven's *King Stephen* overture in one go, for instance, and to me it seemed impeccable, but the first trumpet insisted he had played one wrong note so, as a point of honour, and though it could not be heard, we repeated that bit.'[35] Adrian Boult went so far as to feel guilty when recording a retake: 'I still feel each time I am asked to do a "patch" to be superimposed on my original performance that I am letting the side down for I ought to be able to do the thing in one. Surely we should be able to treat our recording friends exactly as we treat audiences in the concert room?'[36]

One thing that most musicians and most producers would agree on is that it is all too easy to lose the sense of the whole work if one gets too immersed in perfecting tiny details. The musicians have to be able, at some level, to forget that they are playing to microphones, in non-concert conditions, and to capture something of the sense of real performance. This too is something that has not changed, and two reminiscences will illustrate the point.

In the early 1970s, Leonard Bernstein and the London Symphony Orchestra made a quadrophonic recording of *The Rite of Spring*, produced by John McClure of CBS. It was the day after they had performed it at a concert in the Royal Albert Hall in London. McClure had positioned the different sections of the orchestra in separate areas, some of them behind the conductor, in order to be able to separate their sound. Bernstein protested, but was prepared to try it. The work proceeded slowly and somewhat cautiously, as everyone got used to this unusual arrangement. McClure reported, 'After five hours, we were technically covered with what was a very good performance, but everyone missed the ignition of the Albert Hall concert. With only an hour left in the day, Bernstein did a remarkable thing. He asked the orchestra, who had been blowing Stravinsky's murderous phrases all day, if they had the strength and desire to go once straight through the whole piece to create a performance. After a tea break, we reassembled for a do-or-die effort . . . . Sure, you guessed it. The fire ignited, and what you will hear on the new record is the final take with only a few inevitable clams repaired from earlier takes.'[37]

The problems of that session were exacerbated by the unfamilar set-up for a new recording technology. But the same principle can apply just as much in conventional recording, with artists who have been performing the music together for years. In 1959, Peter Pears and Benjamin Britten recorded Schubert's *Die schöne Müllerin*. Pears described the experience in an interview recorded in 1967:

> We had, I think, two weeks put aside at the Kingsway Hall for it. And we worked and worked and worked at it, did it many, many times, in small pieces and in larger chunks, and so on. And then the tapes arrived and we listened to them. And we still, just still, didn't think that they were really anything like good enough. And so we thought we'd go back and do some more. We put by another fortnight. And we thought that we would try and simply go straight through in the first day, and see what we could do from that, working from a complete performance – whether we then would have to patch it or do anything to it. And so we did one complete performance like that. And I think we took it entire for the recording, because it was really much better than any of the other bits, cuttings, scrapings that we'd done before. That, you see, was, if you like, a fortnight wasted, a lot of tape wasted, people's time; but in fact it must have gone towards making that other performance, because we knew what we'd done before. At the back of our minds it was there. We knew what to avoid, even subconsciously. I think it was good.[38]

Learning from recording is something that a great many musicians acknowledge, even those who do not particularly enjoy the experience. But the results of learning feed back not just into more recordings, but also through into concert performance (as the examples of the Florestan Trio showed). And, over time, the habits acquired while recording become part of the general culture of performance, whether in the studio or on the public platform. The most obvious consequence of this has been a gradual rise in standards of accuracy and reliability. But the influence of the recording experience has had a much wider effect, encouraging shifts of technique and style at every level of music-making. The most important of those shifts are the subject of the next two chapters.

CHAPTER THREE

Ensemble and Freedom: Orchestras

Anyone who listens to recordings of the early twentieth century very quickly becomes aware that standards and styles have changed greatly over the last hundred years. Some of the reasons have been touched on already: different levels of rehearsal, different expectations from audiences, the lives musicians lead, and the contrast between habits before and after the birth of recording.

In this chapter and the next, some of these changes will be looked at in more detail, first in orchestras, then in smaller ensembles and soloists. The chapters focus on a subject that is at the heart of changing practices over the twentieth century: ensemble playing, and the freedoms and disciplines that it involves. These are partly to do with rehearsal, and changing levels of competence. But the way people play together is also a matter of style. Even straightforward issues of competence and accuracy are partly stylistic, and the basic techniques of playing instruments involve not just performing accurately, but according to (or sometimes in defiance of) the conventions of the time.

British orchestras in the early twentieth century

Adam Carse, in his book *Orchestral Conducting* published in London in 1929, devotes a section to the subject of rehearsing. Intended as a guide for the aspiring conductor, it incidentally paints a vivid picture of the situation in Britain at the time. There are amateur orchestras, who have 'fairly numerous opportunities for rehearsing'. Then there are 'second-class professional orchestras', in theatres, cinemas, seaside towns and so on. Here, 'the time available for rehearsing is sure to be reduced to a minimum quantity, if, indeed, it is not whittled down to vanishing-point. The players in these orchestras [like Alfred Deahl, who was quoted in chapter 1] are generally good readers, and have little difficulty in playing their parts as far as execution is concerned.' Finally there are 'first-class professional orchestras,' which Carse describes as 'complete, technically efficient, but under present conditions in England, often woefully under-rehearsed'. Furthermore, 'Even though an orchestra bears a name, the individual players may vary from year to year or even from concert to concert . . . . The ordinary rule is one rehearsal for one concert; two rehearsals may occasionally be conceded, but must be regarded as rather exceptional, while for a series of daily concerts at which a familiar repertoire is played, two or three rehearsals a week are all that can be expected.' Carse concedes that important concerts in London sometimes receive more rehearsal, but this is the general standard around the country.[1]

The situation had changed little since the turn of the century. When Richard Strauss was to come to London in 1898 to conduct the British première of *Don Quixote*, the Philharmonic Society offered him two rehearsals, as they usually did to visiting conductors. He was not able to persuade them to give him a third, so he substituted works that orchestral players in London already knew. He had already successfully performed *Don Quixote* with the Berlin Philharmonic, but had found that five rehearsals were only just enough.[2]

In 1895 John Carrodus, who led the concerts of the Philharmonic Society, the Covent Garden Orchestra and the Queen's Hall Orchestra, advised violinists, 'The rehearsals are very trying, especially of the old operas known by heart by myself and others. They are, however, made necessary in consequence of the periodical advent of new conductors, soloists or fresh members of the orchestra.'[3] This is a striking statement from the best-known British orchestral leader of the time. It implies that there is little point in rehearsing if everyone already knows the music. And it suggests that, although shortage of rehearsal time was mainly a matter of money, it was also part of the national culture.

At the beginning of his conducting career, John Barbirolli spent a season in 1926 with the British National Opera Company. 'In one week on tour I did *Romeo and Juliet* (Gounod), *Madam Butterfly* and *Aïda*, each of them for the first time in my life, on three and a half hours' rehearsal for the lot.' For his first concert with the Royal Philharmonic Society Orchestra in 1929, Barbirolli was, like Strauss thirty years before, given two rehearsals for a long programme, including Delius's Cello Concerto and Debussy's *La Mer*. He was allowed an extra string rehearsal only because he paid for it himself.[4]

Carse states that the players in an orchestra may change 'from concert to concert', but the situation was often worse than that. Players in most orchestras were free to send deputies to rehearsals or concerts if they found a more lucrative engagement elsewhere. As Artur Schnabel wryly put it, 'You can easily imagine the consequences of so much *laissez faire*. Instead of an ensemble one might get just an assembly.'[5] The system continued to thrive in Britain and France into the 1920s, and memories of it in Britain were quoted in chapter 1.

The London orchestras who most often recorded in the 1920s were the Royal Albert Hall Orchestra, the London Symphony Orchestra, and the Royal

Philharmonic Orchestra (not the regular body established in the 1940s, but an organization of looser membership that played at Royal Philharmonic Society concerts). Their standards varied greatly. The LSO and the RAHO each recorded Mendelssohn's Scherzo from *A Midsummer Night's Dream* in c.1926, the LSO under Beecham, the RAHO under Ronald. Neither performance is stable or well co-ordinated. In the LSO's performance the strings and woodwind are often at slightly different tempi, partly because the clarinets have difficulty tonguing the quavers (eighth notes) at the tempo and tend to slow down, and the strings, by contrast, tend to hurry. The first beat of the bar is often rushed, so there is a general sense of the players falling over themselves. The RAHO's performance is slightly better, a little more controlled in tempo, but still with some very awkward corners (and, admittedly, hampered by a tuba on the bass line – a reinforcement which was a hangover from acoustic recording, and which was still sometimes used in the early days of electrical recording).

A recording of Beethoven's Symphony No. 5, recorded in 1927 by the Royal Philharmonic Orchestra under Weingartner, has similar problems. The rhythm of the scherzo is vague and imprecise, with entries slightly mistimed and many details blurred and rushed. On the other hand, the same orchestra plays the scherzo of Tchaikovsky's 'Pathétique' Symphony, in a c.1929 recording conducted by Oskar Fried, with remarkable precision considering the very fast tempo, though some phrases are rushed and unclear. And the Royal Albert Hall Orchestra made some impressive recordings under Elgar. *Cockaigne* and the 'Enigma' Variations both have their roughnesses, but the dash and spirit of the playing is striking (Elgar's recordings will be discussed further in chapter 5).

Henry Wood had disallowed deputising in the Queen's Hall Orchestra from 1904, and it became known as the best orchestra in London. Debussy conducted *La Mer* and *Prélude à l'Après-midi d'un faune* in 1908, and wrote to the directors of the orchestra, 'I venture to think that there are few orchestras so marvellously trained. One must admire at the same time their artistic conscience, which is allied to a splendid discipline rarely obtained.'[6]

The Queen's Hall Orchestra was often praised for its performances from the 1890s through to its absorption into the new BBC Symphony Orchestra in 1930. But the standard it achieved was, to judge from its recordings, still far from the standards we are used to in the twenty-first century. The clarity and control of rhythm, and the tuning of the woodwind, were not very much different from those of other London orchestras (the best recordings labelled as being played by the 'Queen's Hall Orchestra' in the 1930s were played by the BBC Symphony Orchestra). The recordings suggest more panache than attention to detail: in Elgar's Violin Concerto with Albert Sammons, rhythmic details are often rushed or unclear. It seems that, like attitudes to rehearsal, some aspects of rhythm and ensemble were habitual.

Harty's recordings, with the other 'regular' body, the Hallé Orchestra in Manchester, tend to be more incisive than Wood's in detail, suggesting that Harty was a musician who paid more attention to such things than Wood. Harty's recording of 'Troyte' from the 'Enigma' Variations is very fast, like Elgar's own performance (which we shall come to in chapter 5), but the Hallé sounds a little more under control than Elgar's Royal Albert Hall Orchestra, even though the rhythms do not sound quite as secure as in modern performances. Harty's Berlioz recordings with the Hallé are among the most impressive and carefully rehearsed British recordings of the period. The 'Queen Mab' Scherzo from Berlioz's *Romeo and Juliet* (1927) is, apart from occasional details, exquisitely delicate and nuanced, and remarkably accurate – in a completely different class from the LSO and RAHO's attempts to play the Mendelssohn Scherzo at about the same date. In the 'Royal Hunt and Storm' from *The Trojans* (1931) Harty and the Hallé begin with beautifully sustained phrases, and accelerating trills in the woodwind. The Storm has great panache, but shows the orchestra's limitations: there are some messy details, and the control of rhythmic detail is loose.

The Proms

Though Henry Wood's Queen's Hall Orchestra had the advantage of regular membership from 1904, it was also the orchestra which played for (one might say endured) the annual season of Promenade Concerts. Although important concerts in the main season could sometimes be given a decent amount of rehearsal, the Proms were famous, or notorious, for the number of concerts accomplished with little rehearsal. At the beginning of the twentieth century the entire season was played by the Queen's Hall Orchestra, and then, from 1930, the BBC Symphony Orchestra took over. John Barbirolli joined the Queen's Hall Orchestra as a cellist in 1916. For the six-week season, with concerts six nights a week, they had three rehearsals for each week of concerts. As Barbirolli remembered, 'We had to sight-read half the stuff when the time came. But old Henry J. was a master of keeping us on the rails.'[7] In 1906, Percy Grainger played Liszt's *Hungarian Fantasy* at a Prom, and reported, 'Wood conducted excellently. We had no rehearsal.'[8]

At a Prom in 1927, a performance of the Brahms Violin Concerto with Daisy Kennedy as soloist ground to a halt during the first movement. Wood had had a piano rehearsal with Kennedy the day before, but had only rehearsed a few passages with orchestra, and Kennedy publicly put the blame on not having had a full rehearsal. A spokesperson for the BBC, which had taken over the running of the concerts that season, wrote (in the tone that has charac-terised BBC utterances ever since), 'All new and difficult works are rehearsed . . . . The Brahms concerto has been performed by the Queen's Hall Orchestra about a hundred and fifty times, so I really do not see that a rehearsal is necessary.'[9] Even today, soloists are allowed little more than a run-through in most conductors' rehearsal schedules. But a soloist would be expected to perform without rehearsal only if standing in for someone who was suddenly taken ill (and indeed such occasions can be memorable because of the extra frisson generated by the emergency).

Three years later, with the new BBC Symphony Orchestra taking over the series from the Queen's Hall Orchestra, the rehearsal schedule had improved. There were four full days of rehearsal before the season began, and then a rehearsal every morning of a concert. It was still a tough schedule, but the proportion of the music which had not been rehearsed was a great deal smaller than in the early years of the century.

There are few recordings of Promenade Concerts before the days of tape-recording, so there is very little recorded evidence to show what standards were actually achieved by Wood during his many years as conductor of the Proms. However, the broadcast parts of a 1936 Prom do survive. They are frankly shocking, even to someone accustomed to recordings of this period. The orchestra is the BBC Symphony Orchestra, by now well established, and the BBC regime of a daily rehearsal was already in place. But there are clear signs of skimped rehearsal, and an unsophisticated level of co-ordination with soloists, even by the standards of the time. Elisabeth Schumann sings the Alleluja from Mozart's 'Exsultate, jubilate'. Wood sets off at a very fast pace, $\downarrow$ = 154, which takes no account of the singer's need to fit in all the notes. Schumann does her best, but is obliged to slither along all the runs and cut corners. In the same concert, Jean Pougnet and Bernard Shore play Mozart's Sinfonia Concertante for Violin and Viola. Wood makes several cuts in the work, omitting most of the opening tutti (bars 18–58, one of the most sublime passages Mozart ever wrote). His tempo is again fast, about $\downarrow$ = 144, and bears no relation to the tempo to which the soloists eventually settle (about $\downarrow$ = 128).[10]

If this was typical of Wood's conducting at the Proms, even with the more generous rehearsal schedule, it was undoubtedly rough-and-ready. Elgar attended a Prom in 1924 and reported in a letter, 'Wood managed to make the grand old Eroica sound commonplace and stupid. I cannot think how it is done! Richter and Nikisch made a noble thing of it.'[11] Several critics voiced the opinion that standards were no more than basic, and their views were summed up by Frank Howes of *The Times* in 1942: 'Every critic, professional and amateur, cuts his teeth on Sir Henry Wood, who has been the teacher of an uncountable host of grateful listeners – none the less grateful if perhaps they ultimately outgrow his interpretations . . . . More sophisticated tastes miss in his work fine shades of expression and find his permanently broad outlines and bold effects apt to be oppressive.'[12] Vaughan Williams was one of those who defended Wood against such criticisms: 'The "Proms" do not appeal, and are not meant to appeal, to the jaded hypercritical Aesthete – they are essentially "popular". The meticulous fidelity of a Toscanini is not only impossible, it is not even desirable in these circumstances . . . . Is not the cult of super-perfection carried too far? If it is to be a question of quality versus quantity, I am for quantity every time. A listener with imagination should want the music, not so-and-so's rendering of it. If the music is intelligibly played and above all with verve and vitality, why should we wish for more?'[13]

Wood's biographer, Arthur Jacobs, who quotes both of these passages, is on the side of Vaughan Williams in this debate. Though admitting that his call for 'quantity every time' seems 'antique', he regards Howes's criticism of Wood as unjust: 'In other words: slog away, dear Sir Henry, while we submit our souls to be ravished by the sophistications of Sir Thomas.'[14] But the hard evidence of those Prom recordings makes it fairly clear that, by 1936, Wood's standards were those of the past. For getting an orchestra through a concert with little or no rehearsal he was undoubtedly second to none. But by the 1930s, Boult with his BBC orchestra and Beecham with his London Philharmonic Orchestra were establishing new standards, and visits from Furtwängler with the Berlin Philharmonic in 1927 and Toscanini with the New York Philharmonic in 1930 had encouraged an appetite for greater sophistication.

Even before the New York orchestra's visit, unfavourable comparisons between British and American orchestras were already appearing in record reviews in the late 1920s. 'K.K.' in the *Gramophone* of September 1929 reviews the recording by Toscanini and the New York Philharmonic Symphony Orchestra of Haydn's 'Clock' Symphony, and uses the opportunity to contrast the British and American approaches to orchestral discipline. 'Here . . . are the fine and comforting fruits of adequate rehearsal . . . everybody knows not only where he is going but – what the members of our inadequately rehearsed native orchestras too rarely fully know – where everybody else is going . . . . I love our British orchestras and long to see them take the place which the talent of our players justify their taking; but until they can get more than two rehearsals for a concert, and do away with the debasing "deputy" system, they never will take a supreme place with those who understand orchestral playing.'[15]

Adrian Boult was already one of the severest critics of British orchestral standards in the early 1920s, when he observed sharply, 'The LSO know they read marvellously and therefore think that a thing as sight-read by them is ready for performance, and even Coates has trouble when he wants hard work out of them. It is a certainty that the Mengelberg standard of ensemble, for instance, is unknown to them: they don't believe they've anything to learn in that or any other way, but worse than this, when they hear it (as when the New York Symphony – Damrosch – people came [in 1920]) they talked about the mechanical precision in a superior way and didn't realise that precision could be learnt from them and need not be mechanical.'[16] In 1930, Boult finally got his chance to demonstrate what could be done with an orchestra of not only regular membership but also regular rehearsal.

Britain in the 1930s and 1940s

In the 1930s, British standards of ensemble improved greatly with the founding of the BBC Symphony Orchestra under Boult (1930) and the London Philharmonic Orchestra under Beecham (1932). Comparisons between British recordings of the 1920s and those of the 1930s almost always show a considerable change in precision, clarity of detail (even allowing for improvements in recorded sound), control and tuning.

The qualities of the three main London orchestras – the two new orchestras and the London Symphony Orchestra – were compared by Alfred Einstein in an article in the *Musical Times* in 1933. He praised the 'calm and distinguished' quality of the BBC orchestra's string tone, and writes, 'What this orchestra can do, with sufficient rehearsal and the full complement of ten double-basses, was proved at its first symphony concert [of the season], under a conductor so calm, thoughtful, and so averse to all mere display as Adrian C. Boult. I have heard the Berlioz "Roman Carnival" Overture sound more French, more inflammable, but hardly ever more magical.' At a concert by the London Philharmonic Orchestra and Beecham, Einstein thought a Haydn symphony wonderful, but the Overture to *Die Meistersinger* as having 'an "open" sound, its splendour unrestrained', the whole performance being 'a show of virtuosity'. Surprisingly, the final section of Boult's recording of *Roman Carnival* (c.1933) is extremely fast. Beecham's (1936) is much slower, with the rhythms more meticulously articulated. Very clear articulation, with more playing 'off the string' than usual, was characteristic of Beecham's approach, and it was one of the features that gave many of his recordings with the London Philharmonic such lightness and clarity.

The London Symphony Orchestra had in 1933 acquired Hamilton Harty as its principal conductor, and was responding to the competition from the new orchestras. Einstein admired the 'noble, gleaming sound' in Sibelius's Seventh Symphony, and the delicacy and precision of their Mozart. A recording by them with Harty of Haydn's Symphony No. 95 (c.1936) indeed shows a much higher standard of precision than in their recordings of the 1920s, and they do achieve considerable delicacy with a reduced body of strings.

Another orchestra established in London in the 1930s was the Boyd Neel Orchestra, a chamber orchestra of predominantly young players which, like the BBC Symphony Orchestra and London Philharmonic, was of a standard not previously heard in Britain. Barbirolli had made some pioneering recordings with his own chamber orchestra in the 1920s, including two of

Elgar's Introduction and Allegro (one under the name of the National Gramo-
phonic Society's Chamber Orchestra). They are very fine for their time,
with a tighter ensemble than in most British orchestral playing. But Boyd
Neel's recording of the same work is even more beautifully finished,
combining higher standards of ensemble with a more refined string style and
lighter portamento. Neel's orchestra made the first recordings of Vaughan
Williams's Fantasia on a Theme by Thomas Tallis (1936), which remains
impressively powerful, and Britten's Variations on a Theme of Frank Bridge
(1938), which was written for them. Their playing balances subtlety of
nuance, intensity and directness.

The change in standard from the 1920s to the 1930s was not just a matter
of rehearsal, but of the rising standard of young string-players. Boult gives a
telling account of the recruitment and early rehearsals for the BBC Symphony
Orchestra in 1930. The auditions produced a 'brilliant group of young and
inexperienced players'. Boult decided to try out the new orchestra with the
third act of *Siegfried* at a concert in the Queen's Hall: 'I said at once that we
must have an extra string rehearsal in order to get on close terms with the
terrible string passages which always frightened players so much. The rehearsal
amazed me, for string technique had progressed so far that Wagner had no
terrors for these young players. In 1930 the scheduled three hours were quite
unnecessary, and we stopped long before time was up.' A few weeks later a
'middle-aged and respected violinist', who had played in the first violins of
London orchestras for years, auditioned to join the BBC Symphony Orchestra.
Boult gave him the final pages of *Götterdämmerung* to play: 'the arpeggios were
unrecognizable. I never found out where he was supposed to be playing, and
this was a man who had played his *Ring* many, many times, and had got away
with it all in the general scramble.'[17]

What was the reason for this sudden rise in technical standards? Had the
training of musicians in Britain suddenly become more rigorous? Not if the
critic W. J. Turner is to be believed. In 1928 he published a damning article
on the standards in the London music colleges: 'If any foreign musician such
as Mr. Casals or Mr. Weingartner were to go to one of the students' concerts
given at the Royal College of Music and were compelled to sit still through
even a quarter of the performance he would probably be carried out fainting
. . . the playing of the students' orchestra at any of its performances that I have
been unlucky enough to hear has been lamentable. Such scraggy incompetence
can exist in few other musical institutions in Europe. And looking closely at
the audience, composed mostly of students and their relatives and friends, I
have been struck by the obvious lack of real musical intelligence in their
attention.' The standard at the Royal Academy of Music is, Turner writes, at
least as bad. 'The explanation of the evil is simple, it may be summed up in one
word, *money*. The fact that both the R.C.M. and the R.A.M. are financially

dependent on the fees of the students damns them utterly as educational bodies . . . . There are large numbers of young people between the ages of seventeen and twenty-five whose parents can afford to let them spend a few years acquiring a musical education that is not expected to be more than what was known in Victorian days as an accomplishment.'[18]

If musical training for string-players was as bad as this article suggests, the most likely explanation for the rise in standards that Boult experienced is that, even as early as 1930, young musicians were already being influenced by recordings. They could hear, as no previous generation could, all the most famous instrumentalists and orchestras, and realised what it was possible to do if one had the talent and the application. No doubt Boult, and Beecham two years later, were also fortunate in recruiting just at the time that cinemas were throwing large numbers of musicians out of work, with the coming of the 'talkies'.[19] Among the thousands of young musicians who had been tempted to go straight into the cinema rather than continue their studies (as Dan Godfrey lamented) there were undoubtedly many of serious talent. And their experience in the cinema, with its wide and ever-changing repertoire, would certainly have developed their basic technical facility and sight-reading skills, if not the refinement of their playing.

The improvement in British orchestral standards continued through to the 1950s. Two new orchestras were founded after World War II: the Philharmonia Orchestra in 1945, the Royal Philharmonic Orchestra in 1946 (again with Beecham as principal conductor). Once more part of the character of both orchestras was the appointment of a new generation of musicians. Walter Legge, who founded the Philharmonia Orchestra specifically to make recordings for the Gramophone Company (later to become EMI), found the core of its players among young musicians who had played in the RAF Orchestra during the war, including principal horn Dennis Brain and principal flute Gareth Morris. With the founding of these two orchestras, 'modern' orchestral playing can be said to have arrived in Britain. There is little in their earliest recordings that would strike the present-day listener as old-fashioned in ensemble.

Continental Europe

In the early years of the twentieth century, the deputy system plagued the orchestras of Paris as well as London. Stravinsky described preparations for the première of *Le Baiser de la fée* in 1928: 'I was generously given four rehearsals with the admirable orchestra of the Opera. They were arduous, because at each of them I had to contend with the dreadful system of deputizing – so fatal to the music when at each rehearsal musicians, without any warning, send others to take their place.'[20] So it was an 'admirable orchestra', but a different one each time. Stravinsky wrote about the advantages of recording sessions, when rehearsal was followed immediately by recording, so that the same people who had rehearsed were in the performance. As in London, the principal players usually made themselves available for important recording sessions – flautist Marcel Moyse, for example, is clearly audible in most recordings of the Straram Orchestra. He played their important concerts too, but it is another question whether he would necessarily have attended all rehearsals for concerts. Because of the continuity between rehearsal and recording, it is quite likely that recordings of this period are of a better standard than most performances at concerts.

Orchestral recordings of Paris orchestras from the 1920s tend to show a standard similar to that of London orchestras. 'Fêtes' from Debussy's *Nocturnes*, played by the Paris Conservatoire Orchestra under Philippe Gaubert (c.1928), has similar problems to the Mendelssohn Scherzo in the hands of the London Symphony Orchestra. The co-ordination of strings and woodwind is very poor: the first woodwind entry is too fast, forcing the strings to accelerate, and several times the strings rush ahead of the woodwind. In the 'Concert et Bal' from Berlioz's *Romeo and Juliet*, played by the Colonne Orchestra under Pierné (1928), the violins often hurry ahead of the accompanying rhythm, creating something approaching chaos.

The Paris Symphony Orchestra was re-formed in 1928, under Pierre Monteux. Stravinsky wrote, 'it was a joy to work with these young musicians, who were so well disciplined and so full of goodwill, and who were forbidden to indulge in the odious habit of deputizing, of which all conductors complain . . . '.[21] Comparison between Stravinsky's recording of *The Rite of Spring* with the Straram Orchestra, which is often very ragged, and Monteux's with the Paris Symphony Orchestra (made shortly before Stravinsky's in 1929) shows that Monteux and his orchestra had more of a grip on the rhythmic details of the work. Many passages are played more accurately together, and with less sense of panic, though the standard of detailed ensemble is not quite that of a modern orchestra. It is difficult to judge how much of the difference between the two performances is caused by the conductors, and how much by the difference in regularity of membership in the orchestras. Monteux was an experienced conductor of exceptional gifts, whereas Stravinsky was comparatively inexperienced as a conductor at this stage of his career – and indeed never acquired Monteux's clarity of gesture.

Monteux's 1931 recording of Berlioz's *Symphonie fantastique* with the Paris Symphony Orchestra is extremely impressive. The second movement, 'Un Bal', has touches of portamento in the violin lines (and not only where Berlioz marks them) and a tempo which is continually in flux, and yet is rhythmically very firm with beautifully shaped and timed phrasing. The woodwind and brass have the distinct French sonorities of the day, strikingly in the 'March to the

Scaffold'. But they are well tuned, unlike the wind of many French recordings from the first half of the century. The big climaxes often accelerate, even where Berlioz gives no indication that they should: the ending of the symphony is played with the wildest abandon. And yet the level of unanimity is remarkably high, and the sense is that the accelerations are meant, not just habitual.

In Berlin and Vienna, orchestral standards were much higher than in London and Paris by the 1920s. Some of the performances of the Berlin Philharmonic Orchestra are quite precise and rhythmically well defined: the Berlin PO under Pfitzner in the 'Eroica' Symphony (c.1929), and the third Brandenburg Concerto under Furtwängler, despite the large number of strings (c.1930). The Vienna Philharmonic under Krauss gives a marvellously deft performance of the overture to *The Marriage of Figaro* (c.1931). Other recordings are less well disciplined, such as the Berlin PO under Kopsch in the overture to *Fidelio* (c.1929) in which the co-ordination between wind and strings is sometimes very loose, and the Vienna PO under Schalk in the third *Leonora* overture (c.1929), in which the final Presto is something of a mess.

Many radio recordings of Furtwängler and the Berlin PO from the late 1930s and 1940s have been reissued on LP and CD. A consistent feature (as far as one can judge from the recordings, which vary in quality) is the depth and weight of tone that Furtwängler obtained from his orchestra. The accuracy of ensemble varies considerably from one performance to the next, but does not noticeably change over the years. Of the recorded performances of the first movement of Beethoven's Fifth Symphony, one of the most tightly disciplined is from 13 September 1939, recorded at a concert ten days after the outbreak of World War II. The whole of this performance is one of the most impressive from Furtwängler's live concerts, with a powerful slow movement, a scherzo in which the trio is most forcefully articulated, and a finale which, at the end, rushes headlong, but with total focus of ensemble. This performance has the sort of powerful emotional unity that Furtwängler and the Berlin PO could only achieve in concert, not in the studio. The 1937 studio recording of the symphony is similar in many ways to the live 1939 performance, but lacks its excitement and sense of urgent common purpose.

The Orchestra of the Berlin State Opera (Berlin Staatskapelle) made a number of fine recordings in the late 1920s, several of them under Richard Strauss. The opening of his *Don Juan* has remarkable rhythmic clarity and incisive dotted rhythms, even though the tempo is brisk. The first movement of Beethoven's Fifth Symphony under Strauss is a tour de force: the tempo is very flexible, with dramatic accelerations and sudden changes of pace, and yet the orchestra manages to stay, apart from one or two details, powerfully together. This is not always the case: its performance of the overture to *The Marriage of Figaro* under Leo Blech (c.1927) is not nearly as well controlled as that of the Vienna PO under Krauss, and the descent in thirds to the recapitulation comes apart completely.

The main characteristics that distinguished the orchestras of Berlin and Vienna from British orchestras before 1930 were not just the amount of rehearsal time or the qualities of conductors, but the regularity of their membership and a sense of tradition. This applied particularly to the Vienna Philharmonic Orchestra, which traced its history back to Otto Nicolai in the 1840s. To be a member of the Vienna Philharmonic – the élite of the Vienna Court Opera orchestra – was to be a respected member of Viennese cultural society, and the upholder of a long tradition stretching back through Mahler to Brahms.

The standing of the Vienna Opera and Philharmonic had been greatly raised by Mahler at the turn of the century. When Mahler made his début at the Vienna Opera with *Lohengrin* in 1897, he was allowed only one rehearsal. At this period, the Vienna Opera had no orchestral rehearsals for operas which were already in the repertoire. Mahler conducted the *Ring* under these conditions. Before the first performance of *Die Walküre*, 'the leader had in fact assured him that everything was much more secure in this opera than in *Das Rheingold*, which had been given so seldom. But the "secure" sections were hardly to Mahler's liking. "The dust of sloppiness and inaccuracy lies an inch thick over the whole thing!"' During this performance the timpanist left before an important roll in the final act, so as not to miss his last train home, leaving the roll to a substitute who missed the entry.[22]

When Mahler became director of the Vienna Opera in 1897 he forbade the use of deputies, and greatly improved the rehearsal routine. For a production of *Die Meistersinger*, for example, he had three orchestral rehearsals and three stage rehearsals.[23] When Mahler took over the conductorship of the Vienna Philharmonic concerts in 1898, he found that they had 'plenty of rehearsals' in contrast to the opera orchestra. For a performance of Mahler's Second Symphony, the Vienna Philharmonic had four rehearsals.[24]

The leader of the Opera and the Philharmonic was Arnold Rosé, Mahler's brother-in-law, who had been in his post since 1881. He remained there until the annexation of Austria by Hitler in 1938, when Rosé and the many other Jewish members of the orchestra were forced to leave. 'Playing together' in such a body was quite different from the casual gatherings of London or Paris, and it shows in their ensemble. Rosé's own style (which Carl Flesch described as that of the 1870s 'with no concession to modern tendencies in our art')[25] informed the corporate style of the orchestra, and particularly of its strings. It was quite distinct from that of any other orchestra of the time, with little vibrato in the strings or the woodwind, and this gave a particularly 'straight' sound to the orchestra. In the 1890s Rosé had denied the brilliant young Fritz Kreisler a place in the orchestra, and the most likely reason is that a player who habitually used a vibrato would not have fitted in to the orchestra's style, in which restraint in the use of vibrato was essential.

The corporate string sound of the Vienna Philharmonic was quite different from that of the Berlin Philharmonic in the 1930s. Whereas Arnold Rosé played in the traditional German style of Joachim, the leader of the Berlin Philharmonic in the early 1930s was Szymon Goldberg, a brilliant young violinist who played with more vibrato (like the young Kreisler). The sound of the Berlin strings during this period is correspondingly warmer, though the wind were as free of vibrato as in Vienna.

Rhythmically, recordings of the pre-war Vienna PO give the impression of a group of people very accustomed to playing with each other, and striving towards a common rhythmic purpose – which is not quite the same as simply 'playing together'. Particularly striking are two live recordings of works by Mahler played under Bruno Walter: the Ninth Symphony (1938) and *Das Lied von der Erde* (1936). Fred Gaisberg, who supervised both recordings for the Gramophone Company, reported that the Ninth Symphony had five rehearsals.[26] It is fascinating to compare the recording of *Das Lied* with later ones conducted by Walter in Vienna and America. The shaping, and the timing of the rhythm, are very much the same, though at slightly different tempi. This first recording with the Vienna PO lacks the precise co-ordination of the later versions, but what it has is a tremendous sense of the players gripping the rhythm, certainly attempting to do it together, but putting the force of the rhythm first, and absolute unanimity second in priority.

For ensemble of a more rigorously disciplined kind, the leading orchestra in Europe in the 1920s and 1930s was the Concertgebouw Orchestra of Amsterdam, conducted by Willem Mengelberg. In particular, their recordings of Tchaikovsky's *Romeo and Juliet* (1930) and Fifth Symphony (1928) are, on the whole, superbly incisive in rhythm. The Concertgebouw had an exceptional amount of rehearsal time, and Mengelberg was renowned for his attention to detail, as the comments of Mahler, Stravinsky and Carl Flesch testify. Much of the rhythmic quality must be attributable to Mengelberg himself. There was no long tradition of a great orchestra in Amsterdam before Mengelberg's arrival in 1895. Recordings made after his departure show that, under his successor Eduard van Beinum, the Concertgebouw's style was rapidly modernised – cleansed of the heavy portamento that Mengelberg fostered, but maintaining much of the rhythmic punch of its brass section.

America

According to Carl Flesch, before World War I the only American orchestra to compare with the best in Europe was the Boston Symphony, with its predominantly Viennese strings, German brass, and French woodwind (including the oboist Georges Longy).[27] It reached its greatest success at that time under Karl

Muck, who was the principal conductor in 1906–7 and for five years from 1912. He conducted the orchestra's first gramophone recordings in 1917, and they convey something of the 'vitality, suppleness and fire' that were reported at the time.[28] The finale of Tchaikovsky's Fourth Symphony has remarkable dash and rhythmic precision, considering the reduced size of the orchestra and cramped pre-electric studio. The dotted rhythms are crisper than those to be heard from most European orchestras before the 1930s, and the wind tuning is also up to the highest European standard.

In 1924, Pierre Monteux, who was then principal conductor of the Boston Symphony, wrote to Stravinsky after conducting *The Rite of Spring* in New York and Boston: 'I myself do not recall having given a performance of the Sacre even approaching these. I must tell you that this orchestra [the Boston Symphony Orchestra] has no equal, that it worked on your score with the *desire* to play it well, and that we rehearsed a great deal.'[29]

The two orchestras of New York, the Symphony and the Philharmonic, both made a few electrical records in the 1920s before their merger in 1928. It was the New York Symphony Orchestra under Damrosch that Boult praised for their discipline compared with British orchestras in the early twenties. Their recordings contain some beautiful moments (lovely French-style bassoon-playing in Ravel's *Mother Goose* c.1927, for example), but the discipline in Brahms's Symphony No. 2 (c.1927) is not as impressive as in Boston at this date – the finale sounds almost British in its scramble. The New York Philharmonic under Mengelberg is much more incisive in the overture to Wagner's *Flying Dutchman* (1925). Toscanini conducted some concerts with the Philharmonic in 1926, and recorded the scherzo from Mendelssohn's *A Midsummer Night's Dream* in that year. The playing is much more precise than in the contemporary recordings by the London Symphony Orchestra and Royal Albert Hall Orchestra, though, as a review in the *Gramophone* put it, 'The scherzo is scarcely that of a band of sprites'.

By common consent, the greatest period of orchestral playing in New York began in 1928, after the merger of the Symphony and Philharmonic Orchestras to form the Philharmonic Symphony Orchestra of New York under Toscanini. The quality of the new orchestra is immediately apparent if one compares that 1926 recording of Mendelssohn's Scherzo with the performance that Toscanini recorded with the combined Philharmonic Symphony Orchestra in 1929. This is not just together, but poised, delicate and almost easy. It makes the London Symphony Orchestra and Royal Albert Hall Orchestra's recordings under Beecham and Ronald sound like a joke. The few recordings that Toscanini and the New York PSO made together have remained classics of the gramophone. They include a famously powerful and refined recording of Beethoven's Seventh Symphony (1936), and a beautifully lyrical and warmly phrased account of Brahms's Variations on a Theme of Haydn (1936). There is also a live recording of Beethoven's Fifth Symphony recorded at a concert in 1933, but not issued at the time. It has not only the power to be expected from Toscanini, but also rhetorical flexibility, which the orchestra carries out with fine bite and depth of tone.

When Toscanini visited London in 1930 with his New York Philharmonic Symphony Orchestra, *The Times* commented, 'The aim of perfection in correlated details which he insisted on in the opera performances of La Scala has been equally pursued with this orchestra, and there could be no question of the absolute finish and clarity of yesterday's performances . . . .'[30] The precision of Toscanini's orchestra was unlike anything to be heard in Europe at this date. By comparison, Stokowski's Philadelphia Orchestra and Koussevitzky's Boston Symphony also had great power and conviction, but details were sometimes as casually placed as in European playing. The Philadelphia's performance of Debussy's 'Fêtes' (1927) tends to hurry, and their *Invitation to the Dance* (1927) slithers over details. The great quality of the Philadelphia Orchestra under Stokowski was its organ-like sonority: broad and deep in both strings and wind, with a fine command of legato phrasing. This was accomplished partly by Stokowski's insistence on free bowing. The orchestra is heard at its best in big late nineteenth-century works, such as Rimsky-Korsakov's *Sheherazade* (1927).

The Boston approach under Koussevitzky was less organ-like than Philadelphia, more muscular and fiery. Their performance of the scherzo from Tchaikovsky's 'Pathétique' Symphony has terrific panache, but this is achieved by good punch at a very fast tempo rather than by precise detail. Particularly impressive are their recordings of Sibelius's Second Symphony (1935) and Rachmaninoff's *Isle of the Dead* (1945). Koussevitzky's performance of the latter makes an interesting comparison with Rachmaninoff's own with the Philadelphia Orchestra (1929). The Philadelphia has a broader, more sustained opening, with darker sonorities; the Boston performance has a more intense and passionate middle section.

When the NBC Symphony Orchestra was founded for Toscanini in 1937, it was widely described as the finest orchestra yet formed. Certainly the sense of corporate intensity is phenomenal, particularly in recordings of live concerts. But it is the intensity of the attack rather than any extra precision which distinguishes their performances from those of the New York Philharmonic Symphony Orchestra. Their recording of Mendelssohn's scherzo from *A Midsummer Night's Dream* (1946) has a sharper edge to the rhythm, but is not actually more together than the NYPSO recording – indeed, one could say that the older version is more remarkable as an example of ensemble, because good unanimity is achieved with greater lightness and sense of ease than in the NBC version. Many of the NBC recordings suffer from harsh and overbearing sound, partly because of the acoustics of the studio where the orchestra most often recorded. But even allowing for this, the differences in orchestral attack between the NBC and the earlier NYPSO performances are often striking. Their Mozart and Haydn tend to be much more fierce and thrusting, and not at all as elegant or easy as, for example, the NYPSO performances of the 'Haffner' and the 'Clock' Symphonies (1929). The NBC Beethoven is extremely muscular, often to very good effect: a 1939 live recording of the 'Eroica' has one of the most powerful and intense climaxes in the funeral march ever recorded. And for sheer virtuosity, it is extraordinary to hear the NBC Orchestra play Paganini's *Moto perpetuo* (1940) straight through without any opportunity for editing, with stunning precision and fire.

Rehearsal methods

What conductors accomplish in rehearsal, and how they do it, is a mixture of the pragmatic and the mysterious. Some can achieve miracles very quickly, some need lengthy rehearsal, and yet others achieve little with long rehearsal. It is partly a matter of what they want to achieve.

One way that Henry Wood was able to cope with very little, or in some cases no rehearsal, was by detailed marking of all the orchestral parts. In this he was following the example of the most efficient conductor in Victorian Britain, Michael Costa. According to Augustus Manns, Costa's parts 'were full of cues, and it was more upon these than upon rehearsal that he relied for a successful performance.'[31] William Alwyn, who began his career as an orchestral flautist in the 1920s, reported:

> Sir Henry Wood used to mark his parts so carefully in blue pencil that you could hardly see the music. He spent *hours* on this – he marked every single piece of expression that he needed, and nothing whatever was left to chance. If anything ever went wrong in rehearsal always his first reaction would be to snarl at the orchestra:
> 'Are these my parts?'
> 'Yes, Sir Henry.'
> 'Well? Haven't I put it in there for you?'
> 'Yes, Sir Henry.'
> 'Very well.'
> And he was right; one was always wrong![32]

The detailed marking of parts was also one of the secrets of Beecham's success. But there was an important difference. For Costa and Wood the markings were a way of dealing with minimal rehearsal. If the orchestra followed what was in the parts, they could expect to achieve a reasonably unanimous result. For Beecham, with greater rehearsal time available to him by the 1930s, and a more regular attendance at rehearsals, the detailed markings had the effect of refining the orchestra's dynamic nuances to an extent not achieved before with a British orchestra. The first concert given by his London Philharmonic Orchestra in 1932 was preceded by seven sectional rehearsals and six full rehearsals (luxury beyond the wildest dreams of Wood earlier in the century). Beecham held separate meetings with each section leader, who then wrote detailed expression markings into the parts.[33] This amount of rehearsal for the important opening concert was exceptional, but the habit of marking in detail was routine throughout Beecham's time at the London Philharmonic Orchestra and, from 1946, the Royal Philharmonic Orchestra.

Several of Beecham's own sets of parts are now in Sheffield University Library. Some works are not heavily marked: the parts of Sibelius's Fourth Symphony, for example, have few indications beyond what is printed. But Mozart's symphonies are marked in extraordinary detail, with virtually every phrase having some extra accent, crescendo, diminuendo, and sometimes fingerings. The same sets of parts were used by the London Philharmonic Orchestra in the 1930s and by the Royal Philharmonic Orchestra from the late 1940s, and it is not easy to establish exactly which markings date from which period. But many of them certainly date from the 1930s, as the opening of Mozart's Symphony No. 40 demonstrates. Music example 3.1 shows Mozart's markings, and music example 3.2 shows the markings in the set of Beecham's parts. These are virtually the same as those in Beecham's published edition of this symphony, dating from 1940, and therefore must have originated in the 1930s.[34] Changes of mind are visible. For example, bar 2 of the cello part is marked in blue pencil to be played in a single bow, as shown in example 3.2, but there is also an earlier pencilled bowing which divides the bar into two halves.

There is no simple equation between the amount of rehearsal time and the results an orchestra achieves. Some conductors have a reputation for clear and expressive gestures, such as Nikisch, Mahler and Toscanini, and can get what they want quickly; others are neither physically elegant nor clear, such as Casals, Szell, and, to judge by film of him, Mengelberg. They all achieved results through lengthy rehearsal.

The contrast between conductors who are obsessional in rehearsal and others who are relaxed goes back to the late nineteenth century. The exceptionally meticulous rehearsals of Lamoureux in Paris and Bülow in Meiningen have already been mentioned in chapter 1. Bülow himself was 'a very peculiar, a very testy, but nevertheless an intelligent, serious, and competent man', according to Brahms, and he conducted from memory even at rehearsals.[35] The members of his orchestra were so well drilled that they were able to perform Brahms's First Piano Concerto without conductor, while Bülow played the piano solo. Eduard Hanslick was even more astounded by their 'flawless' performance of Beethoven's Grosse Fuge, 'a tonal wilderness in which the best

Ex.3.1 Mozart, Symphony No. 40 in G minor, second movement, bars 1–8.

string quartets are prone to lose their way' (a remark that says as much about the string quartets of the day as about Bülow's orchestra).[36]

The other conductor most closely associated with Brahms, Hans Richter, was a very different character from the obsessional Bülow. Richter himself made it clear that he took a much more relaxed attitude to orchestral discipline: 'At times I let myself be guided by the orchestra, since I recognized the instructive freedom of movement, which I should call the individuality of an orchestra, as the proper means of grasping the spirit of a work. That is not to

Ex.3.2 Mozart, Symphony No. 40 in G minor, second movement, bars 1–8. Markings taken from Sir Thomas Beecham's set of parts (Sheffield University Library).

say I could not make my will respected if I wanted to. But I refuse to use the whip, with which many conductors seek to subjugate an orchestra also independent and capable of thinking for itself.'[37] The results of Richter's approach were often magnificent, sometimes scrappy. Weingartner saw Richter at work in the Vienna Opera in 1901: 'I witnessed a performance of Meyerbeer's *L'Africaine*, which he conducted with obvious distaste, and one of *Die Meistersinger*, at which he displayed the full mastery of his leadership.'[38] Dvořák was delighted with Richter's conducting of his third Slavonic Rhapsody in November 1879: 'I have nothing but the highest praise for the performance of the work. It was played with incomparable beauty, and the impression upon me of the Rhapsody, which I had not yet heard, was overpowering. Everyone played with enthusiasm.'[39] Richter conducted many fine early performances of Brahms's works, often with the Vienna Philharmonic, but sometimes the composer was dissatisfied with the level to which he had rehearsed the orchestra. After the second performance of Brahms's First Symphony in 1878, which was 'touch and go', Brahms was reported to have said, 'If someone can't be bothered to study, he should leave it alone. – I didn't ask for this performance. At the very least it is thoroughly disloyal behaviour.'[40]

Mahler's attention to detail, and his insistence on thorough rehearsal, were often described by contemporaries. Schoenberg, however, drew the lesson from Mahler that what matters is knowing how to use rehearsal time:

> I once heard one of his 'colleagues' say that there is no special trick in bringing off good performances when one has so many rehearsals. Certainly there is no trick in it, for the oftener one plays a thing through, the better it goes, and even the poorest conductors profit from this. But there is a trick for feeling the need for a tenth rehearsal during the ninth rehearsal because one still hears many things that can be improved, *because one still knows there is something to be said in the tenth rehearsal*. This is exactly the difference: a poor conductor often does not know what to do after the third rehearsal, he has nothing more to say, he is easily satisfied, because he does not have the capacity for deeper discrimination, and because nothing in him imposes higher requirements.[41]

Adrian Boult visited the Casals Orchestra in Barcelona in the early 1920s, and reported on its exceptionally thorough rehearsals. These were possible because Casals was a wealthy man and could afford to subsidise the orchestra, insisting that every member should attend all rehearsals (even for works in which they were not playing).[42] Casals took five or six weeks to rehearse a series of six concerts, nine sessions per concert. There was careful tuning, and frequent repetition of detail: 'Matters of bowing, and sometimes, too, of fingering, were often discussed, and in all important passages the strings bowed together . . . . Mr. Casals used a heavy stick, and no pretence was made of the modern type of virtuoso conducting with all the expression shown with the point of the stick, as we must do in England when rehearsals are so few. It is surely better to make an orchestra feel the right expression by means of real rehearsing than to rely on the last moment to get the effect needed.'[43] Boult gives a breakdown of the rehearsal times for the concerts he attended. The rehearsals for the first concert were as follows:

	Hrs	Mins
Beethoven Fifth Symphony	6	55
Saint-Saëns *Le Rouet d'Omphale*	2	10
Enesco Romanian Rhapsody in A	3	15
Debussy Gigues	4	45
Bach Overture in D	2	30
9 rehearsals	19	35

What is now unknowable is what standard was actually achieved by this. Boult was certainly impressed, and it must have been better than anything he was used to in England. On the other hand, the Casals Orchestra's recordings from the late 1920s are not impressive now. Their recording of Beethoven's Symphony No. 4 (c.1930) has many moments of vague rhythm, and the cross-rhythms of the scherzo are very confused and rushed. The tuning of the woodwind is also poor.

Mengelberg in Amsterdam had, according to Carl Flesch, 'unlimited rehearsal', but spent too much of it talking. At one rehearsal Flesch timed him, and found that he talked for a total of one and a half hours, and the orchestra played for only three quarters of an hour.[44] Mengelberg was a great admirer of Mahler, and had attended many of Mahler's rehearsals when the composer visited Amsterdam to conduct his own works. Perhaps it was partly through Mahler's inspiration that Mengelberg succeeded in developing the most scrupu-lously rehearsed orchestra in Europe. The results, on records, are in quite a different class from those of the Casals Orchestra. Perhaps Mengelberg had much better players at his disposal. Perhaps also his stick technique was better – though the films of him look more military than expressive. Stravinsky in 1928 attended a performance by Mengelberg and the Concertgebouw of *Ein Heldenleben* (which Strauss dedicated to Mengelberg): 'What horrible music! And how much care and certainty Mengelberg put into its performance.'[45]

By contrast with Mengelberg and Mahler, Nikisch was reported as being very economical in his rehearsals. At the Gewandhaus in Leipzig, where he conducted for twenty-seven years until his death in 1922, the weekly routine during the season was a private rehearsal on a Tuesday evening, a public rehearsal on Wednesday morning, and the concert on Thursday. Boult reported that the first rehearsal often lasted little more than an hour, that Nikisch conducted with absurd exaggerations on Wednesday, and that every-thing fell into place at the concert.[46]

Toscanini was an example of a conductor who was both obsessional and economical. His attention to detail and his frustrated rage when he did not get what he wanted are legendary. But it is less well known that he obtained results very quickly. Boult, again, reported that when Toscanini visited the BBC Symphony Orchestra in the 1930s, 'He was given a generous schedule in London, it is true, but he often stopped the rehearsal an hour early, and he actually cancelled one or two altogether.'[47] Toscanini reported to his wife that he found the BBC orchestra very responsive: 'I've found an excellent, intelligent orchestra that immediately showed me liking and affection.'[48]

Similarly in Vienna in 1933, when Toscanini first conducted the Philharmonic, he declared himself satisfied after the second rehearsal and cancelled the remaining three.[49] Toscanini wrote about the speed with which the orchestra responded to his demands: 'I've begun the rehearsals with Beethoven's 7th and the Brahms variations. The orchestra is good – not excellent, like mine in New York, and above all not as disciplined. You can tell that it's not accustomed to being in good hands. However, it's flexible, because at the first rehearsal it immediately modified itself so as to maintain the rhythm strictly, and it has responded perfectly to all of my demands.'[50] After this first experience, Toscanini returned to Vienna every year until 1937.

Another conductor who rehearsed economically was Leopold Stokowski. But this was partly because he stood against the sort of orchestral discipline that gradually became regarded as the ideal elsewhere during the twentieth century: 'I am completely opposed to standardization, regimentation, uniform bowing, uniform fingering and breathing, and all other conventions which tend to make an orchestra sound mechanical.'[51] His weekly pattern of rehearsal while at the Philadelphia Orchestra was, according to a member of the orchestra, usually as follows: 'Monday: straight through the programme; Tuesday: hard work on difficult spots (rarely more than two hours); Wednesday: reading new music; Thursday: straight through the programme, often with only a few comments. The concerts all took place on Friday and Saturday.'[52]

The contrast between conductors who want as much rehearsal as possible and others who would rather rehearse little, between conductors who achieve a great deal in a short time and others who need many hours, has continued through to modern times. Szell in Cleveland, who was not admired for his stick technique, rehearsed obsessionally and at length, declaring that his orchestra 'begins rehearsing where other orchestras leave off'. The results, in the concert hall more often than on record, were widely regarded in the 1960s as the finest in the world. Rudolf Kempe enjoyed rehearsing more than giving concerts, with which he was usually dissatisfied. By contrast, Gennadi Rozhdestvensky prefers to rehearse little.

Robert Ponsonby, in an obituary of Günter Wand, remembered that, when Wand was Chief Guest Conductor of the BBC Symphony Orchestra in the

1980s, 'He insisted on a minimum of eight rehearsals for a standard programme, a luxury that only a broadcasting organisation could afford to offer. His rehearsals were meticulous and much appreciated by the orchestra, who respected him as part of a vanishing tradition.'[53] Other conductors who continued to demand long rehearsal time into the late twentieth century are Carlos Kleiber and Sergiu Celibidache. But one of the consequences was that they were unwilling to conduct orchestras who could not afford to give them the time, and their appearances were rare. Orchestral rehearsals are very expensive, and multiple rehearsals, as Ponsonby acknowledged, can be afforded on a regular basis only by well-financed organisations.

Anyone who has played in an orchestra knows that some conductors can spend three rehearsals and achieve almost nothing, whereas others can galvanise the orchestra in a very short time. It is partly a question of physical movement, the clarity of the beat, the ability to convey rhythm and impulse by physical means. But it is much more than that: a sense of gathered concentration, the knowledge that serious business is afoot, that time will not be wasted, and that special musical insights are at work.

The routine training of conductors at music conservatoires did not exist in 1900. Conductors in those days started off as orchestral players, pianists and, in many cases, composers, and worked their way up as repetiteurs in opera houses, and by attracting the attention of powerful people. Some of this still goes on, but it is now possible for a music student to set out to have a career in conducting, fresh from a conducting course at a music college, with a competition or two on the way. Not all of these conductors are musicians of stature who command the respect of orchestras. Any conservatoire-trained young conductor can be taught strategies to keep an orchestra in order, just as the modern manager is taught strategies of 'leadership' and 'team-building'. In both fields, the people who command attention are those who make it clear straight away that they have something important to say, and are anxious to help the orchestra to achieve it. Orchestras tend to dislike being rehearsed by many of the nit-picking young conductors they are nowadays faced with. There are exceptions, who are genuinely inspiring, but the run-of-the-mill modern young conductor is essentially a manager, and orchestras tolerate them much as office workers tolerate their bosses.

One of the consequences of the rise of the virtuoso conductor, which began at the end of the nineteenth century and has continued to this day, is that one can easily lose sight of the fact that it is the orchestras who do the playing, not the conductors. Undoubtedly the qualities of the conductor are extremely important in getting an orchestra to play at its best. But an orchestra of regular membership which performs together over years builds up its own style and ensemble, with its players acquiring a knowledge and sensitivity to each other that carry them through concerts with good, bad and mediocre conductors.

Two observations by conductors, one from eighty years ago, one from modern times, will illustrate the point.

In 1922 Adrian Boult was in Prague to conduct the Czech Philharmonic Orchestra. He wrote in his notebook: 'I went to Pilsen next day to hear *Ma Vlást* complete, and it was a marvellous performance. Talich said he had not rehearsed it for two years, but the ensemble was marvellous (quite different from our English idea of ensemble) although they had often rehearsed and played it under other conductors in between: a real case of what the Germans mean when they say a thing "sitzt". When can this be done in England?'[54] What Boult found 'marvellous' in 1922 must, as with the Casals Orchestra, have been much better than what he was used to in England, but it is impossible to know whether we would consider it marvellous now. Talich's three recordings of *Ma Vlást* with the Czech Philharmonic Orchestra (1929, 1941 and 1954) show that the ensemble, in the limited sense of unanimity, was not as good in the 1920s as it was to become later. On the other hand, the 1929 performance of the cycle does show the broad sweep and sonority of the orchestra, and a strong sense of a long-established style of playing.

Eighty years later, Simon Rattle, speaking in 2002, described his experience of conducting the Berlin Philharmonic Orchestra for the first time. He had just performed Mahler's Sixth Symphony in Britain, with a 'marvellous' orchestra. They had been very thoroughly rehearsed, and gave an excellent performance. He then went to the Berlin Philharmonic to perform the same symphony. They had three rehearsals, of which the third was open to the public. At the first rehearsal he took them straight through the symphony, and they played it, Rattle said, as well as the British orchestra had at the concert. He realised 'that I was in the presence of a musical machine the like of which I had never encountered before'. The orchestra already knew the work inside out, and at the second and third rehearsals they were looking up at him just checking that they were doing exactly what he wanted.[55] It cannot be coincidental that the Berlin Philharmonic had been fully funded by city and state since the 1920s, and is one of Germany's national institutions.

The highest standards of orchestral playing are achieved today, as they were a hundred years ago, more by regularity of rehearsal and membership than by the number of rehearsals for a particular event.

Rising standards on little rehearsal

In an interview quoted in chapter 1, Alfred Deahl, Southampton violinist in the 1920s, said, 'we were all good sight-readers, real professionals'. William Alwyn, remembering his days as a deputising flautist in London, said that the British orchestral player's exceptional talent for sight-reading was 'the envy of the world'. Far from regretting the lack of rehearsal in those days, Deahl and Alwyn clearly remembered with pride their ability to cope in difficult circumstances – a characteristically British fondness for muddling through against the odds.

Orchestral standards across the world are, in general, far higher than they were in the early twentieth century. Highly disciplined orchestras were then the exception rather than the rule. Now it is rare, if not unknown, to hear professional orchestral playing as scrappy or ill-tuned as that on many a recording from the 1920s. But is this the result of more and better rehearsal? Some of the high-profile travelling conductors of modern times will turn up only for one or at most two rehearsals, expecting any preliminary work to have been done by someone else. Many modern concerts are in any case achieved on very little rehearsal. On tour, the most an orchestra will usually have in an unfamiliar hall is an hour or less shortly before the concert, and sometimes not even that.[56]

There is something of a paradox in the fact that orchestras' rehearsal time was usually very short at the beginning of the twentieth century, and now is short again, and yet the results achieved are quite different. Perhaps the essential difference is this: that in the early twentieth century orchestras got to know more or less how the conductor wanted the music to go, but, by the standards of our time, few people were concerned with precise accuracy of detail. Now the expectation is that everything will be neat and tidy, whatever the standard of music-making in other ways. This is the result partly of the general drive towards accuracy and clarity, which has been fed by the artificial perfection of highly edited modern recordings, partly of the changing nature and role of conductors, which was discussed above.

The result is that modern performances are often exactly together, very well disciplined, and in tune, but often lack the corporate spirit of messier performances of the past. Even Toscanini, famous in his day as a stickler for precision, was far more concerned with spirit than with literal accuracy. Most of his recordings with the NBC Symphony Orchestra have moments which are looser in ensemble than what one hears from the leading orchestras of today. But the overwhelming impression is that everyone knows exactly what they are doing, and why. His recorded rehearsals make it clear that his driving force was passion: he spent far more of his time trying to get the orchestra to 'sing' than to play accurately. Nowadays everything is exactly together, but sometimes one wonders what the point is. It is the difference between unanimity of purpose and unanimity of execution.

The one most obvious thing that has changed in the last century is that modern orchestras play much more accurately together and much better in tune than most of the orchestras to be heard on records of seventy or eighty years ago. One factor is the individual accomplishment of the players, whose technical standards are very high. Just as Boult found that a new generation of players in 1930 was technically better than the previous generation, now, at the beginning of the twenty-first century, there has been another leap of technical proficiency. This is partly because young players compete for orchestral places across the world. Violinists from Britain, France or Germany are competing with others from America, Japan, Korea and Russia. People from countries that have traditionally been fairly relaxed about standards (particularly Britain) find themselves in competition with people from countries in which intense training and dedication are an assumed part of the culture. The London music colleges are now full of students from many different countries, and the standards are therefore very different from those of thirty or forty years ago. And, far more than in 1930, young musicians of today have the sounds of all the world's finest players in their ears from recordings, which are far cheaper and far more accessible than they were seventy years ago.

High standards make it possible to put a concert or recording together with very little rehearsal, and reach a standard that was unknown until recently. Schedules for orchestral recording sessions routinely describe what is to be done in each session as 'Rehearse/Record'. This means exactly what it says: the conductor and orchestra rehearse, while the engineer sets the microphone levels and makes any necessary adjustments, and when everyone is ready they record. They may not have had any preliminary rehearsal. Often the orchestra will be playing works they have played many times, but not necessarily under that conductor. Sometimes they will be recording works they have never played before.

At a recent recording session in London, one of the top London orchestras was recording oboe concertos with an excellent American oboist. As well as the Strauss concerto, they were recording an American concerto that the orchestra had not played before. The conductor had met the oboist before the sessions, but had not rehearsed with him. The orchestra had had one three-hour orchestral rehearsal, without the soloist. The sessions themselves were the first time that conductor, soloist and orchestra had all met together. In the Strauss concerto, there were only the tiniest of ensemble problems, even on the first reading of each movement. They could perfectly well have played the work at a concert, and few people would have suspected that this was the first time they had all met. It was beautiful and competent playing. The question is, what would it have been like if they had rehearsed thoroughly beforehand? Now that modern players and conductors have got so used to playing like well-oiled machines on no rehearsal, do they actually achieve anything more by rehearsing thoroughly? On the other hand, how deep does the routine competence go? Can there really be any profound sense of a shared interpretation and a common purpose when the casual has become so first-rate?

One of the recurring views expressed about rehearsal over the years is that performance can be too well drilled. One might think that greater precision and clarity are always to be welcomed. But often, when new standards of discipline are reached, there are those who say that something has been lost. This view goes back before the days of recording. Lamoureux, whose orchestra was widely praised from its first appearance in England in 1896, was described by a London critic as a 'perfect musical machine, a musical example of Carlyle's drill-sergeant ideal' compared with Wood, who 'attempts to make his orchestra reflect his own emotional view of a composition'.[57] British reviews of Toscanini's New York Philharmonic Symphony Orchestra recordings in the 1930s were mixed. W. R. Anderson, writing in the *Gramophone* in July 1930, found the phrasing of his 'Haffner' Symphony 'exquisite throughout', and thought the finale 'polished to perfection'. But a month earlier he had written of their recording of preludes from Verdi's *Traviata*, 'Every hair in every bow seems to be numbered and regimented .... I see no point in reproducing such slight music with all this show and energy.' Today, this review is incomprehensible when one hears the extraordinary sweetness of tone and beautiful shaping of phrases in that recording.

When Toscanini and his orchestra appeared in Vienna, the correspondent for the *Musical Times* made a striking comparison to put their efficiency in its place: 'Comparison with Vienna's Philharmonic – a body justly famous and recognised in all European capitals – was as near at hand as it was difficult. Toscanini's watchword is unconditional subordination of his men; the Vienna men are given the liberty to "sing" to their heart's content, to be co-ordinate, not subordinate to their leader. In discipline and precision the New York players are therefore superior, but the question remains how the comparison would stand if the two orchestras had the same opportunity for rehearsal. If the New York orchestra be superior in drill, the Viennese men appear to us to be the more "creative".'[58]

More understandable are the criticisms levelled at some of the NBC Symphony Orchestra recordings, with their fierce accentuation and ruthless drive. But to describe them as over-drilled is not accurate. It is the character of the playing which is sometimes relentless. As was mentioned above, accuracy is not always perfect: details are often slightly messy by modern standards, and the tuning of the woodwind, particularly the oboes, can sometimes be surprisingly raw. As for the accusation of ruthlessness, it is not always easy to separate the effect of the playing from the effect of the often dry and harsh recording quality. It is noticeable that, when NBC recordings have been remastered for CD issue, some of the *performances* sound less aggressive than they did on LP. The same is true of Szell's recordings with the Cleveland Orchestra. Now that remixing for CD reissues has taken the edge off some of the Cleveland recordings, the playing itself sounds more musical, as it did in the concert hall.

Competence and style

The trend over the twentieth century from under-rehearsed laissez-faire to modern accuracy and clarity is clearly audible on recordings. But, as some of the examples quoted above suggest, matters of ensemble and discipline are not just to do with accuracy. A powerful sense of unanimity of spirit can survive serious vaguenesses and inaccuracies of detail (as in Elgar's recordings with the London Symphony and Royal Albert Hall Orchestras). And it can positively be enhanced by slight lack of discipline, because moments of inaccuracy make one aware of the efforts of eighty people attempting to play the music together. Some examples from live recordings conducted by Klemperer and Ančerl were mentioned in chapter 2. Such touches of roughness were taken for granted in the best recordings of the 1930s and 1940s, for example in Beecham's recordings with the London Philharmonic, Mengelberg's with the Concertgebouw, Walter's with the Vienna Philharmonic, Toscanini's with the NBC Symphony Orchestra, Koussevitzky's with the Boston Symphony Orchestra, Stokowski's with the Philadelphia Orchestra. By comparison, some of the super-accurate, super-clear performances of today can sound dehumanised (particularly when sanitised by scrupulous editing).

The much less well-controlled performances from the 1920s and 1930s raise more of a question about competence and style. Many details in orchestral recordings of this period now sound somewhat skimped, even chaotic. To hear Albert Coates conducting British players in the overture to Borodin's *Prince Igor* (c.1926) or the first movement of the 'Eroica' Symphony (1926) is to hear performances of terrific panache, but nothing resembling the level of firmness in detail that is now routinely required. Piero Coppola and the Paris Conservatoire Orchestra take the finale of Schumann's Symphony No. 3 (c.1934) so fast and with such nervous placing of accents that it is almost a surprise to hear them reach the end of the movement. In these recordings, and hundreds like them, groups of semiquavers (sixteenth notes) are often no more than flurries, dotted rhythms are very overdotted, and tempi accelerate whenever the music is agitated. These are all things that modern style and taste require to be kept under firm control.

By modern standards, such orchestras were incompetent. The best amateur orchestras today are, in standard of ensemble, far better than many professional orchestras in the 1920s and early 1930s. But it is not quite as simple as that, and we cannot just dismiss all the old orchestral recordings that now sound messy. When Elgar conducted the new BBC Symphony Orchestra and London Philharmonic in the early thirties, he was delighted by them. But when it was suggested in 1933 that he should replace his old recording of *Cockaigne*, in which he had conducted the Royal Albert Hall Orchestra, with a new one conducting the BBC Symphony Orchestra, he asked whether there was 'anything the matter' with the old recording.[59] Putting the two performances side by side reveals much more control and rhythmic clarity in the BBC performance, particularly in the patterns of quavers and semiquavers that dominate the work. By comparison the RAHO performance is a little more casual and hasty. But if the BBC performance now therefore sounds 'better', the RAHO performance has extra dash.

In 1938, Stravinsky praised the Berlin Philharmonic Orchestra, with which he had recorded *Jeu de cartes*, describing it as 'magnificent'.[60] But his suggestion that they should record *Petrushka* together, to replace his 1928 recording with the Straram Orchestra, was to take advantage of 'the latest technological improvements' of recording, not because of the messiness of the Straram performance. He says nothing about the superiority of the Berlin orchestra, which was in quite a different class from the Straram Orchestra.

How much of this is to do with levels of rehearsal, and how much is stylistic? Orchestras which were adequately rehearsed, such as the New York Philharmonic Symphony Orchestra or the Concertgebouw Orchestra, under conductors with a firm grasp of orchestral discipline and style such as Toscanini and Mengelberg, undoubtedly achieved quite different results from the more casual orchestras of the time. But the hurrying and lightness of detail to be heard in so many orchestral recordings from the 1920s are matters of more than competence. As we shall see in discussion of recordings of chamber and piano music, such stylistic traits were common even among the most thoroughly rehearsed groups and the most renowned of soloists.

Woodwind

Changes in woodwind sections of orchestras over the century also raise issues which are to do partly with competence, partly with style. The general standard of professional woodwind-playing has improved greatly over the last hundred years. Woodwind as out of tune as some to be heard on early twentieth-century recordings is never encountered in modern professional orchestras, nor even in good amateur orchestras. Players of period woodwind instruments, which are often more difficult to play in tune than their modern equivalents, play with much better tuning than many early twentieth-century players on their more modern instruments.

Harry Blech remembered how unreliable the standards of wind tuning were in British orchestras when he started the London Wind Players in the 1940s: 'I used to get letters from conductors: "The first time I hear wind-playing in tune and with reasonable balance." I remember sitting in the BBC Symphony Orchestra and listening, and I'd think, "Well, that's a marvellous first oboe, but what the hell's the second oboe doing? I mean it's neither balanced nor in tune." I was very critical.'[61]

The general standard of tuning has risen over the last century. Serious problems, which were routine in the early twentieth century, are rare today, and even the less extreme instances of poor tuning of the 1950s and 1960s are largely a thing of the past. Of course, editing creates the impression on CDs that tuning is now always perfect. That is not quite true in the concert hall, even now, and period instrumentalists in particular can still have problems. But there is no doubt that tuning standards are now incredibly high compared with any time in the last hundred years (and probably before that).

But the development of woodwind-playing involves more than just rising standards. The styles of individual instruments, and the concept of how they should blend together, changed through the twentieth century. The broad trend was towards a blend of sound in which the timbres of the instruments are as closely matched as possible. From our modern perspective, some of the recorded orchestral sonorities of the 1920s and 1930s can sound varied and unblended compared with those of the modern orchestra. This is most shocking when the standard of tuning is low (as it often was). But even a carefully tuned ensemble of woodwind and brass was often a combination of distinct timbres.

French orchestras in the early twentieth century had particularly distinctive woodwind, in which the separate characters of instruments were more important than their ability to blend together. Recordings of Berlioz's *Symphonie fantastique* provide good examples, and the effect in the 'March to the Scaffold' is particularly striking. The march opens with two horns, which are then joined by the remaining two horns and the four bassoons. The blend of modern orchestras, and the prevalence of German Heckel-system bassoons, together with reeds designed to produce a smooth, un-reedy tone, means that the listener is not particularly aware of any difference between the sounds of the horns and bassoons (particularly if Berlioz's instruction that the horns should be hand-stopped is ignored). The combination might as well be all horns, or horns and trombones, or even all trombones – modern horn tone has tended to move closer to trombone tone, with the wider bore of most instruments and the more cupped mouthpieces that many players use. In French recordings of the 1920s and 1930s, the pungent, nasal tone-colour of the French bassoons gives a sinister edge to the sonority as they enter. This is particularly effective in Monteux's 1931 recording with the Paris Symphony Orchestra, only a little less so in Pierné's 1928 recording with the Colonne Orchestra. The later entries of the bassoons in the march also have quite a different effect in the old French recordings: nasal and whining at their high entry (bars 25ff.), reedy and mocking in their running staccato (bars 49ff.). The smoother, darker, more solid tone of modern players on their Heckel-system bassoons produces an altogether pleas-anter, more polite effect in this march. Even players on period instruments aim for something approaching modern blend. The bassoonists of the Orchestre Révolutionnaire et Romantique under Gardiner (1991) sound fairly reedy and un-polite in the high passage, but they blend with the horns almost like modern bassoons at the opening. How much is this because bassoons and reed-styles of c.1830 sounded like that, and how much is it the result of the modern taste for a blended sound, applied to old instruments? Could it be that the stark contrasts of sonority to be heard in French recordings of the early twentieth century might be closer to what Berlioz had in mind?

Similarly, the opening of the 'Scène aux champs', in which cor anglais and distant oboe answer each other like shepherds piping across the valley, has changed in effect noticeably over the last eighty years. Today, both players can generally be relied upon for beautiful tone, elegant phrasing, and modern vibrato (the 'live' London Symphony Orchestra/Colin Davis recording from 2000 is a good example). Period performances are not very different: in Gardiner's recording the cor anglais sounds very much like a conventional modern instrument, played with a pleasant vibrato in conventional modern fashion. The echoing oboe is a little less vibrant, but otherwise modern in style. The fundamental approach, in both period and conventional modern performances, is highly refined. Could Berlioz have meant this, given his intention to evoke shepherds' piping? He marks the melodic lines with accents and staccato marks. These too are smoothed over in modern performance.

Recordings of the 'Scène aux champs' from the 1920s and 1930s tend to be much 'straighter', less refined in their phrasing, with less vibrato, and with a more pungent tone. The cor anglais of the Paris Symphony Orchestra in 1931 has only a slight quiver, that of the Paris Conservatoire Orchestra in 1939 has hardly any vibrato at all. In both cases the echoing oboe has a little more vibrato, but still nothing like modern oboe vibrato. Clarinettists in French recordings of that period also have a characteristically pungent tone, often with an intermittent rapid tremor (as in Stravinsky's 1931 Paris recording of *The Soldier's Tale*). French flautists already played on metal flutes, in many cases with a confident vibrato which sounds virtually modern (Moyse being the most famous example). Putting these highly individual woodwind-players together in an orchestra produced an ensemble quite unlike that of the modern woodwind section. Even in France the tendency in recent years has been towards a more homogeneous blend, and a rounding out of the pungent tone-qualities of earlier generations. Some prominent conductors have encouraged French players to abandon the traditional French bassoon in favour of the German (Barenboim required German bassoons for the Orchestre de Paris in the 1970s), though there has been resistance to this trend, and even outside France there is now something of a revival of interest in the French bassoon. Perhaps the most impressive use of traditional French woodwind timbres is to be heard in the recordings from the 1950s and 1960s of the Suisse Romande Orchestra, based in Geneva, and conducted by Ernest Ansermet. The pungent sonorities, guided by Ansermet's ear for clarity and texture, produced marvellously subtle and characterful results in the works of Debussy and Ravel.

In Britain in the early twentieth century, as in France, blending was not the first priority for woodwind. Oboes tended to be powerful and penetrating, epitomised by William Malsch, the principal oboe of the Queen's Hall Orchestra until 1904. Flutes were almost always wooden, with a broad tone, sometimes almost saxophone-like on the lower notes. Clarinets had a characteristically 'woody' quality, and bassoons were French, and reedy in tone. Unlike in France, vibrato was used little by any of the woodwind. Woodwind-playing like this can still be heard in many recordings from the 1920s, often with poor tuning and rather crude balance and blend.

Over the twentieth century, British woodwind-playing underwent great change. It began with the appointment of a Belgian oboist, Henri de Busscher, to succeed Malsch in the Queen's Hall Orchestra, and the adoption of the German bassoon by Archie Camden, first in the Hallé Orchestra and then in the BBC Symphony Orchestra. De Busscher played with greater delicacy and flexibility than Malsch, and with a French-style vibrato. It was he who inspired Leon Goossens, who then developed the vibrato, brightness of tone, and flexibility of phrasing in a highly personal way. Goossens, in turn, influenced other woodwind players to play more flexibly and with vibrato, notably clarinettist Reginald Kell and bassoonist Gwydion Brooke, his fellow-principals in Beecham's London Philharmonic in the 1930s. The principal flautist of the orchestra, Geoffrey Gilbert, had studied with a French flautist, and played with French-style vibrato and silvery tone on the metal flute.

The influence of the new style, with its vibrato and greater flexibility, gradually spread in Britain. Still elements of the old style remained: oboes were sometimes quite pungent into the 1950s, and many clarinettists and bassoonists resisted vibrato. Some flute players were still playing on the wooden flute into the 1960s, but now with some vibrato. The general trend, however, was towards a flexible, highly expressive style of woodwind-playing, compared with the British style of the early twentieth century.

In Vienna and Berlin, woodwind style was not as pungent in the early twentieth century as it was in France and Britain. The tone of oboists, clarinettists and bassoonists was darker and more mellow, with broad, smooth phrasing, and rarely any trace of vibrato. This style persisted right through to the 1950s without much change. Although a little vibrato was sometimes heard on the flute, it was never continuous. The overall woodwind sound, both in Berlin and in Vienna, was steady and broad, with the instruments tending to blend together in ensemble in a more organ-like way than in France or Britain. In more recent years, prominent vibrato has been adopted by both flautists and oboists in Berlin and Vienna, but hardly at all by clarinettists.

America, as Furtwängler already observed in the 1920s, became the melting-pot of orchestral styles. In woodwind instruments, the predominant influence was French. Pupils of French flautists Paul Taffanel and Philippe Gaubert were principal flautists in the orchestras of Boston, Philadelphia, Chicago and New York in the early years of the twentieth century, and taught many of the next generation of Americans.[62] Pupils of oboist Georges Gillet were principals in the orchestras of Boston and Philadelphia. One of them, Marcel Tabuteau, was principal oboe of the Philadelphia Orchestra from 1915 to 1954, and was highly influential as a teacher. His fast vibrato became a hallmark of American oboe-playing for the rest of the twentieth century. But the woodwind sound of American orchestras was not straightforwardly French. Oboists tended to have a darker, more mellow tone than those in France. German bassoons were widely used, but most often played with some French-style flexibility and vibrato. Clarinettists mostly played in a more Germanic style, with broad phrasing and little or no vibrato (perhaps as a reaction to the growing use of vibrato in jazz-playing). And there had developed in America by the 1930s a sensitivity to the blending of the woodwind section as a whole that was rarely matched in Europe at that time. Partly this was because the standard of tuning was generally higher than in most of Europe. The wind of the New York PSO play the opening chorale of Brahms's Variations on a Theme of Haydn, in 1936 under Toscanini, with a modern standard of tuning, phrasing and blend. It does not sound very different from, for example, the Cleveland Orchestra under Szell in the 1960s.

Worldwide, the modern blend of woodwind styles involves compromises between different traditions. Many modern oboists and clarinettists, for example, play with combined elements of German and French styles – darker in tone than the old French, brighter than the old German, with a little vibrato (which Germans have rarely used in the past); modern bassoonists generally play on the German-style bassoon, but often with vibrato and flexibility of phrasing which owe more to French tradition. The coming together of traditions in this way, which is first heard in recordings of American orchestras from the 1920s and 1930s, has spread round the world.

Global homogenisation of wind

By the end of the twentieth century, this sharing round of diverse styles had coalesced into a level of homogenisation that could never have been dreamed of by Furtwängler and his contemporaries. In the first half of the twentieth century orchestras in different countries sounded quite different from each other. By the end of the century it was often difficult to tell where an orchestra came from, just from its recordings. There had grown up a norm for a smoothly blended orchestral sound and style, based, particularly in the wind, on an American/European compromise, in which there was much less room for diversity than there used to be. There are still orchestras that have distinct chacteristics of their own, but the differences are narrowing all the time.

The sound of Russian brass is a particularly striking example. The impact of the Leningrad Philharmonic Orchestra when they visited Britain in the 1960s was overwhelming not just because of the power and intensity of the playing, but because it was utterly different from that of British and other Western European orchestras. The blaring vibrancy of the brass in the great climaxes of Tchaikovsky's 'Pathétique' Symphony was something that few in the audience had ever heard in a concert hall. When the orchestra returned to Britain in the 1990s, as the St Petersburg Philharmonic, the brass style was undergoing change. They brought two brass teams with them, the 'old guard', who still played in the vibrant Russian style, and a younger team whose playing was much more westernised, with little vibrato and a less brash sound.

This changing Russian brass style is clearly audible on recordings. In a 1949 recording of Tchaikovsky's Fifth Symphony by the Leningrad Philharmonic Orchestra under Mravinsky, the horn solo in the second movement is extremely vibrant, and the trumpets in the climaxes are very fierce, with noticeable vibrato. Russian recordings from the 1990s are still impressive, but have to some extent been tamed. In recordings of the same symphony by the Russian National Orchestra under Pletnev (1996) and the Russian Philharmonic Orchestra under Friedmann (1995), the horn vibrato is much more delicate, the brass climaxes less vibrant and fierce, and with a broader, more Western sound.

Other orchestral brass styles have undergone similar, though less dramatic, changes. Horn vibrato in France reached a peak in the middle of the century (for example in the Paris Conservatoire Orchestra's recordings of the 1940s to 1960s), but has tended to become more subtle in recent years. The Concert-gebouw Orchestra under Mengelberg had a characteristically fiery, rasping brass style, very exciting in Tchaikovsky's climaxes. The same orchestra in the 1990s still has a fierce edge to the brass (for example in Chailly's 1998 recording of Tchaikovsky's Fifth Symphony), but has lost some of the wildness of the pre-war recordings.

One can easily demonstrate how homogenised the sounds of most of the world's orchestras have become by playing a game of 'blind tasting'. Take two or more modern recordings of orchestras from different parts of the world, and see if anyone can guess where they come from. Put side by side, for example, the principal horns of the 'Georges Enescu' Bucharest Philharmonic Orchestra, playing the solo at the end of the first movement of Brahms's Symphony No. 2,[63] and of the New Zealand Symphony Orchestra playing Delius's *Brigg Fair*,[64] and it is impossible to detect any serious difference in style or tone between them. Indeed, such is the mobility of the modern orchestral player that orchestras across the world are as likely to have principal players from Japan, Korea, Australia or France as from the local country.

Similar narrowing of styles applies to woodwind. Until the 1940s flautists in Germany and Austria played on the wooden flute, with little or no vibrato. French players, led by the great Marcel Moyse, played on the metal flute with a very vibrant style as early as the 1920s. By the 1970s this distinction in national styles had been eroded to the extent that the principal flautist of the Berlin Philharmonic Orchestra played in the most flamboyant of French styles (James Galway, an Irishman). In the first half of the century French and German oboe and bassoon styles were highly contrasted, the French pungent and often with vibrato, the German darker, smoother, and with an organ-like steadiness of tone and breadth of phrasing. Now most of the prominent oboists and bassoonists of the world play in some version of a compromise style, and the German bassoon predominates.

Portamento

A subject that has been touched on from time to time during this chapter is portamento. There was an enormous change over the twentieth century in the use of portamento in orchestral string-playing. In the early decades of the century much heavy sliding was to be heard in recordings, and this gradually diminished during the 1930s and 1940s. By the 1950s, portamento was generally used discreetly, and by the end of the twentieth century it was usual for most orchestras to play with little audible sliding. That is a generalisation, and the role of portamento is more complex than that summary implies. The subject is explored in some detail in my *Early Recordings and Musical Style*, and many examples can be found there.[65]

Portamento in a small ensemble highlights the individuality of every line, as each player creates particular emphases. In an orchestra, the effect of portamento is more complex, and often more diffuse. Only in the most highly rehearsed orchestras are matters of fingering discussed to any great extent, and composers rarely indicate specific fingerings in orchestral parts. String-players in an orchestra do not habitually play with matching fingerings, now any more than in the early twentieth century. In the modern orchestra, in which audible portamento is largely avoided except for special effect, the fingerings of individual players are not particularly noticeable most of the time. Even when a composer has specifically indicated a portamento (as Mahler does from time to time, Richard Strauss and Elgar occasionally), the modern tendency is to treat it very discreetly – even with an air of embarrassment. In the early twentieth century the approach was quite different. In a culture in which frequent, prominent portamento was used, both for deliberate effect and as a routine manner of changing position, the placing and prominence of portamento in an orchestra could be expected to be, to a large extent, random and variable.

The most startling examples are to be heard in British orchestras of the 1920s. In the slow movement of Grieg's Piano Concerto, recorded in c.1927 by the Royal Albert Hall Orchestra under Landon Ronald, with de Greef as soloist, the violins slide ten times in the first eight bars of the theme (example 3.3).

Ex.3.3 Grieg, Piano Concerto, second movement, bars 1–8. Portamenti played by Royal Albert Hall Orchestra, conducted by Ronald.

There are only twenty-six intervals in those bars, so they slide across 38 per cent of the available intervals, usually slowly.

To modern ears this sounds grotesquely lugubrious. It is difficult to believe that, even in London in the 1920s, any one player would have played all those slides. Solo and chamber playing never reached quite those heights of absurdity. So presumably the overall effect results from different players sliding at different times. What we hear, therefore, is a composite of different fingerings, adding up to a melodic line with almost continuous sliding.

That is an extreme example. Less extreme, and to modern listeners more genuinely expressive, is the playing of the same orchestra under Elgar in the 'Enigma' Variations. In the theme, the strings play a total of 18 clearly audible slides during the course of 78 intervals, a rate of about 23 per cent. Many of the slides are slow, as in the Grieg example, but others are faster, and they vary in shaping and prominence. This is caused partly by the very flexible phrasing, but must also result from the fact that different numbers of players are joining in each of the slides. Some changes of position are popular, others are less so. At the big, climactic leap near the end of the theme, everybody slides (certainly all the cellos), and the result is strong and purposeful. Some of the smaller intervals have only a delicate portamento, presumably because a shift at this point is only one of several options, and only a few players have chosen it.

British portamento became refined through the 1930s and 1940s. In the thirties a certain amount of warm portamento was still used, but it was rarely as heavy as in the twenties, and it was becoming more discreet in Classical than in Romantic music, rather than being applied equally to music of all periods. By the forties, with the new Royal Philharmonic Orchestra and Philharmonia, sliding was yet more refined, even in the Romantics. In the prelude to Delius's *Irmelin*, the London Philharmonic in 1938 plays several warm portamenti (example 3.4). The slide up to C double sharp in bar 51 is particularly beautiful, and must have been a carefully rehearsed effect. The Royal Philharmonic in 1946 plays fewer slides, avoids downward portamenti (which had become unfashionable), and slides much more subtly than the London Philharmonic.

Ex.3.4 Delius, *Irmelin* Prelude. Portamenti played by London Philharmonic Orchestra (solid lines) and Royal Philharmonic Orchestra (dotted lines), conducted by Beecham.

a) bars 27–30

b) bars 51–52

Orchestras in France went through a broadly similar process of refinement to that in Britain. In Vienna and Berlin the orchestras already slid less heavily than the British in the late 1920s and early 1930s, but the sense of a network of alternative fingerings is similar. In Vienna, Walter seems to have encouraged a 'cleaner' style than other conductors: his recording of the 'Adagietto' from Mahler's Fifth Symphony is strikingly chaste (it will be discussed in chapter 5). Example 3.5 shows the opening of the third movement of Brahms's Third Symphony in two recordings by the Vienna Philharmonic, one conducted by Krauss (1930), the other by Walter (1936). Krauss's recording has quite warm and frequent slides. Walter's recording has as many slides in the cellos, but far

Ex.3.5 Brahms, Symphony No. 3, third movement, bars 1–23. Portamenti played by Vienna Philharmonic Orchestra, conducted by Krauss (dotted line) and Walter (solid line).

fewer in the violins, and even in the cellos they are somewhat lighter. Though this is nothing like the heavy sliding of 1920s Britain, the close succession of portamenti in some places – up and down at bars 9–10 – suggests that one is still hearing a network of different players shifting in different places. The Berlin Philharmonic under Furtwängler (1949) plays this passage with about as many slides as the Vienna Philharmonic in Walter's recording (the Berlin string style had changed little since the 1930s).

In Europe one orchestra, the Concertgebouw under Mengelberg, continued to play with very prominent portamenti right through the 1930s, in defiance of the general trend elsewhere. It is clear from recordings that this was not just a broad habit, but that, certainly in some instances, Mengelberg required specific fingerings at particular places. Some of the slides in his recordings are too eccentric to have been the result of more general instructions. There are striking examples in Tchaikovsky's Fifth Symphony (1928, music example 3.6).

In the extract from the first movement, the placing of the portamenti is so unusual that it must have been carefully planned. The slide up after a rest (at bars 428 and 432) is very rarely heard in orchestral playing. Solo violinists, notably Kreisler and Heifetz, frequently use it, and it has the effect of a sort of swooping accent. At the climax of the melody, Mengelberg again does something

Ex.3.6 Tchaikovsky, Symphony No. 5. Portamenti played by Concertgebouw Orchestra (solid lines) and Berlin Philharmonic Orchestra (dotted lines), conducted by Mengelberg.

a) first movement, bars 425–438

b) second movement, bars 45–48

unexpected. Having avoided the obvious portamenti up to the two highest points of the melody, he places a slow portamento down from G sharp to F sharp after the climax. In the second movement, the very slow downward portamenti in bars 47–48 must, similarly, have been a carefully rehearsed effect.

Also shown in these examples is the sliding of the Berlin Philharmonic at a concert under Mengelberg in 1940. Mengelberg was a guest conductor, and the difference compared with the playing of his own orchestra is dramatic. The Berlin Philharmonic slides only once in the extract from the first movement – a light upward portamento at the end of the passage. They play none of the 'special effects' Mengelberg rehearsed with his own orchestra (admittedly there is a gap of twelve years between the two recordings, but Mengelberg's taste for heavy portamento did not diminish during the 1930s). Did Mengelberg leave the Berlin orchestra to play in the style they were used to under Furtwängler? Did he attempt to persuade them to play in the Concertgebouw's style and fail? Without other evidence one can only guess, but this example suggests that the characteristic sliding of the Concertgebouw was something that Mengelberg cultivated over years, and that he could not just apply it when visiting other orchestras.

In America, the great specialist in portamento was Stokowski with his Philadelphia Orchestra. As with Mengelberg, this was clearly a style that Stokowski and his orchestra developed through regular rehearsal over the years. But, as Stokowski's statement quoted above makes clear, his method was quite different from Mengelberg's. He was opposed to all uniformity of bowing and fingering, and remained so to the end of his life. The sliding of the orchestra must have been the result of a more general policy. It also has a different character, tending to be more smooth and languorous than in the Concertgebouw.

If the sliding in the Philadelphia Orchestra was less specifically rehearsed than in the Concertgebouw Orchestra, it was nevertheless different from the casual sliding of British orchestras in the 1920s. In music example 3.7, from Brahms's Second Symphony (c.1930), the cellos slide almost as frequently as those of the Royal Albert Hall Orchestra under Landon Ronald (c.1925). But the effect is quite different. Whereas the British players sound as if they are sliding for convenience, and all the portamenti are much the same, the Philadelphia vary the speed and prominence of the sliding considerably, playing the big intervals with slow and prominent slides, other intervals more subtly. Though Stokowski did not want uniform fingering, he did achieve coherent expression: the sliding is an essential part of the shaping of the melodic line.

When Eugene Ormandy took over as conductor of the Philadelphia Orchestra in 1938, the style of the strings underwent considerable change. The rich sonorities remained, but the portamento was refined, becoming less frequent and more subtle. In this Ormandy was bringing the style into line

Ex.3.7 Brahms, Symphony No. 2, second movement. Portamenti played by Philadelphia Orchestra, conducted by Stokowski.

with that of other American orchestras. Sliding is to be heard in recordings of Toscanini's New York Philharmonic Symphony Orchestra, and Koussevitzky's Boston Symphony Orchestra, but it is never as heavy or as frequent as in Stokowski's Philadelphia Orchestra. The refinement has continued through to the present day, as in Britain and the rest of Europe.

The change in use of portamento over the twentieth century was complex. At any one time, orchestras in different places had different approaches. The general trend was towards a cleaner style, but it went at a different pace in different orchestras. By the end of the century, orchestras across the world, which used to have such diverse approaches to portamento, were now almost universally 'clean' and, in their restrained use of portamento, almost indistinguishable from each other.

The cleaning up of portamento, like the cleaning up of ensemble in general, can be viewed from different perspectives. On the one hand, modern playing is neat and tidy. Not only do orchestras play together, but the absence of routine portamento gives clear definition to the rhythm and to the melodic lines. This in turn enhances the effect of everything being together. On the other hand, just as slight roughnesses in ensemble make one aware of eighty individuals struggling to achieve unanimity, so the old-fashioned habit of portamento makes one aware of the physical process of individuals sliding up and down the fingerboards of stringed instruments. Now that we receive most of our music through loudspeakers, rather than in the physical presence of musicians, it becomes easier and easier to forget that the music was actually played by musicians. If you hear the Royal Albert Hall Orchestra sliding, you may or may not like it, but you cannot be unaware of the physical process of playing. It is as if the musicians are sitting there in front of you. Despite the high quality of modern digital sound, one is less aware of the players in present-day recordings of orchestras, because the modern, clean style of orchestral string-playing has become more remote from the physical process. The orderly, smoothly blended sound of the modern orchestra, in which everyone moves neatly and apparently effortlessly together, has become more machine-like, and less obviously human, than it used to be.

CHAPTER FOUR

Ensemble and Freedom: Chamber Groups and Pianists

A chamber group is in some ways simpler than an orchestra, in some ways more complicated. There are fewer people involved, but each musician is separately audible. In an orchestra, it is impossible to know whether an individual string-player is using vibrato on a particular note, or playing a portamento over a particular interval, or phrasing in a particular way. What one hears is the combined effect of what everyone in the section is doing. In a string quartet everything that any individual does can be heard.

A chamber group is therefore open to a far greater range of subtle interplay between musicians than an orchestra, and how musicians relate to each other is more complex. Orchestras sometimes play absolutely together, sometimes with various degrees of raggedness. The blend of the instruments varies – the woodwind sometimes blending together, sometimes remaining distinct, for example. In chamber ensembles, all of this applies, but there is also more room for freedom in the relations between one musician and another. Subtle irregularities of timing or emphasis, the placing of a portamento, one musician playing slightly later than another, these introduce into chamber playing an element of flexibility in the relations between musicians which is not often possible in orchestral playing, where the aim is that everyone should play (more or less) together.

It may come as a surprise to find pianists named separately in the title of this chapter. But pianists are, in effect, playing an ensemble of their own. Just as the lines of a string quartet have a musical relationship with each other, so do the various lines that a pianist plays. At a simple level, one can hear a relationship between the two hands; at a more complex level, there are relationships between melody and bass, and between any two notes in a texture.

In chamber and piano playing, as in orchestral playing, the approach to all of these things changed greatly over the twentieth century. As with orchestras, it is partly a matter of discipline, partly a matter of style. But with the extra freedom that is possible once individuals are in sole charge of each musical line, the questions of style become more subtle and more interesting.

Co-ordinating phrasing and interpretation

Generally speaking, the best ensembles of today rehearse so that everyone agrees, not just about tempo but also about details. There is still room for a certain level of individuality, but if a theme passes from one instrument to another, it will not be played in a radically different way by each player. In early twentieth-century recordings, there are sometimes startling contrasts between two or more musicians playing together.

In c.1928 Adela Fachiri and Donald Tovey recorded Beethoven's Violin Sonata in G Opus 96. They play the first movement with fundamentally different approaches to the rhythm (see example 4.1). There are frequent changes of pace, which they carry out more or less together (when they are both playing). But their interpretation of rhythmic details is not co-ordinated at all. Tovey plays with many more tenuti than Fachiri. Sometimes his tenuti emphasise a strong beat (bars 20–21), sometimes they create a slight pause before the following phrase (as on the first notes of bars 33, 35 and 37), sometimes they mark the climax of a phrase (on the highest notes of bars 17, 38 and 40). Often Tovey plays unequal groupings of quavers, lengthening the first of a pair or the first of a triplet. He does this to pairs of quavers in bar 9, and in bars 47–48 the first note of each triplet gets longer as he slows down.

Tovey was a great admirer of Joachim, with whom he played concerts, and his use of tenuti and 'agogic accents' echoes descriptions of Joachim's own playing. Despite the fact that Fachiri was actually a pupil of Joachim, there is hardly a trace of such rhythmic adjustments in her playing of this movement. She gives a generally much straighter performance of the rhythm – though with the occasional portamento, which creates its own rhythmic emphasis. Such a contrast of interpretation between violinist and pianist in a sonata would not be possible in modern performance.

By comparison with Fachiri and Tovey, Fritz Kreisler and Franz Rupp (1935) play the opening movement of Beethoven's Opus 96 in a completely straightforward manner, apart from an occasional anticipation by Kreisler, and a few, highly characteristic portamenti. On the other hand, when Kreisler and Rachmaninoff play together, they sometimes seem to be approaching the music from completely different directions, and playing in totally different styles, with no attempt to compromise with each other. In 1928 they recorded Grieg's Third Violin Sonata in C minor. The slow movement begins with the theme played by the piano, and then the violin enters and repeats it. Rachmaninoff plays the theme with characteristic and highly expressive rubato (example 4.2). Most of the pairs of quavers are played unequally, slightly dotted, rather as Tovey pairs many of the quavers in the Beethoven sonata. Kreisler enters and plays the same theme with deliberately even emphasis on each note. It is as if someone in conversation had said, 'What I think is . . .', and someone else had answered, 'Well yes, up to a point, but I think you'll

Ex.4.1 Beethoven, Sonata in G major for Violin and Piano Opus 96, first movement, bars 1–59 (Fachiri and Tovey).
‾ = lengthened note ˘ = shortened note ⁄ = early note

Ex.4.2 Grieg, Violin Sonata No. 3 in C minor, second movement, bars 1–8 (Rachmaninoff).

find . . .'. Again, modern performance of this movement would never have such contrasting approaches. The players would expect to rehearse an agreed way of phrasing the theme (as, for example, Lydia and Elena Mordkovitch do in their 1992 recording).

Kreisler and Rachmaninoff's contrasting approach to recording has already been mentioned in chapter 2. Rachmaninoff was much more critical of each take than Kreisler, and insisted, according to his own account, on recording five takes of each side of the Grieg Sonata. The fifth take was the one chosen in each case (except for side 5, which is actually take 6). This makes their unco-ordinated phrasing all the more striking. Rachmaninoff was very fussy about detail, and he can surely not have been unaware of this contrast in style. About their records of the Schubert Duo in A major, he wrote to Kreisler, 'I consent to their release. It irritates me a little bit that in some places we do not play absolutely together. This is because we were too far away from each other. This defect is very small but you and I will notice it and that is why I am not satisfied with them.'[1]

A particularly striking example of non-agreement is another Kreisler recording, one of a series he made with the tenor John McCormack. In an arrangement of Schubert's 'Ave Maria', recorded in 1914, Kreisler and McCormack perform the first eight bars of the melody together in unison. But 'together' is hardly the word. Kreisler slides where McCormack does not, and McCormack slides where Kreisler does not. And the one time they slide over the same interval (down a tone in the first bar of the melody) Kreisler slides later and more slowly than McCormack, so the two portamenti are separately audible. This invariably raises a smile from modern listeners, and if a singer and violinist of today were to perform this arrangement, they would undoubtedly take care to co-ordinate their performance much more closely than McCormack and Kreisler. But what would be the point? One might argue that the whole purpose of putting a violin with the voice on this line is to have the distinct impression of two musicians performing it, not one. The closer the two performances were to come to each other, the less audible the violin would be. The heterophony of Kreisler and McCormack's interpretation is surely not accidental.[2]

Rubato in ensemble

Generally speaking, the smaller the number of people playing together, the easier it is for there to be freedom between them without the ensemble being endangered. One particular aspect of this freedom is a kind of *tempo rubato* which, though it has more or less died out in modern playing of classical music, had a long pedigree, stretching back from the early twentieth century to the time of Mozart and beyond.[3] This is a rubato in which the melody becomes freed from its accompaniment, so that the two are rhythmically dislocated for a time. Eugène Ysaÿe was particularly renowned for this kind of freedom: Carl Flesch described him as 'master of the imaginative rubato'.[4] Emile Jaques-Dalcroze, who played the piano in recitals with Ysaÿe, described Ysaÿe's approach to the ensemble between them while they were rehearsing Beethoven's 'Kreutzer' Sonata, and his 'meticulously ordered' rubato:

> In *rubato* melodic passages, he instructed me not to follow him meticulously in the accelerandos and ritenutos, if my part consisted of no more than a simple accompaniment. 'It is I alone', he would say, 'who can let myself follow the emotion suggested by the melody; you accompany me in strict time, because an accompaniment should always be in time. You represent order, and your duty is to counterbalance my fantasy. Do not worry, we shall always find each other, because when I accelerate for a few notes, I afterwards re-establish the equilibrium by slowing down the following notes, or by pausing for a moment on one of them.' . . . In the train he would try to make up violin passages based on the dynamic accents and cadences of the wheels, and to execute 'rubato' passages, returning to the original beat each time we passed in front of a telegraph pole.[5]

Ysaÿe's rubato, and his freedom in relationship to the pianist, are strikingly audible in his recordings of 1912. The most extreme example occurs in his recording of a Rondino by Vieuxtemps, by whom he was taught. The manner in which he sways either side of the beat, while the piano maintains an even rhythm, is very much as described by Jaques-Dalcroze – free but highly disciplined. In slower music, such as the 'Prize Song' from Wagner's *Die*

Meistersinger, it is the beauty of Ysaÿe's tone and his liberal use of portamento which are most striking. But the rhythmic freedom in relation to the piano is an essential part of the effect, as he lingers, hurries, anticipates and delays. Indeed, one of the functions of his portamento is often to blur the precise position of a beat, so that the violin floats above the piano, rather than remaining rhythmically tied to it.[6]

Ysaÿe did not record any concertos, but the freedom of his concerto-playing was described by Henry Wood, who wrote of his 'marvellous singing quality and perfect rubato . . . if he borrowed he faithfully paid back within four bars'.[7] Ysaÿe's mastery of this subtle art was unusual. But it is not uncommon to hear soloists in concertos momentarily freeing themselves from the orchestra in early twentieth-century recordings. A passage which used to be treated in this way by some pianists is the beginning of the development section in the first movement of Beethoven's Piano Concerto No. 3 (bars 249ff.). Schnabel (1933) stays close to the orchestra, though his dotted rhythms at the start of the passage are markedly overdotted, and answered by woodwind playing the rhythm more literally. Rubinstein, in a 1944 live recording with Toscanini and the NBC Symphony Orchestra, plays the dotted rhythms more strictly, but then (from bar 260) is much freer than Schnabel, starting each phrase slightly early, and using the extra time to expand. The orchestra, playing regular, repeated quavers (eighth notes), is momentarily thrown off balance by this. But Marguerite Long (1939) takes this sort of freedom much further. She, like Rubinstein, tends to start phrases early, and, to a much more exaggerated extent, slows down the beginning of the phrase and then catches up as it finishes. Indeed, she is sometimes barely with the orchestra at the end of the phrase. This is the sort of procedure to which Henry Wood refers when he writes of Ysaÿe 'paying back'.

The slow movement of Saint-Saëns's Cello Sonata No. 1 in C minor is played in a fascinating manner by the cellist Paul Bazelaire and the pianist Isidor Philipp (1935). When the cello and piano play the opening theme together at the start of the movement, they synchronise with each other quite closely. But when the theme is repeated by the piano, with the cello playing the running semiquavers (sixteenth notes) in the bass, Philipp plays noticeably behind the cello. Then when the cello takes up the melody, with the piano playing the bass, Bazelaire sometimes anticipates at the beginnings of phrases. The effect, curious to modern listeners, is to add grandeur to the piano statement of the theme, and to add passion to the cello line.

Freedom of the melody in relation to an accompaniment is often found in early recordings of singers. Adelina Patti (1905) sings Cherubino's aria 'Voi che sapete', from *The Marriage of Figaro*, with a great deal of freedom, beginning phrases early, stretching them out, varying the tempo, adjusting rhythms, and introducing languid portamento. The overall effect is much like Ysaÿe's violin-playing, and the pianist, Landon Ronald, follows her overall pace but leaves her to be free either side of each beat. Frieda Hempel (1911) uses a similar, though less exaggerated, style of rubato in the Queen of the Night's first aria from *The Magic Flute*, 'Zum Leiden'. In the slow section, she begins phrases early, lingering on the highest notes and then accelerating back into tempo to rejoin the orchestra. Selma Kurz shows similar freedom in her 1905 recording of the same aria. Conchita Supervia sings Cherubino's second aria from *The Marriage of Figaro*, 'Non so più', with an unusual degree of freedom for the date (c.1928). The sort of stretching which Patti, Kurz and Hempel applied to slow music she employs in this fast aria. She slows down certain phrases, such as the third, 'ogni donna cangiar di colore', so that her line comes apart from the accompaniment to an almost dangerous extent. It is a vivid way of illustrating the words of the aria, in which Cherubino describes his confused emotional state.

This is a particularly striking example of rubato. It would be a mistake to suppose that all singers in the early part of the twentieth century sang with such freedom, but less extreme instances are very common in recordings of singers from a wide variety of backgrounds. By contrast, Amelita Galli-Curci (1917) sings 'Non so più' with absolute rhythmic precision and regularity of emphasis, to the extent that she seems barely aware of the meaning of the words (though admittedly the tuba on the bass line helps to give an almost military effect). Galli-Curci sang with a certain amount of freedom in slow music, but in this fast aria she seems almost rigid.

By the second half of the twentieth century, singers rarely performed either with the freedom of Patti, Kurz, Hempel and Supervia or with the instrumental blandness of Galli-Curci. Singers were by now expected to convey the meaning and emotional force of the words, but within quite strict rhythmic limits. Suzanne Danco, an admired Cherubino of the 1950s, illustrates the ideal of the time. She sings 'Non so più' (1955, in the set of *Figaro* conducted by Erich Kleiber) with great charm and expressive intensity. But she does it by enunciation, colouring and phrasing within the rhythms as written (as we might now say): there is no sense that she is ever parting company with the orchestra, any more than there is any sense of her just playing her vocal instrument, like Galli-Curci.

String quartets

String quartets of the early twentieth century often show a variety of approaches to phrasing, and particularly portamento, which today seems ill co-ordinated. An extreme example is the fugal finale of Mozart's Quartet in G major K.387, recorded by the Léner Quartet in 1929. There is absolutely no co-ordination in the way the members of the quartet place portamenti in the five notes of the fugal subject. At different times a portamento occurs between notes 1 and 2, 2 and 3, 3 and 4, or the subject is played without portamento. In the two series of fugal entries, at bars 1–17 and bars 143–159, the subject is never played the same way twice in succession (see example 4.3). The effect of this apparently random placing of portamenti sounds strange, even perverse, to a modern listener. But why should the theme always be played the same?

Ex.4.3 Mozart, String Quartet in G K.387, fourth movement (Léner Quartet).

a) bars 1–17

b) bars 143–159

One could argue that something repeated should always be looked at in a new light. Clearly, this individual freedom in the shaping of phrases was intentional, and an essential part of the Léner Quartet's style. There is no question of a string quartet as well established and constant in its membership as the Léner Quartet failing to co-ordinate through inadequate rehearsal.

The placing of a portamento highlights an interval in the melodic line. With the oldest generation of middle-European string quartets on recordings – among them the Bohemian, Léner, Rosé and the original Budapest Quartet (led by Emil Hauser) – the highlighting can seem rather heavy and quaint to a modern listener. The same is true of the Capet Quartet – Capet, though French, was highly influenced by Joachim. The portamento of the Flonzaley

Quartet tends to be less heavy (as with others brought up in the Franco-Belgian school), and the next generation – the new Budapest (led by Josef Roisman), Busch, Pro Arte and Kolisch Quartets, who all recorded in the 1930s – treated portamento with greater refinement.

Comparing the Rosé (1927), Capet (1927–8) and Busch Quartets (1936) in the first movement of Beethoven's Quartet in C sharp minor Opus 131 shows this change of approach clearly (see example 4.4). For substantial stretches of the movement the portamenti are infrequent in all three performances, but where they occur they are generally slower and more prominent in the Rosé and Capet than in the Busch, and the Busch play fewer than the others. This is most noticeable in bars 20–26, where the first violin and cello of the Rosé and Capet answer each other with the opening phrase of the fugue subject, each time playing the rising third with a portamento (the cellist of the Rosé plays one more portamento than the cellist of the Capet). This gives the climactic moment an insistent plangency which modern players would not think appropriate. The Busch Quartet avoids this repetitive sliding. But Busch himself slides twice in quick succession in bars 25–26 as he approaches the climax, the second portamento emphasising the sudden drop down at the end of the crescendo. Rosé does the same. This too is an effect that modern players would generally avoid.

Ex.4.4 Beethoven, String Quartet in C sharp minor Opus 131, first movement, bars 1–31. Portamenti played by Busch Quartet (solid lines), Capet Quartet (dotted lines above) and Rosé Quartet (small dots below).

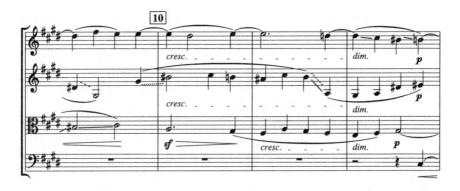

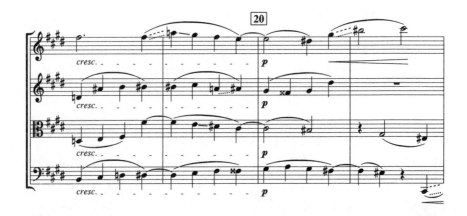

The Busch Quartet was, in portamento, vibrato, bowing, and rhythmic emphasis, much closer to modern style than the Léner, but the placing and prominence of some of its portamento still give a characteristic old-fashioned emphasis. In this movement, only the viola entries are played with portamenti in the fugal subject itself, and this gives a particular inflection which is different from the 'clean' entries of the other instruments. Elsewhere, occasional, quite heavy portamenti in each line give a sense (as with the Capet, Rosé and Léner) of an ensemble of distinct individuals which is never felt to this extent in modern performances. The Calvet Quartet (1938), a younger French quartet than the Capet, avoid all sliding over bars 20–26, restricting themselves to the occasional discreet portamento elsewhere in the movement.

The slow movement of Beethoven's Quartet Opus 59 No. 1, played by the original Budapest Quartet (1927), is as old-fashioned as the playing of the Capet and Rosé Quartets (see music example 4.5). The opening melody in the first violin is repeated by the cello. In the eight bars of the theme, the first violin plays eight portamenti, many of them slow, the cellist plays ten, most of which are even slower. In the half-bar of transition between the end of the violin's statement of the theme and the beginning of the cello's (bar 8), the viola plays a descending portamento, and the second violin plays a rising portamento, gently drawing attention to the movement of the inner parts.

The sense of individuality in the members of an ensemble is influenced by all aspects of style – portamento, phrasing, vibrato and rhythm. Among string quartets, one of the most striking examples of an ensemble with a old-fashioned attitude to all these things is the Bohemian Quartet (also known as the Czech Quartet). Their portamento is often slow and prominent, as with the Léner Quartet, but is sometimes most beautiful, even to modern ears. At the opening of the slow movement of Smetana's First Quartet in E minor, the cellist plays his introductory passage with wonderfully free and expressive portamento. Just as striking is the use of portamento where the three other instruments enter. After the heavy melodic portamento of the opening cello solo, the first violinist plays the first few bars of the melody without any portamento at all. It is the second violin and viola who slide, and this has the effect of highlighting the contrapuntal texture of the writing. But more than that, each portamento is placed to emphasise a move of particular harmonic significance, such as a chromatic shift. There is nothing random about it.[8]

A passage such as this makes one realise how carefully thought out the playing of the Bohemian Quartet is, even though a first impression suggests a rather easy-going, informal approach to ensemble, portamento and rhythm. There are certainly aspects of their ensemble which are not at all the way things are done now. They play the opening of Dvořák's 'American' Quartet in what now seems a curiously 'loose' manner. Close listening reveals that every aspect of their technique and style contributes to this impression. The 'problems' begin with the very first notes. The pattern of semiquavers (sixteenth notes) in the violins is not smooth and even, as in modern performance: each pair is slightly uneven. When the theme enters on the viola, the note-values are not timed to coincide exactly with the accompanying semiquavers. The dotted rhythms are slightly overdotted, the slurred semiquavers hurry. Compared with a modern performance, it is as if the jigsaw does not quite fit. This impression continues where the first violin takes up the theme. The lack of vibrato in his playing makes the entry sound rhythmically underemphasised, and this adds to a slight feeling of insecurity. As soon as the first violin has finished the opening phrases, and the semiquavers become continuous, the tempo takes off, rising from ♩ = 112 at the opening to = 130 at bars 11–15. As each group of slurred

Ex.4.5 Beethoven, String Quartet in F major Opus 59 No. 1, third movement, bars 1–16. Portamenti played by Budapest (Hauser) Quartet.

semiquavers rushes by, the other players seem to be scampering to fit in the dotted rhythm.

Throughout the movement, there is an impression that each player is functioning as an individual. Each responds to the behaviour of the others, but there is little impression of pre-planned details. They have simply got used to each other's behaviour and have learned to live with it. This all sounds very negative, but there is no reason to think that our modern way of rehearsing such a work is inherently superior. It is only convention and habit which insists that today everything should sound absolutely co-ordinated and clean. The Bohemian Quartet had played together for many years by the time they made that recording, and had worked with Dvořák on his quartets. As with the Léner Quartet, their way of playing together could not have been the result of inadequate rehearsal. They simply were not aiming for our modern notions of ensemble.

In the early decades of the twentieth century the Bohemian Quartet sometimes attracted reviews that make it clear that their combination of individual freedom and apparent unanimity was unusual even at the time. They visited London for the Czecho-Slovak Festival of 1919. *The Telegraph* observed, 'The fire, the passion, and the fervour of their playing remains absolutely unimpaired, while the requisite balance, the perfect unanimity of tone and feeling, are as wonderful as they ever were.' But *The Times* made a point which chimes more with the impression that their recordings give now: 'The Smetana, in particular, is the favourite warhorse of the quartet, and their performance of it is one of the curiosities of musical execution; apparently everyone does just what he likes and how he likes, yet there is never any question of the slightest misunderstanding.'

Perhaps, therefore, the Bohemian Quartet is an extreme example. Compared with them the Flonzaley Quartet, the most highly rehearsed quartet of the 1920s, sounds much closer to modern style. This is partly because of the more continuous, though delicate, vibrato, partly the firmer, more assertive bowing. Both of these features are characteristic of the 'Franco-Belgian' school of playing in which these players were trained. There is also a greater sense of rhythmic unanimity than with the Bohemian Quartet. But there are still elements of the Flonzaley's playing which sound strikingly old-fashioned. In particular, their ideas of relative note-values, rhythmic clarity and control of tempo are not those of the twenty-first century.

Their recording of Beethoven's Opus 18 No. 2 in G (1926) is wonderfully deft, but extremely volatile. Not only are the tempi of the fast movements very fast, but many of the rhythms are very light and quick, to an extent that now sounds casual. The slurred demisemiquavers (thirty-second notes) in the opening theme are thown off as swirls. The pairs of semiquavers (sixteenth notes) in the scherzo are very fast. Tempi sometimes accelerate in an excitable manner, especially in the finale. And yet everyone in the quartet is expecting these rhythmic eccentricities (as we might now call them): although the ensemble is somewhat loose in detail, it is clear that the music has been rehearsed at great length. Their very light approach to rhythm gives particular wit to their Haydn, most notably 'The Lark' Opus 64 No. 5 (1928).

The opening movement of Mozart's Quartet in D minor K.421 (1929) is even more striking, perhaps the most characteristic and 'unmodern' of the Flonzaley's recordings.[9] It is the timing of, and emphasis of, rhythmic detail which sound most old-fashioned. The relationship between longer and shorter note-values is, again, not as clear-cut as in modern performances. There is a subtle use of rubato and agogic accents, which tend to lengthen longer note-values and shorten and weaken shorter values. Dotted rhythms tend to be over-dotted, and continuous semiquavers rush off. The beginnings of phrases are often emphasised by tenuti, with subsequent notes hurried in compensation. Occasionally entries are played slightly early, much as a pianist of the time might underline an entry in the bass (more of that habit later in the chapter). The Flonzaley's use of portamento is less old-fashioned than the Bohemian's or the original Budapest's, but its placing is sometimes, to modern ears, rhythmi-cally disturbing, because of its tendency to blur the precise placing of the beat. Often the effect is to create a momentary rubato against the other instruments.

Once more, it is easiest for a modern writer to describe these features in predominantly negative ways, because the general impression to a listener unaccustomed to this manner of doing things is of an ensemble which is looser and less tightly co-ordinated than a modern string quartet. But this is just another way of saying that we are now used to regularity of rhythm, clarity of detail, unambiguous placing of beats, and a sense of control at all times. The Flonzaley Quartet's performance is a highly refined example of a style in which subtle emphasis of detail, by lengthening, shortening, emphasising with portamento, hurrying and displacing, form a continuous and ever-changing characterisation of the music, of where it is going, of how each part relates to the whole. All of this is accommodated within a performance in which the four players clearly know what to expect, and play together (though not with the absolute precision of a modern ensemble). But the hierarchies of emphasis are not at all what we are accustomed to in modern performance, and our ears hear their varied and subtle placing of detail as a slightly casual lack of control and clarity.

Not just in portamento, but in all aspects of rhythm and ensemble, the next generation of quartets recorded in the 1930s gives the impression of having taken a large step from the style of the early twentieth century towards the firmness, clarity and control that we expect today. The 'Russianised' Budapest Quartet, led by Josef Roisman from the early 1930s, played in quite a different style from the Flonzaley. Their c.1936 recording of Mozart's Quartet in F K.590 is absolutely firm and controlled from the first bar. There are no heavy portamenti, semiquavers do not rush off, there are no anticipations at entries. It is delicate and expressive, but in an even, modern way, without the Flonzaley's constant negotiating of rhythmic freedoms. The more constant vibrato also adds to the sense of firmness (another widespread difference between generations).

In fast movements, the Busch Quartet still preserves some of the freedom of the Flonzaley, with an extra element of risk-taking which makes their performances particularly exciting. The risk is that the ensemble will disintegrate altogether. Sometimes they seem to be playing right at the edge of what they find physically possible – for example in the fugal finale of Beethoven's third 'Rasumovsky' Quartet (1933), which begins dangerously fast and gets faster. In the finale of Schubert's G major Quartet (1938), an exhausting tour de force even for a modern quartet, the relentless jig rhythm often sounds unstable, with the quaver upbeats hasty, and with the breathings in Busch's phrasing not always coinciding with the regular rhythm of the other instruments. The result seems highly articulate but bordering on chaotic. In this movement, the Kolisch Quartet (c.1934) shows a level of control and unanimity which is ahead of its time. Both in technique and in style their approach is much more literal than that of the Busch Quartet (or that of the Flonzaley, who recorded a cut version of this quartet in 1929), and much closer to the way modern quartets play this movement.

With orchestral recordings it is reasonable to attribute some of the hit-and-miss character of the early twentieth century to lack of rehearsal, at least in Paris and London. But with the Bohemian, Rosé, (original) Budapest, Flonzaley, Léner and Busch Quartets, there can be no doubt that what we hear as 'loose' ensemble in various ways is an essential stylistic feature of their playing. The idea that individuals playing together have freedom to play things slightly differently from each other, and to shape phrases in ways that create a loosening of strict unanimity, is an assumption at the heart of early twentieth-century ensemble. It is possible to find examples just as striking in vocal performance: the ensembles in the famous Glyndebourne recording of *The Marriage of Figaro* (1934–5), in which characterisation sometimes takes precedence over precision and vocal blend, or the quintet from *Die Meistersinger* led by Elisabeth Schumann (1931), in which the individual performances are more clearly differentiated, and the ensemble less strict, than in modern performance.

The Joachim Quartet

Carl Flesch, always an acute observer of the scene, makes a striking comparison when he writes about the Bohemian Quartet, whom he first heard in 1894: 'Hitherto, one had been accustomed to see in quartet ensembles chiefly a foil for the dominating leader, as was the case above all in the Joachim Quartet . . . here for the first time one heard *ensemble* playing by four congenial individualities who were on the same technical level.' And he concludes, 'The steadily rising development of quartet playing in our own day can be traced back to this revolutionary phenomenon. The "Capet", "Flonzaley", "Léner", "Kolisch", "Brussels", "Pro Arte" and "Guarneri" Quartets would be unthinkable without the electrifying example of the "Bohemians".'[10]

According to this analysis, the Bohemian Quartet, whose recordings now sound so old-fashioned, initiated the development of modern quartet-playing. If this is true, what can the Joachim Quartet have been like? Joseph Joachim made a few recordings with piano in his (for those days) old age but did not record with his string quartet, which is tantalisingly just out of reach. This is a pity, because it was the most celebrated chamber ensemble of its day. Richard Strauss wrote in 1884, 'It's the finest quartet in existence – that has ever existed, I think. The sheer beauty of the sound, the purity, the ensemble, the wonderful nuances, everything you could possibly ask for is there.'[11]

If we were to take such a report at face value, we might assume that the Joachim Quartet was more modern in style than anything to be heard on early twentieth-century recordings. But, even without Flesch's comments, there have been enough eulogies to past performers already quoted in this book for it to be obvious that 'finest' in the 1880s could not have meant what it would mean today. Recordings show how loose and informal early twentieth-century chamber playing was. It is inconceivable that modern ideas of ensemble, which have only recently developed, existed some time in the nineteenth century or earlier and were lost by the time of early recordings.

The most detailed contemporary description of Joachim's playing is to be found in J. A. Fuller-Maitland's biography (1905). He describes the great freedom of Joachim's playing, and in particular his characteristic use of agogic accents to mould phrases, declaring that 'none have ever carried out the principle so far or with such fine results as Joachim has done'. And he concludes, '. . . his powers as an interpreter are perhaps most prominently exhibited in association with the members of the famous Joachim Quartet, in whose company he is of course perfectly free to indulge in the mood of the moment, knowing that the other members will divine his intention, though it be formed without premeditation.'[12]

The level of freedom that Fuller-Maitland seems to be describing is surely closer to what is heard in early recordings than to modern notions of good ensemble. Joachim's few recordings, all of solo or duo works, indeed demonstrate much use of agogic accents. These form part of a very flexible and rhythmically nuanced style, like a more exaggerated version of the Bohemian Quartet's playing, with tenuti, overdotting, hurrying, irregular pairing of notes, slow portamento, and rubato which takes him out of synchronisation with his pianist. If one imagines this style applied to quartet-playing, one must inevitably conclude that the ensemble was, by modern standards, very loose, allowing far more individual freedom than would be acceptable now. The same conjecture applies to the Ysaÿe Quartet, if one imagines his very free rubato applied to quartet-playing.

One aspect of Joachim's playing which suggests a more relaxed attitude to ensemble than we are accustomed to is the fact that for several years 'The Joachim Quartet' consisted of more than one team. The famous quartet of Joachim, Karl Halir (from 1897), Emanuel Wirth and Robert Hausmann did not visit England until 1900. For a period of more than three decades before that, Joachim played quartets in London with different players: Louis Ries, Henry Blagrove and Alfredo Piatti in the 1860s, Ludwig Straus, Zerbini and Piatti regularly on later visits. This team was engaged regularly for the Popular Concerts at St James's Hall in Regent Street.[13] Reviews were always enthusiastic, as two examples from three decades apart illustrate:

> . . . he led Beethoven's Posthumous Quartett, Op. 130, in B flat, with even more than his accustomed powers both of execution and expression. At the next concert the 'Rasoumowski' Quartett of Beethoven, in C major, was as finely performed as we ever heard it, . . . the artists Messrs. Joachim, L. Ries, H. Blagrove, and Signore Piatti, seeming to vie with each other in giving the utmost meaning to the minutest portion of the composition. (1867)[14]

> After the first few bars it was apparent that the *ensemble* of the four artists was perfect. Dr. Joachim has, so to speak, impressed his idiosyncrasy on his fellow executants, and they play literally as 'one man'. The performance of the great work in C sharp minor was truly remarkable. (1898)[15]

The four players 'vying with each other' suggests real chamber-music playing, though perhaps of a somewhat improvisational kind; on the other hand, the idea of the leader 'impressing his idiosyncrasy' on his fellow players is hardly behaving like the leader of a modern string quartet. Szigeti (who never heard Joachim himself, but met many people who did) quotes descriptions of Joachim in his role as quartet leader which suggest an extremely temperamental player. One is from Klemperer, who heard Joachim when he was a student: 'When he was not bothered by nervousness he played in a manner that carried one away. The last movement of the C sharp minor Quartet for instance he played like a fiery Hungarian fiddler, not at all in the "classical manner".'[16] A musician who sometimes played with Joachim reported, 'To play with "The Old Man" is damned difficult. Always a different tempo, a different accent . . . .'[17] Taking all the evidence together, it becomes clear that the Joachim Quartet played with a degree of spontaneous freedom which is absolutely incompatible with modern notions of 'good ensemble', and that they must have played with even more 'looseness' of ensemble than the Bohemian or Léner Quartets.

Regular and casual ensembles

If it is important not to use modern expectations to imagine the playing of the Joachim Quartet, it would equally be a mistake to suggest that the change over the twentieth century was from rough-and-ready chamber ensembles to modern groups perfectly drilled and co-ordinated in every detail. Throughout the century there were both regular, dedicated chamber groups, and more casual groupings of players who spend most of their time as soloists. Joachim was as much in the second category as the first (as was Ysaÿe), being regarded as the finest solo violinist of his time, but also admired for his exceptional qualities as a chamber musician. Jascha Heifetz used to lead chamber groups, which made famously high-powered recordings. The impression they give is of a group of soloists competing with each other for attention, with the dominant personality of Heifetz inevitably winning. Other well-known soloists have also led chamber groups: Isaac Stern (including the famous Schubert String Quintet with Casals), Yehudi Menuhin, Arthur Grumiaux (whose recordings of Mozart's chamber music are particularly fine), Henryk Szeryng, Pinchas Zukerman, Itzhak Perlman. Present-day chamber music concerts include not only the regular, dedicated groups, but also András Schiff or Steven Isserlis 'and friends', and Alfred Brendel playing chamber music with younger string players. Such groupings are guaranteed to fill the hall because of the fame of the central figure. On the other hand, their musical success as ensembles is extremely variable, depending on the particular group assembled for the occasion. The interplay between powerful musical personalities can be highly engaging, even when the amount of rehearsal rules out the sort of mature interpretations that the best permanent chamber groups achieve. On the other hand, there are occasions when the mixture simply does not produce more than the sum of its parts, and sometimes less than that.

The piano trio is a particularly interesting phenomenon through the twentieth century, because there never was a regular piano trio comparable to the famous string quartets until the second half of the century. The most famous piano trio of the first half of the century was formed in 1905 by three of the finest musicians of the time, Thibaud, Cortot and Casals. The trio was so successful that it lasted thirty years. But the three players spent little of their time together. Casals described their relationship: 'We understood each other perfectly in our music, and we formed a marvellously gratifying team – not only as an ensemble but as friends. We began the custom of devoting one month each year to travelling together to give chamber-music concerts.'[18]

The success of the Cortot–Thibaud–Casals Trio was produced by the inter-action of three very different musical personalities. In an interview with Roger Nichols, Jean Bérart, a leading figure in the recording industry in France in the 1920s, described the differences between the three players: 'Casals represented a sense of security, along with a certain ruggedness, and of course incomparable phrasing. He was the outstanding cellist of his day. But when Cortot took up the same phrase, he was one step closer to fantasy – a little less controlled, a little more subtle. And always that wonderful tone. And then Thibaud: well, Thibaud represented pure inspiration. There was a very personal, floating quality to his playing. The contrast in their three styles was quite remarkable.'[19]

The recordings of Cortot, Thibaud and Casals are still greatly admired nearly eighty years after they made them. But it is this interaction of very different musical personalities which gives them their unique appeal. The contrast between the ways in which the individual players shape the music is often striking, with the two string-players, themselves highly individual, tending to form a kind of duo, and with Cortot as the odd one out (an effect exaggerated by the recorded balance, with the piano rather distant). And the tiny number of their recordings, including the 'Archduke' and Schubert's B flat Trio, represents most of the repertoire that they played regularly. They never played Schubert's great Trio in E flat, and very rarely played Beethoven's three Opus 1 trios.[20]

Robert Baldock, in his biography of Casals, argues that the Trio survived so long 'precisely because its partnership was intermittent rather than permanent. The three men had quite different temperaments, and the creative tension that resulted was clearly a factor in the brilliance of their performance.'[21] There was even greater tension in the trio of Jascha Heifetz, Emanuel Feuermann and Arthur Rubinstein, which came together only briefly in 1941 to make recordings. Heifetz's biographer, Artur Weschler-Vered, wrote that Heifetz and Rubinstein had very different approaches to the music: 'Heifetz complained that Rubinstein liked to linger over romantic passages. The pianist found the violinist too aggressive in his playing, always thrusting ahead.'[22] Rubinstein himself wrote that he admired Heifetz's playing, but 'when it came to the interpretation proper there was often a fundamental discord between us'. Feuermann, by contrast, was 'an artist after my own heart. A supreme master of his instrument, he was a source of inspiration throughout our recordings.'[23] When the three players were sent the different takes of the recordings for selection, Feuermann wrote to Rubinstein, saying that he had occasional criticisms, and found his own playing disappointing. But then he happened upon the Cortot–Thibaud–Casals recording of the 'Archduke', which was playing when he walked into a music shop in New York. This completely changed his view: 'Now I am absolutely enchanted by US, I am overwhelmed. I find our trio-playing – individually and as an ensemble – perfect . . . .'[24]

Feuermann died the following year, so there was no opportunity for the trio to develop into a long-standing ensemble. But to judge by the reports of the relationship between Heifetz and Rubinstein, they could hardly have worked together for long. In 1949 Rubinstein and Heifetz did form a trio again, with

Gregor Piatigorsky, and made some recordings in 1950. Rubinstein and Heifetz once more disagreed on fundamental issues, and they never played together again. This has not stopped these trio recordings, like those with Feuermann, becoming 'classics'. They are undoubtedly impressive, but, as with Heifetz's other chamber recordings, they are classics of tension and competition, rather than interpretations by an ensemble of players who understand each other at a deep level. Menahem Pressler, pianist of the Beaux Arts Trio, was asked by Nicholas Delbanco what he thought of such groupings of virtuosi: '"Truly a trio it isn't," he says, when asked about such great exemplars as Cortot, Casals and Thibaud, or Rubinstein, Piatigorsky, and Heifetz. He admires them as virtuosi – "Just to hear them tune would have been sufficient!" – but insists on the ongoing demands of ensemble. "What you hear are three splendid fellows," he says. "You don't hear Schubert or Brahms."'[25]

Not many people would put it quite as strongly as that. But Pressler's view does highlight the fact that the Beaux Arts Trio was, from its formation in the 1950s, the first piano trio to rehearse and perform as regularly as the top string quartets. When Delbanco wrote his book on the Beaux Arts in 1985, two of the members had (like Cortot, Thibaud and Casals) been playing together for thirty years (the violinist Isidore Cohen had joined in 1968). The great difference was that they met not just for one month of the year, but for an average of a hundred concerts per year. Their level of unanimity and precision was at quite a different level from any piano trio composed of players with careers as solo virtuosi. On the other hand, unanimity of ensemble did not mean obliteration of individuality. The description of them by their producer, Volker Straus, has much in common with Bérart's description of Cortot, Thibaud and Casals: '. . . they're so different, so absolutely different, what they bring. Bernie's the rock. The fundamental [Bernard Greenhouse, the cellist]. He has a metronome in his head, he's absolutely exact. And Izzy [Isidore Cohen, violinist] is the artist, the philosopher, a little bit of Gypsy in him, too. And Menahem [Pressler] is, how would you call it, energy? The driving force.'[26]

In the twenty-first century, the separate qualities of individuals are still valued in a piano trio. Writing about the Florestan Trio, Andrew Clements of the *Guardian* wrote, 'Like all successful ensembles, the members of the trio preserve their separate musical identities while still creating a collective persona.'[27]

These observations illustrate the point that there is not a simple progress from casual music-making of the past to the precision of today. The most admired chamber groups (and orchestras, for that matter) of the twenty-first century are not simply those whose ensemble is most efficient, but those who manage to achieve a modern level of discipline and yet retain strong musical personality, both as a team and individually. Similarly, any idea of the string quartet as a homogeneous and musically democratic body only goes so far. From the Amadeus and Végh Quartets onwards, the string quartets that have been most successful in the last half-century have often been those in which the personality of the ensemble has very clearly been set by the personality of the leader (Peter Cropper of the Lindsays and Levon Chilingirian of the Chilingirian Quartet are two of several present-day examples). This is partly in the nature of the music: the fact is that the first violin part in most string quartets carries the melodic line more often than the other parts, and is generally more virtuosic. There are examples of modern quartet teams in which the leader is a particularly sensitive ensemble player rather than a dominant personality (such as Edward Dusinberre of the Takács Quartet and Erich Höbarth of the Quatuor Mosaïques), but even here the musical characters of the four musicians retain a certain distinctness despite the requirements of modern unanimity. These are subtle distinctions, however, and the fact is that the level of co-ordination and corporate thinking of the modern ensemble is something that was unknown in chamber music a hundred years ago. It can be argued whether something has also been lost in this drive towards perfection, but the process itself is unmistakably demonstrated by recordings.

Pianists

The general informality of co-ordination in the early twentieth century applies not just to ensembles of musicians, but also to the playing of pianists, in the relationship between bass and treble, and between any two notes in the texture. In effect, any piece of piano music is an 'ensemble', and the question is how the different voices perform together.

The habitual spreading of chords and non-synchronisation of bass and melody notes is familiar to anyone who has heard recordings of Paderewski, Pachmann and dozens of other early twentieth-century pianists. Writers interested in historical keyboard style have sometimes been uncomfortable with this old-fashioned habit, and have tried to argue that it represents little more than early twentieth-century sloppiness. Jean-Jacques Eigeldinger, for example, quotes Saint-Saëns on the difficulty of playing freely in the right hand while maintaining the rhythm in the bass: 'This way of playing is very difficult since it requires complete independence of the two hands; and those lacking this give both themselves and others the illusion of it by playing the melody in time and dislocating the accompaniment so that it falls behind the beat; or else – worst of all – content themselves with simply playing one hand after the other.' Eigeldinger takes the view that much of the pianoplaying heard on early twentieth-century recordings, including Pachmann, Paderewski and Rosenthal, is like this, and that their loose co-ordination is not to be taken seriously.[28]

Richard Hudson, in his study of rubato, argues that early twentieth-century performers preserved only a crude vestige of true nineteenth-century rubato (and, in particular, that of Chopin), often amounting to little more than a failure to play the hands together.[29] But this is to dismiss too lightly most of the famous pianists of the early twentieth century, some of whom formed their playing style under the guidance of nineteenth-century players such as Clara Schumann, Liszt, Leschetizky, Anton Rubinstein and pupils of Chopin. If we want to understand the real functioning of nineteenth-century rubato, then the playing of the oldest generation of pianists preserved on early recordings is surely the best place to start, even if much of their playing seems, at first hearing, to offend against modern notions of taste (this being at the root of the objections posed by Hudson, Eigeldinger and others).

Such judgement of early twentieth-century piano-playing derives from the modern expectation that playing chords together, and precisely synchronising bass and melody notes, is the norm, and that any non-synchronisation is a deviation from it. But it is quite clear from recordings that such a norm only developed later in the century, and that, in piano-playing as in ensemble playing, modern discipline was not expected nor, in most cases, aimed for. Pianists varied in their approaches. Some, such as Josef Hofmann, played with almost modern synchronisation, and argued against looseness (though his playing was very free in other ways).[30] But the vast majority of early twentieth-century pianists played with considerable freedom of 'ensemble'.

Extreme examples, such as Paderewski and Pachmann, if played to musicians who are unaccustomed to them, tend to raise a smile these days. They sound impossibly sloppy, and not to be taken seriously as part of a historical performing style. Subtler examples are more difficult to ignore. Raoul Koczalski, who was taught by Chopin's pupil Mikuli, is an example of a pianist who used arpeggiation and dislocation with refinement and clear purpose. There are striking instances in the opening of Chopin's first Ballade (recorded 1938). The beginning, with its rising octaves, is absolutely 'clean'. But as soon as the texture becomes more complex, the relationship between the different layers of the texture is clarified by dislocation (see example 4.6). Already at bar 9, where a regular pattern of accompanying crotchet (quarter note) chords begins, Koczalski plays the chords irregularly, placing the first chord (the second beat of each three-beat bar) slightly early, almost like a very subtle version of the traditional Viennese waltz rhythm. Where the bass notes coincide with melody notes, at bars 10, 12, and similar places, this early placing of the bass has the effect of dislocating it from the melody, so that it is clearly audible on its own (example 4.6a). At bar 24, where a melodic fragment is repeated in the bass, the first note of each phrase (marked in the score with an accent) is played almost a quaver (eighth note) early, with a long tenuto, so that it is completely separated from the note in the treble (example 4.6b).

To modern listeners, these dislocations and rubati sound like 'liberties'. At a recent research conference, a member of the audience reacted to this example by observing that what Koczalski was doing 'seemed to have nothing to do with Chopin'. What he meant was that it sounded to a modern listener as if Koczalski was taking great liberties with what was indicated on the printed page. But it is making a great leap of imagination to assume that what sounds like a 'liberty' to us, in our literal-minded, text-based world, would necessarily

Ex.4.6 Chopin, Ballade No. 1 in G minor (Koczalski).
⁻ = lengthened note   ╱ = early note

a) bars 8–17

b) bars 24–26

have sounded like that to an earlier generation. What Chopin himself might have thought of this is a subject for conjecture, though contemporary reports make it clear that separation of melody and accompaniment was an important part of his own style. If one puts aside questions about the authority of the text, the effect of Koczalski's 'liberties' is elegant, and his expressive purpose is clear. By rhythmically separating two things that are happening at the same time, he makes them separately audible. By playing accented notes early, he makes them stand out without having to play them louder.

Other refined exponents of the old art of dislocation include Rosenthal, Friedman, Hambourg, Moiseiwitsch and Rachmaninoff. Paderewski, Pachmann, Fanny Davies and Frederic Lamond are among those who, to judge by their recordings, used the device in a less subtle way. And there are also a large number of less distinguished pianists on early recordings who show that it was a very widespread assumption that chords were not necessarily to be played with all the notes sounding together. Even when there is no specific expressive reason for it, there is in many pianists a general habit of softening the impact of a chord by slight arpeggiation.

There are some particularly interesting examples of piano records made by musicians who are not principally remembered as pianists, and who played in this old-fashioned way: Sir Thomas Beecham, accompanying Dora Labette in songs by Delius (1929); Elgar playing improvisations, with every single chord arpeggiated (1929); Ernest Newman illustrating the leitmotivs from Wagner's *Tristan* (1928); and Bruno Walter accompanying Kathleen Ferrier in Schumann's *Frauenliebe und -leben* at the first Edinburgh Festival in 1949. This last is a remarkably late example of a rhythmically relaxed style of piano-playing that goes right back to the beginning of the century. It is utterly unlike the clean and disciplined playing which had become the rule by the late 1940s, but extraordinarily touching in its old-fashioned nuancing of the rhythm.

It is difficult to draw a clear distinction between rhythmic dislocation for deliberate expressive effect and a general habit of not playing the notes of chords together. Some of the piano-playing accompanying early recordings of singers sounds routinely vague in the placing of right and left hand. It is hard, from a modern perspective, to imagine that there is much purpose in it. Some of the recordings of Paderewski and Pachmann can sound galumphing, others marvellously free in expression. What is clear is that this habit or style in piano-playing was part of the same expressive world in which duo-players were not always expected to keep absolutely together, and members of string quartets had the freedom to take their own time for moments of expressive shaping, even if it caused momentary lack of co-ordination or vagueness of rhythm.

Other liberties in early twentieth-century piano-playing are closely related to those in other kinds of music-making. The lightness of rhythmic detail – overdotting of dotted rhythms, flurries of semiquaver (sixteenth note) groups instead of the deliberate articulation we expect today, the tendency to accelerate when there is a lot of activity – is simply the pianist's version of what can be heard in recordings of chamber ensembles and orchestras. It can be found in pianists across many different schools and nationalities: in the playing of Rachmaninoff (Russian), Bartók (Hungarian), Schnabel (Austrian), Cortot and Poulenc (French) and Kathleen Long (English), to take a sample across nationalities. There were important differences between them, but they shared a common understanding of what might be called the rhythmic environment of their time.

One could take a similar sample at the end of the twentieth century: Brendel (Austrian), Uchida (Japanese), Pletnev (Russian), Argerich (Argentinian), Donahoe (English), Schiff (Hungarian), Lupu (Romanian). There are important differences between these pianists too, but again they share a common understanding of what the modern world expects: clarity, control and precise placing. Even Martha Argerich, the most volatile of this list of pianists, does not go beyond what can be accomplished clearly and securely. The 'looseness' and 'casualness' of the past have gone.

With pianists whose recording career extends over a long time, we can hear their styles of playing changing in reponse to the general shift in practice. Arthur Rubinstein's playing of Chopin changed considerably between the 1930s and the 1960s. In the mazurkas, his rhythmic nuances and changes of tempo are more sudden in the earlier recordings, more subtle and more even in the later recordings, with the tempo changes usually being less extreme. As with many other pianists over this period, it is not just that the range of tempo becomes narrower, but specifically that accelerations, which tend to be uninhibited in the earlier recordings, are more controlled in later years, making his whole approach less volatile. Striking examples are the Scherzo in C sharp minor (1932 and 1959), the Piano Concerto in F minor (1931 and 1958) and the Barcarolle (1928 and 1966). Similarly, Wilhelm Backhaus plays the finale of Beethoven's 'Pathétique' Sonata in a more volatile manner in 1927 than in 1958, and Wilhelm Kempff's playing undergoes much the same change in Beethoven's Sonata in A flat Opus 110 (1936 and 1964). Claudio Arrau, who became thoughtful to the point of pedantry in some of his later recordings, was lighter and faster in his earlier years. Compare, for example, his recordings of Beethoven's Sonata in E flat Opus 31 No. 3 (1947 and 1965), and Schumann's Piano Concerto (1945 and 1963). Of course, one has to be cautious in making judgements about tempo from a comparison between 78 rpm records, recorded one short side at a time, and LPs recorded on tape and edited, but without the old time-constraints. Yet the change in general approach shown in these and countless other examples is unmistakable.

The elements of ensemble

A fundamental point that applies to ensemble of all kinds, whether literally a group of several musicians or the one-person ensemble of piano-playing, is that what happens in one strand of the ensemble affects everything else. A note in one line cannot be early without making the other lines seem late, or vice versa. Any alteration of the placing of a note shifts the perception of where the beat is, or (particularly with portamento) makes it less clearly defined. This is one of the main effects that makes much early twentieth-century ensemble sound uncomfortable to modern listeners, until they get used to it.

It is not only in matters of rhythm that all strands of an ensemble affect each other. In tuning, timbre, vibrato, phrasing, articulation, all the members of an ensemble are interdependent. Anyone who has ever played in an ensemble knows that it only takes one member to play out of tune to destabilise the entire group. And in a more subtle way, the balance of the ensemble can be changed by contrasts of vibrato and tone-colour. A leader with a somewhat flabby vibrato affects the impression given by the whole quartet (Jenö Léner and, later, Norbert Brainin of the Amadeus Quartet were both sometimes criticised for this). A player who uses more vibrato than the others can seem to dominate by warmth rather than volume. When Josef Roisman first joined the Budapest Quartet in the late 1920s as second violinist, the Quartet was still led by Emil Hauser, a violinist of the old school who played with restrained vibrato and heavy portamento. In recordings from this period, Roisman can be heard discreetly fitting in with Hauser, and being careful not to dominate from the second desk. This is noticeable on their recording of the cavatina in Beethoven's Quartet in B flat Opus 130 (1928), as Roisman answers Hauser with just a touch more vibrato. When the Quartet recorded the work again in c.1937, with Roisman leading and Alexander Schneider playing second violin, that contrast between old and new styles had gone.

Some of the oldest quartets to make recordings are very sparing in their vibrato. This gives a particularly transparent, one might even say, naked, character to the ensemble. Details of tuning are mercilessly exposed, because there is no ambiguity about the pitch of each line, as there is when vibrato is used. This is true of the original Budapest Quartet, the Capet Quartet, and the Rosé Quartet, which, in sustained passages, sometimes sounds almost like a consort of viols. In the Bohemian Quartet, the leader's vibrato varies greatly: in lyrical phrases a rather slow vibrato swells up, but elsewhere it is virtually absent. In the Flonzaley the vibrato is faster and more continuous, though still delicate (in the 'Franco-Belgian' style of Ysaÿe). This, together with their light approach to rhythm, gives a characteristically warm and mercurial quality to their playing. The new Budapest Quartet, led by Roisman, combines a more continuous, firmer vibrato with a more assertive style of bowing. Adolf Busch also has these qualities, but with a variety of vibrato and articulation greater than that of any other quartet leader. This gives his quartet the means to achieve the range of emotion and texture for which it is still so admired.

Ensembles in which strings and wind are combined present particularly interesting examples of the relationships between different instruments, and the way that different styles of playing can affect the perceived balance. Some of the issues are vividly shown by two recordings of Ravel's Introduction and Allegro, both of which were made by players known to Ravel himself. The scoring is for harp, flute, clarinet and string quartet.

The first recording of the work was made in London by British players in 1923, and conducted by Ravel.[31] The string quartet is led by George Woodhouse, who plays in the usual English style of the time, with a modest amount of vibrato which comes and goes, and with some heavy sliding. The flautist is Robert Murchie, who was of the old English school, playing on the wooden flute with broad, largely un-nuanced phrasing and scarcely a trace of vibrato. The clarinettist, Haydn Draper, similarly plays with no vibrato and no detailed nuances. This results in an expressive balance in which the flute and clarinet are heard as companions, the 'straight' duo, in contrast to the much more heavily nuanced string-players, with their vibrato (even if modest).

A recording of 1938 was made by French musicians who knew Ravel, though the recording was made after his death. The flautist is Marcel Moyse, with clarinettist Ulysse Delecluse, harpist Lily Laskine, and the Calvet Quartet. Moyse was one of the leading exponents of the French school of flute-playing founded by his teacher Paul Taffanel. He played on the metal flute, with prominent and flexible use of vibrato, detailed dynamic nuances, and a brilliant, silvery tone. The clarinettist plays with an occasional tremor, but most often with none, and the string-players have the continuous vibrato which was becoming the norm by that date. The expressive balance is rather different from that of the 1923 recording: here the clarinettist seems the odd one out, the 'straight man', and the flautist most often seems the expressive companion of the first violinist.

Even today, many clarinettists play with little or no vibrato, whereas virtually all flautists (except period instrumentalists) play with a substantial amount of vibrato, certainly in twentieth-century French music. The perception of the clarinettist as the straight member of the ensemble is therefore common in modern performance, as in that 1938 recording. The old English balance, with flute and clarinet as a straight pair, would be thought most odd today.

Not only vibrato and nuances affect the expressive balance of an ensemble. Tone-colour has an effect on the prominence of each instrument, and on the blend of the ensemble as a whole. In that English recording of Ravel's Introduction and Allegro, part of the reason why the flute and clarinet sound like a pair is that Murchie's low notes on the flute have an almost saxophone-like tone-quality which closely approaches the tone of Draper's clarinet in this register. Stravinsky's various recordings of *The Soldier's Tale* show how tone-qualities have a fundamental effect on ensemble. His earliest recording is quite different from his later ones, mostly because of the different tone-colours of French and American instrumentalists.

His first recording, recorded in Paris in 1932, has very pungent tone-colours, which are individual and distinctive. The clarinet is particularly sharp-toned, with a slight quiver, and the bassoon has the characteristic reediness of players on the French instrument at that time. The cornet and trombone are bright-toned, clearly using the narrow-bore instruments then current in France, and the cornet is played with a light quiver which gives a nervous edge to the tone. The result is an ensemble which does not blend in a modern way, but is a collection of separately characterised voices.

Stravinsky next recorded the work in 1954 in New York with American players.[32] Here, the wind instruments achieve a blend of tone which was obviously not intended or attempted in the earlier, Paris recording. This is made possible because the individual instruments are more mellow in tone, and less distinct from each other. The clarinet is smoother and darker, and so is the bassoon, which is clearly the broader-toned German instrument. The trumpet (rather than cornet) has a more rounded tone than the cornet in the French recording, and the player uses a more confident-sounding, almost jazz-style vibrato. The overall effect is of a much more homogeneous group of players. To modern ears it sounds more comfortable, but you could argue that it has less character because the individual instruments are less distinct.

Ensemble, conversation and expression

An ensemble is like a conversation, and to answer the question 'What is good ensemble?' one might ask 'What is good conversation?' Of course, in a sense the composer has already written the conversation. The players are merely acting, or performing it. But the analogy does help to focus attention on what works or does not work, and how ways of playing together change over time.

There are two possible extremes in ensemble-playing: utter chaos, and inhuman efficiency. Both became the aim of some composers in the later twentieth century, but in music as performed through most of history no one has been in favour of either extreme. The question is, how much chaos is allowed, and how much efficiency is needed? As we have seen, answers to that question have changed greatly over the last hundred years.

One could compare a chaotic ensemble to an incoherent conversation, in which people talk over each other, shout each other down, and in which argument is obscured. A merely efficient ensemble is like a conversation in which everyone already agrees, and nothing new is said. But there are more subtle things to be observed both in the way musicians play together and in the way people converse. There are different kinds of relationship, different modes of expression, different levels of self-consciousness, different levels of dominance or imbalance, different voices, different levels of listening and response.

Ideal conversationalists are good thinkers, good speakers and good listeners. If challenged, or presented with an unfamiliar point of view, they consider it seriously and respond with thought and consideration. A conversation between people like that is one in which everyone has something to say, is heard, and listens. Perhaps the best musical ensembles are like that too.

How much each musician in an ensemble 'speaks' is laid down by the composer. But the way musicians speak, and the impact that their contribution has on the ensemble as a whole, depend on how they perform. The word 'balance' is often used to describe the relationship between musicians, but it is widely taken to mean simply how loud everyone is. The interplay between the members of an ensemble is far more subtle than that, and, as the examples presented in this chapter have shown, there are many ways in which an individual can be more or less dominant.

There is another useful analogy to be drawn between music-making and conversation, and that is to do with the role of physical movement. 'Body-language' has become a familiar concept in descriptions of how people communicate with each other. Music-making too has its body-language. In the physical presence of musicians we see the expressions on their faces, and the way they hold or interact with their instruments. We can see how tense or relaxed they seem when faced with technical difficulties. We see them taking breath, swaying, remaining still, turning or looking towards each other in an ensemble. In a concert, the most subtle physical indications can convey to an audience the intensity with which the players are listening and reacting to each other.

Recordings remove us from most of this. But there are physical aspects of music-making which do survive the recording process. We hear, though we do not see, musicians grappling with aspects of technique, some of which have changed greatly over the last hundred years. Portamento is an obvious example. The old-fashioned habit of sliding frequently and slowly makes one aware of the musicians moving their hands up and down the instrument. This is often carefully disguised in more recent string-playing. In less obvious ways the physical reality of musicians' playing is conveyed by early twentieth-century recordings in which ensemble is not strictly together, either because of failure to co-ordinate, or because of deliberate rubato. Modern recordings, in which this freedom is generally absent, make one forget that musicians are going to the effort of co-ordinating with each other, because they do it so smoothly and accurately.

The trend during the twentieth century towards the smoothing over of the physical aspects of performance, and the removal of audiences from the musicians by recordings, have gone hand in hand with changes in attitudes to the music itself. The mid-twentieth century saw the rise of the 'Urtext', the supposedly definitive publication of the great composer's works in accurate scholarly editions. While correcting mistakes and removing misunderstandings about what composers had actually written, this encouraged scholars and musicians to think that the principal job of the performer was to give an accurate reading of the text. Already the trend in performance had been towards an emphasis on clarity, control and accuracy of ensemble, and away from the freedoms of the past. This new emphasis on composers' texts encouraged the tendency towards a more objective and literal interpretation of the notes, free of 'distortion'. Among these distortions are the very features of early twentieth-century performances that endanger accurate co-ordination. This new purism in turn fed into the period instrument movement that accelerated from the 1960s onwards, encouraging the view that much of the tradition of performance in the earlier twentieth century was suspect.

This trend towards objectivity and literalism has passed its peak, and the current interest in historical recordings is one sign of that. Just as musicians in the field of period instruments have come to discover unsuspected freedoms in the performing practices of earlier centuries, musicians, audiences and scholars are discovering that there is more than inaccuracy and sloppiness to be found in some of the supposedly corrupt freedoms of early twentieth-century ensemble-playing One of the lessons they have learned from historical recordings is how the concept of 'faithfulness to the composer' is itself subject to the vagaries of taste and fashion. The late twentieth-century, literal-minded version of it was nothing more than its latest incarnation, born of a world which values clear-cut and efficient answers.

Recordings have preserved the performances of many musicians of the past who believed passionately in being true to the score and to the composer's intentions, but who had quite different ideas from ours about how this was to be achieved. Schnabel is often cited as an early example of a musician who set great store by the composer's text. But his recordings of Beethoven's piano sonatas (1932–5) together with his edition (1935) contain a wealth of evidence to show that Schnabel's idea of 'faithfulness to the composer' was quite different from that of the scholars and performers of the late twentieth century and beyond. At the heart of this is Schnabel's understanding of rhythm. His illumination of the score relies on a free treatment of the relationship between one note and another, and one passage and another, so as to create a vivid sense of how everything relates to everything else. He characterises each rhythmic detail, underlining the differences between the accented and the unaccented, the short and the long, and distinguishing between points of repose and points of transition. His pupil Clifford Curzon reported, 'His rhythm . . . was never produced by extraneous accents, which he spent a lot of time removing from our performances, but by the most careful placing of each sound. As he frequently put it to us, "Rhythm is a matter of proportion, not of accent".'[33] This echoes something that Schnabel's teacher Leschetizky told him: 'You must speak the piano.' In practice this means almost constant, subtle changes of pace from phrase to phrase, and a very flexible approach to the relationship between long and short notes. Schnabel's volatile way of doing all this is 'free', and not much of it is to be found in Beethoven's text. But it is the very freedom which gives us the impression of drawing closer to an understanding of what Beethoven's text means.

What is true of Schnabel's playing is, in different ways, true of much playing from the early years of the twentieth century. The nuances of the Flonzaley or Busch Quartets, the rubato of Ysaÿe or Rachmaninoff, help to convey the meaning of the music much as the inflections of speech convey the meaning of words in a sentence. This is even more clearly true of singers, who, in the early years of the twentieth century, were freer than they are today to adjust the note-values to be more like those of speech. Harry Plunket Greene, singing Schubert's 'Der Leiermann' in English in 1934, at the age of nearly seventy, is able to convey the narrative with startling clarity, because the conventions of the time allowed him to sing the notes and words in much the same rhythm as if he were speaking them. This would, in the twenty-first century, be thought cavalier. The rubato of singers mentioned earlier in this chapter has the effect not only of freeing the vocal line from the regular rhythm of the accompaniment, but, in effect, of freeing the words from the regularity of the music as notated.

Much that has happened in the years since has been to reduce such inflections, elevating instead a more even level of expression. Later twentieth-century styles of rubato are smoother and more regular. Any points of emphasis are carefully incorporated into the whole, nothing is allowed to stand out in relief, or to interrupt the seamless flow of tone which, in string-playing and singing, is rendered yet more seamless by a constant vibrato (at least until the influence of period string-playing begins to spread). Musicians of the past used the repertoire of rhetorical gestures to 'tell the story' of the music. By comparison, musicians from the late twentieth century onwards are more inclined to trust the music to tell the story for them.

Perhaps the finest musicians of each generation would agree that there is an infinite range of possible ways of playing a piece, within obvious constraints. But the question that has to be asked in each generation is, what are the constraints? Today, a group would say that you need to rehearse to the point where you know what is going to happen when you go out onto the platform. Tempi may vary slightly, details may acquire a slightly different emphasis, but nothing must come as a surprise to the other players. You are playing an agreed interpretation. A hundred years ago, a group might have said that this is unnecessarily constraining. That, given the infinite range of possibilities, much can be left open in performance. That a suddenly different tempo, or a different emphasis which loosens the strict 'ensemble', is acceptable. The purpose of performance is to have a living dialogue about the piece as one performs it, not to reproduce something fixed.

On the other hand, the modern group might say that freedom is allowed in performance, and that rehearsing in great detail allows those freedoms to occur without chaos ensuing. And the old group might have said that of course you need to agree the broad interpretation in advance. But the evidence of recordings, and the experience of going to concerts, demonstrate that the level of pre-determination required has greatly increased over the last century. The freedom available to the modern performer is much more limited than in the days when looseness of ensemble, and actual disagreement in matters of phrasing or emphasis, were part and parcel of the performance practice of the time.

CHAPTER FIVE

Questions of Authority:
the Composer

The issues

Problems of how to interpret notation, and how to deduce what was meant by the composer, should have become much simpler when composers began to make and supervise their own recordings early in the twentieth century. Surely, one might think, if a recording exists of the composer's performance, it is a straightforward matter for other musicians to listen to the recording, and to do what the composer does. But composers are not necessarily the best performers of their own works, and even if they are, their views may not be fixed. A composer's recording gives us only what was done on one occasion, in particular circumstances. Composers, like other musicians, live in a world of conventions and habits of performance. These change over time, so that retracing our steps, perhaps many years later, to the world of the composer involves much more than imitating what the composer did, even if that were desirable. Despite all these caveats, it is a fact that the existence of recordings associated with composers gives us valuable evidence of the composer's intentions beyond what is printed in the score. What sort of evidence is it, and how can we use it?

CD reissues of composers' own recordings, and of any recordings associated in some way with a composer, often include booklets in which words like 'authoritative' or 'definitive' are enthusiastically used. It is natural that the existence of a composer's recording from long ago should provoke excitement. After all, if recording had been invented a century earlier than it was, we would have records of Beethoven playing the piano before he went deaf. To have recordings of Rachmaninoff, Elgar and Stravinsky is perhaps not quite as exciting as that, but it is important enough. It is an astonishing thought that we are the first generation in the history of music to have the privilege of being able to hear long-dead composers perform.

The list of composers of the past who made recordings includes Bartók, Brahms (one cylinder only), Britten, Copland, Debussy, Elgar, Fauré (piano rolls only), Grieg, Hindemith, Kodály, Lehár, Leoncavallo, Mahler (piano rolls only), Mascagni, Messiaen, Milhaud, Poulenc, Prokofieff, Rachmaninoff, Ravel, Saint-Saëns, Shostakovich, Stravinsky, Tippett, Vaughan Williams and Villa-Lobos. There are countless others, and there are also many living composers who perform and record their own works. But inevitably the recordings which arouse the greatest interest are those by major composers who are no longer alive to be consulted.

Each of these composers also had favoured performers who made recordings, often with the composer. Indeed, composers can have several different levels of involvement with a recording, and it might be a useful starting-point to draw up a checklist of the various ways in which a recording can be connected, directly or indirectly, with a composer. There are:

1. Recordings performed by the composer (sound recordings and piano rolls, which raise different problems)
2. Recordings directed/conducted by the composer
3. Recordings made while the composer was present
4. Recordings approved by the composer
5. Recordings made by musicians who worked with the composer or who were taught by him/her
6. Recordings made by musicians who heard the composer perform or direct
7. Recordings made by musicians of the composer's time and place

The relationship between composers and recordings in recent decades has varied greatly. But even confining ourselves to conventional composition, performance and recording, it would be possible to extend the above checklist almost indefinitely, for example by applying all of these categories to a pupil of the composer, or to a pupil of a pupil. And in every category there are questions to ask.

A sample of the sorts of questions that can be thrown up is provided by the CD reissue of Pierre Monteux's 1931 recording of Berlioz's *Symphonie fantastique*, which has already been mentioned for its fine ensemble and striking wind sonorities. The booklet quotes Monteux's reminiscences of Edouard Colonne, with whom he worked as assistant conductor in Paris. Monteux writes that Colonne 'had known Berlioz and had seen him conduct at the Opéra and at the Conservatoire'. Monteux had 'never forgotten the "Berlioz" way', and possessed scores in which he had noted down 'the various ways Colonne exposed Berlioz's desires'.[1] Monteux's recording of the *Symphonie* is certainly brilliant. But how close does his link through Colonne take us to Berlioz's own ideas? What did Colonne see Berlioz conduct, and how often? How much of what he passed on to Monteux was really from Berlioz? How much of what Monteux does in the recording was derived from Colonne, let alone from Berlioz? Gabriel Pierné, who also worked with Colonne and succeeded him as conductor of his orchestra, recorded three movements of the *Symphonie fantas-tique* in 1928. A reissue of that recording describes Pierné as 'definitely the leader of the pack' of French conductors in the interwar years.[2] Pierné could no doubt claim the same access to 'the Berlioz way' as Monteux. But Pierné's performances are, by comparison with Monteux's, dull and heavy. How are we to assess the comparative authority of these two recordings, and their possible connections to Berlioz's own interpretations?

By comparison with such tenous links to a composer, a composer's own recordings provide much stronger evidence for interpretative intentions. But even here, there is much that needs to be asked, and the answers are not often straightforward. The examples that follow are just a small sample from this rich vein of historical evidence. They include recordings played and conducted by composers, and others that have more indirect links. Elgar, Stravinsky, Mahler and a trio of French composers (Fauré, Debussy and Ravel) are considered at some length, to give an idea of the complexity of the subject. Then there are briefer notes on Rachmaninoff, Bartók and Schoenberg which raise some other issues worth exploring.

Elgar

Much has been written about Elgar as a composer, and the researches of Jerrold Northrop Moore have unearthed important details about his recording sessions.[3] There is a great amount of material with which to try to evaluate his recordings. But, beyond enthusiasm and sentiment (which are fully justified), little has so far been written about the characteristics of Elgar's performances on record, and what we are supposed to make of them seventy years after his death.

Elgar conducted most of his major works for the gramophone, many of them twice (though the earlier, acoustic versions are in many cases cut, and with reduced orchestration). There is ample evidence that he was satisfied with the recordings that were published. Yet, in line with the practices of his time, their standards and styles of ensemble are very different from those of the twenty-first century. A good example of the style and limitations is given by the 'Enigma' Variations, which he recorded in 1926 with the Royal Albert Hall Orchestra. The fast variations are taken daringly fast: 'Troyte' is one of several variations that are taken even faster than his printed metronome marking (o = 84, compared with 76). But the most strikingly 'unmodern' feature of the performance of this variation is the tendency to accelerate: in patterns of minims (half notes) and crotchets (quarter notes), the crotchets hurry forward, giving an impression of nervousness and instability. No modern orchestra would play it like that. If a conductor tried to take the variation at that tempo, and found that the crotchets hurried, then the tempo would be reduced a little so that details could be more firmly controlled. Indeed, it is rare for a modern performance of 'Troyte' to be taken quite as fast as Elgar took it, even though his own recording is by now widely known.

Elgar's own recordings supply countless instances in which he either disobeyed his own instructions or added to what he wrote in the score. The outer movements of his First Symphony are subjected by Elgar to continual changes of pulse that are not marked in his score. In the allegro of the finale, which has a single metronome marking of 𝅗𝅥 = 84, Elgar begins at 76, rises to 108 by figure 118, and drops to 80 at figure 130. The first movement of the symphony is in a state of constant flux, from the very first bars of the allegro. Modern conductors take these movements with a certain flexibility, but only those who know Elgar's own recording adopt anything like his approach, and they rarely attempt such a level of volatility.

One of the most celebrated examples of Elgar's flexibility of tempo is 'Nimrod' from the 'Enigma' Variations. The metronome marking in the published score is ♩ = 52. Elgar begins at 40, gets into his stride at 48, and accelerates to about 56 before the climax. Just at the point where he pushes forward most noticeably, the marking in the score is 'largamente'.

One might imagine that this indicates that Elgar attached little importance to metronome marks. But in fact he had thought long and hard about this particular marking over the years since he wrote the work in 1899. A sketch for 'Nimrod' at the Elgar birthplace has an original pencil marking of ♩ = 66. Elgar rubbed this out and replaced it with 72, but then reverted to the original decision for the published score. Four years later, in 1903, he wrote to his friend Jaeger (the original inspiration for 'Nimrod') at Novello, 'I always take "Nimrod" slower than M.M. in score. Cowen [Frederic Cowen, composer and conductor] says it should be altered, what do you think?'[4] Jaeger agreed, and the marking in the score was changed to 52. But this gives little idea of what Elgar did in practice in his 1926 recording.

What might be the reasons for this discrepancy between Elgar's tempo instructions and his practice of starting 'Nimrod' slowly and accelerating? At least four possible reasons suggest themselves: first, that Elgar accelerated because he was anxious not to run out of space on the record; secondly, that he had simply changed his mind again between 1903 and 1926; thirdly, that he was not very good at judging the speed of actual performance when considering metronome markings (there was, after all, no recording from which to check his own practice when he was changing the marking in 1903); and fourthly, that flexibility of tempo was something that he took for granted, and that he regarded metronome markings as nothing more than a rough guide.

The first possibility is one that is easily forgotten in these days of CD transfers, in which the original 78 rpm sides are joined seamlessly together. Speeding up a performance in order to fit a section onto a side was not unusual, though drastic examples became less common after the advent of electrical recording in 1925. If there was a choice between breaking the music at an inappropriate moment and taking a slightly faster tempo, then the latter might be the more 'musical' choice. Elgar would certainly not have wanted to break 'Nimrod' in half. But in Elgar's 1926 recording, 'Nimrod' and the preceding variation are both fitted onto a single side. If the preceding variations had been distributed differently over the sides, 'Nimrod' could have had a side to itself (though Elgar would admittedly have had to lose the crucial sustained note which joins it to the preceding variation). In any case, Elgar's tempo for most of 'Nimrod' is actually *slower* than the revised metronome marking. So, all in all, it is surely unlikely that Elgar accelerated to a substantially faster tempo for the recording than he would have done in the concert hall. This is not to say that he always conducted in the same way. Several reports make it clear that he was an unpredictable conductor of his music, taking different tempos depending on his mood on the day.

As to the second option, it is quite possible that Elgar conducted 'Nimrod' differently in 1926 from the way he had done in 1903. Twenty-three years is a long time, and in his old age Elgar was not only unpredictable in mood but also subject to bouts of depression. There might also be some truth in the third possibility. His documented changes of mind about this marking suggest some uncertainty. In performance his tempo might also be influenced by the acoustic of the building in which he was performing, taking the music more slowly and steadily in a cathedral, more quickly and with more acceleration in a dry studio.

As for the fourth suggestion, this must surely be the heart of the matter, whatever the truth about the other options. Elgar made a habit of moulding his music flexibly, and critics of the time make it clear that flexibility was the hallmark of Elgar's conducting style in the concert hall. He conducted the 'Enigma' Variations at a concert in London only two days before making his 1926 recording. One critic wrote, 'Credit is due to the orchestra for its response to Sir Edward's uneasy, wilful beat' and another described the orchestra as 'responsive to Sir Edward's very personal *rubato*'.[5] Elgar himself wrote, in another letter of 1903 to Jaeger, that he wanted his music to be played 'elastically and mystically', not 'squarely and . . . like a wooden box'.[6]

If we accept that Elgar's 1926 recording of 'Nimrod' shows, broadly speaking, how he habitually conducted it, then it is fascinating, and somewhat puzzling, to put it side by side with modern recordings of the same variation. Most modern performances of 'Nimrod' are much slower than Elgar's, and therefore also substantially slower than the metronome marking, and if they accelerate they do so only subtly. Simon Rattle with the City of Birmingham Symphony Orchestra, to take a modern recording more or less at random, begins at scarcely more than half the published metronome marking, and well below Elgar's starting tempo, and reaches 36 as he approaches the climax compared with Elgar's 56. And yet Rattle is a conductor who does take an interest in historical recordings, and his phrasing of the theme of the 'Enigma' Variations makes it clear that he knows Elgar's recording of this work. There are nuances of phrasing and points of emphasis that he could not have acquired from any other source. Why, then, does Rattle, like most modern conductors, ignore the evidence of both the metronome marking and Elgar's own recording when deciding on a tempo for 'Nimrod'? He is not alone in this: Mackerras, who similarly knows Elgar's recording, in his 1992 recording of the Variations takes much the same approach to 'Nimrod' as Rattle, beginning at 28 and rising to 38 before the climax.

The obvious explanation is that this music has become associated with funerals and ceremonies of remembrance. These sombre religious overtones cannot have been in Elgar's mind when he wrote it. In 1899 he and his inspiration for the piece were close friends in the prime of life (Elgar was forty-two, Jaeger was thirty-nine). The lack of elegiac character in the variation is confirmed in his recording. But it is difficult for the modern conductor to escape the weight of this tradition, and to recapture something like Elgar's own approach, even though the evidence of both score and recording is absolutely clear.

The other striking difference between Elgar's recording of 'Nimrod' and any modern performance is the portamento of the Royal Albert Hall Orchestra. At the beginning, virtually every interval is joined by a slide. The question of whether the sliding of British orchestras at this period was a matter of mere habit, style or both has been raised in chapter 3. Here, the question is whether this practice is an essential part of what the composer expected, or merely something he accepted because he was surrounded by orchestras that did it. Modern recordings never have the frequent portamento of Elgar's recordings. Occasionally conductors get orchestras to slide at particular points for emphasis, but modern orchestras do not slide habitually. Even the occasional indication of portamento that Elgar writes into a score is nowadays usually treated gingerly.

Is portamento part of the essential 'Elgar style', or is it just something that was the habit of the times, and not part of the composer's intentions? Just as the rhythmic practice and the woodwind style of orchestras was changing during the last years of Elgar's life, so was their approach to portamento. When Elgar conducted the new London Philharmonic Orchestra and BBC Symphony Orchestra, he was pleased, and seemed to have no reservations about them. Just as he had described the London Symphony Orchestra as 'a jolly fine orchestra' in the early years of the century, he found the new BBC Symphony Orchestra 'marvellous'. But the two orchestras at these two different periods played quite differently. The BBC orchestra, like the LPO, was more thoroughly rehearsed, they had tighter control over rhythmic detail, and their string-playing was more refined, with more discreet portamento.

Nor was Elgar disturbed by the revolution in woodwind vibrato. He seems never to have commented on the plain style of oboe-playing that dominated early twentieth-century Britain, but about the vibrant Leon Goossens in the LPO he wrote, 'Leon G's oboe passages in *Froissart* are divine – what an artist!'[7]

There are similar problems in arriving at Elgar's 'preferred' style of playing and interpretation for his Violin Concerto. He wrote it in 1909–10, when most of the violinists he heard in England still played in the Joachim-inspired style of the late nineteenth century, with heavy portamento and very restrained vibrato. But he composed the concerto for Kreisler, who played with a characteristic (and revolutionary) warm, constant vibrato. Others with whom Elgar happily performed the concerto include violinists from both the old and the new schools of playing: Marie Hall, an old-style violinist with whom he recorded an abridged version of the concerto in 1916 (already mentioned in chapter 2), and Albert Sammons and Yehudi Menuhin, both of the new school.

It was with the teenage Menuhin that Elgar made his famous 1932 recording. That complicates the issue still further. Elgar had conducted the concerto many times, with Kreisler, Ysaÿe and Sammons. Sammons had been playing it for fifteen years, and was widely acknowledged as a great interpreter of the concerto. He had already made a fine recording of it with Henry Wood in 1929 (though there are questions, mentioned in chapter 2, about some of the tempi in the first and last movements, which may have been speeded up to fit the music on the sides). Menuhin had only just learned the concerto, had never performed it in public, and had only one brief piano rehearsal with Elgar two days before the session (though not as brief as Menuhin later claimed).[8] Elgar was deeply impressed by Menuhin, but comparison between the recording, the score and Elgar's recordings of his other works suggests that Elgar was persuaded by Menuhin's beautiful playing to let him take some of the music more slowly than the composer would otherwise have done. In the first movement, Elgar shoots off at the tuttis, while letting Menuhin take his time during the solo passages in a way that is quite at odds with Elgar's usual manner in his large-scale works. The *lento* at figure 29 drops to $\boldsymbol{\downarrow}$ = 36 in Menuhin's recording, compared with 64 in Sammons's recording with Wood. The slow movement has a tempo marking of $\boldsymbol{\downarrow}$ = 52, the pace adopted by Sammons. Menuhin and Elgar take it at about 48. Elgar and the orchestra often lag behind Menuhin's already expansive phrasing, suggesting that Menuhin had unsettled Elgar's sense of the pace of the movement (and there are similar problems of ensemble in the first and third movements).

This interpretation of the problem is conjectural, but the idea that Elgar was swayed from his normal way of doing things by Menuhin is supported by an observation of Basil Maine, who was present during the recording of the concerto. It was memorable and touching, he writes, to watch the old man and the boy discussing points during the breaks in the recording session: 'The enthusiastic admiration of each for the other appeared in Menuhin's eager suggestions as to incidental expression or pace or phrasing, and in Elgar's quiet acquiescence to some of these.'[9] Interestingly, Menuhin's later recording of the concerto with Boult (1966) is less inclined to languish. Figure 29 in the first movement is at ♩ = 46, the slow movement at ♩ = 52 as marked, and much more flowing than in 1932. The impression is that Menuhin's command of the structure of the concerto was (not surprisingly) much more developed in 1966 than it was in 1932. Elgar never gave any indication that he was at all dissatisfied with Menuhin's interpretation, and defended him from criticism by, among others, Ernest Newman. But against the advantage of recording it with the composer himself has to be put Menuhin's lack of experience in the concerto, and the fact that he recorded it one side at a time. It is not surprising that the result, though beautiful, is rather different in character from Elgar's recordings of most of his other works, when he was in sole command of pacing, working with musicians who knew his music and his interpretations well.

Significantly, Elgar's only other electrical concerto recording, of the Cello Concerto with Beatrice Harrison (1928), has none of the ensemble problems of the Menuhin recording, and is much closer in character to Elgar's interpretations of other works. The orchestra, the Royal Albert Hall Orchestra (called the 'New Symphony Orchestra' on the labels), has the warmth and impetuousness of its recording of the 'Enigma' Variations, and the same slight roughnesses and casual details. Elgar and the orchestra do not catch every subtlety in Harrison's accelerandi at the start of the finale, but the problems of ensemble are minimal compared with the serious lagging in the Menuhin recording, even in the very tricky scherzo of the Cello Concerto. Harrison had worked with Elgar over many years, ever since she had made a cut recording of the concerto in 1919–20. Her way of playing the concerto was in close sympathy with Elgar's own approach, and this shows in their ability to co-ordinate much more accurately than Elgar and Menuhin were able to.

The evidence of most of Elgar's recordings that he habitually took his music fast is, like his flexibility of tempo, confirmed by reviews of his concerts. Writing about the concert performance of the 'Enigma' Variations that took place two days before the 1926 recording, the *Musical Times* reported, 'It is indeed a privilege to have great music interpreted by its author when it so happens that he is incomparably its best interpreter. Sir Edward has a drastic way of hacking at his music. All sorts of things which other conductors carefully foster, he seems to leave to take their chance. He cuts a way through in a fashion both nervous and decisive. At the end we realize that detail and rhetorical niceties have been put in their right place, and that the essential tale has been vividly told.'[10] But if witnesses of his concerts confirm that Elgar's way of performing his music was highly personal, they also report that it varied considerably from one concert to another. Boult wrote, 'with Elgar anything might happen. I have heard him slash through things when he was in a bad temper for no reason at all that one could find, so much so that if I made a mark in my score I used to put the date as well because he did things so very differently at different times.'[11]

A recording by Elgar therefore presents only one way in which he might have performed the work. Perhaps Menuhin did take Elgar away from his usual manner of performing his work, but on the other hand Elgar might have favoured that way of playing it on some days, in certain moods. There is certainly no sign that Elgar was at all dogmatic about how other musicians should play his music. In a humorous and self-mocking letter to Compton Mackenzie, Elgar praised the recording Barbirolli made of his Introduction and Allegro in 1928, finding the tempi 'mainly correct', but observing that he 'here and there makes a pause somewhat longer than the composer . . . . I do not know how long the pause is, but I know that Mr. Barbirolli is an extremely able youth and, very properly, has ideas of his own . . . .'[12]

One question, which applies to Elgar as to any composer, is whether musicians who knew him, and heard his own performances, have a particular advantage, or even authority, in their interpretations. Among conductors, Barbirolli and Boult were the two musicians who seemed most to represent an 'Elgar tradition' in Britain through to the 1960s. And yet their recordings show that their approach moved far away from Elgar's as they grew older and took slower tempi. In their earliest recordings of the 'Enigma' Variations, Boult and Barbirolli were fairly close to Elgar in their tempi for the fastest variations: in 'Troyte' (Variation 7), Boult's tempo in c.1936 was $\mathbf{o}$ = 84 (the same as Elgar, but more controlled in rhythm), and Barbirolli's in c.1947 was 82. By the early 1960s, they had slowed down considerably: Boult to 78, Barbirolli to 74. In Variation 2 ('H.D.S.-P.'), Elgar's tempo is $\decrescendo$. = 80 (faster than the score's 72). Boult in c.1936 has 86, and in the 1960s 68; Barbirolli has 84, and in the 1960s 72.

Similarly, comparison between Barbirolli's recordings of the Introduction and Allegro shows that his interpretation became altogether bigger and more stately in tempo over the years. Boult's interpretation of Elgar's Second Symphony, which was extremely vigorous when he first recorded it in 1944, became grander and slower in his later recordings.

As for flexibility of tempo, both Barbirolli and Boult had, at least in their later years, a much more controlled approach than Elgar himself. All of their recordings of the symphonies date from long after Elgar's death, when their tempi had in any case tended to slow down. But their tempo ranges in the First Symphony make a striking comparison with Elgar's own. In the allegro of the finale, where Elgar ranges from $\decrescendo$ = 76 to 108 (at figure 118), Boult (1967) has 72 to 80, Barbirolli (1963) has 64 to 76.

The opinion often used to be expressed or implied that non-British conductors are at a disadvantage in understanding the character of Elgar's music. Elgar's close association with, and praise of, Richter suggest otherwise (though Richter never made any records). Toscanini's approach to Elgar attracted lively debate when he conducted the 'Enigma' Variations on his visits to London in the 1930s. When he conducted his own New York Philharmonic in the work in 1930, *The Times* reported: 'Probably never has the "Troyte" variation been played with more electric energy, or "Nimrod" attained such an overwhelming tonal climax. The playing was wonderful, and Signor Toscanini had perfectly definite ideas of every number, which he brought out with complete mastery. But his ideas were too definite for a satisfying reading of Elgar. Those who value his music and this work in particular for a certain elusive quality, and a mentality at one moment almost excessively confidential, and at another withdrawing into half statements and hints of feeling, cannot be wholly at ease in listening to this highly organized interpretation.' When Toscanini returned to conduct the BBC Symphony Orchestra in the 'Enigma' Variations in 1935, 'W. McN' wrote: 'Shall an Italian interpret Elgar? He did, and a good deal better than some Englishmen. As Sir Landon Ronald put it in a letter to *The Times*: "We had the Variations from Toscanini exactly as Elgar wished them to be played, plus the genius of a great master of the orchestra."'[13]

There is a recording of this concert with the BBC Symphony Orchestra. How does it compare with Elgar's own approach, recorded nine years before? The theme is, unusually, as slow as in Elgar's performance, though not as volatile, hardly speeding up in the middle section. Variation 2 is very fast, and almost as messy as Elgar's with the Royal Albert Hall Orchestra. Variation 4 is exceptionally fierce, Variation 6 ('Ysobel') much slower than under Elgar, but beautifully poised ('exquisite' according to W. McN). 'Nimrod' is slower than Elgar, but not nearly as slow as it is usually taken in modern times, and with a fine and intense climax. And the finale is a little more controlled than with Elgar, less abandoned in the accelerations, less flowing, but powerful.

All in all, it is not quite Elgar's approach, but it is no further away from it than the noted Elgarians Barbirolli and Boult, and in some variations (particularly 'Nimrod') is closer in spirit to Elgar's own view, even though, presumably, Toscanini never heard Elgar conduct.

Stravinsky

It would be difficult to imagine two musicians more contrasted than Elgar and Stravinsky, both in their compositions and in their views on performance. Elgar wanted his music played 'elastically and mystically'. Stravinsky famously railed against 'interpreters', and insisted that all he required of a conductor was 'a very clean and finished execution of my score'.[14] In his own recordings, however, he supplies ample evidence that he himself changed his view of what constituted 'clean and finished execution'.

Stravinsky conducted his own recorded performances over a period of more than thirty years. His earliest recordings were made with French musicians in the late 1920s and early 1930s. From the 1940s to the 1960s he recorded in America. The differences between the earlier and later recordings are very striking, in tone-colours, rhythm, discipline and tempi. His earliest attempts at *Petrushka* (1928), *The Firebird* (1928), *The Rite of Spring* (1929) and *The Soldier's Tale* (1932) are full of passages which, from a modern perspective, are taken faster than the musicians can comfortably manage. They are full of the same sort of haste and roughnesses of co-ordination as in Elgar's recordings with the Royal Albert Hall Orchestra – and given the similar problems of the deputy system in Paris as in London, which Stravinsky himself describes, that is not surprising. In Stravinsky's music, with its clear-cut and complex rhythms, the balance between excitement and chaos is much more uncomfortable than in Elgar. The 'Ritual of Abduction' in Part 1 of *The Rite of Spring* is taken, in Stravinsky's first recording with the Straram Orchestra, at about ♩ = 138, faster than the printed metronome marking of 132. The general effect is exciting, but the ensemble is very messy and the rhythms indistinct. Both of the later American recordings (1940 with the New York Philharmonic, 1960 with the Columbia Symphony) are slower, at about the tempo of the metronome marking, and rhythmically much more clearly defined and unanimous. In the 'Infernal Dance' from *The Firebird*, the 1928 performance by the Straram Orchestra is taken at ♩ = 172. Again, the musicians sound almost out of control: in particular, the brass tend to hurry the ends of the offbeat phrases (like the brass of the Royal Albert Hall Orchestra in Elgar's 'Troyte'). The Columbia Symphony Orchestra in 1960 is still fast, at ♩ = 156, but there is no impression that the orchestra is having difficulty, and every detail of the rhythm is firmly in place.

This is one of a number of instances in Stravinsky's scores where he changed the metronome marking when he revised the score. The original 1910 score of *The Firebird* has, for the 'Infernal Dance', ♩ = 168; the revised version published in 1945 has ♩ = 152. Is it a coincidence that the 1928 and 1960 recordings are, respectively, close to the tempi of the first and second editions? The changing of the marking in the score might suggest that by 1945 Stravinsky had decided that he wanted a higher standard of precision than could be achieved at the original fast tempo.[15] And yet, there is nothing to suggest that Stravinsky was dissatisfied at the time with the standards achieved in his early Paris recordings. Far from it: in his *Autobiography* of 1936, having bemoaned the deputy system, he spells out in detail the opportunity for obtaining high standards at recording sessions, and the value of the results:

> . . . these recordings, very successful from a technical point of view, have the importance of documents which can serve as guides to all executants of my

music. Unfortunately, very few conductors avail themselves of them . . . . Is it not amazing that in our times, when a sure means which is accessible to all, has been found of learning exactly how the author demands his work to be executed, there should still be those who will not take any notice of such means, but persist in inserting concoctions of their own vintage? . . . This is all the more regrettable since it is not a question of a haphazard gramophone record of just any performance. Far from that, the very purpose of the work on these records is the elimination of all chance elements by selecting from among the different records [i.e. takes] those which are most successful . . . . I do not for a moment regret the time and effort spent on it. It gives me the satisfaction of knowing that everyone who listens to my records hears my music free from any distortion of my thought, at least in its essential elements. Moreover, the work did a good deal to develop my technique as a conductor. The frequent repetition of a fragment, or even an entire piece, the sustained effort to allow not the slightest detail to escape attention, as may happen for lack of time at any ordinary rehearsal . . . all this is a hard school in which a musician obtains very valuable training and learns much that is extremely useful.[16]

When we hear these recordings today, the idea that they represent sustained attention to 'the slightest detail' conjures up a wry smile. Incidentally, the 'frequent repetitions' are not borne out by the take numbers. Stravinsky's Paris recording of *The Rite of Spring* (1929) consists entirely of first and second takes (see Table 1 on page 40). Perhaps he was referring to attempts which were abandoned part-way through a side, or preliminary rehearsals and run-through, none of which would have been listed as take numbers.

There can be no doubt from Stravinsky's *Autobiography* that he regarded his early Paris recordings as a great success — or, at the very least, that he wished to promote them as a great success. One can read between the lines for indications that they could have been even better. That the discs were free from distortion of his thought 'at least in its essential elements' perhaps implies an acceptance that there are roughnesses. The acknowledgement that the sessions helped to develop his conducting technique is also an admission that he was inexperienced at that time. Although he had conducted two concert performances of *The Rite* with the Straram Orchestra the previous year, his control over tempo and rhythmic detail was undoubtedly far looser than that of his champion Pierre Monteux (whose own recording had already appeared). Monteux had conducted the famous première in 1913, and was a thoroughly experienced conductor.[17]

Most startling of all is the recording Stravinsky made of the *Symphony of Psalms* in 1931. He made this recording shortly before conducting the première in Paris. He writes, 'The performance could not fail to benefit by this, as the rehearsals had to be conducted with that exceptionally minute care which, as I have already pointed out, is demanded by all records.'[18] The chorus, both in the recording and at the concert, was the Alexis Vlassoff Choir. Their extremely wobbly tone and poor blend and tuning, particularly when unaccompanied, make their performance intolerable to modern listeners. Stravinsky's later recordings, made in Canada in 1946 and America in the 1960s, have choirs in quite a different class and style. But Stravinsky seems to have been satisfied with what he heard in 1931.

Comparing Stravinsky's early Paris recordings with those he made in America from the 1940s to the 1960s is always startling. The tuning, the clarity of rhythm and texture (even allowing for the greater clarity of the recordings themselves), the precision of ensemble (even allowing for editing), and the control of detail and of the overall tempo, make the later recordings sound comfortable to modern ears, as the earlier recordings do not. It would be interesting to know what Stravinsky in the 1960s thought of his early attempts at recording. But despite his comments on his own and others' recordings of later years, he seems to have drawn a discreet veil over these pioneering efforts. He did, however, go so far as to acknowledge in 1968 that 'one performance represents only one set of circumstances'.[19] This shows a considerable softening of attitude to performance compared with his earlier demand for 'finished execution' and nothing more.

There are also matters of changing styles and national differences to consider. Instrumentalists in different countries played in radically different styles in the 1920s and 1930s, as we have seen. This is clear in Stravinsky's recordings of *The Soldier's Tale*, which have already been discussed in chapter 4. In his *Autobiography*, he singles out for particular praise the 'admirable group of Paris soloists' who took part in his early recordings, including several who participated in the 1932 recording of *The Soldier's Tale*.[20] And yet, in this as in all Stravinsky's Paris recordings, the pungent and distinct timbres of the wind instruments are quite different from the smoother, more blended ensembles of his American recordings.

The recording Stravinsky made of *Jeu de cartes* in 1938 is stylistically different both from the playing of Paris orchestras, and from the American playing he was to encounter later. The orchestra is the Berlin Philharmonic. The woodwind and brass are smooth-toned and broadly phrased, and there is no vibrato. The flute-playing makes a particularly striking contrast with that of Marcel Moyse in Stravinsky's Paris recordings. Moyse's tone is bright and vibrant, the epitome of what was to become familiar as modern French flute-playing. The German flute-tone is softer and organ-like in its steadiness. Wooden flutes were still in use in the Berlin Philharmonic, whereas Moyse played on the metal flute.

One might imagine that obvious differences like these would have struck Stravinsky forcefully. If so, he seems to have kept his impressions of different instrumental styles to himself, and to have accepted them. He did, however, drop one revealing remark about national differences between orchestras. In 1965 he published an analysis of three recordings of *The Rite of Spring*, conducted by Karajan, Boulez and Robert Craft. He was highly critical of all of them as 'interpretations', but he also said something about the orchestras – the Berlin Philharmonic, the French Radio Orchestra, and the Moscow State Orchestra. Stravinsky wrote, 'Whereas the music sounds French in the French recording, and German in the German, the Russians make it sound Russian, which is just right.'[21] This is particularly interesting in the light of the fact that *The Rite of Spring* was first performed by French musicians, and not by Russians until years later. And if it was important for *The Rite of Spring* to sound Russian, one might think it would be even more important for *Petrushka*, with its overtly Russian character. Stravinsky recorded extracts from *Petrushka* at a concert in Moscow with the Moscow Symphony Orchestra, during his visit to Russia in 1962, and those too sound very 'Russian', earthy and vigorous.

Even if Stravinsky did find in the 1960s that he liked a Russian sound for these works, Russian orchestral playing in the 1960s must have been very different from Russian playing in 1913 when *The Rite* was written, or even earlier when Stravinsky was still living in Russia. A recording of the Letter Scene from Tchaikovsky's *Eugene Onegin*, made in St Petersburg in 1906–7, has none of the later Russian vibrancy. The horn player shows no trace of vibrato, and there is little vibrato from the other players in the chamber group accompanying the singer – none on the oboe, and little even on the violin. Clearly the culture of the time was one of restraint in the use of vibrato, and that must be what Stravinsky encountered in his youth. Again, Stravinsky has nothing to say on this subject.[22]

Mahler

Elgar survived just long enough to record many of his major orchestral works in electrical recordings. Stravinsky recorded many of his works two or more times over a long period. Mahler is the most frustrating example of a composer who died just at the beginning of the period of recordings, leaving only Welte piano rolls (recorded in 1905) of the first movement of his Fifth Symphony, the finale of the Fourth, and some songs. Something can be made of tempi, perhaps, though allowance has to be made for the tendency of a pianist to play faster than a full orchestra. And the spread chords, melody notes out of synchronisation with the bass, and fast and light rhythmic detail, show only that Mahler was a pianist of his time.

The reason the rolls are so frustrating is that Mahler was often described as the greatest of all conductors, and he died too early to leave direct evidence of it.

Egon Wellesz described him as having the rhythm of Toscanini and the heart of Bruno Walter.[23] But even though there are no recordings of Mahler conducting, we do at least have recordings of his music conducted by four conductors who knew him and worked with him: Bruno Walter, Otto Klemperer, Willem Mengelberg and Oskar Fried. How far do these take us to Mahler's own interpretation of his music, and in what way are they 'authoritative'?

Oskar Fried has the distinction of having made the first ever recording of a major work by Mahler, his Second Symphony, recorded in the pre-electric studio in 1923–4, with a reduced orchestra and choir. One could hardly expect the great choral finale to work under these conditions, but the rest of the symphony is, within obvious limitations, remarkably successful, rhythmically much more incisive than most pre-electric recordings of orchestras (as was observed in chapter 2). But how close is it to Mahler's own ideas?

Fried had first met Mahler in 1905, when Mahler was music director at the Vienna Opera and Fried was beginning to make his own name as a composer. Mahler asked to see him, to discuss performing his opera. Mahler was so impressed with Fried's interpretative ideas that he said, 'You will conduct my second symphony in Berlin. I shall come to hear it myself. You will do it splendidly.' The concert took place in November of that year, and the rehearsals culminated in Fried losing his temper and throwing his stool into the stalls. Mahler calmed him down and took him back to his hotel. The following day Fried announced to the orchestra, 'Gentlemen, I have been rehearsing it all wrong. Tonight, I will take completely different tempi.' Mahler wrote to his wife Alma, 'Fried is very docile and knows how to take a hint. Yesterday he took it all too fast by half!' The performance was a triumph, and it was the first time that the Second Symphony had been well received in Berlin. Mahler afterwards wrote to Fried and thanked him, ending with the words, '*Please*, remember at your rehearsals all the things I told you.'[24]

Fried's eleven discs of the Second Symphony were made nearly twenty years after that Berlin performance, and thirteen years after Mahler's death. If Fried's original tempi were 'all wrong', and Mahler had to plead with him to remember what he had told him, does this recording give us Mahler's tempi, or Fried's tempi, or some compromise between the two, possibly further affected by the constraints of side-limits?

One striking feature straight away is that Fried's opening tempo is closer to Mahler's (rare) metronome marking than most later recordings, even those by other conductors who knew Mahler. In a note in the score, Mahler gives the tempo of the opening phrases in cellos and basses as ♩ =144, settling to ♩ = 84–92 at the 'a tempo'. Fried's opening is very forceful and abrupt, at about ♩ = 140, settling to ♩ = 84. Bruno Walter made a piano duet arrangement of the symphony in 1899, which reproduces Mahler's note on the opening metronome marks, and suggesting ♩ = 84 for the eventual tempo. Walter's live

1948 performance with the Vienna Philharmonic opens at 124, settling to 76. His later American recording (1958 with the New York Philharmonic) is slower, starting at ♩ = 112, and settling to ♩ = 72. Klemperer, both in a live 1951 recording and in his 1962 studio recording, begins at about 120, falling to 88 in 1951 and 84 in 1963.

Is Fried unusually close to Mahler's intentions at the opening of the symphony? It might seem so on the face of it, but inconveniently Mahler wrote to Fried before the 1905 performance, 'The note on the first page of the score is no longer applicable.' What did this mean? Are other conductors right to take the opening more slowly than Mahler's marking? If Fried follows Mahler's note which is 'no longer applicable', is he ignoring Mahler's subsequent advice?[25] Whatever the truth of this, it seems clear that Fried's vigorous approach to the basic tempo of the first movement must be closer to Mahler's intentions than some of the grand, slow performances recorded in the late twentieth century. Most extreme is Leonard Bernstein in a live 1987 recording. After a fast opening (♩ = 136), he drops to a portentous 64 at the 'a tempo'. At figure 2, where Mahler's autograph (and Walter's 1899 piano duet arrangement) has ♩ = 100, Bernstein is still at 64, becoming even slower and more languishing in the violin phrases that follow. Rattle (c.1987) is also very slow, setting a basic tempo of 72, and broadening still further after figure 2.

It is difficult to know what to make of Fried's tempo for the third movement. Mahler published no metronome marking, but there is one in his autograph score: ♩. = 52, rising to 58 at bar 14. Walter's duet arrangement has ♩. = 52 rising to 60–63 at bar 14. Most conductors have taken the movement at least as fast as Mahler's marking. But Fried takes it more slowly, at 45, with abrupt phrasing and marked overdotting. Was this what Mahler told him to do? And if so, why did Klemperer and Walter not do the same thing (Walter takes it at 56–60 in 1948, 56 in 1962, Klemperer at 60 in 1952, 56 in 1962)?

Letters suggest that what Mahler most valued in Fried was his close attention to detail in performance, something about which Mahler himself was obsessional. He had got this impression of Fried even before the Berlin performance of the Second Symphony. In May 1905 Mahler wrote to Fried from Strassburg, where he was to conduct at the first Alsace-Lorraine Music Festival: 'I'm conducting my Vth here on the 21st. I don't know whether I should advise you to come. On such occasions you just have to let things ride a little and conduct the large vision. People "of our ilk" loathe to dispense with detail. But today's conductors call that "*the grand manner*"!' After the very successful performance of the Second Symphony conducted by Fried, Mahler wrote again, comparing Fried favourably with Nikisch. Fried's performance he regards as 'a ray of hope in one's life'. Nikisch, on the other hand, had just conducted the *Kindertotenlieder*, and, according to Mahler, 'didn't look at' the work before the performance. Earlier in the year Nikisch had conducted the Fifth Symphony in Berlin. Mahler writes to Fried dolefully, 'Perhaps you will still be able to rescue these works from the grave where Nikisch hurled them (together with the Vth) some time ago.' But one must not make too much of Mahler's approval of Fried. It was at the end of this same letter that Mahler wrote, '*Please* remember everything I told you during your rehearsals!' – something that he would hardly have written if he thought that Fried could be completely relied upon to understand his intentions in future.[26] And, just to make an already complicated situation even more so, there is a third-hand anecdote suggesting that Mahler might not have enjoyed Fried's conducting of the Second Symphony at all. De la Grange reports that the conductor Harold Byrns, a close friend of Alma Mahler, heard from Franz Röhm, son of the musicologist Max Friedländer, that Friedländer stated that he 'had attended the concert with Mahler, that Mahler had refused to shake Fried's hand in the wings, and finished the evening with Friedländer in a restaurant'. When Friedländer asked Mahler what he had thought of the performance, according to this story he responded, 'in his resonant baritone voice: "Oh! Ah! I turned in my grave!"'[27] A third-hand anecdote is not much to put beside Mahler's own letters, but it makes it clear that the opinions of a long-dead composer about a performance that took place a century ago are not easily established beyond doubt.

At Fried's 1905 performance of the Second Symphony, the off-stage band in the finale was conducted by an immensely tall twenty-year-old student by the name of Otto Klemperer. His memory of that occasion remained vivid more than sixty years later when Peter Heyworth interviewed him in 1969: 'Mahler came to the last rehearsal, and afterwards I went to him and asked, "Excuse me, but was it all right?" He said, "No. it was much too loud. It should sound very quietly from behind." I said, "But it says *sehr schmetternd* [very blaring] in the score." He replied, "But from a long way away; it was much too close." It wasn't possible to get that far away, so I said to the musicians, "Play it *piano*: the whole thing." They did so and the performance was an enormous success. Mahler embraced Fried on the stage and when he came into the artists' room he shook my hand and said, "Very good." I was proud.'[28] Two years later, Klemperer made a solo piano arrangement of the Second Symphony, which Mahler pronounced 'splendid', though it was not published and was later lost.[29] Klemperer played the scherzo to Mahler in Vienna, from memory. Mahler was impressed by Klemperer's talent, recommended him for a post in Hamburg, and wrote a testimonial for him.[30] This 'opened every door' for Klemperer and set him on his conducting career, which began with three years at the German Opera House in Prague.

Mahler presumably never saw Klemperer conduct any of his works (apart from his participation in Fried's performance of the Second Symphony), but Klemperer saw Mahler conduct on several occasions, including his Third and Eighth Symphonies. He described Mahler as 'a hundred times better than Toscanini', but regarded his qualities as 'unteachable'. As for the qualities in Klemperer that Mahler admired, we have to put out of our minds the increasingly frail, dogged old man who became familiar in concert halls in the 1960s, and imagine the immensely imposing, fiery manic-depressive he was in his prime. He terrorised orchestras almost as thoroughly as Mahler himself, and was often compared to him. When Klemperer made his own Berlin début in 1921, conducting Mahler's Second Symphony, the critic Oscar Bie wrote, 'Once again, one had the impression of seeing and hearing Mahler. No emotionalising, ⬅ no trivialisation, no softness, no rhetoric, only power and necessity.'[31]

Klemperer's earliest Mahler recordings date from many years later. A concert performance of the Second Symphony recorded in Amsterdam in 1951 makes a particularly impressive comparison with his 1962 studio recording of the work. Fine though the later performance is, the earlier one has much greater urgency and bite, with many sections at faster tempi. In the first movement the differences in tempo are slight. The second and third movements are both slower in 1962 than in 1951. And in the finale, the differences become substantial. After figure 14, the tempo is ♩ = 144 in 1951, 118 in 1962, sounding very stolid by comparison. Before figure 19, at 'kräftig', the tempo is ♩ =136 in 1951, 116 in 1962, dropping to 104 by figure 19. Klemperer was already aged sixty-six in 1951, and one can imagine that his grip of tempo and rhythm would have been yet stronger when he conducted this work with 'only power and necessity' in 1921, at the age of thirty-six. Perhaps from this we can also imagine something of the qualities that Mahler admired in him, even though he never heard Klemperer conduct this work.

The two conductors who had most direct contact with Mahler, and who might be expected to carry something of his 'authority', are Bruno Walter and Willem Mengelberg. Of the two, Walter was far closer to Mahler for much longer periods of time. He worked with Mahler as a repetiteur at the opera house in Hamburg from 1894, aged only eighteen, and then, having twice been invited by Mahler to join him as a conductor at the Vienna Court Opera, finally did so in 1901. Of all Mahler's disciples and hangers-on, he was the closest and most faithful, and the one whom Mahler most consistently supported. He shared with Mahler the criticism and anti-Semitism heaped upon him in Vienna. When he first joined Mahler in Vienna in 1901, he was described as following him slavishly, to the extent of imitating his gestures as a conductor. But Mahler had great faith in him from the first. Walter's début at Vienna, conducting *Aida*, elicited the comment from Mahler that 'every tempo and every musical intonation filled me with serene satisfaction'.[32] It was Walter whom Mahler chose to prepare piano duet versions of his first two symphonies, and he entrusted many important opera performances in Vienna to him. When Mahler left Vienna for America in 1907, he wrote to Walter,

'Neither of us need waste words on what we mean to each other. I know of no-one who understands me as well as I feel you do, and I believe that for my part I have entered deep into the mine of your soul.'[33]

Walter became a devoted champion of Mahler's music after the composer's death. Mahler had sent him the score of *Das Lied von der Erde*, asking him to conduct it, and Walter gave the première in Munich. He made important recordings of *Das Lied von der Erde* and the Ninth Symphony in Vienna in the 1930s, shortly before Hitler's annexation of Austria and the dispersal of many of the members of the Vienna Philharmonic who had played under Mahler (including the leader, Arnold Rosé, Mahler's brother-in-law).

All this gives Walter a level of authority in his association with Mahler that is matched by no other conductor. But because they worked so closely together, there is a lack of documentary evidence of Mahler's detailed views about Walter as a conductor, and in particular there is almost nothing about his views of Walter as a conductor of Mahler's own music. Mahler preferred to conduct his own works whenever he could, though Walter was certainly the conductor he felt was most able to replace him. In 1904 Mahler wrote about the possibility of his Fifth Symphony being performed in Munich: 'I would almost advise a performance conducted only by myself or Walter. Or else Mottl or Weingartner, who are naturally "hors concours" and who would certainly do the work no harm.'[34]

There is far more comment from Mahler about Willem Mengelberg. This is not because he held Mengelberg in higher esteem, but because Mahler only encountered Mengelberg from time to time, when he visited Mengelberg's orchestra in Amsterdam to conduct his works, and they therefore needed to correspond. There are letters to Mengelberg full of appreciation for his careful preparation of the orchestra, and letters about Mengelberg and his orchestra to Alma and others. There are few such letters about Walter, because they spent so much of their time together, and because most of Walter's contacts with Mahler, unlike Mengelberg's, were to do with performances of the works of other composers. In that way, Mengelberg is privileged over Walter in the amount of material that exists about his role as a conductor of Mahler's works.

When Mahler's Fourth Symphony was performed in Amsterdam on 23 October 1904, it was played twice in one evening. According to Alma Mahler, Mahler conducted the first time, Mengelberg the second, to Mahler's great satisfaction. But other evidence makes it clear that Mahler conducted both performances that day, and that Alma, who was not present, must have mis-remembered comments by Mahler about Mengelberg's conducting of other works. Mahler did sometimes share a concert with Mengelberg, Mahler conducting his own works and Mengelberg the rest of the programme, and Mahler commented on an 'excellent performance' by Mengelberg of Schumann's Fourth Symphony during that same visit to Amsterdam.[35]

Mahler's praise of Mengelberg, and his faith in him as an interpreter of his music, is therefore based mostly on Mengelberg's preparation of his orchestra which Mahler then conducted at final rehearsals. It is unlikely that Mahler actually heard Mengelberg conduct any of his works, because the only times that they met were when Mahler had come to Amsterdam specifically to conduct. Mengelberg did take detailed notes of Mahler's instructions during rehearsal, and believed that he learned from Mahler exactly how he wanted his music to be performed, as he wrote in 1926: 'His rehearsals in particular established a precedent for our future performance practice of his music. At these rehearsals he would analyse his works in the minutest detail, and explain his views on every single phrase. Thus we learned exactly how he wanted his work to be performed. "Das Wichtigste steht nicht in der Noten", he used to say: the most important part is not in the notes.'[36] Perhaps Mengelberg's notes were accurate, but it is impossible to know. When Mahler's performance of his Seventh Symphony in Amsterdam in October 1909 was followed by a tour of the work conducted by Mengelberg, critics 'generally agreed that Mengelberg's interpretation matched Mahler's'.[37]

A violinist in the Concertgebouw Orchestra, Max Tak, wrote in his memoirs about the rehearsals for that 1909 Amsterdam performance of the Seventh Symphony. He writes of meticulous preparation, but also provides a rare piece of evidence that Mengelberg's approach might not always have been the same as Mahler's:

> Mengelberg needed a week to prepare Mahler's Seventh with the orchestra. Rehearsals were held in the morning and evening. The rehearsal atmosphere was highly charged. I can't imagine there was ever a work as thoroughly studied as this. Then Gustav Mahler arrived. A small, thin man with a high forehead, beneath which two eyes, hidden behind frameless glasses, fired rockets into the orchestra. Something that pleased none of the orchestra was the fact that, in the very first bar (which introduces the figure for the following tenor horn solo), Mahler remarked on the way Mengelberg, with his exact attention to metrical division, had taken this figure. This caustic observation created an atmosphere of conflict such as so frequently surrounded Mahler's personality. The Mahler rehearsals progressed under the smouldering threat of incident, but there were no actual explosions, mainly because Mengelberg was present at all the rehearsals. Thanks to Mengelberg's exemplary preparation, the performance, sublimely conducted by Mahler, was an unforgettable experience.[38]

This presents us with a problem similar to that of Fried and the Second Symphony. Did Mahler's correcting of Mengelberg's interpretation of the opening bars result in Mengelberg incorporating that correction into his own later performances, when Mahler was not present? There seems to be no

Mengelberg recording of the Seventh Symphony from which to judge, even if we could deduce what the difference between their approaches to the opening bar actually was. The only recordings of Mahler symphonies conducted by Mengelberg, at least currently in circulation, are a gramophone recording of the Adagietto from the Fifth Symphony, recorded in 1926, and a recording of a concert performance of the Fourth Symphony from 1939. Can we really know how close they are to Mahler's own ideas?

The conductor of the Smithsonian Chamber Players, Kenneth Slowik, implies in a CD note that Mengelberg's recording of the Adagietto with the Concertgebouw Orchestra is closer to Mahler's intentions than Bruno Walter's with the Vienna Philharmonic, and he uses Mengelberg's recording as a model for his own performance. He writes, '[Mengelberg's] 1926 recording is a fascinating document of orchestral *rubato* and *portamento*, both of which were trademarks of Mengelberg's painstakingly-prepared Amsterdam interpretations.' The recording shows 'not only the remarkable rhythmic elasticity and vitality of Mengelberg's approach but also his insistence on carefully coordinated and markedly audible slides between certain notes in the melody designed to heighten the lyricism and expressiveness of the music. Bruno Walter's 1938 Vienna Philharmonic Orchestra rendition . . . seems almost sterile by comparison, despite Walter's deserved reputation as a Mahler disciple.'[39]

Richard Taruskin, in a characteristic piece in the *New York Times*, acclaims Slowik's recording as an antidote to the 'cleanup crew' of Norrington, Gardiner et al.: 'How refreshing, then, to find a group of excellent musicians – "early" musicians, yet – who are making a stand against militant sterility.'[40] But to take the Vienna Philharmonic and Walter's approach to Mahler as an example of 'sterility' is a strange thing to do. Though their performance of the Adagietto does begin without any of the Concertgebouw's portamenti, there are traces later on, as there are in their famous live recordings from the same period of *Das Lied von der Erde* and the Ninth Symphony, which nobody could describe as sterile. There is some evidence that Walter encouraged the Vienna Philharmonic to play in a somewhat 'cleaner' style than some of his contemporaries did (as discussed in chapter 3). Perhaps Walter thought that the simplicity of the opening of the Adagietto invited a 'pure' approach. But Taruskin's view is simply that 'Compared with Mengelberg, Walter is practically Roger Norrington'.

An important question, which neither Slowik nor Taruskin addresses, is whether there is any evidence that Mahler would have preferred the Concertgebouw playing to the Viennese playing in these two recordings. To this, as to most questions about dead composers' views, there is no straightforward answer. An important difference between the Concertgebouw Orchestra and the Vienna Philharmonic in the decades before World War II is that the Concertgebouw Orchestra was exhaustively rehearsed and trained by Mengelberg, and its technique and style were moulded exclusively by him.

He himself had built the orchestra into one of the most famous ensembles in the world, and his rehearsals were lengthy and exhaustive. By contrast, the Vienna Philharmonic had a long tradition, stretching back well into the nineteenth century, which did not owe its style or standard to any single conductor, and it did not rehearse with the habitual thoroughness of the Concertgebouw. It was not in any sense Walter's orchestra, as the Concertgebouw was Mengelberg's. Its style was that of the Vienna Philharmonic, and its concertmaster, Arnold Rosé, had been in his post since 1881. Both the Vienna Philharmonic and the Vienna Opera orchestra, from which the Philharmonic's members were and are drawn, had for several years been conducted by Mahler himself (Vienna Opera, 1897–1907; Vienna Philharmonic concerts, 1898–1901). His period at the Vienna Opera from 1897 was often described as the greatest period in the history of the house. The contrast which Slowik describes is therefore not just between the performances of Mengelberg and Walter, but between two orchestras of utterly different backgrounds, one of which was virtually created by Mahler's champion Mengelberg, the other of which was an orchestra with strong traditions of its own, which were an integral part of Mahler's own background. What is more, Mahler's association with Amsterdam began precisely when he was music director at the Vienna Opera, so he could have written in detail about the contrasting styles of the two orchestras at that time if he had wished to. He did not, and one therefore has to ask whether he can have had a strong preference for the style of one orchestra or the other, even though their styles were (to judge by their recordings made twenty to thirty years later) very different.

It is certainly true that Mengelberg's Concertgebouw Orchestra plays with a great deal more portamento than the Vienna Philharmonic in Walter's recording. The sliding is much more frequent, and much heavier. In the first section of the movement (to figure 2, a total of 38 bars) the Vienna Philharmonic plays only four clearly defined portamenti, though a suggestion of the sound of shifting can also be heard elsewhere. The Concertgebouw Orchestra plays thirty clearly defined portamenti during the same passage (part of the violin and cello lines is shown as music example 5.1). Its sliding, as in the example discussed in chapter 3 (music example 3.6), gives the impression of having been carefully rehearsed; it is not like the playing of British orchestras of the time, in which audible sliding was simply a habit, and largely unco-ordinated. At bar 23, Mengelberg uses an effect which is rarely heard in orchestral playing: at the repeated Cs, the first violins play the first C on the A string, and the second C on the D string, sliding up to it, producing a sort of expressive 'gulp'. The Smithsonian Chamber Players faithfully reproduce this fingering, as well as most, but not all, of the Concertgebouw's other portamenti, in their Mengelberg-inspired recording. They play 19 portamenti in the first section of the movement, compared with the Concertgebouw's 30.

Ex.5.1 Mahler, Symphony No. 5, fourth movement 'Adagietto'. Portamenti played by Concertgebouw Orchestra, conducted by Mengelberg (violin 1 and cello).

a) bars 1–16

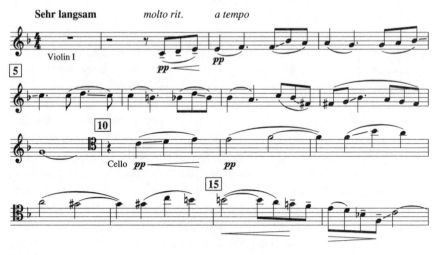

b) bars 23–24

To suggest that Mengelberg's performance is closer to what Mahler wanted than Walter's, as Slowik does by implication, is to take an enormous leap of the imagination. Did Mengelberg prepare the orchestra to play Mahler's lines in this way for the composer's performances in the early years of the century? Or was this a particular expressive style that he cultivated for his own performances, and perhaps developed over later years? If the contrast between the string-playing in Vienna and Amsterdam was as startling when Mahler visited as it was in the late 1920s and 1930s, would we not expect Mahler to have commented on it? Could he have preferred such a style in Amsterdam without having said so? Mahler's letters to Alma certainly praise Mengelberg and his orchestra frequently, from the time of his first visit to Amsterdam in 1903. In October 1904, rehearsing for the double performance of the Fourth Symphony, he wrote, 'I rehearsed the Fourth today and the orchestra plays it so cleanly that I'm enchanted.'[41] And two years later, 'The orchestra *splendidly rehearsed in advance* and a performance equal to any in Vienna.'[42] In 1907 he was unable to come to Amsterdam, and suggested that Mengelberg should perform his Sixth Symphony without him. And in 1909 he wrote to Alma, about plans to perform the Eighth Symphony in Amsterdam: 'The conditions would in any case be perfect in so far as I should have a well-trained chorus and orchestra, rehearsed as only he [Mengelberg] can, at my unrestricted disposal.'[43] Nowhere does Mahler write that he prefers the *style* of the Concertgebouw to that of the Vienna Philharmonic. His emphasis is always on the care of preparation, the attention to detail, and the availability of as much rehearsal time as he needs, conditions which delighted him after the struggle he had to achieve high standards in Vienna. In this he is echoing Brahms's praise of Hans von Bülow and his exceptionally rehearsed Meiningen Orchestra, which has similarly been elevated into more than it probably meant.

The idea that Mengelberg might have been Mahler's ideal interpreter is put firmly in its place when the composer writes to Alma about his dislike of travelling abroad, after that double performance of the Fourth Symphony: 'The only moments of such a journey when I feel really comfortable are the rehearsals. If only I had reached the stage at which conductors understood the style of my works! I could go for a stroll through Heiligenstadt instead.'[44] Clearly, even Mengelberg could not wholly be trusted by the highly demanding Mahler.

Mengelberg and Walter both claimed unique 'authority' in their performances of Mahler, and their approaches were very different. In the case of the Fourth Symphony, there survive not only recordings conducted by Mengelberg and Walter, but also Mahler's own piano-roll recording of the finale, and the copy of the score sent to Mengelberg by Mahler, to which Mengelberg added notes of his own during Mahler's rehearsals. The first page of this score has been repro-duced from time to time.[45] It is covered with annotations by Mahler and Mengelberg, including one referring to the end of the third bar which states that Mahler said at the rehearsal, 'Please play the rall. as though we are beginning a Viennese waltz in Vienna'. For the tempo at bar 4, there are two different pencilled metronome indications, $\downarrow$ = 69 and $\downarrow$ = 76–80. Neither of these bears any relation to Mengelberg's tempo in his 1939 concert, in which his tempo is a very fast $\downarrow$ = 112. This is after an extremely drawn-out rallentando which seems quite grotesque (and far more exaggerated than in any recording of the Vienna Philharmonic beginning a waltz). Walter, both in a 1946 studio recording and in a 1955 live recording from Vienna, has a much less exaggerated rallentando, and then settles to a tempo of $\downarrow$ = 84 (close to one of the rival markings in Mengelberg's copy of the score). This is much nearer to most conductors' way of starting the movement, and seems less contrived than Mengelberg's. But is there any way of knowing who is closer to Mahler's own approach?

Fascinating though comparison between these different views is, the lesson that emerges is a simple and unhelpful one, perhaps best expressed by Mahler himself in answer to Walter's observation that some passages in the symphonic repertoire 'can only be thus and not otherwise'. Mahler advised him, 'The only right way is to see everything afresh and create it anew.'[46]

Fauré, Ravel, Debussy

These three composers can conveniently be considered together, because a number of important performers worked with all three of them. Their own performances on record are rather limited.

Debussy was, according to Marguerite Long, 'an incomparable pianist. How could one forget his suppleness, the caress of his touch. While floating over the keys with a curiously penetrating gentleness, he could achieve an extraordinary power of expression.'[47] Fauré and Ravel were not notable performers themselves, though they did give public performances of their own piano music. Fauré's playing was 'characterised by precise accentuation, strength, and delicious tenderness, all qualities required for the performance of his music. He had an altogether personal way of striking the keys, heavy and supple at the same time. His rather heavy hands produced a beautiful sound, a kind of round sound that I associate with the "Fauré style of playing".'[48] Ravel played in public, but was not considered to be remarkable either as pianist or as conductor. Emile Vuillermoz stated baldly, 'M. Ravel is continually brought out as a pianist or as a conductor, whilst he cannot possibly shine in either of these two specialities.'[49] Ravel was aware of his own limitations as a pianist. In 1923 he wrote to the Belgian violinist Désiré Defauw, who was organising a concert of Ravel's music. He suggested that his Piano Trio should be included, but 'without the participation of the composer, who will be absolutely incapable of playing the piano part', though he did offer to accompany a singer and to play some solo pieces. On the other hand, a number of writers stated that his limited technique conveyed musical power: 'His performance in the Violin and Piano Sonata, and his accompaniment to the songs, were vitally rhythmical and extremely authoritative in style, which is not always the case with composers. Even if not invariably accurate, it did not seem to matter . . . .'[50] '. . . he accompanied his Violin Sonata and from the musical point of view he was fantastic. He made lots of mistakes – that was because he didn't practise enough. But he gave a very good idea of what he meant. I prefer Ravel with mistakes to anyone else without them.'[51]

Unfortunately, it is impossible to gauge the accuracy of these judgements from the recordings that the three composers made. Debussy was recorded in 1904 accompanying Mary Garden in extracts from *Pelléas*, and three of the *Ariettes oubliées*. The *Pelléas* extracts have such spare accompaniment that little can be deduced about Debussy's style of playing. His playing in the *Ariettes oubliées* shows fluency and, perhaps, delicacy. But the recording is too primitive to convey any real impression of tone-colour, textures or 'the caress of his touch'. There are piano rolls of all three composers, which contain some useful information about tempi and rhythm (notably an unmarked tempo-change in Debussy's performance of 'La Cathédrale engloutie' which has only recently been accepted by editors). But in music which requires such sensitivity, the limitations of the recording and replaying mechanism are more obvious than with other music. Even the most sophisticated of player-pianos did not record the precise volume of each note, and so the 'loose' rhythmic style of the time, with its arpeggiations, unequal pairing of notes, and dislocation of melodies from their accompaniment, often sounds clumsy or incomprehensible, to an extent that sound recordings rarely do. Fauré, Debussy and Ravel all show this rhythmic looseness in their piano rolls, without the finesse in the reproducing mechanism to make it sound coherent.

Listening to Fauré play his Barcarolle No. 1 in A minor Opus 26, we can hear that the melody, in the middle of the texture, has an independent life of its own.[52] Often it does not quite coincide with the accompaniment above and below, which contains many rhythmic nuances and agogic accents. But we are left to imagine the tonal and dynamic relationship between melody and accompaniment which would have made it work: the piano roll reproduces the timing of the notes, but clearly does not have the sensitivity to layer the dynamics as Fauré presumably intended. The resulting texture is thick and confusing. Debussy plays the opening of 'Soirée dans Grenade' with a similar rhythmic separation of melody and accompaniment.[53] But some of the rhythms sound tentative and misplaced, because they do not make sense without their accurate dynamic relationship. The same applies to the rhythmic irregularities in Debussy's performance of 'Dr Gradus ad Parnassum' from *Children's Corner*,[54] and in Ravel's rolls of the Sonatine (movements 1 and 2) and other pieces.[55]

The most important recordings which give some idea of what these composers wanted are those made by musicians who worked with them, and of whom they approved. For Debussy and Ravel, by far the most important pianist was Ricardo Viñes (1875–1943), who premièred much of their solo music, and to whom both composers dedicated works: Ravel's *Menuet antique* and 'Oiseaux tristes', Debussy's 'Poissons d'or', as well as Falla's *Nights in the Gardens of Spain*. He premièred, among other works, Ravel's *Jeux d'eau* (1902), *Miroirs* (1905) and *Gaspard de la nuit* (1909), Debussy's *Estampes* (1903), *L'Isle joyeuse* (1904), *Images* (both sets, 1905 and 1908) and several *Préludes* (1910–13), and Fauré's eight *Pièces brèves* (1902). He had been a friend of Ravel since teenage years, when they would spend days together at the piano, and they were fellow students at the Paris Conservatoire.

Viñes did not always accept Ravel's views on interpretation. He disagreed with him about the second movement of *Gaspard*, 'Le Gibet'. Ravel complained, 'He said that if he observed the nuances and tempos that I wanted, *Le Gibet* would bore the public. He was never prepared to change his mind about it.' This is similar to the famous row between Ravel and Toscanini about *Boléro*, which Toscanini refused to take as slowly as Ravel wanted (Ravel's own recording is indeed unusually slow). But Viñes was acknowledged by composers and fellow musicians as the master performer of the new French music. Poulenc was taught the piano by him, and remembered: 'He was some kind of a strange hidalgo with an enormous moustache, a brown sombrero in true Barcelona style and button boots with which he used to kick me on the shins whenever I was clumsy at the pedals.' It was subtlety of pedalling that Poulenc most admired in Viñes: 'No one could teach the art of using the pedals, an essential feature of modern piano music, better than Viñes . . . . [He] somehow managed to extract clarity from the very ambiguities created by the pedals.'[56]

Subtlety is a quality which comes across from Viñes's recordings, subtlety not only of pedalling, but also of the layering of dynamics, and the placing of rhythms, in order to clarify textures. In Debussy's 'Soirée dans Grenade' (1930), he sets up the habanera rhythm at the opening with a slightly overdotted rhythm. The melody below it is played with delicate rhythmic freedom, so that it seems quite independent of the habanera rhythm. Comparing this with Debussy's own piano roll of the same piece, it is tempting to think that Debussy's rhythmic freedom would have sounded similarly subtle if accurately reproduced. In 'Poissons d'or' (1930), which Debussy dedicated to him, Viñes's playing is full of nervous energy, with lightly flicked upbeat demisemiquavers (thirty-second notes) at the opening, and a powerful climax.

Marguerite Long (1874–1966) was the most energetic champion of Fauré's piano music. For a period of ten years she worked with him and gave numerous premières. Fauré became a friend of Long and her husband (the writer Joseph de Marliave). Long regarded herself as an authority on the interpretation of Fauré, Debussy and Ravel, and wrote somewhat arrogantly about her relationship with each of them. About Fauré she wrote, 'I worked with him from 1902–1912, and during those years the validity of the interpretation of so many of his works firmly established itself with us. It is this that I pass on today, because its validity has been testified by Fauré himself. He would often say to me after one of our working sessions that he had "just made a discovery about his music", and I knew that after this he would require from others playing his music just what we had realised together.'[57]

Of course this does not necessarily mean that Fauré regarded Long as the supreme interpreter of his music. Indeed, it is quite clear that his attitude to her was ambivalent. On the one hand he greatly valued her work on his behalf, on the other hand Fauré's treatment of her at the Paris Conservatoire, where he was Director, indicates that he did not think of her as the finest of French pianists. Long was appointed as a professor in the Classe Préparatoire at the Conservatoire in 1906. But she was twice refused promotion to the Classe Supérieure when vacancies came up in 1907 and 1913, and was finally promoted only in 1920. On the first of these occasions, Cortot was appointed instead of Long, and Fauré wrote to his wife, 'there will be much, much opposition when it ought to go through of its own accord, since Cortot is infinitely superior to other possible candidates, whom I know only too well, alas!'[58]

When Cortot was appointed, Fauré's letter of explanation to Long was firm and unapologetic: 'You know how interested I am in your career, you know how I wish to provide you with opportunities that highlight your talent, but you also know – and I believe my life as an artist is a good example – how I prefer things to happen in due time.'[59] According to Long, Fauré promised her the next vacancy, but when it occurred in 1913, she was refused again, and her relationship with Fauré declined: 'For my part, I got used to (not without difficulty) separating my admiration from my resentment . . . . Between Fauré and us, never a word of explanation came. From one day to the next, he ceased to come and sit at our dinner table, where his place was always set.'[60]

But just as it is a mistake to take composers' praise for musicians who perform their works at face value, so it would be a mistake to deduce from this that Fauré did not appreciate Long's playing. He sometimes praised it highly. After a concert in 1904 he wrote, 'Let me . . . thank you for having played my piece with the most ideal perfection.'[61] Even so, there can be no doubt that he considered Cortot by far the finer musician (and not just as a pianist), though Long was the more faithful champion of his music.

Long's recordings of Fauré are characterised by clarity and energy. She begins the Impromptu No. 2 in F minor (1933) at $\downarrow$. = 90, very fast compared with the printed 69. According to Long, Fauré often said to her, 'It always gives me great pleasure to hear myself played with verve. On the pretext of getting involved in the work, people always play me as if the blinds were down, just the way they think you have no need for a voice to sing my songs.'[62] Whether or not that quote is to be trusted, perhaps Fauré would have enjoyed this performance. There is, however, a question mark over the bars which end the first section of the Impromptu (bars 65–70, later repeated). The score is clearly marked 'sans presser' at this point. Long writes, 'To lead in the end of the first episode – and its repeats – the movement should be lively so that the passage runs swiftly and lightly. Fauré agreed entirely that one should ignore the marking "do not hurry" which the printed score nevertheless bears.'[63]

It is impossible to know whether Fauré really said this, or whether Long was simply justifying her own practice. Perhaps Fauré liked what she did, but would not necessarily have approved of anyone else doing it. The effect is certainly charmingly reckless, exaggerating the sudden change of pace already created by the switch from $\frac{6}{8}$ to $\frac{2}{4}$, though it is not at all what a pianist of the twenty-first century would do. Kathryn Stott, for example (1994), scrupulously observes the instruction 'sans presser', even though she already plays the first section of the Impromptu with greater firmness and less dash than Long. This has more to do with rhythmic control than the basic tempo, which is very similar to Long's.[64]

Even more unfashionable today is the rhythmic 'swing' with which Long plays the left hand of Fauré's Nocturne No. 4 in E flat (1937), hurrying to the second quaver (eighth note) of each group. This creates an effect almost like that of the traditional Viennese waltz rhythm. In her book on Fauré, she writes at some length about the interpretation of this Nocturne, but she makes no mention of this rhythmic nuance. Once again we are left wondering whether or not Fauré would have approved of it in principle, or only as an exception for Marguerite Long, or not at all. Not surprisingly, there is no trace of this rhythmic adjustment in the performance by Kathryn Stott (1994), who plays the Nocturne with even quavers (though with modern long-term flexibility across whole phrases) and much more slowly than Long: $\downarrow$ = 50 compared with Long's 80. This is much closer than Long to the printed metronome marking of 56. Long's recording, at 4 mins 29 secs, does fill one side of a 78 rpm record, which raises the suspicion that she might have taken it a little more slowly if the space had been available. This is reinforced by the suggestion in her book that the Nocturne should be taken at $\downarrow$ = 66 – much slower than her recorded performance, though still faster than the marking in the score. Nevertheless, the rhythmic irregularity of Long's interpretation is clear and unambiguous.

It is in lyrical music, such as this Nocturne, that it is easiest to guess at Fauré's reservations about Long's musicianship compared with that of Cortot. Cortot at his best achieves a subtlety of balance, a fluidity of rhythm, and a singing tone, which make Long's playing sound dry and matter-of-fact, charming though it can be. Cortot's recording of Fauré's First Violin Sonata, with Jacques Thibaud (1927), is a good example. At the very opening Cortot achieves a wonderful balance between the singing line in the treble, the light, rippling quavers in the middle of the texture, and the clear bass line which is firm but not at all heavy. Because of the delicacy of the accompanying layers, the melody sings out without having to be pushed, and it continues to do so in counterpoint with the violin when it enters. Cortot's shaping of each phrase is beautifully rounded, but he does not lose sight of the longer line: despite each wave of the melody, the entire passage from the beginning until the violin entry is perceived as a single span.

Ravel's opinion of Marguerite Long's playing seems to have been less equivocal than Fauré's. After the première of the G major Concerto, which he wrote for her, most critics were full of praise for Long's playing. Henry Prunières, however, wrote that her interpretation was technically correct but lacked sensitivity and poetry. Ravel published a reply, in which he insisted that her interpretation fully revealed his intentions and should be considered a model for future performers.[65] Ravel himself conducted the première, and then toured Europe with Long, introducing the concerto in twenty cities.

Something of what Ravel appreciated in Long's playing can perhaps be deduced from his reported remarks about her performance of *Le Tombeau de*

Couperin. It was the first of his works with which she was publicly associated, and she gave the première in 1919. Long played the Prélude very fast, and she later reported that 'When a pianist came to Ravel to play the prelude he received this advice: "Not so quick as Marguerite Long." "Why do you always say that?" I asked him one day. "Either my tempo is wrong, or you underestimate the ability of your interpreters." He replied: "Because so far as you are concerned one is sure to hear all the notes." Poor dear Ravel. Is one ever sure?'[66] If this is accurate, perhaps, as in Fauré's Impromptu in F minor, the composer liked what Long did even though it was not what he had originally intended.

Long recorded the G major Concerto in April 1932, three months after the première. The labels of the published recording claimed that it was conducted by Ravel, and this has been repeated on later reissues.[67] But it later emerged that it had actually been conducted by the Portuguese Pedro de Freitas-Branco, who had shared with Ravel the programme at which the concerto had been premièred. Ravel supervised the recording from the control room, insisting on retakes late into the night. 'I could have killed him, but I did it all the same', Long was reported as saying.[68]

Presumably, therefore, the result was in the end more or less what Ravel wanted. The performance has the same nervous and hasty struggling for co-ordination as in Stravinsky's Paris recordings of this period (and the anonymous 'Orchestra Symphonique' probably contained many of the same musicians as the Straram Orchestra). The rhythmic details in the orchestra are often chaotic by modern standards, and the tempi of all three movements are very fast. The first movement, marked $\downarrow$ = 116 in the published score, begins at about $\downarrow$ = 128. Rhythmic detail in the orchestra is often rushed, particularly pairs of quavers (eighth notes) in the opening theme, and co-ordination with the piano is uncertain. But Long's own playing in the outer movements is characterised by dash and clarity, reminding one of Ravel's reported comment on her playing of the Prélude of *Le Tombeau de Couperin*.

Comparison with any modern recording of the concerto highlights both the nervous energy and the uncontrolled orchestral detail of Long's recording. Jean-Yves Thibaudet and the Orchestre Symphonique de Montréal under Charles Dutoit (1995) set off at $\downarrow$ = 120, very close to the printed tempo marking. Many details in the orchestra are more audible because of the modern recording, but the greatest difference is in rhythmic control, achieved not only by the slightly slower tempo but also by the careful placing of detail. The co-ordination is firm and controlled, whereas in Long's recording the quavers hurry, particularly in the violins, and render the rhythm unstable.

Marguerite Long quotes Ravel as saying, 'I do not ask for my music to be interpreted, but only for it to be played.'[69] This is very like Stravinsky's attack on interpreters, and it throws up similar questions. Would Ravel have preferred the more exact performances of his music which have now become

commonplace to the vaguer approximation of the recording which he supervised? He would certainly have been astonished by the precision of the
Montréal orchestra, which he could not have heard from any French orchestra
of his day. But would he have liked the sense of complete safety? Or would he
have found it cold and dull? The level of instability in the 1932 recording can
hardly have concerned Ravel very deeply at the time of the recording,
otherwise he would presumably have insisted on a slightly slower tempo for
the sake of firmer control. It would have been quite possible to break the sides
at an earlier point in the score in order to allow for this (the first movement in
Long's recording lasts 7 mins 22 secs, with the side-change coming at 4 mins
20 secs, so there is no question of the movement being hurried in order to fit
on the two sides). But there is no way of knowing what Ravel would have
thought of modern clarity and precision. All we do know is that he was
satisfied with a performance which now seems scrappy. The slow movement,
similarly, is at a faster tempo than the printed metronome marking: $\flat$ = 82,
compared with 76 in the score. Again, the movement could have been broken
earlier if Ravel had wanted a slower tempo: the first side lasts 4 mins 36 secs,
the second side 4 mins 4 secs.

Cortot was also an important player of Ravel's music, and his recordings
include *Jeux d'eau*, *Ondine*, the Sonatine, and the Concerto for Left Hand. He
gave the première of the Violin Sonata with Georges Enesco in 1927, and
conducted the première of *Shéhérazade* in 1904. Cortot's famous piano trio with
Thibaud and Casals was well known to Ravel, and his high regard for them is
indicated by a letter of June 1921. He writes to Cortot, 'Jacques Thibaud should
have come to take me last Tuesday to the Conservatoire to hear you rehearse
my trio. I waited for him in vain. But I am not worried [*je suis tranquille*]. I hope
to be able to come and hear you on the 30th [that is, at the concert].'[70] Given
Ravel's reputation for exactness, he would hardly have been 'tranquille' if he
had had any doubts about the trio's playing. But it is impossible to know what
he thought of the comparison between Cortot and Long.

What is clear from recordings is that Cortot brings a particular singing quality
to Ravel, as he does to Fauré, which is quite different from Long's playing. This
is striking if one compares Cortot's 1939 recording of Ravel's Concerto for the
Left Hand with Long's 1932 recording of the G major Concerto. Cortot's lines
sing out, whereas Long's slow movement hums to itself.

Ravel was very particular about how his works should be performed, as
several musicians reported. The violinist André Mangeot, who had known
Ravel since 1913, made the first recording of Ravel's String Quartet in 1927,
and wrote an article about it in the *Gramophone*. He led the International
Quartet, whose other members were British, and they had made several attempts
at recording the quartet. Mangeot had not been satisfied with the results.
'Luckily for me Ravel himself came to London just then . . . . He consented to

hear the records we had made, and he heard them in a little cubicle at the Aeolian Hall, which was soon thick with cigarette smoke. I had the score with me, and as the records were played he marked it wherever there was an effect or a tempo that he wanted altered. It was very interesting. He is most precise – he knows exactly what he wants – how, in his mind, that quartet, every bar of it ought to sound. So, armed with such authority, we had another recording at the studio and my colleagues and I rehearsed hard for it over those little details.'

Mangeot then visited Ravel in Paris with the new recording: 'He was much pleased with the records, which we listened to from the terrace . . . . The old cook gave us a very simple and perfect dinner (Ravel is a firm bachelor), and we left him at 10.30 after a delightful visit, and afterwards he wrote the charming letter of appreciation which allows us to call our records of the Quartet an "interpretation of the composer". Not only do I regard this as one of the finest compliments ever paid to our quartet, but, as Ravel said to me, "It will constitute a real document for posterity to consult, and through gramophone records composers can now say definitely how they meant the works to be performed."'[71] Ravel wrote a testimonial for publication: 'I have just heard the discs of my Quartet recorded by the International Quartet. I am completely satisfied as much with the sonority as with the tempi and the nuances.'

One might think, therefore, that the International Quartet's recording should provide the definitive interpretation of Ravel's Quartet, to which all later performers could refer. But Ravel also supervised a second recording, by the young Galimir Quartet of Vienna (Felix Galimir and his three sisters). This took place in 1934, and it is quite different from the earlier recording, both in playing style and in interpretation. The International Quartet has, like much British playing of the period, frequent and leisurely portamenti. The Galimir Quartet is more sparing in portamento, and the slides which it does use are faster and more discreet. It also has a more modern approach to vibrato and bowing: the vibrato is more constant, the bowing more assertive (Galimir was a pupil of Carl Flesch). And, apart from these basic stylistic differences, the Galimir Quartet's performance is generally faster than the International Quartet's. This is most noticeable in the first movement: the International Quartet takes 7 mins 28 secs, the Galimir Quartet takes 6 mins 33 secs.

Evaluating these differences is not straightforward. Ravel approved the International Quartet's performance, but was not present at the recording. He was present at the Galimir Quartet's recording, but there are contradictory reports about his alertness during the session. He was already suffering from a brain condition which impaired his memory and co-ordination. According to one witness he said almost nothing, but according to Galimir himself he did comment on their performance, judging each side as it was finished, and they recorded several retakes.[72] Galimir recorded the work again in 1982 when he was in America, and his tempi are more leisurely. He was, however, in his seventies by this time (he was only twenty-four at the time of his first recording).

Ravel, like Stravinsky, was renowned for his exact requirements of performers, and his annoyance when his instructions were ignored. But, again like Stravinsky, Ravel nevertheless accepted strikingly different styles of playing in his music. This is vividly illustrated by the flautists who worked with Ravel. Ravel himself conducted the first recording of his Introduction and Allegro in 1923, as already discussed in chapter 4. This is by a group of British players, including the flautist Robert Murchie and the clarinettist Haydn Draper. Murchie, who played on a wooden flute in the traditional English style, has hardly a trace of vibrato. The duet of flute and clarinet which opens the piece is played with organ-like steadiness, and even the melodic solos later are played entirely 'straight'. This is very different from the style of flute-playing Ravel was accustomed to in France, where the school founded by Paul Taffanel was dominant with its metal flutes, bright tone, and highly expressive use of vibrato. One of the leaders of this school, Marcel Moyse, often played this work under Ravel, and recorded it with the Calvet Quartet in 1938. The difference compared with Murchie has already been described. Moyse's vibrato is very flexible and subtle. At the beginning, in duet with the clarinet, it is barely noticeable. But as the flute-line expands later on, the vibrato, and the brightness of Moyse's tone, bring an expressive warmth which is quite absent from Murchie's playing.

The Introduction and Allegro was premièred in Paris in 1907 with Taffanel's pupil Philippe Gaubert as flautist. Gaubert's recordings show that he already played with the now-familiar French brightness of tone, and with a fairly fast, light vibrato. Ravel presumably had the sound of French players in mind when he wrote the work. But he seems to have had no difficulty in accepting quite different styles of flute-playing, just as Stravinsky did.

Rachmaninoff, Bartók and Schoenberg

Rachmaninoff's characteristic tenuti have already been mentioned in chapter 4. He plays the opening of the slow movement of Grieg's Violin Sonata in C minor with many pairs of quavers (eighth notes) played unequally, like *notes inégales* in French Baroque style. He often applies this nuance to his own music, together with a repertoire of arpeggiation and dislocation of rhythm. His rubato consists of subtle adjustment of rhythmic detail, rather than the languishing mini-rallentando that tends to characterise the rubato of later pianists in Romantic music. As a result, his rubato does not hold up the flow. The way he plays the principal theme of the slow movement of his Second Piano Concerto (1929), or the famous melody that forms Variation 18 of the Variations on a

Theme of Paganini (1934), makes a striking comparison with later pianists. Modern pianists have tended to make more of a meal of such moments. Vladimir Ashkenazy, for instance (c.1987), plays Variation 18 much more slowly than Rachmaninoff (there is no metronome marking). His rhythm is more even, but he draws out the upbeat group that starts each phrase of the melody. Rachmaninoff, by contrast, keeps the music moving all the time. Instead of stretching out the whole of the first upbeat group, he plays it irregularly, with tenuti on the first three semiquavers (sixteenth notes), then a shortened final semiquaver which gives an impulse onto the first beat of the next bar. He does the same with the upbeats over the next three bars, in subtly varying ways. Rachmaninoff also arpeggiates chords, and, at the seventh bar of the theme, brings out an internal melodic counterpoint by playing notes early. Ashkenazy does none of this, and there is no indication in the score that he should. But it gives Rachmaninoff's playing a unique 'speaking' quality.

In faster music Rachmaninoff's playing has great verve and brilliance, but without the massive weight of many later pianists. His tempi are often very fast, and the rhythms light and snappy – for example in his Prelude in G minor (1920), in which the pairs of semiquavers are played fast. Often his fastest tempi are faster than his printed metronome markings, even when there is plenty of room left on the 78 rpm side. In the outer movements of his Piano Concerto No. 2 Rachmaninoff, with few exceptions, plays the fastest sections more quickly than marked, sometimes dramatically so. Few modern pianists attempt the combination of energy, lightness and detailed flexibility shown in Rachmaninoff's own recordings (though a performance of the Rhapsody by Stephen Hough at the 2002 Promenade Concerts in London came remarkably close to the spirit of Rachmaninoff's recorded performance).

Bartók's piano-playing also has characteristics that could not be deduced from his scores, and that are unlike modern performances of his works. He was taught by a pupil of Liszt, and his playing sounds surprisingly 'Romantic' in its freedoms. In a concert recording of Beethoven's 'Kreutzer' Sonata with Szigeti (1940) chords are arpeggiated to a startling extent. The first chord of the piano entry is virtually the only chord in the whole of the slow introduction in which Bartók plays all the notes together. Here, and in the theme of the slow movement, almost every chord is slightly arpeggiated, with the bass note leading.

In fast music, Bartók is vigorous and dashing, like Rachmaninoff, but he often plays groups of semiquavers more impressionistically than modern demands for clarity allow. This is striking enough in Scarlatti (the Sonata in G Kk427, 1929), but more so in his own music, which is now generally played very incisively. In the *Allegro barbaro* (1929) semiquavers vary in speed considerably, tending to be played fast where they end a phrase, and accelerating where they are continuous. This, as in many of his other recordings, suggests the swirl and fluidity of dance much more vividly than the more controlled clarity of modern performance.

It would be difficult to deduce Bartók's manner of playing from contemporary reports. Klemperer comes nearest to describing what is recognisable from the recordings: 'The beauty of his tone, the energy and lightness of his playing were unforgettable. It was almost painfully beautiful. He played with great freedom, that was what was so wonderful.'[73] On the other hand, when Bartók played in London in 1922 Percy Scholes reported 'a hard, cold rattle of a keyboard, violently attacked in chance combinations of keys and notes, with the stiffened metal muscle of a jerkily rhythmic automaton'.[74] Bartók's recordings sound anything but hard and mechanical, and it is now difficult to imagine what Scholes was hearing.

Some recent players, notably András Schiff, have expressed admiration for Bartók's recorded performances of his own works. But the general approach to Bartók's music has, from the second half of the twentieth century onwards, been very different from the composer's own. Modern pianists play his music with a more percussive edge, and treat his rhythms and tempos more strictly, than Bartók did himself. The result is usually much more mechanistic, and less dance-like, than Bartók's own playing. And his freedom with arpeggiation is (not surprisingly) never emulated by modern pianists, any more than Rachmaninoff's is. Bartók himself did one thing to encourage a literal-minded approach to his music, which was to publish not only metronome markings but also precise timings of each of his movements, as if he insisted on exact adherence to his instructions. But, according to Joseph Szigeti, this is not what Bartók meant. Szigeti was struck by the difference between Bartók and Alban Berg in this respect. Berg gives as the duration of his Violin Concerto '25–30 minutes', whereas Bartók specifies the duration of each piece to the precise second. Szigeti asked Bartók for the reason, and Bartók replied, 'It isn't as if I said: "this *must* take six minutes, twenty-two seconds" . . . but I simply go on record that when *I* play it the duration is six minutes, twenty-two seconds.'[75] But even this is not quite the whole truth, as his recordings show. Bartók did not stick rigidly to his published tempi, but sometimes played faster and sometimes slower than his instructions suggest. Paul Griffiths has demonstrated the complexity of this issue in fifteen of the pieces from *Mikrokosmos* that Bartók recorded. He compares Bartók's printed timing with the duration of his own recording. He also deduces a timing from Bartók's printed metronome marking. In several cases the timing based on the metronome marking is not even the same as the printed duration, and the duration of Bartók's recording often differs significantly from one or both of the printed indications.[76]

Bartók himself writes about the value of recordings in preserving the composer's intentions, but in the next sentence cautions against thinking that the composer has a fixed view: 'It is a well known fact that our notation records the composer's idea on music paper more or less inadequately; hence the existence of contrivances with which one can record precisely the composer's every idea and intention is indeed of great importance. On the other hand, the composer himself, when he is the performer of his own composition, does not always perform his work in exactly the same way. Why? Because he lives; because perpetual variability is a trait of a living creature's character.'[77]

Schoenberg was not a noted performer, and only directed one recording, *Pierrot Lunaire*, led by Rudolf Kolisch (1940). But he made a number of comments on performance and particular performers, expressing strong, but sometimes inconsistent, views. The musicians of whom he approved make for interesting comparisons. In the early years of the twentieth century his chamber works were championed by the Arnold Rosé Quartet, who premièred *Verklärte Nacht* (1903) and the String Quartet No. 2 in F sharp minor (1908). In 1918 Schoenberg founded the Society for Private Music Performances, which was dedicated to the thorough rehearsal of new music (rarely less than ten rehearsals per work).[78] One of those who participated was Schoenberg's pupil Rudolf Kolisch. When Kolisch formed his string quartet in 1922, they memorised their repertoire, which in time included all of Schoenberg's string quartets.

Schoenberg described the Kolisch Quartet as 'the best string quartet I ever heard'. When the Quartet recorded Schoenberg's four string quartets in 1936-7 (a private recording at a Hollywood film studio, later released for sale), Schoenberg recorded some comments, including the following at the end of the first movement of the Second Quartet: 'Although the première of this quartet was exceptionally well presented by Master Rosé and his wonderful string quartet, one knows that perfection cannot be expected at the very first performance. So it was this Second String Quartet about which a gentleman once asked me whether I had heard it already in a perfect manner. I had to answer, "Yes, during the composing." Now, since the Kolisch Quartet exists, and thanks to my friend Alfred Newman, who gave me the opportunity to record these compositions, everybody – and even myself – are in a position to hear it in a perfect manner, in a perfect performance.'[79]

In 1950, when Schoenberg was living in Los Angeles, the Hollywood Quartet, with additional viola and cello, came to play *Verklärte Nacht* to him before making a recording. Schoeberg pronounced their performance very good, and after the recording was made sent them a signed photograph with the inscription, 'To the Hollywood String Quartet for playing my *Verklärte Nacht* with such subtle beauty'.

Schoenberg therefore praised in turn the Rosé, Kolisch and Hollywood Quartets. But recordings make it clear that the Rosé Quartet on the one hand, and the Kolisch and Hollywood Quartets on the other, were on opposite sides of the great divide in string-playing in the early twentieth century. Rosé and his colleagues played in the old manner, with very restrained vibrato, prominent portamento, and the gentler old style of bowing, Kolisch and the Hollywood Quartet in the new style with more or less continuous vibrato, restrained portamento and firmer, more assertive bowing. The Rosé Quartet did not record *Verklärte Nacht*, but from their recordings of Beethoven it is easy to imagine that their première of it would have sounded quite different from the delicately vibrant, highly refined performance of the Hollywood Quartet. Similarly, the Rosé Quartet's première of the Second String Quartet must have been very different from the recording by the Kolisch Quartet. And despite what Schoenberg said, the 'perfect performance' that he imagined when he wrote the score in 1907–8 could not have been like that of the Kolisch Quartet, because such a style of quartet-playing did not yet exist.

Do Schoenberg's other comments shed any light on this conundrum? They seem, on the contrary, to complicate the situation. In an article on 'Vibrato', written in about 1940, he comments on both vibrato and portamento:

> Vibrato has degenerated into a mannerism just as intolerable as portamento-legato. Even though one may at times find the latter unavoidable, and admissible for purposes of lyrical expression, its almost incessant use even for intervals of a second is as reprehensible technically as from the point of view of taste.
>
> But I find even worse the goat-like bleating used by many instrumentalists to curry favour with the public. This bad habit is so general that one could begin to doubt one's own judgement and taste, did one not occasionally have the pleasure, as I did recently, of finding oneself supported by a true artist. I listened on the radio to Pablo Casals playing the Dvořák Cello Concerto. Extremely sparing vibrato, exclusively to give life to long notes, and carried out with moderation, not too quickly, not too slowly, and without detriment to intonation. *Never* that sentimental portamento. Even intervals not easy for the left hand to join smoothly are bridged without adventitious help, simply by the artistry of his bowing. And when the occasional portamento does occur, it is only to lend a lyrical *dolce* passage the tender colouring that expresses the mood of such a passage all the more piercingly.[80]

This article was written when Schoenberg was already living in America. Probably what he is objecting to, therefore, is the exaggeratedly sweet and 'soupy' style to be heard in Hollywood films and other popular American music genres. But his condemnations of both excessive portamento and excessive vibrato are interesting in the context of his acceptance of changing string fashions in the quartets that he worked with.

Schoenberg's other writings about performance are contradictory. On the one hand, in an article written in 1923–4, he allows the importance of the interpreter in bringing a work to life: 'It should not be denied that in making the author's ideas and their flow comprehensible, a good deal can be done through a certain liveliness in rhythm and tempo, a certain emphasis in the delivery of phrases, in contrasting, opposing and juxtaposing them, a certain build-up in tempo and dynamics, a purposeful distribution of *espressivo* and its opposite . . . . But, on the other hand, an outstanding soloist (Kreisler, Casals, Huberman, among others) has a way of working at his part; he tries to make even the tiniest note sound, and to place it in correct relationship to the whole.'[81] On the other hand, Schoenberg writes, in 'About metronome markings' (1926): 'Has not the author at least the right to indicate, in the copies of the work he *himself* publishes, how he imagines his ideas should be realized? . . . Anyone who has learned at his own expense what a conductor of genius is capable of, once he has his own idea of a work, will no longer favour giving him the slightest scrap more freedom. For instance, if such a man has got into his mind a "powerful build-up", which means he has found a place where he can begin too slowly and another where he can finish too fast, then nothing can hinder him any longer in giving rein to his temperament.'[82] But by 1948, Schoenberg is complaining about the present-day rigidity of tempo, attributing it to 'the style of playing primitive dance music'.[83]

The most likely explanation of these apparently condradictory views is that, in each case, Schoenberg was reacting to particular performances that were fresh in his memory at the time he was writing, and that it is useless to try to construct a general principle out of them. His objection to the 'rigidity' of performance that he heard in America made him, perhaps, nostalgic for the sorts of flexibility that were part of the normal language of musical discourse in middle Europe in the 1920s. On the other hand, even in the 1920s, he objected to some of the modern conductors who were more intent on making an impression on the audience than adhering to the composers' instructions – though he does not say whom he had in mind.

The composer's authority and its limits

The opportunity to contrast the comments of great composers of the past with recordings by them or their close associates is valuable, though also frustrating if one is looking for certainty. On the one hand, each of them had an idiosyncratic approach to the performance of their own work, which could not be deduced simply from their scores. On the other hand, all of them in different ways accepted much of the styles and standards of the times and places in which they worked. Recordings prove that this applies even to the acerbic Stravinsky and the meticulous Ravel, with their stated dislike of 'interpretation'. Composers' opinions need to be considered in their context, and cannot be taken at face value. At the same time, composers rarely have fixed ideas of how their music should actually go, even in basic matters of tempo, rhythm or instrumental styles.

It would be a mistake to imagine that such problems and contradictions are restricted to the early twentieth century and the more distant past. More recent composers are just as unlikely to have fixed or consistent views about how their works should be performed. And, like the composers of any period, they are bound to be influenced by the performing world in which they live, and by particular musicians they have heard.

The pianist Peter Hill has described his experience of studying Messiaen's *Vingt regards sur l'enfant Jésus* with the composer.[84] In No. 5 of the set, 'Regard du Fils sur le Fils', there is a passage marked 'un peu plus vif', at which the piano breaks into birdsong. The dynamic marking in the score is *piano*, but Messiaen said that he wanted it quite loud. Peter Hill had thought it should be quiet and distant, like an ecstatic liberation after the intricate canon of the preceding bars. He then turned to the recording by Yvonne Loriod (Messiaen's wife), who had given the première, and found that she played it quite loud. Messiaen had written the *Vingt regards* in 1944, and Loriod had made her recording in 1973. Was this a case, Hill wondered, of a performer corrupting the composer's memory? When he came to make his own recording in 1991, Hill decided to obey the instruction in the score, rather than Messiaen's later preference. This was one of a number of instances when Hill found himself disagreeing with Messiaen, and thinking that the composer had lost sight of what he originally meant.

From such experiences Hill realised the importance of distinguishing between composers' instructions which are universally applicable and instructions which arise as the composer's response to a particular performer's idiosyncratic playing. For this reason he has come to the conclusion that it is bad for him say to a student, 'this is what Messiaen told me to do'. If another player had come to Messiaen and played in a different way, he might have said something different. Hill later amplified this point: 'I think that on the whole Messiaen was remarkable in that he didn't interfere much with what I was doing if it was working, and indeed he appeared to encourage me not to play in the Loriod manner – he could hear when I wasn't being true to my nature. In that sense one could see he was a very skilled teacher. But there were a few instances when after careful thought all my instincts rebelled. Thank heavens my producer, Anthony Pople, said to me "If in doubt do it your way". Excellent advice.'[85]

There are countless examples of composers changing their minds when they hear their works played, or over time, or not remembering what they meant when they wrote the piece. A few years after writing *Ulysses Awakes* for viola and string orchestra, one of his most frequently performed works, John Woolrich admitted, 'When I go to rehearsals now, if they ask me questions I simply can't answer them. If they say, "Should this be faster or slower, louder or softer?" it's gone – completely. And those decisions, which are very important decisions, are probably best answered by a performer now.'[86] For

John McCabe, the response of the performer is crucial. If he, as the composer, attends a rehearsal of one of his works, he regards it as his job to help the musicians achieve their vision of the music in a way that works, not to impose his own interpretation.[87]

Alexander Goehr held a working session with the Florestan Trio in 2002, rehearsing his Piano Trio which he wrote in 1966.[88] It is a work of immense complexity, in which the musicians sometimes have to play in different metres simultaneously. His main concern in these passages was not that they should be absolutely accurate, but that the gestures in each line, which were based on folk-music, should have their independent character. 'Try to play accurately, but don't sacrifice the character. It doesn't matter if it comes apart a bit.' It was important 'not to count too much'.

There was one point where Goehr had forgotten what he originally meant. The opening of the movement is repeated, with the instruction that it should be played *piano* the first time and *fortissimo* the second time. But then there is a *Da Capo* with no repeats, and the score does not say whether it should be *p* or *ff*. Which should they play? Goehr admitted, 'I don't remember what I intended. You could play either.' Then, after a pause looking at the score, 'probably *fortissimo*'.

There was another point about which he had changed his mind. In the 1960s, when he wrote the Trio, he liked long glissandi. But they had now become something of a cliché in modern music, and he was tired of them. The way the cellist, Richard Lester, was playing the glissandi in the second movement was the way Goehr thought of them when he wrote the piece; but he now preferred them to be played faster. As for tempi, Goehr said that, generally, if the tempo is right the detail will come out right. Most wrong performances come about because the tempo is wrong – and this applies not just in contemporary music but in earlier repertoire. When it came to the second movement, which has an extremely slow metronome marking ($\flat$= 46), Goehr said at first that he thought the Florestan Trio played it too fast. But later he said that he meant it sounded too fast 'in character, but not necessarily in tempo', adding that a performance which seems slower in character can actually be faster in tempo than a performance that seems faster.

Goehr admitted that he did not have a fixed view of how his music should be played: 'Some composers, such as Kurtág, think there is only one ideal performance which must be imposed on performers. I don't think like that. Every performance is different, and I am willing to learn from that. What seems right to me is usually the last performance I remember.' Goehr remembers that Ligeti was delighted when a work of his was played exactly as he wanted it. But then he heard the same performers later when their performance had evolved, and he was furious that they were no longer playing it as he had instructed.

A number of points emerge from this session. The first is that, even in the work of a composer who notates things very precisely, the relationship between notation and performance is not straightforward. The *character* of a tempo is more important than the actual metronomic tempo. Rhythmic characterisation is more important than strict accuracy. The composer's own views change over time, and he cannot always remember what he intended. He has precise ideas about many performance matters, but he learns from performers, and is influenced by them.

Not all composers are like this, but most are to a greater or lesser extent, and recordings make it clear what kinds of flexibility composers have had since the early twentieth century. In recent decades, the relationship between composers and recordings has varied greatly. In some cases the traditional relationship between composer and performer ceases to exist, and this in turn changes the nature of any authority residing in a recording. At one extreme, development of computer technology has enabled composers, of whom Babbitt and Stockhausen were early examples, to create works in which there is little or no intervention of a performer. In such cases often the work *is* the recording. At the opposite extreme, some composers, such as John Cage, developed the use of chance elements to such an extent that the concept of a 'work' which was to be 'performed' ceased to be meaningful. A performance was simply an event in which the composer had set up certain conditions in which anything was allowed to happen. In such cases a recording is (even more than in conventional music) nothing more than a record of what happened to take place on a particular occasion.

In jazz and other popular music forms, the relationship between composer and performer tends to be looser than in most forms of classical music, so questions of authority or authenticity rarely arise in quite the same way. The element of spontaneity in jazz performance is so strong that there has always been considerable resistance to the idea of repeating what has already been done. The point of performing a jazz 'standard' is to do something different with it (though there have also been some attempts at reconstructions of historical jazz styles). The composer's authority is a side-issue, or not an issue at all. This is a subject for other books and other writers. But one of the points that recordings make is that performance of classical music used to have rather more of the free elements of jazz performance. In the twenty-first century, the freedoms of jazz and the strictness of classical performance are poles apart. In the early twentieth century some of the freedoms we now associate with jazz were still allowed in classical music. The old rubato in which the melody frees itself from the accompaniment – a practice for which there is evidence as far back as the seventeenth century – is the essence of jazz performance but is now frowned upon in performance of classical music. Indeed, it is possible that its adoption and exaggeration in jazz and other popular genres is one of the reasons that classical performers began to adopt a more literal interpretation of the composer's notation. In the days when such freedom was usual in classical performance, there was a greater rhythmic freedom in the interpretation of what the composer had written than there is today.

The freedoms exercised by composers in their own works, and allowed by them in other musicians' performances, have a particular fascination for a later generation. If it were not for recordings, we would have no idea how Elgar, Rachmaninoff, Bartók, Stravinsky, Poulenc and others performed their own music. We would be left with reminiscence, as we are (apart from an almost incomprehensible cylinder) with Brahms. There are plenty of descriptions of Brahms's playing and conducting, from which we gain a vivid impression that his performances were forthright, free and highly expressive. But the most telling comments are those which suggest that his own way of doing things was highly personal, and could not be imitated: 'Brahms' interpretation of his works frequently differs so inconceivably in delicate rhythmic and harmonic accents from anything to which one is accustomed, that the apprehension of his intentions could only be entirely possible to another man possessed of exactly similar sound-susceptibility or inspired by the power of divination.'[89]

Similar things were said of Elgar, and in his case recordings allow us to hear what was meant, many years later. The question is, what do we learn from him about how to play his music? What sort of freedom is involved, and should we try to reproduce it? Why is it not in the notation? Elgar himself was reported to have expressed frustration that his very detailed performance instructions still led many musicians to perform his music quite differently from how he intended: 'Beethoven and Brahms ... wrote practically nothing but allegro and andante, and there seems to be no difficulty. I've done everything I can to help musicians, but my efforts appear only to confuse them.'[90]

But if there is 'no difficulty' establishing how to perform Beethoven and Brahms (a debatable point in itself), perhaps this is precisely because we do not know quite how they performed themselves. Like Elgar, they must certainly have had their own inimitable ways of performing. If we had recordings of them, we would know the intimate details of how they played and conducted. Would this make life simpler or more complicated for the modern performer? We only have to listen to the recordings of the early twentieth century, let alone the early nineteenth, to realise the answer to that question.

The unnotated levels of freedom and nuance in the performances of Elgar, or any other composer or performer, are like the gait of a walker, or the inflections of a person's speech. The question is not 'Why is it absent from the notation?' but 'How could notation ever be expected to convey all that?' Nobody imagines that the words on a page of a play include all the instructions needed to give a performance. If Elgar were a great dramatist or poet, and had recorded his own works, we would have his own personal style of speech, with its accent, rhythm, tone, sonority, inflection, preserved for us to hear nearly a century later. What would we do with such information? Would we set about imitating his voice, like a TV impressionist? Certainly not. We would absorb what his style of delivery has to tell us about the work, and let it inform our own way of doing it. Elgar's and Rachmaninoff's recordings show us valuable things: how lightly they mean *tenuto* marks to be interpreted, how volatile their tempi are, beyond the markings in the scores. But they are of no value if we merely imitate them. Their value lies in their ability to help us understand their music, and what they meant by it. Recordings, in other words, do not provide a short cut to how to perform the works of the composers, but only a further level of clues to their ways of thinking.

CHAPTER SIX

Questions of Authority: Schools of Playing

Recordings of the composer, or of musicians in some way linked to the composer, will always hold a particular fascination, even though their claims to be authoritative are sometimes exaggerated. There is a broader category of performers for whom great claims are made in CD booklets. These are musicians who were representative of important schools of performance. Some of these schools were themselves directly linked in their origins to composers of the past, others were not. But the ability of a performer to state that he or she was taught by a famous teacher, or even by the pupil of a famous teacher, carries a certain cachet. Like the association with composers, the association with a school needs to be examined.

As this book has already made clear, recordings show that styles of playing in the early twentieth century were a great deal more diverse than those in the early twenty-first (putting aside the contrasts between modern 'period' and 'conventional' performance). Ways of playing in different countries, and according to different traditions or schools, used to be strongly contrasted with each other, and pianists, string-players and wind-players can be heard performing in radically different styles on early twentieth-century recordings. The same is true of singers, who are beyond the scope of this book.[1] This chapter looks at some of these schools, the individuals who belonged to them, the contrasts and similarities between them, and the way their significance changed over the twentieth century.

Pianists

Among the many pianists who made records in the first half of the twentieth century were a number who studied with important late nineteenth-century teachers – Franz Liszt, Clara Schumann, Anton Rubinstein, Theodor Leschetizky, and several pupils of Fryderyk Chopin. These in turn taught a younger generation of pianists. Recordings make it possible for the first time to trace the influence of teachers from one generation to another, and to establish the differences and similarities between fellow pupils.

Pupil-teacher relationships are very varied, and recordings do not reveal a simple pattern of influences. This is hardly surprising. All prominent pianists, before and after the invention of the gramophone, have made their reputations mainly by their own insights and individuality, whatever they may have learned from their teachers. The picture is further complicated by the fact that many early twentieth-century pianists studied with more than one teacher.

Leschetizky's pupils included Ignacy Paderewski, Ignacy Friedman, Mark Hambourg, Benno Moiseiwitsch and Artur Schnabel, all of whom made recordings. There are also piano rolls (but not gramophone recordings) of Leschetizky himself. The differences between these pianists are much more striking than their similarities, but recordings of Friedman, Hambourg and Moiseiwitsch do have in common a wonderfully subtle layering of textures. In Hambourg's performance of the Mélodie from Gluck's *Orfeo ed Euridice* (1929), the very soft accompaniment allows the melody to project although played very quietly, so that it acquires a floating, gently singing quality. Friedman similarly plays Chopin's Nocturne in E flat Opus 55 No. 2 (1936) with a very quiet accompaniment, so that the melody sings without being pushed, and details in the accompaniment tell with only the slightest emphasis. Moiseiwitsch, who was particularly admired by Rachmaninoff, plays his Prelude in B minor Opus 32 No. 10 (1940) with the most beautiful shading of phrases and balancing of the inner voices. Friedman, Hambourg and Moiseiwitsch also share a very refined approach to rubato and the rhythmic dislocation of chords. Slight arpeggiation of chords and anticipation of important notes in lower parts are used very selectively.

Schnabel stands somewhat apart from other Leschetizky pupils, partly because of the repertoire which he recorded, notably the famous 'Beethoven Society' recordings of all the sonatas (recorded 1932–5). He is often characterised as the great 'Classical' pianist, as opposed to the 'Romantics' Friedman, Moiseiwitsch and Hambourg. Certainly he gives the impression of a very analytical mind, but, as was said in chapter 4, this is achieved by a highly individual and free treatment of rhythmic detail. What he has in common with other Leschetizky pupils is a command of subtly layered textures, which enables him to clarify Beethoven's counterpoint in an extraordinary way. His pupil Clifford Curzon reported, 'If he played a chord of six notes, all six notes were thought individually, were coloured individually. He never played an undifferentiated chord.'[2] Schnabel also shares with many pianists of his generation a preference for fast tempi in fast movements, even when this means occasional loss of precision. His attempt to play Beethoven's 'Hammerklavier' Sonata at something like the composer's metronome markings is famous

(1935). Other examples of Leschetizky pupils playing with great brilliance include Moiseiwitsch in Weber's *Perpetuum mobile* (1922), and Hambourg in the finale of Beethoven's Sonata in C Opus 2 No. 3 (1926), which he takes at extraordinary speed ($\boldsymbol{\mathmarkdown}$. = 152) and with the jig rhythm lightened by short and snappy quavers (eighth notes).

The most famous and successful pupil of Leschetizky was Paderewski, but his recordings, which are very mixed, present something of a puzzle to the modern listener. By the 1930s, when he made his later recordings, he was in his seventies, and an important political figure with, presumably, much less time to maintain his piano-playing than in earlier years. But throughout his recording career his performances reveal a bewildering mixture of considerable charm and dexterity (as in Liszt's 'La Leggierezza', 1923) and what now sounds like clumsiness (as in Chopin's Nocturne in F major Opus 15 No. 1, from his first ever session in 1911). Paderewski's use of dislocation is particularly striking in Chopin's Mazurka in C sharp minor Opus 63 No. 3 (1930). Where the melody is played in canon (bars 65ff.), Paderewski uses this technique to separate the two parts to a remarkable extent.[3]

There were therefore considerable differences between the pupils of Leschetizky. In particular, Schnabel and Paderewski had little in common. Because Leschetizky himself made only piano rolls, it is impossible to judge quite what his playing sounded like. But one thing is clear from his recording of Chopin's Nocturne in D flat major Opus 27 No. 2 (1906), and that is that he used as much dislocation of bass and treble as Paderewski at his most extreme. On this evidence, none of his pupils apart from Paderewski played with as much rhythmic dislocation as Leschetizky himself.

As for pupils of pupils of Leschetizky, what if anything is left of the 'Leschetizky School'? The most distinguished example of a pianist who studied with a pupil of Leschetizky is Clifford Curzon, who was taught by Schnabel. Curzon said that Schnabel taught him to let the music 'breathe', and his sense of timing and placing of detail do, within the constraints of a more modern style, have something in common with Schnabel. But since Schnabel's own style was highly individual, and very different from that of other Leschetizky pupils, Curzon cannot in any useful sense be considered 'a grand pupil' of Leschetizky.

There are similar problems with the 'Liszt Tradition'. Liszt's pupils included Moriz Rosenthal, Arthur de Greef, Arthur Friedheim, Frederic Lamond, Emil von Sauer and Eugen d'Albert, all of whom made records. None of these were in their prime by the time they recorded. Lamond retains a fair amount of brilliance in his recordings of Liszt. His tempi are very volatile, not only in Liszt and Chopin, but also, more surprisingly to modern ears, in Beethoven (Sonata in C minor Opus 13, 'Pathétique', 1926). D'Albert's rubato includes much uneven pairing of notes (in the manner adopted more subtly by Rachmaninoff). All of these Liszt pupils make much use of dislocation between melody and bass. In Brahms's Capriccio in B minor Opus 76 No. 2 (1928), Lamond produces an extraordinary 'galumphing' effect by the continual anticipation of the bass. Von Sauer, in his recording of Liszt's Concerto No. 1 (1938), not only dislocates melody and bass in the piano part, but also creates accents by playing melody notes ahead of the orchestra. Friedheim (in Liszt's *Hungarian Rhapsody* No. 2, c.1917) and Rosenthal (in Liszt's *Soirées de Vienne*, 1936) show the light and snappy playing of short notes characteristic of so many pianists of their generation.

Rosenthal is, to the modern listener, probably the most impressive Liszt pupil on record. Some of his later recordings show him limited by old age, with the dislocation becoming unsubtle. But a 1930 recording of Chopin's Berceuse reveals a wonderfully delicate and fluid lyricism. And in Chopin's Nocturne in E flat Opus 9 No. 2 (1936) the smooth and quiet melodic line seems to float independently above the bass, because of the finesse with which Rosenthal places it in relation to the rhythm of the accompaniment.

The problem for anyone wanting a simple family tree of teachers and pupils is that Rosenthal studied not only with Liszt, but also with Liszt's pupil Tausig, and with Chopin's pupil Karol Mikuli. When he appeared in Vienna at the age of twenty-one, he made a mark as a fiery virtuoso in the Liszt mould, but Eduard Hanslick disliked the 'unlovely violence with which the keys were pounded in fortissimo passages'.[4] It was later that he developed a reputation for the delicacy of his soft playing. It would be neat if Rosenthal acquired his gentle qualities from Mikuli, and his brilliant virtuosity from Liszt. But his three years with Mikuli were from the age of nine, before he studied with Liszt.

A number of pianists who made records studied with pupils of Chopin. Like Rosenthal, Alexander Michałowski and Raoul Koczalski both studied with Mikuli, who was one of Chopin's most important pupils. Michałowski's recordings include Chopin's Polonaise in A major (c.1907), played very vigorously, but with light dotted rhythms. He also recorded two versions of the 'Minute' Waltz, one a 'straight' version, played with considerable dash, the other, more surprisingly, a virtuoso rearrangement of the kind which was popular in the early years of the century. Koczalski is perhaps the most important link with the 'Chopin School', because, unlike his fellow pupils Rosenthal and Michałowski, he did not move on to other teachers after studying with Mikuli (he was, however, only eleven when he finished studying with Mikuli, and did not make his first recordings until about twenty-seven years later). Koczalski is also the most impressive of pianists in the Chopin line to have recorded. The Scherzo in B flat minor (c.1936) is much lighter than most modern performances, volatile in tempo, very clear in texture, with sparing use of the sustaining pedal, and with beautiful, free rubato in the melody of the second theme, over an accompaniment which maintains a strong forward impulse.

Koczalski's rubato at the beginning of Chopin's first Ballade has already been discussed in chapter 4. The big question is how much of this kind of freedom might derive from Chopin himself, via Mikuli. Only a pupil with no ambitions would play exactly like their teacher, let alone their teacher's teachers, even if such a teacher was someone as important as Chopin. But given the many descriptions of the freedoms which Chopin employed in his own playing, and particularly his well-documented habit of playing a melody with considerable freedom over a rhythmically firm bass ('Let your accompanying hand be your conductor'), it seems quite likely that Koczalski's freedoms to some extent derived from that tradition, even though they must undoubtedly be his interpretation of such freedoms rather than Chopin's or Mikuli's.[5]

Alfred Cortot and Marguerite Long were also taught by a disciple of Chopin, though not actually a pupil, Emile Decombes. In the 1930s and 1940s Cortot was probably the most widely admired of all Chopin players, but his style was very individual. The singing of his melodic lines had a particular intensity, greater than that of any of the Leschetizky pupils. His approach to tempo was sometimes wayward, but his precise pinpointing of the character of each moment nevertheless creates an impression of command of structure. No one has played Chopin's twenty-four Preludes with such mercurial beauty, and yet with such a sense of the set as one continuous work (he recorded it three times, but the 1933–4 version is the most impressive). His 1931 recording of Chopin's Sonata in B minor contains many detailed tempo changes and points of emphasis (very different from the more straightforward, muscular brilliance of Percy Grainger in 1925), and is memorable for moments of exquisite shading and lyricism. But the work as a whole also sounds coherent, even when stitched together from the 78 rpm sides. Cortot's volatile responsiveness to musical character made him particularly suited to the music of Schumann, notably the Concerto (1927) and *Carnaval* (1928).

There was also an official 'Schumann Tradition' passed down from Clara Schumann to her pupils, who included Fanny Davies, Adelina de Lara and Mathilde Verne. Schumann herself was renowned as a thoughtful and serious-minded pianist, who rejected the effects of the fashionable virtuosi. One of the consequences of this seems to have been that she passed on to her pupils an unusually (for the time) disciplined approach to flexibility of tempo. Mathilde Verne ran a famous piano school in Kensington, where her pupils included Solomon and Moura Lympany. Lympany recalls,

Once I sat down to play her the Schumann Piano Concerto, and I had just played the first entry, allegro affetuoso, and settled down to the next phrase, the beautiful solo, at about half the pace, when to my shock and dismay she tore my hands off the keys.

'Why are you playing half-time?' she demanded.

'Because it is always played like that', I replied mildly.

'Has Schumann marked another tempo there?' she asked.

'No', I replied meekly.

'Well then', she instructed sharply, 'play it as it is written – the same tempo as the entry'.[6]

Lympany's recorded performances of this movement are unusually 'straight', but even she does not play the second piano entry literally in tempo. In her recording issued in 1959 the movement opens at $\downarrow$ = 152, and the second entry is at 108. Fanny Davies in 1928 begins at about 152, with the second entry at 96.

Mathilde Verne herself made no recordings. The playing of her fellow Schumann-pupils Fanny Davies and Adelina de Lara now seems rather plain in style, apart from a great deal of loose co-ordination between the hands – quite different from the volatile Cortot, who might well have displeased Clara Schumann. In De Lara's recordings, all made in her late seventies, some of this might be attributable to old age. But Davies, who was in her fifties, shows a similar style in, for example, the opening piece of *Kinderszenen* (1929), with the bass anticipating the melody on almost every beat, in a charming but somewhat routine, Paderewski-like manner.

This rhythmic trait of Schumann's pupils was not passed on to the next generation. There is no trace of it in Moura Lympany, nor in Solomon, who studied with Verne as a child prodigy (an experience he later described as 'terrible, terrible').[7] By the time Lympany and Solomon rose to prominence in the 1940s, the dislocation of bass and treble had become seriously unfashionable.

Anton Rubinstein was an important influence on a number of pianists, but he took only one private pupil, Josef Hofmann, who studied with him for two years. Hofmann wrote that 'He would follow every note of my playing with his eyes riveted on the printed page. A pedant he certainly was, a stickler for the letter – incredibly so, especially when one considers the liberties he took when he played the same works!'[8] This paradox is echoed in descriptions of Hofmann's own playing, in which he is variously 'without equal among Romantic pianists', and 'the dramatic orchestrator of the piano whose playing evoked the forces of nature and of humanity', and yet 'a modernist, with far fewer mannerisms than any pianist of his rank', who plays 'with a mixture of classic purity and romantic elegance'.[9] Hofmann's recordings now sound 'modern' in one sense, which is that they contain hardly any trace of the old-fashioned separation of bass and treble (as early as 1909 he advised amateur pianists, 'This "limping", as it is called, is the worst habit you can have in piano playing . . .').[10] He has an extraordinary technique, a very wide range of tone-colour and dynamics, and a singing legato. In public recital, where, according to those who heard him, the 'real' Hofmann was to be heard, he took liberties which now sound anything but modern. His recital at Casimir Hall recorded in 1938 includes some of his own virtuoso display-pieces, a lugubrious chromatic re-writing of Schubert's *Moment musical* in F minor, and an arrangement of Chopin's 'Minute' Waltz, with an independent inner part added at the reprise. These were the traditional stock-in-trade of the virtuoso pianist, and they are delivered with glittering panache. Chopin's Ballade in F minor is played with dramatic contrasts of volume and tempo, and the overall impression is of a larger-than-life performance of exceptional power. The Polonaise in E flat minor seems much more wilful, and it begins with a very portentous, slow introduction.

Rachmaninoff and Josef Lhévinne were both acquainted with, and influenced by, Anton Rubinstein while they were at the Moscow Conservatoire, though neither was his pupil. They had in common with Hofmann a commanding technique – surprising in Rachmaninoff, who had never intended to make a career as a concert pianist. Rachmaninoff's highly individual style of rubato has already been discussed. Both he and Lhévinne exercised a much stricter control of tempo than Hofmann. In Lhévinne's recordings, the impression is of very firm projection of tone, and a steely brilliance in virtuoso passages, as in Schulz-Evler's arrangement of *The Blue Danube* (1928 – Lhévinne's Ampico piano rolls of this and other works, already discussed in chapter 2, give a false impression of feathery lightness). Like Rachmaninoff, and unlike Hofmann, Lhévinne uses subtle anticipations and delays to emphasise melody notes, as in a marvellously glittering performance of Liszt's arrangement of Schumann's *Frühlingsnacht* (1935).

The most prominent heir to this 'Russian School' was Vladimir Horowitz, who was taught by another student from Rubinstein's classes, Felix Blumenfeld. Horowitz revered Hofmann, and has more in common with him than with Rachmaninoff or Lhévinne, combining a phenomenal technique with a huge range of tone, touch and dynamics, and a very free approach to tempo. His early recordings, made in the early 1930s, already reveal the disturbing mixture of qualities which persisted throughout his career. Beethoven's Thirty-two Variations in C minor (1934) alternate between athleticism and sudden moments of calm beauty. Busoni's arrangement of Bach's *Nun freut euch* (1934) is very fast and mechanical. And yet nothing conveys more natural and easy grace than Schumann's *Arabesque* (1934), in which the singing second theme is poised above its accompaniment by the most delicate of rhythmic separation. Horowitz uses the same technique to point the melodies of Scarlatti's Sonata in B minor Kk87 (1935) and Chopin's Mazurka in E minor Opus 41 No. 2 (1933), one of his earliest and most highly acclaimed recordings. Despite the undoubted power of the big works (the live 1943 recording of Tchaikovsky's Piano Concerto No. 1 with Toscanini is particularly impressive), it is Horowitz's quietest moments which stay longest in the memory.

In England in the first half of the twentieth century there developed what can loosely be called an 'English School' of piano-playing. Tobias Matthay was an important figure, teaching, among others, Myra Hess, Irene Scharrer, Harriet Cohen and Harold Craxton. Hess in turn taught Stephen Kovacevich (Bishop), Craxton taught Denis Matthews, Peter Katin and Noel Mewton-Wood. Matthay wrote densely worded analyses of the physical aspects of piano-playing, notably *The Act of Touch* (1903). But he was also an important teacher: Hess and Scharrer continued to go to him for advice until his death in 1945. The sobriety and lack of display of Matthay's pupils had something in common with the Clara Schumann school. Finesse and quiet intensity of tone were characteristic of both Hess and Scharrer. Scharrer's few recordings include some beautifully poised performances of the gentler works of Chopin. Hess's recordings range from Bach and Scarlatti through Mozart, Beethoven, Brahms and Schumann to a few twentieth-century works, notably the Sonata of her friend Howard Ferguson (1940). Hess's Scarlatti has gentle wit, her Brahms combines clarity and weight with warm-toned lyricism. In later life she was particularly renowned for her performances of the late Beethoven sonatas, to which she brought a quality of spiritual intensity. Harriet Cohen was especially noted as a friend and champion of Bax, and she was also chosen by Elgar to record his Piano Quintet in 1933.

But if there was an English School, it extended beyond the pupils of Matthay. It included Moura Lympany (taught by Mathilde Verne), Kathleen Long (a pupil of Herbert Sharpe), Clifford Curzon (a pupil of Schnabel) and Solomon. These all shared with the Matthay pupils a tendency to understatement which was far removed from a Hofmann or a Horowitz, and had more in common with Schnabel or Edwin Fischer. At their best they had a penetrating sensitivity which was all their own.

The case of Solomon demonstrates how difficult it is to draw any sensible distinctions between schools of playing in his generation. As a child prodigy he studied with Mathilde Verne, and later he went to Simon Rumchiysky and Lazare Lévy. He shared with the best of his British contemporaries a certain reserve and absence of show, adding to it a characteristic clarity and delicacy, achieved with a seemingly effortless technique. Solomon's rubato was always restrained, his tempi were never self-indulgent. But these were not negative qualities in Solomon. His playing was notable for its power. Did any of Solomon's qualities come from Mathilde Verne, passing on the seriousness of her teacher Clara Schumann? Not according to Solomon, who denied that he learned anything more than basic technique from Verne. It is likely that Solomon owed more to Lazare Lévy, with whom he studied as a young adult at the Paris Conservatoire – Clara Haskil, another pupil of Lévy (but also of Cortot and Busoni), shared these qualities of clarity and restraint.

But the essential qualities of any great pianists can owe only a limited amount to their teachers. This is true of two of the most admired Chopin-players of the twentieth century, Alfred Cortot and Arthur Rubinstein. Cortot's training was French (Emile Decombes and Louis Diémer at the Paris Conservatoire), Rubinstein's was German (Karl Heinrich Barth in Berlin, who also taught Wilhelm Kempff). But their personalities as pianists cannot be defined just in relation to their teachers. Rubinstein's early development was strongly influenced by Joachim, who supervised his musical education. Rubinstein often heard Joachim and his musical circle, played for his masterclasses, performed concertos with Joachim conducting, and was encouraged by him to absorb as much as he could of the rich cultural life that Berlin had to offer in the early years of the twentieth century. Rubinstein himself wrote in his memoirs about his capacity for throwing himself passionately into the world around him, musically and personally.[11] Cortot has already been mentioned in this chapter, because one of his teachers was of Chopin's circle. But just as significant is the fact that Cortot was far more than a pianist. He was one of the most important French conductors of his generation, conducting the first performances in France of Wagner's *Götterdämmerung* and *Parsifal*, and Brahms's *German Requiem*.

The schools of piano-playing through the twentieth century therefore present a complex picture. Certainly, in the early years of the century, there were prominent pianists who represented important links to nineteenth-century teachers. But the distinctions between their styles of playing were not clear-cut, and the differences between pupils of the same teacher were, in some cases, as great as their similarities. By the 1940s, the distinction between schools had become yet vaguer. No doubt the younger generation still learned valuable things from distinguished teachers, but the element of any traditional method or style was much weaker than in the previous generation.

String-playing

As with piano-playing, it is possible to categorise string-playing in the early twentieth century into separate schools and traditions. But, again, the distinctions only go so far, and become less and less distinct as the century wears on.

Violin schools in the late nineteenth and early twentieth centuries are generally described as having three main branches: the German (led by Joachim), the Franco-Belgian (led by Ysaÿe) and the Russian (led by Leopold Auer who, though Hungarian, taught at St Petersburg from the 1860s). There are a number of features that distinguish these schools, but as with piano-playing, the differences are not always clear-cut. And the role of the schools diminished over the first half of the twentieth century as the influence of particular players came to dominate (partly through recordings).

One distinguishing feature of the three schools was their contrasting styles of bowing. The German tradition was to keep the elbow of the bowing arm low, as had been general in earlier nineteenth-century violin-playing. Franco-

Belgian and Russian methods raised the elbow higher. With this went differences in the manner of gripping the bow, which Carl Flesch describes in *The Art of Violin Playing* (1923–8).[12] In the old German grip, with the low elbow, the fingers are close together, and roughly at right-angles to the bow. In the Franco-Belgian grip, the hand is tilted more towards the index finger, which is therefore pushed away from the other fingers. In the 'Russian' grip this is taken to an extreme, with the hand further tilted so that the index finger curls round the bow.

Flesch declares the Russian grip to be superior to the other two. He writes that it allows 'the most effortless method of tone production', principally because of 'the powerful outward rolling of the lower arm', and because the curled index finger allows the hand 'to take possession of the stick, control it and compel it to do its will . . .'.

Many players at the beginning of the twentieth century adhered to the old German style of bowing. The trend through the first half of the century was towards the adoption of the Franco-Belgian and Russian styles, or versions of them. This development, as Flesch's espousal of the Russian method suggests, is to do with far more than technique. The different methods were associated with different approaches to style of violin-playing, and these are clearly audible on early twentieth-century recordings. Differences in power and quality of tone (to the extent that they can be assessed on early recordings), styles of phrasing and articulation, do fall to some extent into the three schools. And with these different approaches went distinct attitudes to vibrato, with the older style favouring discretion, the newer styles using vibrato as an intensifier of tone, rather than just an ornamental colouring.

Joachim made a few recordings in 1903, and contemporary descriptions of his playing, some of which were quoted in chapter 4, show that almost nothing of his charismatic personality as a musician comes over from the recordings. What is clear is his broad style of bowing and phrasing, with very little vibrato, and languid portamenti in sustained melodies (such as his own Romance in C). Restraint in vibrato was firmly advocated by Joachim in his teaching: 'A violinist whose taste is refined and healthy will always recognize the steady tone as the ruling one, and will use the vibrato only where the expression seems to demand it.'[13]

A number of Joachim's pupils made recordings, and to a large extent they share his characteristics of broad bowing, restraint in vibrato, and slow portamenti. They include Maria Soldat-Roeger, Adela Fachiri and Karl Klingler (leader of the Klingler Quartet). But the survival of the old 'German' way of playing extended far beyond Joachim's direct influence. Different versions of it can be heard in recordings of the Rosé, Bohemian, Capet, and the original Budapest Quartet (led by Hauser), and many English violinists of the early twentieth century also played in this style. The so-called German school was therefore not just a narrow group associated with Joachim, but a wider culture of violin-playing which, for a time, resisted the trend towards more powerful and assertive styles. Its preference for a broad style of bowing, and little vibrato, was a continuation of early nineteenth-century practice.

French and Belgian violinists, from Baillot in the 1830s onwards, had experimented with a greater variety of bow-strokes, including different types of springing bowing that are familiar in modern playing, and which Paganini had encouraged.[14] The raising of the elbow partly facilitated the new variety of articulation, partly assisted tone-production. The player who was regarded as the outstanding example of the Franco-Belgian school in the early years of the twentieth century was Eugène Ysaÿe, who, according to a Belgian colleague, 'realises, in his playing, the most perfect union of fullness of sound, immateriality, intensity and expressive gradation of feeling'.[15]

Ysaÿe's free rubato has already been discussed in chapter 4. The agility and crispness of his bowing, both on and off the string, can clearly be heard in his recording of the Rondino Opus 32 No. 2 by Vieuxtemps (1912). The sweetness of his tone, and his delicate and variable vibrato, are best heard in the 'Prize Song' from Wagner's *Die Meistersinger*. 'Ysaÿe's vibrato,' wrote Flesch, 'which followed every mood of his admirable personality, became the ideal goal of the generation around 1900.'[16] Adolfo Betti, leader of the Flonzaley Quartet, the outstanding Franco-Belgian quartet of the early twentieth century, similarly played with light agility of bowing and a sweet and delicately vibrant tone (though not quite Ysaÿe's intensity, to judge by the recordings).

The Russian style of bowing was associated with pupils of Leopold Auer. Of these the most famous and influential was Jascha Heifetz, in whose playing a new power of tone and assertive crispness of bowing can be heard, coupled with an intense, fast and virtually continuous vibrato.

It is in the spread and intensification of vibrato that any simple idea of schools becomes blurred as the twentieth century gets under way. The greatest single influence in the use of vibrato was Fritz Kreisler, an Austrian taught by the Parisian Massart. As Flesch writes in the 1920s, 'It was *Kreisler* who forty years ago, driven by an irresistible inner urge, started a revolutionary change in this regard, by vibrating not only continuously in cantilenas like *Ysaÿe*, but even in technical passages. This fundamental metamorphosis has put his indelible stamp on contemporary violin-playing, whether one agrees with it or not.'[17]

Where did this continuous vibrato come from? Was it 'Franco-Belgian' in origin, or was it Kreisler's personal invention? Kreisler himself claimed that Massart liked him 'because I played in the style of Wieniawski'. Wieniawski, Kreisler said, 'intensified the vibrato', and Vieuxtemps, Ysaÿe and Kreisler then took it up.[18] This all sounds very convincing, but Kreisler never heard Wieniawski or Vieuxtemps, and Ysaÿe's vibrato was neither as wide nor as continuous as Kreisler's. It seems therefore that Flesch was probably right in surmising that Kreisler's style of vibrato was largely the result of his own 'inner urge', Franco-Belgian though his training may have been.

The Russian style is also far from simple in its pedigree. Leopold Auer himself wrote in 1921, 'I have taught for many years and I still take pride in the fact that I have always insisted on the one great principle – that my pupils express *themselves*, and that they must not try to express me.'[19] This is confirmed by the great differences between Auer's most famous pupils, Efrem Zimbalist, Samuel Dushkin, Mischa Elman, Jascha Heifetz and Nathan Milstein. Of these violinists, Dushkin and Zimbalist played with less aggressive bowing and less intense vibrato than their younger colleagues Heifetz and Milstein. Joseph Szigeti even doubted whether the 'Russian bow-hold' described by Flesch derived from Auer at all. Szigeti points out that Auer recommends the older 'German' style of grip in his published violin course, and he thought that the new 'Russian' approach was probably developed by some of Auer's pupils independently.[20]

There are similar problems in attributing the intense vibrato of Heifetz to any teaching of Auer. Auer himself wrote, 'violinists who habitually make use of the device – those who are convinced that an eternal *vibrato* is the secret of soulful playing, of piquancy in performance – are pitifully misguided in their belief'.[21] This sounds like the advice of Joachim, by whom, to make matters even more confusing, Auer was himself taught. Recordings reveal that Auer's own vibrato was more prominent than Joachim's but still very delicate, and not continuous even in a flowing melody such as Tchaikovsky's *Souvenir d'un lieu cher* (1920).

Another violin teacher who stands somewhat apart from any national schools was the Czech Otakar Ševčík. He is famous for his system of fingering, but like Auer he seems not to have imposed a particular style of playing on his pupils. They included Jan Kubelík and Marie Hall – both players of the 'old school' with restrained vibrato and heavy portamento – and Rudolf Kolisch and Wolfgang Schneiderhan – players of a new generation, not only in age but also in approach to bowing, vibrato and portamento.

All of this seems to confirm Szigeti's view: 'The neat "genealogical tables" showing how twentieth-century violinists descend from this or that "Chef d'École" of the past are not as dependable as the authors of these books would like to make them seem.'[22] By the time the twentieth century was under way, the spread of new approaches to violin-playing seemed to be due more to the influence of charismatic individual performers (especially Kreisler and Heifetz) than to any particular schools, national or otherwise. As an example of a player who defies categorisation, one might take Albert Sammons. In the early years of the twentieth century he was the first English violinist to be regarded as a great player on the level of Kreisler or Heifetz. He taught a number of distinguished violinists of the next generation, including Hugh Bean, and could be regarded as having founded a kind of 'English School'. But he himself had no clear pedigree. He was taught as a child by his father, then had some lessons from two pupils of Ysaÿe and a few more from a pupil of the German Bernhard Molique. But as a teenager he was already too busy earning his living in hotels and cafés to devote time or money to formal training.[23] Broadly speaking one could describe his style as being modelled on that of Kreisler, though with a characteristic directness and lack of mannerism (perhaps the violinist's equivalent of Solomon). He was an example of a violinist of exceptional natural gifts who needed little help from teachers.

In cello-playing, as in violin-playing, there was a great change in the early years of the twentieth century. Even more than in violin-playing, it was attributable to the influence of a particular performer rather than to schools of teaching. Pablo Casals is widely credited with revolutionising cello technique and style. This was partly, as in violin-playing, a matter of freeing the bowing arm. Nineteenth-century cellists, such as Alfredo Piatti, had played with a low elbow, with the cello held between the knees and not supported by an end-pin. Casals himself had first been taught in the 1880s to bow with a book clutched under his armpit. In his own teaching he advocated 'complete freedom in the movement of the right arm, including the elbow', so as to make 'the whole bow technique stronger and easier'.[24] Casals's fingering involved the use of stretching to avoid many of the traditional shifts. This was far more than a technical advance, as Emanuel Feuermann wrote: 'He has shown that the 'cello can sing without becoming overly sentimental, that phrasing on the 'cello can be of the highest quality. He adopted a technique according to the musical requirements. The enormous reaches seem to have disappeared; so have the ugly noises theretofore considered an integral part of 'cello playing. He has set an example for the younger 'cellists and demonstrated what can be done on it.'[25]

The teacher who most systematised Casals's stretching technique was Joachim Stutschewsky. He wrote, 'The best fingering is the one restricting the changes of position to a minimum .... When choosing a fingering, the composer's intention will have to be decisive and not the personal ease.' Stutschewsky's methods were endorsed by his teacher Julius Klengel, principal cellist of the Leipzig Gewandhaus Orchestra for many years, who wrote to him, 'I do not mind stating that I shall try in my old age to touch up my left hand.'[26]

The reforms of Casals and Stutschewsky, and of the teacher who collaborated with Casals, Diran Alexanian, undoubtedly had a great influence on cellists. The routine, heavy sliding from one position to another, which is so much a feature of early twentieth-century recordings of the cello, gradually became a thing of the past. Schoenberg's appreciation of Casals's playing has already been quoted in chapter 5. Schoenberg particularly admired his avoidance of sentimental portamento: 'And when the occasional portamento does occur, it is only to lend a lyrical *dolce* passage the tender colouring that expresses the mood of such a passage all the more piercingly.'[27]

Casals's recordings are remarkable not just for the discretion with which he uses the portamento, but for the great variety with which he plays it, usually delicately, sometimes firmly, fast or slow depending on the musical circumstances. His recording of Elgar's Cello Concerto (1945) contains many examples. In the slow movement Casals plays ten portamenti within the first twenty-six bars. W. H. Squire (1930), a player of the old school taught by Piatti, plays twenty-three portamenti, and his sliding is mostly slow and unsoftened by diminuendi. By contrast, Casals's sliding is extremely varied and subtle. It is, partly, the difference between a player for whom portamento was a necessary device to move around the cello, and a player who had to a large extent overcome this problem. This is a little unfair to Squire and the old school, but the musical discrimination of Casals's portamenti is most striking in comparison.

Casals was highly influential on later cellists, but as with schools of violin-playing, the trend was not straightforward. It was not the case that, before Casals, all cellists slid around indiscriminately, and after him, all played cleanly. There were still considerable divergences of opinion about the amount of portamento desirable in cello-playing.

David Soyer, cellist of the Guarneri Quartet, was taught by Diran Alexanian, Casals's pupil, whose method Casals endorsed. Then Soyer went to Emanuel Feuermann. Feuermann had quite a different approach to portamento: 'Feuermann . . . was less prone to use extensions and made somewhat more frequent use of glissandos. Alexanian had been very strict in that regard; you weren't allowed to make a glissando unless you had five excellent reasons for doing so. When I came to Feuermann I was a pretty brash kid, so I asked, "Why do you slide so much?" As he was a pretty brash guy, he didn't mind that. "I slide," he said, "because I'm not playing the clarinet; I'm playing the cello. When I put my fingers down I'm not just covering holes. The slide gives a sense of fluency and a vocal quality. Try singing a phrase and not sliding and see how far you get. It's a perfectly natural way of playing.'[28]

And who was Feuermann's teacher? The same Julius Klengel who had endorsed Stutschewsky's methodical avoidance of unnecessary portamento. Nor is the comparison between Casals and Feuermann as straightforward as Soyer's description suggests. Recordings give the impression that the difference between Feuermann and Casals in their portamento was as much in the manner as in the frequency. In an arrangement of Chopin's Nocturne in E flat Opus 9 No. 2, Feuermann (c.1938) actually slides slightly less frequently than Casals (1926). But Feuermann's shaping of the portamenti is less varied than that of Casals, falling into a somewhat more predictable pattern. The listener is left with the impression, therefore, that Feuermann has used the portamento more than Casals, when he has not.

One important point about teachers is that they vary greatly in the extent to which they are systematic, and the extent to which they wish to impose a particular way of playing on their pupils. William Pleeth was taught by Julius Klengel and said about him, 'Klengel never encouraged us to copy, and if you look at the wide range of playing from his many pupils you will see how different they all are.' Klengel's pupils included not only Pleeth, Feuermann and Stutschewsky, but also Guilhermina Suggia (who later studied with, and married, Casals), Paul Grümmer and Gregor Piatigorsky.[29] Pleeth's view of Klengel as undogmatic echoes a point already made about Leopold Auer, and, among pianists, Theodor Leschetizky.

The contrasting approaches of teachers is illustrated by Yfrah Neaman, who studied with Carl Flesch and Flesch's pupil Max Rostal, and with Jacques Thibaud. Flesch's approach to violin teaching was highly analytical and systematic, and so was Rostal's. Thibaud was quite different: 'Rostal went even farther [than Flesch], and codified and organised the movements in the right arm and in the left arm, and how you change position and how you change bow, and so on. So everything was highly organised. Thibaud, on the other hand, was a natural player. What one got from Thibaud was simply the stimulation of being with someone who was an artist to their toe-nails .... It was no good saying to him, "Why do you do that?", or "How do you do it?" The why and the how didn't exist. It was just "Well, how else? That's it. I just feel it." And fortunately he had immaculate taste, so he could do things by instinct.'[30]

This is not to say that a teacher is necessarily either systematic or instinctive. Casals was clearly both, combining a highly analytical brain with a refined emotional sensitivity. Bernard Greenhouse described the lengths to which Casals went in order to equip him with a vibrato with a full expressive range:

He said, 'You know, you're very gifted, but there's a slight vulgarity to your playing, and it's because you do not use the vibrato to make music. You have an automatic motion to your left hand, which means that there is no help to the bow arm in what you do.'

It meant that I had to change my whole left-hand technique. He sent me back to my studio to work without any vibrato at all. 'Come back next lesson without any vibrato. But I want a musical performance in spite of the lack.' Well, I found that enormously difficult to do – because my hand had become accustomed to constant motion. At length I was able to satisfy him.

Then we started producing vibrato in several different manners, using different parts of the arm. One was an arm vibrato for the lower strings; another was an elbow vibrato for the middle strings; a finger vibrato for the upper, higher register. This ability to vary the speed and the width of the vibrato changed my whole approach to phrasing. It was like a whole new spectrum – instead of having just the three primary colors, or perhaps one of the primary colors, you have the entire spectrum.[31]

Woodwind

Different styles of woodwind-playing and their development over the twentieth century have already been discussed in the context of orchestral ensemble in chapter 3 (and briefly in chapter 4). The evolution of woodwind styles in the first half of the century is examined in my *Early Recordings and Musical Style*, and there is no need to go into detail here.[32] In the early twentieth century there was great diversity of approach, and the different styles to a large extent fell into distinct national schools. The clearest distinction was between French woodwind, with its somewhat pungent tone-colours and frequent use of vibrato, and German/Austrian playing with its darker, smoother tone-colours and avoidance of vibrato. Over the century the influence of French style, particularly on the flute and oboe, spread around the world.

It is worth looking at the origins of this influential style. The most famous figure in the history of French woodwind-playing was the flautist Paul Taffanel. He is generally credited with the creation of the French school of flute-playing. But, as with schools of piano- and string-playing, it is difficult to establish the true extent and nature of his influence, and to distinguish it from that of his pupils. Taffanel had, at the end of the nineteenth century, established at the Paris Conservatoire a school of flute-playing using the metal flute rather than the wooden instrument. This was the foundation of the French school that became the dominant influence in flute-playing through the twentieth century. The brilliance of tone, flexibility of phrasing, and prominent use of vibrato – features that are still familiar in modern flute-playing – were established early in the twentieth century. But the evidence for Taffanel's own influence on this style, and particularly on the use of vibrato, is not straightforward. In the *Méthode* that Taffanel wrote with his pupil Philippe Gaubert, the authors argue against vibrato on the flute as strongly as Joachim and Auer did on the violin: 'There should be no vibrato or any form of quaver, an artifice used by inferior instrumentalists and musicians . . . . It is a serious error and shows unpardonable lack of taste to use these vulgar methods to interpret the great composers.'[33]

Taffanel and Gaubert's *Méthode* was published in 1923, but Taffanel had died in 1908. Was his attitude to vibrato as severe in practice during his lifetime as it might appear from this version of his instructions published after his death? Taffanel made no recordings, so there is no direct evidence of how he himself played. None of his pupils (or at least none of those who made recordings) adhered to these instructions against the use of vibrato. And several descriptions of Taffanel's teaching suggest a rather less austere approach, though reports are somewhat contradictory. Louis Fleury wrote that Taffanel stressed the importance of 'the search for tone, and the use, for this purpose, of a light, almost imperceptible *vibrato*'. This too was published after Taffanel's death, in an article drawing on his teaching.[34] Marcel Moyse, the most influential of all

Taffanel's pupils through the twentieth century, wrote an article in 1950, 'The Unsolvable Problem: Considerations on Flute Vibrato', in which he talks about the three 'magnificent teachers' who taught him in Paris, Adolphe Hennebains, Paul Taffanel and Philippe Gaubert: 'They didn't have much trouble making me understand that beating and quivering worked havoc with a good tone', he writes.

As for Taffanel's own playing, 'Every note had its place in relation to the whole; clear or resonant, the groups of notes were flexibly connected without vibrato, without any function other than that of serving as an embellishment to the principal notes. And when he spoke to us of notes with vibrato or expression, he told us with a mysterious air that these notes, forte or piano, seemed to come from within himself. One had the impression that they came directly from the heart or soul.'[35] It is difficult to interpret this passage clearly. One moment Moyse is talking of the danger of 'beating and quivering' and Taffanel's groups of notes 'connected without vibrato', and the next moment about Taffanel's 'notes with vibrato or expression'. It becomes clearer later in the article that what Moyse himself objects to, and what he says his teachers objected to, is vibrato used without expressive purpose: 'I still prefer a careful execution without vibrato to a quivering execution where the sound attracts the attention to the detriment of the musical phrase and runs the risk of evoking thoughts that no longer have anything to do with the music.' Even though Moyse may have urged restraint and discrimination in the use of vibrato, the fact is that a prominent vibrato is one of the most noticeable features of his playing, throughout his recording career. But, in contrast to many other flautists of the (broadly) French school, Moyse does indeed use vibrato with clear expressive purpose, not just as a constant and routine colouring. Among his early recordings, Debussy's *Prélude à l'Après-midi d'un faune* (with the Straram Orchestra, 1930) shows the great flexibility of his phrasing, enhanced by vibrato that varies from inconspicuous to quite prominent.

One might suspect that the severe attitude to vibrato expressed in Taffanel and Gaubert's *Méthode* came from Gaubert rather than Taffanel himself. But this possibility is ruled out by Gaubert's own playing. The recordings that he made in 1918–19 have a limited frequency range, but his tone is recognisably bright and rich, and is accompanied by a clearly audible, moderate-speed vibrato – lighter than that of some later French flautists such as Moyse, and variable in prominence, but never absent for more than one or two notes at a time.

Despite the strictures of the *Méthode*, the confident use of vibrato to enliven the silvery tone produced on the metal flute is an essential element in the playing of all Taffanel's pupils. This is not to say that they all played in the same way. Moyse's vibrato is not only more prominent than Gaubert's, it is also slower. Georges Barrère, on the other hand, played with an exceptionally fast vibrato, which was shallow but more constant than the vibrato of Gaubert and

Moyse. As with Taffanel, Gaubert and Moyse, there is some contradiction between what Barrère did and what he said. In the 1940s he complained about the use of vibrato by modern flautists: 'For the fifty years I had been tooting on my instrument, my daily care was to *avoid* the *vibrato*.'[36]

Just as pupils of Taffanel played with different styles of vibrato, so the more general spread of the French school produced varying results. Barrère played in the New York Symphony Orchestra from 1905, and his very fast vibrato was highly influential in America. His pupil William Kincaid played in the Philadelphia Orchestra from 1921 to 1960, and his vibrato was even faster than Barrère's. A very fast vibrato became characteristic of much American flute-playing in the second half of the twentieth century. In Britain, the French influence came later and had a somewhat different effect. Geoffrey Gilbert, principal flautist in Beecham's London Philharmonic Orchestra from 1935, had studied with René le Roy, a pupil of Gaubert. Gilbert was the first prominent flautist in Britain to adopt the metal flute and play in the French style. He played with a medium-speed vibrato, and a flexibility of phrasing and tone-colour to rival that of Moyse (as can be heard in a 1939 recording of Debussy's *Prélude à l'Après-midi d'un faune* with the London Philharmonic under Beecham). Other British flautists in the 1930s and 1940s tended to adopt a similarly moderate speed of vibrato, in contrast to the fast vibrato of many Americans. This makes British flute-playing of the period sound more relaxed, American playing more tense, a distinction that to some extent continued into later years.

How much of all of this can be attributed to Taffanel? Certainly he was an inspirational figure, but his pupils already show a diversity of styles, and perhaps to some extent contradict his approach to vibrato (like pupils of violinist Leopold Auer). By the time Taffanel's pupils, and the pupils of other French flautists, are playing in orchestras across the world, and are to be heard on recordings, the influence of the French school becomes generalised. And within woodwind sections players are responsive to each other. In England the very flexible and vibrant oboe-playing of Leon Goossens (inspired by the Belgian Henri de Busscher) directly and indirectly influenced not only other oboists but also clarinettists and flautists. In the Philadelphia Orchestra, flautist William Kincaid sat next to oboist Marcel Tabuteau, a pupil of Taffanel's contemporary at the Paris Conservatoire, Georges Gillet. Tabuteau, like Kincaid, played with a fast vibrato (which his teacher, Gillet, seems not to have done, to judge by a very dim 1905 recording). Tabuteau and Kincaid were beautifully suited to each other in style, and must surely have had some effect on each other's playing.

After World War II the spread of 'French' woodwind vibrato becomes very widespread, and it is difficult to separate one influence from another. Not only were there more and more woodwind-players adopting flexible phrasing and vibrato, but vibrato on stringed instruments was universal. The 'straight' woodwind sounds of the early twentieth century gradually succumb to this general shift of style, even in the orchestras of Berlin and Vienna.

In the second half of the twentieth century, the melting-pot of woodwind styles extended round the world. For a time, traditional distinctions survived to some extent: darker oboe tone in Germany, a more plangent tone in Vienna (which still used its own, traditional design of oboe), a certain pungency in some British players (a distant echo of the Old English style), a brighter, reedier sound in France. Clarinettists also preserved some national characteristics: brighter in France, dark and smooth in Germany, creamy and often with a little vibrato in England. Czech clarinettists in the late twentieth century had a characteristically rustic and vibrant tone, though it had more in common with contemporary Russian clarinet-playing than with the older, more Germanic style heard in earlier Czech recordings. In England a few flautists continued to use the wooden flute, but none of them played without vibrato, as flautists such as Robert Murchie had done earlier in the century. In the Berlin Philharmonic a heavy vibrato was already in use by flautists and oboists by the 1960s, in contradiction of the tradition that had survived right through the first half of the century. Despite minor differences in style and in the designs of instruments, towards the end of the twentieth century it became increasingly difficult to tell the difference between oboists and flautists around the world.

Tradition and the authority of the past

There were still fine teachers on all instruments at the end of the twentieth century, and some of them could trace their 'descent' back to famous teachers of a century before. But their powers to uphold tradition were more limited than they had been, and they were in competition with many other influences. The reason that instrumental style had become so globalised by this time was not that teachers across the world had, in some mysterious way, pooled their knowledge and traditions, and come to an agreement about how things should be done. It was, above anything, the fact that everyone could hear the best players all the time on recordings. If you were an oboist, you did not have to go to America to hear Ray Still in the Cleveland Orchestra, or to Germany to hear Lothar Koch in the Berlin Philharmonic. These and all other famous oboists could be heard on recordings and on the radio, and their influence was audible in colleges, spreading internationally far beyond their own pupils. Similarly, there were still famous violin and cello teachers, taught by the great teachers of the past, but the recordings of Heifetz, Oistrakh, Grumiaux, Rostropovich and Fournier were readily available, whoever you were taught by.

This meant that the most famous individual soloists were highly influential, but in a more general way it meant that 'the best' was constantly in the ears of young musicians. By the twenty-first century, the fact is that, if one turns on the radio and hears instrumentalists playing, the standard is generally very high, but it is usually impossible to tell where they come from, or who they were influenced by. Musicians of strong personality still stand out, as they always have, and can be recognised. But this is for their personal idiosyncrasies rather than the characteristics of any school or national style.

One of the consequences of this availability of the world's finest musicians is that the custodians of traditions have faded in importance. At the beginning of the twentieth century it was possible for rival schools of teaching and playing to advocate quite different approaches, and to coexist side by side. Joachim and his disciples at the Berlin Hochschule preached the old virtues of purity and classicism, of which the most obvious technical manifestations were a traditional approach to bowing and vibrato. Meanwhile Ysaÿe, Kreisler, Flesch and others were simultaneously advocating a quite different style, with more vibrato and more assertive bowing. Over the decades fashions swung heavily in favour of the new approach, and the old 'German' style came to seem dry and old-fashioned.

Among pianists, the habit of arpeggiating chords and dislocating melody and bass in the early twentieth century was more exaggerated in some pianists than in others. To a limited extent this was associated with different schools of playing – Liszt's and Clara Schumann's pupils did it to a greater extent than pianists associated with Anton Rubinstein. But what every school of playing had in common was that, as the century went on, a gradual trend against such freedom overrode any other considerations. By the 1940s playing chords together was generally regarded as a necessary part of modern neatness, and any lapse from it was thought sloppy. Recordings from that time onwards are free of the habit, except in the case of a few very elderly pianists (such as Adelina de Lara and Bruno Walter).

Fashions have come and gone throughout history, but the later twentieth century was the first time that, through recordings, all the options were available to everyone who had access to a record player or radio. Teachers who upheld a particular tradition or espoused a particular view were far less able than before to isolate their students from the influences that were all around them. A number of consequences have flowed from this. One is a sort of democratisation of musical styles. Even the best teachers of today are no longer the figures of authority that their predecessors once were. Unimaginative students may still do just what they are told by their teachers, but there are plenty of other sources of stimulation, and the best students seek it out with an appetite. We shall return to this important point at the end of the next chapter.

Leon Botstein has written bluntly about the kind of teacher who still claims to be handing on a tradition:

> I once taught a seminar as a guest on interpretative practice at a leading American conservatory. Each student was given an entire class period at

which he or she presented a work and defended the interpretative strategy and choices. The first student, a pianist, chose a Chopin Ballade. When questioned about the opening phrase, the articulation, and the tempo choices, the student had no explanation except for an appeal to the authority of the teacher who was not only famous but a pupil of a pupil of a pupil who had studied with Karol Mikuli and Julian Fontana, Chopin's amanuensis. When I asked whether the student had ever played the child's game of telephone [Chinese Whispers], he replied yes. It took no time for this student to realize the complexities and illusions associated with a generalized appeal to the authority of an allegedly stable tradition passed down through teaching over generations.[37]

This story echoes the problems that arise with performers who claim authority from composers, as discussed in chapter 5. Of course, no musician has ever made a successful international career just by imitating a teacher. It is precisely the individual insight into the music that we most value in the playing of Schnabel or Gilels, Feuermann or Rostropovich. In the end, the audience is not much interested in who they were taught by. But something new has crept into the view of teaching and tradition in recent decades. It is a belief, stated or implied, that the tradition is fundamentally corrupt, that what is being handed down is, as Botstein says, a kind of Chinese Whispers. Though traditional teachers have much of value to offer, many modern musicians take the view that what such teachers are passing on has to be taken with a pinch of salt, and that there are other important sources with which they need to concern themselves. The root of this is the realisation that an old man telling a pupil how to play Beethoven may not know any better than the pupil how people would have played in Beethoven's day.

This has, since the 1970s, led to a split in the culture of musical tradition and teaching, and a new approach has become pervasive. There are still teachers teaching in the traditional ways. But overlaid on top of this tradition (or under-lying it) is a parallel culture which is fundamentally archaeological. It is based on the notion that, in order to perform the music of J. S. Bach or Beethoven, our job is not to receive a living performance tradition, but to re-awaken something from the past which was dead. Together with the ongoing oral tradition passed from teacher to pupil, we have a culture based on evidence, historical documents, studies of performance practice, and the avoidance of error. Ironi-cally, the dwindling of the oral tradition has taken place just as people have become aware of historical recordings: so the oral tradition of the past, with all its schools and teachers, has itself become part of the objectively analysed evidence on which we now base our painstakingly constructed 'style'.

CHAPTER SEVEN

Questions of Authority:
the Archaeological Approach

From the second half of the twentieth century onwards, a major focus for thinking about what gives performers their authority has been the field of 'Early Music' and its associated period instrument movement. Asked to name pioneers in the field, many people today might think of David Munrow's Early Music Consort and Michael Morrow's Musica Reservata, which were both active from the 1960s. Before that there were famous recordings by the Swiss group Schola Cantorum Basiliensis directed by August Wenzinger, and the New York Pro Musica with Noah Greenberg and Russell Oberlin. From the 1970s onwards the period performance movement gathered pace, dispersed to a wider and wider public by recordings and broadcasts.

But the work of earlier pioneers stretches back into the nineteenth century, and recordings of what was then known as 'Old Music' were made from the early years of the twentieth century. Though most of these recordings are now little known, they shed fascinating and revealing light on the whole concept of 'period' performance, and its interaction with the fashions of the day. This chapter therefore begins with a discussion of some of the most important of the pioneers preserved on early recordings.

Pioneers of Early Music performance

The Columbia History of Music, a series of records which first started appearing in 1929 and was edited by Percy Scholes, included a number of recordings by the Dolmetsch family: Arnold on the clavichord, Rudolph on the harpsichord and virginals, and viol consorts in which Arnold and Rudolph were joined by Cécile, Carl, Nathalie and Mabel. The series also included madrigals conducted by the great editor E. H. Fellowes, and early choral works conducted by Sir Richard Terry. An associate of the Dolmetsch family, Violet Gordon Woodhouse, made the first recordings on the harpsichord, though her fame was later eclipsed by the charismatic Wanda Landowska.

Landowska established the Ecole de Musique Ancienne near Paris in 1925, and during the 1930s a number of important pioneers of Early Music were based in Paris. In 1932 a beautifully produced edition of Couperin's harpsichord pieces was published by Editions de l'Oiseau-Lyre, one of the first ventures of the publishing house founded in Paris by the Australian Louise Dyer. L'Oiseau-Lyre also published recordings from the 1930s onwards, the early issues including a number of French composers of the seventeenth and eighteenth centuries: François and Louis Couperin, De Lalande, Rameau and others.

A major recording enterprise was supervised by the German musicologist Curt Sachs, who worked at the Musée de l'Homme in Paris and taught at the Sorbonne. Sachs had already in 1930 supervised an anthology on twelve discs called Two Thousand Years of Music, which ranged from ancient Greek and Jewish chant to the eighteenth century. In Paris during the 1930s he began an immense enterprise called L'Anthologie Sonore, an ongoing series which continued into the 1950s, eventually totalling more than 150 records. It ranged across music which was mostly unknown outside history books, from the tenth to the eighteenth century. Meanwhile, the great teacher Nadia Boulanger was installed at the Ecole Normale, inspiring young composers and becoming known as a conductor, and performing and recording Monteverdi's madrigals with a vocal group.

These are only some of the most prominent musicians working in the field of early music in the first part of the twentieth century. What impact did they make, and how does their work strike us now, from the perspective of a world steeped in the sounds of period instruments and vocal groups?

Reviews of the early Dolmetsch recordings make interesting reading, because they acknowledge the importance of the enterprise while warning delicately of its limitations. In October 1929, the editor of the *Gramophone*, Compton Mackenzie, wrote an editorial welcoming their consort recordings, and remembering his first encounter with the Dolmetsch family in the early years of the century, when, as an undergraduate, he took part in a revival of an Elizabethan play in one of the college gardens in Cambridge: 'Both before and after the play the audience was beguiled by enchanting music played by the Dolmetsch family, they too dressed in Elizabethan costumes. I have seldom enjoyed music as much as I enjoyed the music on that fine summer afternoon a quarter of a century ago . . . . But I cannot expect that many of my readers are going to be able to conjure up from the past, from one Columbia disc, the pictures that I have been able to conjure up, and so, to speak frankly, I shall have to warn them that they may find these fantasies for viols a little dull.'[1] Another reviewer in the same magazine wrote, 'That the performances of the Dolmetsch family are not always perfect is well known. Their value lies at times more in spirit than in truth; but the influence of the craftsmanship and art that the family has been carrying on for the last fifteen years at Haslemere has been deep and profitable for music.'[2]

The recordings, of viol consorts by Weelkes, Norcome and Dowland, now sound very plain and at times rather tentative, with Cécile Dolmetsch singing Dowland's 'Awake sweet love' like a reluctant treble at a school speech day. But any tendency to scoff ought to be put firmly in its place by the realisation that these were truly pioneering recordings. They were essentially amateur music-making, and indeed Arnold Dolmetsch was proud to call himself an amateur.[3] In this sense, one could argue that these recordings were closer to being 'authentic' than any of the Early Music recordings of the late twentieth century. For whom, after all, were Elizabethan viol consorts and songs written, and by whom were they originally performed?

Arnold Dolmetsch, the head of the family, was first and foremost a craftsman, as few later performers of early music have been. He was one of the most important figures in the growth of historical performance, historical instrument-making, and the revival of 'Old Music'. His father was a maker of pianos, and his grandfather was an organ-builder, and as a young man he learned both crafts from them in their workshops in France. The turning-point in his career came when he was a student at the Royal College of Music in London. He wrote about it in an article in 1929, the same year that his family's consort recordings began to appear: 'In 1889 in the British Museum, I found an immense collection of English Instrumental Music of the 16th and 17th centuries. Although well aware of the contempt of musical authorities for the little of that music they had seen, I was struck by its interest and beauty. Fortunately I felt from the first that that this music would only be effective if played upon the instruments for which it was written. Viols, lutes, virginals and clavichords had not yet become the prey of collectors. I had no great difficulty in procuring some. Having failed to find anybody who could put these instruments in sufficiently good playing order to satisfy my requirements, I remembered that I was a craftsman. I soon rigged up a workshop in the attic of my house and began to work.'[4]

The list of people who encouraged Dolmetsch, and for whom he made instruments, includes William Morris, Edward Burne-Jones, W. B. Yeats, Joseph Joachim and George Bernard Shaw. Shaw heard and tried a clavichord that Dolmetsch made for the Royal College of Music in 1894 (and which is still in the College's Museum of Instruments), and described it as 'a little masterpiece, excellent as a musical instrument and pleasant to look at, which seems to me to be likely to begin such a revolution in domestic instruments as William Morris's work made in domestic furniture. I therefore estimate the birth of this little clavichord as, in a modest computation, about forty thousand times as important as the Handel Festival.'[5]

Arnold Dolmetsch was, by all accounts, a remarkable player on the clavichord. He pioneered recordings on it, including the beginning of what was planned by Columbia as the first complete recording of J. S. Bach's 48 Preludes and

Fugues. But he was old and increasingly ill, and he completed only a few of them. They give little idea of what he must have been like in his prime, and are at times stumbling and hesitant, particularly in the Chromatic Fantasia and Fugue, which accompanied the first, and only, volume recorded in 1931. But they do show a remarkable musician putting his scholarship to expressive effect. In his famous book *The Interpretation of the Music of the XVII and XVIII Centuries,* which he had first published in 1915, Dolmetsch quotes writers who describe the practice of 'notes inégales', in which pairs of notes are played unevenly. He uses this nuance very expressively in his performance of the Prelude in F minor from Book 2 of the '48'. Together with the very loose relationship between left and right hands, this creates a fascinating mixture of scholarly practice and early twentieth-century habit.

Of the other members of the Dolmetsch family, the most notable were Arnold's sons: Carl, who became distinguished as a recorder player, making the first solo recordings on that instrument, and Rudolph, who was a brilliant harpsichordist. Tragically, Rudolph outlived his father by only two years, dying at sea in 1942, so he made few recordings. Those that he did make show a wide range. In Scarlatti he played with great flair, on one of the big concert harpsichords built by Arnold. But Rudolph Dolmetsch also recorded Elizabethan music on the virginals, playing in a straightforwardly neat and rhythmical style appropriate to the intimate nature of the music. His approach is a great deal more 'modern' than the rhythmically looser and freer style of his father, even though his first recordings appeared in that same Columbia History of Music in which the family's viol consort performed in 1929.

Closely associated with the Dolmetsch family was the player who first recorded on the harpsichord, and whose fame was second only to that of Landowska. Violet Gordon Woodhouse was born in 1872 and trained as a pianist. She met Arnold Dolmetsch in 1910, and two years later bought from him a harpsichord and a clavichord. She, like Arnold Dolmetsch, acquired an impressive circle of friends and admirers: George Bernard Shaw, T. E. Lawrence, Ethel Smyth, Serge Diaghileff, Vaslav Nijinsky, Thomas Beecham, and Frederick Delius, who wrote a harpsichord piece for her. We owe her recordings partly to the fact that she and her husband, Gordon Woodhouse, who devotedly furthered her career, ran out of money after the First World War, and for some years she became a full-time concert performer. In 1922 a review appeared in the *Musical Times* with the title 'Old Music': 'Many were drawn to such concerts as those given by Mrs Gordon Woodhouse by the air of respectability conveyed in the words "old music", and by the notion that the hall-mark of good taste nowadays is to be susceptible to the quaint, old-fashioned, even primitive charm of these soothing strains. They are learning, however, that there is no need for these patronising adjectives. No musically-inclined person could hear Mrs Woodhouse play the B flat Bach Partita without feeling that the music is as alive and full-blooded as most of the modern romantic stuff that audiences are brought up on.'[6]

Violet Gordon Woodhouse was indeed a performer of strong character, with a particular feel for rhythmic freedom and tempo rubato. But her rubato, like that of Arnold Dolmetsch, is as much a nuance of her time as a historical adoption. Dolmetsch had written in his famous book on interpretation, 'It is obvious that emotional feeling, if there be any, will cause the player to linger on particularly expressive notes and to hurry exciting passages. If there are people who think that the old music does not require *tempo rubato*, it is because they are ignorant of the fact that it was as common formerly as it is now.'[7] But when Dolmetsch wrote those words, 'now' was 1915, when generally held ideas of rhythmic freedom were very different from the ideas of the early twenty-first century. In those days it was perfectly acceptable for the melody in the right hand to free itself rhythmically from the accompaniment in the left, and Dolmetsch showed in his book that such a technique had its origins at least as early as the eighteenth century. Violet Gordon Woodhouse demonstrates this style of rhythmic freedom, and its application to eighteenth-century music, very vividly in the slow movement of J. S. Bach's Italian Concerto (1927), in which the melody moves with great freedom, while the accompaniment keeps up a steady pulse (though one which fluctuates in pace).[8]

The year 1912, in which Woodhouse acquired her Dolmetsch harpsichord and clavichord, was also the year in which Wanda Landowska took delivery of a harpsichord made to her own specification by Pleyel of Paris. Landowska is the most famous name in twentieth-century harpsichord-playing, and with good reason. Despite the pioneering work of the Dolmetsch family, Violet Gordon Woodhouse and others, it was Landowska more than anyone who achieved the rehabilitation of the harpsichord as a concert instrument worldwide. Like Woodhouse, she began her career as a pianist, but she was already playing the harpsichord in public by 1903. Armed with her massive iron-framed Pleyel harpsichord, she created a sensation wherever she went, and taught many distinguished pupils in Germany, France, and, for the last part of her life, America. J. S. Bach was the mainstay of her repertoire. In 1933 she first performed the Goldberg Variations, a work which was, up to that time, admired in theory, but rarely actually played by pianists. She also championed a wider repertoire of harpsichord music, including Scarlatti, Couperin, Rameau and Handel, as well as writing passionately about the harpsichord and its music. She did not see herself as a kind of musical archaeologist, and she wrote with something approaching contempt against the notion that it might be possible to give narrowly 'authentic' performances of old music:

> How can we men of today have the presumption to believe that we feel and play exactly like Bach, Couperin, their predecessors and contemporaries? It is altogether folly, lack of intelligence and of assimilated culture. We follow

musicological discoveries step by step with great attention. We study deeply, trying our best to understand ancient precepts to the letter. With all our heart we approach as closely as we can this remote music and these revered masters. But between them and us Beethoven, Chopin, Wagner, Debussy, Stravinsky and so many others have existed. We represent an accumulation, and we are powerless against that fact. And why should we rebel? Let us submit consciously to this transformation of matter. At no time in the course of my work have I ever tried to reproduce exactly what the old masters did. Instead, I study, I scrutinize, I love, and I recreate.[9]

As many writers have observed, Landowska was at her most impressive in rhythmically exuberant music, such as Scarlatti's more boisterous sonatas, or J. S. Bach's Fantasia in C minor. Her performances of these works were meticulously orchestrated with changes of registration, a style that set the standard until the development of a more directly historical approach to harpsichord registration from the 1970s onwards. In gentler music, Landowska tends towards a sort of dogged wilfulness. But one thing is certain, that much of her personality is missing from the records. As with Paderewski, whose exceptional status is a mystery to anyone who has only heard his recordings, so with Landowska there was clearly something magnetic about her physical presence at concerts that does not come over on the recordings. People who saw her describe the extraordinary contrast between this delicate, graceful little woman and the astonishing energy of her playing. It is also clear that her harpsichord is ill-served by the recording process of her day. Its power and variety, supplied by Pleyel to her specification, were deliberately designed for modern concert conditions, but the recordings convey a hard, clanging sound. One gets a better idea of how brilliant it must have sounded from later players on the Pleyel harpsichord, notably the impressive first recordings of her pupil Rafael Puyana, made in the 1960s.

What does come over on all Landowska's recordings is the unusual sense of control and coherence in everything she plays. There is nothing 'loose' in her playing, and that immediately makes her seem a more modern player than Violet Gordon Woodhouse, despite her eccentricities. In Couperin she has a meticulously rhythmical way of playing all the elaborate ornaments, which can often seem fussy or rambling in less disciplined hands. The six records of Couperin that she recorded for HMV's 'Couperin Society' edition in 1934 were the first substantial collection of his pieces to be recorded. Up to that point, Couperin had generally figured only as the supplier of occasional character-pieces as tasteful encores in piano recitals.

The use of period instruments for old music was not widespread in the 1920s and 1930s. Editions de L'Oiseau-Lyre, who published their edition of Couperin two years before Landowska's recording, also made recordings of their own, of Couperin, De Lalande, Rameau and other French composers. The 'Orchestre de

L'Oiseau-Lyre' played on conventional modern instruments. Roger Desormière conducted them in movements from De Lalande's *Musique pour les soupers du Roi*, with a full-blooded string sonority very different from modern approaches to this music. The bassoonist Fernand Oubradous directed a chamber group in the fourth of Couperin's *Concerts royaux*. This recording is still a delight. The rhythms, particularly the dotted rhythms, are very pointed, with the ornaments snappily executed. And although the instruments are modern, not period, the pungent tone of Mystil Morel's oboe and, particularly, of Oubradous's French bassoon in effect gives an almost 'period' sonority, quite different from the smoother, blander sound of modern woodwind.

Period instruments are to be heard in the early issues of L'Anthologie Sonore, which began in 1933, and whose performers were chosen 'to render these works scrupulously faithful to the originals'. Curt Sachs himself conducted eighteenth-century suites with a conventional modern string orchestra, which, like the orchestra conducted by Desormière for L'Oiseau Lyre, now sounds rather thick-toned, with the occasional portamento. More striking are the contributions by the American conductor and musicologist Safford Cape, who specialised in the realisation of thirteenth- to sixteenth-century music, and had recently formed the Pro Musica Antiqua of Brussels. Their recordings for L'Anthologie Sonore include vocal works by the fifteenth-century composers Dufay, Obrecht and Brassart. These incorporate conjectural realisations of instrumental parts, played convincingly on viols, lutes, trombones and other wind instruments. The vocal parts have more of the character of the recording period, tending to be rather swoopy and warbly.

The same is true of the St George's Singers, the choir conducted by E. H. Fellowes, and named after St George's Chapel Windsor, where Fellowes was the director of music from 1927. They recorded a number of Elizabethan madrigals, in which the rather loose vibrato and portamento make their singing sound quaint to modern ears. Indeed, it is difficult to find choral singing of the inter-war period which does not sound strange in this way to listeners used to the refinements of modern period singing. Of the vocal groups performing English repertoire, the English Singers still retain some charm. They did more than anyone to popularise the English madrigal in the early years of recording. Originally a vocal quartet who sang at St Martin-in-the-Fields, London, they augmented themselves to a sextet to sing madrigals in public at the suggestion of the tenor Steuart Wilson, and with the encouragement of Fellowes. They gave their first concert in 1920, and made their first recording the following year, 'Six noses crowded into the single horn' as Wilson described it.[10] For their concerts, they adopted the custom of singing while sitting round a table, an arrangement for which original editions of madrigals were often intended. Like most ensemble singing of the inter-war years, the recordings of the English Singers sound very much of their period. But there is a clarity and intimacy to the sound of their single voices, and to their pronunciation and timing, which make them still charming to listen too, with the slight waywardness of a well-rehearsed string quartet of the period.

The madrigal recording of the 1930s which has remained most famous is the collection of Monteverdi recorded in 1937 in Paris by a group of eight singers directed by Nadia Boulanger. There is nothing drily 'authentic' about these performances: no period violins or bows, no harpsichord. Boulanger directs the singers from the piano, in itself a feature which roots them firmly in her own period. They have extraordinary intensity of spirit: highly atmospheric and dramatic in 'Hor ch'el ciel e la terra', a level of concentration in 'Lasciatemi morire' which makes them sound almost like a Russian choir, and wonderful buoyancy of rhythm in 'Chiome d'oro'. The other ingredient which has made these recordings survive to the present day is the very French quality of the singing, particularly the quivering lightness of the tenors Paul Derenne and Hugues Cuénod – a style that has something in common with the famous French chansonniers such as Charles Trenet.

It is a general truth that the qualities that make early twentieth-century recordings of 'Old Music' endure, and still be enjoyed seventy or eighty years later, have very little to do with the extent to which they approach any later notions of 'correct' period performance. Landowska cuts through the years with her rhythmic power, Boulanger's group with their sense of conviction, and their combination of intensity and lightness. And the same applies in the larger instrumental works of the eighteenth century. String orchestras that sound heavy-footed, like those conducted by Desormière and Sachs, are no longer of great interest. But the chamber orchestras directed by Adolf Busch and Boyd Neel still convince in their Bach and Handel, even though they do not sound like modern players.

The Busch Chamber Players were formed in 1934, and first gave concerts in Florence and in Basel, where Adolf Busch was then living as an émigré from Nazi Germany. Then in October 1935 they travelled to London and performed the six Brandenburg Concertos in two concerts at Queen's Hall. The reviews make one regret not having been there:

> No one then present (and the hall was full) is likely to forget the joy of hearing the six Brandenburg Concertos played under practically ideal conditions. The Concertos – as one heard them – seemed to come straight from Bach himself. What Bach's inner ear had heard, we now heard, as it were, with himself – and in actual outer hearing it may well be that the players of Bach's day never gave him anything quite so beautiful as the Busch renderings. All worked together, in an ensemble that had the initiative and intimacy of true chamber music, together with the rich resilience of orchestral tone – an ensemble the more remarkable because in 18th-century fashion there was no conductor.

The only departures from the material of Bach's own day were in the substitution of a piano for the harpsichord, and in the greater sonority of the string instruments. As Serkin made the piano sound like a heavenly harpsichord, there was nothing to cavil at in the first; as to the second, only antiquarians would prefer the weaker-toned violins of old.[11]

These views are now unfashionable. We have had ample opportunity to get used to the 'weaker-toned violins of old', and the antiquarian sound of them is now a commonplace. The tone and texture of Busch's chamber orchestra is more substantial than is now thought appropriate for Bach, and although solo pianists still play Bach, a piano as continuo instrument is now a rarity in the concert hall. But there is no mistaking the beauty of sound and phrasing on the recordings of the Concertos that Busch made in 1935.

The Busch Chamber Players returned to London the following year to repeat their performances of the Brandenburg Concertos, together with Bach's Orchestral Suites. Again the reviewer in the *Musical Times* was full of praise for their daring in performing Bach as chamber music: '. . . once again the courage displayed in performing these intricate works in true chamber music style without a conductor justified itself. Where many players are involved the risk is great, but if the feat succeeds, so is the gain. With Adolf Busch to lead, failure becomes unthinkable. His dominance, however, is so kindly that he sometimes makes one think of a shepherd, with Rudolf Serkin as a sort of enchanting sheep-dog of music, to help him marshal the flock.' But the reviewer also found a more sombre resonance to these concerts, in which German and British musicians sat side by side performing German music in England in 1936: 'It was a moving thing to hear the musicians playing from their very hearts, and it was moving to see the rapt response of the audience. Yet touching beyond all it was to remember Bach who, unknown to himself, by his spiritual strength and steadfastness has become for thousands today their main point of stability in a world of mental and moral chaos.'[12]

Busch and his Chamber Players recorded the Brandenburg Concertos in 1935 and the Orchestral Suites in 1936. Busch re-formed his Chamber Players in America in the 1940s, mostly with American players, and they recorded the Handel Concertos Opus 6 in 1946, this time with harpsichord continuo.

Several things are particularly striking about the Busch performances. One is their sense of rhythmic freedom and lightness in fast movements. There is a strong element of the dance in the way they point rhythms, often with quick short notes, and particularly with overdotted dotted rhythms. The third movement of Handel's Concerto Opus 6 No. 10 is a characteristic example. The semiquavers (sixteenth notes) are on tiptoe, the quavers (eighth notes) pointed, the dotted rhythms overdotted (particularly the last of each group, giving a push to the next beat). The phrasing breathes, and there is not a moment in the short dance without a sense of rhythmic impulse and direction. The same is true of the first bourrée from the Orchestral Suite No. 1 in C. The pairs of quavers are fast and light, and the dotted rhythms crisply overdotted.

This has little to do with Bach scholarship. Though Busch adopted a harpsi-chord in his 1946 Handel recordings, the style of rhythm in the 1935–6 Bach recordings with piano is much the same. There has been, since Busch's day, much research and debate concerning the treatment of dotted and other rhythms in eighteenth-century music. It is clear that Busch knew little of such matters (he does not double-dot French overtures). His style of rhythm is the same as that in his recordings of Beethoven as a soloist and with his string quartet. Again, there is more knowledge now of Bach's stringed instruments and bows than there was in the 1930s. Busch played on gut strings not for reasons of 'historical awareness', but because he preferred them.

Overall, one has the impression not of a scholar who has researched the way things were done in Bach's day, but of a player with a natural flair for rhythm and phrasing, who, for all his German seriousness of purpose, never forgot the days and nights he and his brother and father spent playing dance music in the villages round their home town of Siegen in Germany. It is with these fundamental qualities of musicianship that he and his Chamber Players brought the music of Bach and Handel to life, making the large-scale performances conducted by Henry Wood, Furtwängler, Stokowski, Koussevitzky and others seem leaden and bloated by comparison.

The modern Early Music movement

The development of the modern Early Music and period instrument movement got into its stride in the 1950s and 1960s, and took off with remarkable success from the 1970s. August Wenzinger had founded the Schola Cantorum Basiliensis at Basel in Switzerland as long ago as 1933 (Wenzinger played viola da gamba in Busch's recording of the Brandenburg Concertos), but it was with their recordings from the 1950s onwards that they became known to a wide public. Gustav Leonhardt led the Dutch Early Music field from the 1950s, becoming one of the central figures of Early Music performance. One of the Dutch circle, Frans Brüggen, rose to fame from the late 1950s as a recorder player. His brilliant and highly expressive playing raised the status of the instrument to a completely new level, attracting the attention not only of Early Music enthusiasts but also of contemporary composers. Nikolaus Harnoncourt founded Concentus Musicus in Vienna in 1953, and in the same year Noah Greenberg started the New York Pro Musica. David Munrow's Early Music Consort, Michael Morrow's Musica Reservata, Anthony Rooley's Consort of Musicke and Franzjosef Maier's Collegium Aureum followed in the 1960s. John Eliot Gardiner's English

Baroque Soloists, Christopher Hogwood's Academy of Ancient Music, Roger Norrington's London Classical Players, Andrew Parrott's Taverner Choir and Consort, and Trevor Pinnock's English Concert were all founded in the 1970s. There were other figures who, though not working principally with period instruments, were important in promoting early repertoire or historical practices. Among these was Raymond Leppard, whose colourfully dramatic reworkings of the operas of Monteverdi and Cavalli in the 1960s and 1970s attracted mixed praise and criticism. Charles Mackerras pioneered the use of appoggiaturas and other eighteenth-century ornamentation in the operas of Mozart in the 1960s, long before their general acceptance.

The modern Early Music phenomenon and its earlier origins have been described in fascinating detail by Harry Haskell in *The Early Music Revival.*[13] The list of performers and groups who rose to prominence in a short period of time is astonishing, and the success of the movement was profound and long-lasting. With the easy availability of long-playing records and later CDs the performances of the period instrument groups were spread round the world very rapidly. The period violinist Simon Standage put the importance of recordings bluntly. Asked, in a BBC radio programme, whether the English Concert would have succeeded without recordings, he said, 'Would the whole movement have succeeded without recording? I doubt it. If orchestral sounds have changed, it's because of the constant bombardment of recordings. A concert series here or there wouldn't have had the same effect on public taste.'[14]

At first, the greatest successes were in music that was previously known only to specialists, such as the New York Pro Musica's reconstruction of the medieval *Play of Daniel* (1958), and the wide range of medieval and Renaissance music recorded by the Early Music Consort and Musica Reservata. To hear such music performed with vividness and enthusiasm, in concert as well as on record, opened the ears of a generation of listeners. The performance of such early repertoire has remained at the heart of the Early Music movement, and many of the performances over the last thirty years, both instrumental and vocal, have been revelatory.[15] But a parallel strand has been the gradual encroachment of period instrumentalists on repertoire which had previously been performed by conventional musicians on modern-style instruments.

There had been some elements of this overlap for many years, notably in Landowska's recordings of J. S. Bach and Scarlatti, which were listed in record catalogues alongside performances on the piano by Edwin Fischer, Vladimir Horowitz and others. But as the period instrument movement grew, with its alliance of scholars and practitioners, it came to pose a serious challenge to conventional performers. At first this was focussed mainly on Baroque repertoire, particularly J. S. Bach and Handel, but later it moved on to Haydn and Mozart, Beethoven, and eventually through to Brahms and even Mahler and Elgar.

In the early years the challenge to modern orthodoxy tended to be carried out with self-confidence bordering on arrogance. Famous figures from the world of conventional Bach performance were spoken of with disdain. The word 'authenticity' was much used, with the implication that conventional performance with its baggage of tradition was founded on accumulated error. Musicians talked of 'stripping away the layers of discoloured varnish to reveal the true colours' of Bach or Mozart, without stopping to ask themselves whether music really had any useful analogy with a painting.

As early as 1951 Theodor Adorno wrote a paper entitled 'Bach defended against his devotees' in which he railed against the 'purists' and 'Philistines' whose favourite argument was that the work 'need only be performed asceti-cally in order to speak. . . . At times one can hardly avoid the suspicion that the sole concern of today's Bach devotees is to see that no inauthentic dynamics, modifications of tempo, oversize choirs and orchestras creep in.'[16] Adorno was writing specifically about German post-war attempts at 'authentic' performance, before the ideas of Leonhardt and others began to produce a much more flexible approach to Baroque expression. But accusa-tions of such a false asceticism have surfaced from time to time as period instrumentalists have moved through the repertoire. Richard Taruskin's attack on Norrington's recording of Beethoven's Ninth Symphony in 1988 was, in essence, not very different from Adorno's criticism of German Bach-performance more than thirty years before: by sticking rigidly to the letter of Beethoven's score, and throwing out what Norrington regarded as corrupt accretions (particularly unmarked tempo changes), Norrington had trivialised the symphony. Taruskin concludes

> This, then, is the ultimate resister's Ninth, a Ninth to mollify and reassure those many of us who have come to hate the piece – or rather, who hate what the piece has come to stand for. The question is whether what the piece has come to stand for – that sublimity, that naïveté, that ecstacy of natural religion, that bathos – is something inherent in the Ninth, or something that has accreted to it. To take the latter view is, I firmly believe, the easy way out, and that is what Roger Norrington and his forces, with magnificent dedication, conviction, and technical panache, have accomplished. In so doing, Norrington has again shown himself, as he did with the Second and Eighth, to be a truly authentic voice of the late twentieth century.[17]

One aspect of Early Music purism, which has also been attacked by Taruskin and others, is its insistence on the 'right' instruments for whatever repertoire is being played. This has gone through a number of phases over the years. Until the 1960s a harpsichord was 'right' for Bach, and a piano, to those of a historical bent, was 'wrong'. For a time around the 1970s it was fashionable for the proponents of authenticity to deride the very idea of Bach played on the piano, even when the careers of Glenn Gould and Rosalyn Tureck were at their peak. But it took a long time for the Early Music movement to arrive at the use of harpsichords that Bach himself would have recognised. The massive, iron-framed Pleyel of Landowska was rapidly falling out of favour, but the harpsichords played in the 1950s by Thurston Dart, Ralph Kirkpatrick, George Malcolm and others, though lighter than the Pleyel, were still big, solidly constructed instruments equipped with a sixteen-foot stop, a row of pedals with which to change registration in mid-flight, and sometimes a Venetian swell with which to create a crescendo and diminuendo. Similarly, the concern with orchestral forces playing Bach in the 1950s was simply that they should be small. The instruments themselves were not yet, for the most part, 'period'.

All this changed over the next two decades, as skilfully constructed copies of the old instruments gradually became available. The harpsichords played by Gustav Leonhardt were no longer sturdy modern instruments designed specifically for use in large concert halls, but copies of historical instruments of Bach's and Couperin's day (or sometimes the originals), specifically German or French in design. Increasingly, Baroque music was played on Baroque-style stringed instruments with the bows of the period, and instrument-makers made, and players learned to play, the wind instruments of the time. A century on from Arnold Dolmetsch's early clavichords, the role of the craftsman had again become central to the development of period instruments. Landowska's mighty Pleyel harpsichord came to seem like an absurd anachronism.

This might seem a straightforward trajectory towards a brave new world in which Bach and other 'early' composers were to be rescued from the accumulated corruptions of later centuries. But two elements, among others, conspired to make the situation more complex than that. The first is that old instruments are, in many cases, difficult to play accurately and in tune, particularly by musicians who have only been brought up on their modern counterparts. Controlling an eighteenth-century oboe or bassoon, with its cross-fingerings and different designs of reed, or an eighteenth-century bow on gut strings, or pitching the notes on a narrow-bore valveless horn, requires great skill which cannot be acquired in a hurry. But the market for Early Music and period performances was booming, there was a spirit of pioneering excitement in the air, and musicians were anxious to throw off the dead weight of modern convention and move forward.

There is, not surprisingly, a rough-and-ready character to many of the period-instrument recordings of the 1970s. In a fascinating study of the social structure of Early Music, Laurence Dreyfus wrote in 1983 about the mediocrity inherent in the ramshackle equality and versatility of some Early Music groups.[18] Some of them took pride in a kind of challenging amateurism, distantly related to the amateurism of the Dolmetsch family in the early years of the century. The roughness could, in the best groups, take a highly invigorating turn: Musica

Reservata, encouraged by its director Michael Morrow, brought a palette of raucous instrumental and vocal tones to medieval and Renaissance music, partly inspired by the sounds of Middle Eastern, African and other musical traditions. But as the fashion for period performance gathered pace, there were musicians jumping on the bandwagon of Early Music who would not have done very well in the mainstream (as conventional musicians were quick to point out). Hans Keller in 1984 observed tartly, 'most of the authentic boys just aren't good enough as players to make their way without musicological crutches'.[19] This is unfair to the best of the period instrumentalists, but it is undoubtedly true that it was possible to get away with a lower standard of technical expertise in much of the repertoire of Early Music.

In unknown early repertoire, these variable standards could pass as all part of the spirit of discovery. But when it came to the performance of eighteenth-century music, musicians could not avoid comparison with the existing culture of smooth efficiency that was already in place for conventional music-making. There was therefore great pressure for standards to match those on conventional instruments. Over the years, much of the gap has been closed, partly by the musicians becoming more skilful on the old instruments, but partly by adaptation of the instruments themselves to make them easier to play.

In many cases the instruments in modern period performances are not quite those that would have been used in earlier centuries. Instrument-makers have devised ways of making the old instruments more reliable and better in tune. The most extreme example is the modern 'natural' trumpet, which Robert Barclay describes: 'Most current players have taken to using machine-made instruments with as many as four finger-holes placed in their tubing near to pressure nodes, so that the so-called "out-of-tune" harmonics of the natural series . . . will not be unpleasant to modern sensitivity. The vented instruments that have resulted from this recent "invention of tradition" are often equipped with so many anachronistic features that the result is a trumpet which resembles its baroque counterpart only superficially. . . .'[20]

On the genuine Baroque trumpet, the 'out of tune' notes can only be pulled more into tune if they are played quietly, and even then not entirely. The finger-holes have the effect of shifting the pitch into tune. This means that the modern Baroque trumpeter can play high melodic parts both loudly and in tune, a combination that would have been impossible in J. S. Bach's and Purcell's day. The vent-holes therefore do not just correct a 'fault', they encourage players and conductors to bring the volume of the trumpet closer to that of the conventional modern instrument.

The pressures to compromise in this sort of way have increased over the last thirty years. The public and critics have been trained to expect perfection and impact in performance, and so musicians are increasingly nervous of sounding tentative or of exposing themselves to unnecessary risk. When it comes to recordings, mistakes cost money. A group needs to be as reliable as possible, in order to cut down on time in the studio. Musicians are not always entirely candid about these compromises and short-cuts. Trevor Pinnock, celebrating twenty years of his period orchestra, The English Concert, in 1993 wrote: 'Some of the publicists' myths about "authenticity" have been exploded, but for us the simple fact remains the same: we like to use the tools designed for the job in hand. Instruments good enough for Bach should surely be good enough for us.'[21]

The problems have not entirely gone away. Standards on period instruments do not always reach those on conventional instruments, even today. People who listen only to recordings are, to a large extent, protected from this unreliability. Most recordings of period instrumentalists are, like most other recordings, heavily edited. Correspondence between the producer at Nimbus, Adrian Farmer, and a period instrument group, the Hanover Band, was quoted in chapter 2. The producer wrote that the small amount of editing he had already carried out had made their playing 'of a total quality which is actually beyond the competence of the Band to reproduce in a live concert'. That was in the early 1980s. Although standards have generally risen in the last twenty years, editing still disguises a great deal. A producer who specialises in recording early music said in conversation recently that he was about to record some virtuoso twentieth-century piano music 'for a change'. It would, he said, involve much less editing than most of his early music records, even though the music was far more complicated. When the reaction to this was surprise, he explained, 'Nobody goes into a studio to record virtuoso piano music without being sure that they can play it.'

There are some very fine period instrumentalists and vocal groups. One of the most successful growth areas in recent years, in terms of standards of instrumental playing, has been the orchestra. For Classical and Romantic music, there is a large international pool of period players who are extremely good. Many of them spend part of their lives in the period field, part of it playing in conventional ensembles. They switch from one to the other, the string-players in many cases using the same instrument for both purposes and changing the strings and, sometimes, the bow. This cross-fertilisation has led to a tendency for styles and standards to become increasingly merged. Period orchestras not only sound better than they used to, they sound more like conventional orchestras than they used to. And one feature of period orchestras that has encouraged this is the role of the conductor.

The 'period' conductor is the ultimate example of modern compromise. Conductors enable the best period-instrument orchestras to give performances which are virtually modern in discipline, tuning and neatness, and with the modern sense of interpretative unanimity. John Eliot Gardiner's recordings with the Orchestre Révolutionnaire et Romantique of Beethoven symphonies

(1992–3), in terms of discipline, tuning and sophistication of ensemble, bear comparison with any conventional modern orchestra (no doubt the usual amount of editing was carried out, though some of the symphonies were at least compiled from live recordings). But the conductor as we know it is a recent invention. The first conductors who took command of the expressive as well as mechanical aspects of orchestral playing were Bülow and Nikisch in the late nineteenth century. Conducting barely existed at all before the nineteenth century, and what Gardiner, Norrington and others do in front of their orchestras is in the modern tradition rather than anything earlier.

Is compromise in order to achieve modern reliability and unanimity necessarily a bad thing? It partly depends what musicians are claiming to do. There was a time when 'authenticity' was the motto of much of the Early Music movement. But when musicians use the word today, it is usually to distance themselves from such a simplistic notion. Nikolaus Harnoncourt said in an interview in 1993, 'For me, authenticity is ridiculous. If Mozart performs one of his piano concertos himself, this is authentic. My performance is authentic me; I cannot give an authentic performance of any composer.' Roger Norrington in the same year wrote about his recent recordings of Brahms, 'I have spent thirty years trying to let great pieces of music speak to us today without too many "traditional" accretions of intervening fashion . . . . In no sense did such a procedure ever aim to be "authentic" (its result will inevitably tell future generations more about us than about the composers).'[22]

This more realistic attitude to 'historically aware' performance came about partly because of some of the published attacks on over-confident assertions of the 1970s. Richard Taruskin famously demolished naïve ideas of authentic time-travelling in an essay in *Early Music* in 1984, following it up with a piece in the *New York Times* in 1990, 'The modern sound of early music'.[23] Taruskin writes, 'what we call historical performance is the sound of now, not then. It derives its authenticity not from its historical verisimilitude, but from its being for better or worse a true mirror of late-twentieth-century taste.' This sort of writing provoked some furious reactions from aggrieved musicians. But some of the best of them could always see what they were really doing, and were aware of the limitations of the exercise. Michael Morrow, director of Musica Reservata, and one of the most radical thinkers in the Early Music field, wrote an article in 1978 in which he scotched any idea that he and his colleagues were reproducing genuine medieval or Renaissance performances:

Where there is no surviving tradition – and performing style is something that can only be learned by imitation, not from books – any piece of music, medieval, renaissance, baroque, what you will, offers the modern performer the potentiality of countless possibilities of interpretation: one medieval piece, for instance, could be played in a dozen ways and the result would almost certainly appear to be twelve quite different pieces of music. Of course, one of these performances could, by sheer chance, be more or less historically correct. But how are we now to judge which? And supposing a medieval or renaissance listener could hear a modern performance of a chanson by Binchois or a Dowland lute solo, for instance, would he say (I use modern English of course) 'How can anyone ruin such fine music in this way?'; or would he exclaim 'What the hell is that? Some Moorish barbarity no doubt.' . . . Some time ago a friend of mine was at a lecture on singing and, as an illustration, the speaker played a recording of Melba: the audience giggled. In a few years time a similar audience will almost certainly be reduced to hysterics by a recording of Kathleen Ferrier singing *Kindertotenlieder*.[24]

It is surely a sign of growing self-confidence and realism in the period-instrument movement that its leading lights should now be so anxious to state the limits of what they are aiming to do. Comparing Harnoncourt's recording of Beethoven's *Missa solemnis* with Gardiner's, or Gardiner's recording of Berlioz's *Symphonie fantastique* with Norrington's, is not an exercise in determining which of the two is closer to what Berlioz or Beethoven expected, which is largely unknowable, but a judgement of the vividness with which they put over the music, which any listener is entitled to make. Just as we value some of the early twentieth-century attempts at performing Old Music for their sense of conviction rather than their historical correctness, so future generations will no doubt judge period performances of our time by a similar yardstick of musical insight.

If the claim were still being made that modern period performances sound like they would have done in the eighteenth century, then the compromise instruments that are now in use could be regarded as a deception. Perhaps some of the rough-and-ready performances of forty years ago were nearer to 'the real thing', just as Arnold Dolmetsch and his viol consort had an amateurism that was historically truer to the sixteenth century than more refined modern groups. But now that ideas about time-travelling have been put to one side, the ethics of compromising with modern taste and expectation are less of a problem. One fact that makes this inevitable is that the sound of an instrument is not a fixed thing. There are different views on how a harpsichord should be regulated and tuned, all kinds of subtleties in construction that produce different results. Identical copies of the same historical instrument never sound quite the same as each other. And with wind and stringed instruments, two players can make an identical instrument sound quite different, sometimes to a shocking extent.

At a meeting of the Historic Brass Society in Paris in 2000, Hermann Baumann, the doyen of hand-horn players, gave a masterclass. A student played the finale of a Mozart horn concerto extremely well – accurately, with rhythmic point and elegance. There then followed a discussion about the student's horn. It turned out that Baumann's hand-horn was by the same maker, and that his mouthpiece was almost the same as the student's. These niceties over, Baumann told the student that she was playing the movement far too delicately. 'This is hunting music', he said, and taking his horn he produced the most raucous, rasping sound. The student had a go, and sounded a little more brazen than she had before. Baumann rasped away again and encouraged her to do likewise. The student had another go, and sounded just a little more like Baumann, but not much. There was an unbridgeable gulf between them. They were playing virtually identical instruments, but each had a quite distinct idea about what it should sound like in this music.

Dennis Brain began his career playing on the old narrow-bore French horn, on which his father Aubrey insisted. About 1950 he changed to the wider-bore German-style horn. Comparison between recordings he made before and after this change show that, in his hands, the two instruments sound very similar. This is partly because he kept his French-style mouthpiece, which was almost conical, in preference to the more cup-shaped mouthpiece commonly used on the German instrument.[25] But it is mostly because he had a clear idea of what he wanted the horn to sound like. Whatever horn Dennis Brain had played on, he would still have sounded like Dennis Brain.

The comparative unimportance of having precisely the 'right' instrument has in recent years been proved by musicians achieving more or less period style on modern instruments. Roger Norrington, having spent some years working principally with orchestras of period instruments, has recently been conducting conventional modern orchestras, but persuading their string sections to play without vibrato. Having listened to recordings from the 1920s and 1930s of the Vienna Philharmonic and other orchestras, he had grown enthusiastic about the sound of vibratoless strings in music as late as Brahms and Mahler. The startling thing is how a modern orchestra of conventional players can instantly be converted into an orchestra with period-sounding strings, even though they are all playing on 'wrong' instruments. At the 2002 Promenade Concerts in London Norrington conducted the Salzburg Camerata, of which he became principal conductor after the death of Sandor Végh, in a concert including Beethoven's Violin Concerto with Joshua Bell. Turning on the radio in the middle of the performance, without knowing who was playing, was a striking, and somewhat bewildering, experience. It sounded like a period string orchestra with modern wind, simply because the strings were playing without vibrato.

Whether this is a good thing or not is a current subject of debate. Should orchestras have their own style, built up over the years, as they did in the past, or should they be able to switch from style to style at the bidding of the conductor? Many aspects of style are routinely flexible: no orchestra these days plays Mozart as it plays Brahms. But for a conductor to turn off an orchestra's

vibrato, and completely change the string sound, is something more fundamental. Norrington writes, 'The reason to do so is not because pure tone is
"authentic", but because it is beautiful, expressive and exciting.'[26] Nevertheless,
his argument is also based on how the orchestras of Vienna and elsewhere
played until the mid-twentieth century. He draws on historical recordings to
support his taste in this matter. Why, in that case, is Norrington not interested
in the equally traditional portamento of those orchestras? Because he does not
like it. There is an uncomfortable feeling, despite the selective appeal to history,
that the orchestra has become like a young boy's train set, which he is free to
take to pieces and rearrange whenever he gets bored with the current layout.

Clive Brown used a different analogy in the early 1990s, when he criticised
the commercially motivated race to push period-instrument record performance ever more rapidly into the nineteenth century: 'There is serious
concern that where a search to rediscover the sounds and styles of 19th-century
music conflicts with the exigencies of the recording studio and the need to
obtain a neat and tidy, easily assimilable product, it is the latter that are regarded
as paramount . . . there is infinitely more to historically sensitive performance
than merely employing the right equipment, and the public is in danger of
being offered attractively packaged but unripe fruit.'[27]

It is when one starts referring to recordings of the early twentieth century for
historical justification that the crunch comes for any ideas of period re-creation.
Norrington skilfully edges round the problem of historical reconstruction,
claiming that he is not attempting anything of the kind. For anyone who does
try to travel back to the early twentieth century we can make direct comparison
between the modern re-creation and 'the real thing' preserved on old recordings.
The most prominent attempt of this kind is the New Queen's Hall Orchestra.

The New Queen's Hall Orchestra started out with radical ambitions. The
programme for their first concert, in London on 21 February 1992, billed them
as 'The reformed New Queen's Hall Orchestra . . . founded 1895 by Sir Henry
Wood', and, furthermore, 'the world's only truly authentic symphony
orchestra'. How did the orchestra's founder, John Boyden, justify such claims?
By the use of gut strings, brass and woodwind instruments from the turn of the
century, and the use of portamento, which 'is back with a vengeance', Boyden
wrote in the programme leaflet. On the other hand, 'the New Queen's Hall
Orchestra has no intention of mimicking, or imitating, any old recordings.
Such a concept would be a complete denial of everything we are striving to
create, and to sustain into the future.' In an interview published before that first
concert, Boyden spoke of the early twentieth-century players' 'greater gift for
shaping melodies', and their 'true sense of *legato*' which has often been lost.
The leader of the orchestra, John Ludlow, was quoted as saying that 'slides,
portamenti, were less prevalent in the strings than we sometimes think. They
weren't used terribly imaginatively when they were used – and I hope that,

while still remaining "authentic", we can introduce a greater variety of slides to explore a greater range of expression.'[28]

The message was very mixed. On the one hand, this was the only 'authentic' symphony orchestra. On the other hand, there was to be no 'mimicry'. Furthermore, they hoped to improve upon the 'unimaginative' portamento of the early twentieth century.

So what is the point of such an experiment. Re-creation? Yes and no. The aim was to use selected practices of the period, but adapt others, and to recreate the spirit rather than the literal sound of the early twentieth century. In part, it was a reaction to the excesses of the modern symphony orchestra, its 'aggressive' playing, and its heavy brass section. And the high-flown ambitions of the launch have proved difficult to fulfil. Late-Romantic portamento is a particularly hard nut for modern players to crack. It goes against all their training, and the prevailing taste in which they are brought up. When the New Queen's Hall orchestra played Elgar's 'Enigma' Variations in December 1993, nearly two years after their launch, the portamento was still very discreet. In conversation after the concert, some of the woodwind players admitted that they were longing to hear more portamento from the strings. But you cannot take a group of modern string players, most of whom spend a large part of their time playing in conventional symphony orchestras, and expect them to abandon modern taste and metamorphose into an orchestra of Edwardian gentlemen. Charles Mackerras describes how he attempted to persuade the Royal Philharmonic Orchestra to play Elgar's 'Enigma' Variations with portamento somewhat like that of the Royal Albert Hall Orchestra in Elgar's own recording. He told the audience that they were to hear an attempt at 'period' portamento. The critic of *The Times* reported that it was a good thing he had told them, because the difference from normal playing was inaudible. Mackerras said, 'They couldn't do it, because they were used to playing "cleanly"'.[29]

Interestingly, John Boyden had, in the two years since the New Queen's Hall Orchestra's début, somewhat modified his expectations for the orchestra, expressed in the programme booklet. Gone is the claim that this is the only 'authentic' symphony orchestra. Instead he writes, 'The New Queen's Hall Orchestra does not claim a monopoly of integrity in performing particular pieces, nor does it lay sole claim to the high ground in any debate over style .... The reasoning behind the New Queen's Hall Orchestra's re-formation is simply that some attempt should be made to solve the problems of internal balance wrought by 20th century changes in the manufacture of instruments and that some of the spontaneity which seems to have been lost in so much music-making should be revived.'[30]

These are modest claims compared with those of the launch. From an attempt to get back to the style of c.1900, with all the 'authentic' baggage that implies, the New Queen's Hall Orchestra is aiming at more general targets of 'freedom' and 'spontaneity'. Though the style intended is different from Norrington's, with his rejection of both vibrato and portamento, the basis is the same in both cases: an appeal to modern taste and feeling, with an element of nostalgia, drawing on selected aspects of historical evidence that can comfortably be made to support them.

The various 'historically aware' conductors – Hogwood, Gardiner, Brüggen, Harnoncourt, Mackerras – share this combination of appealing to history and tailoring it to suit modern taste and expectations. None of them now claims to be 'going back', and all say, in one way or another, that they are simply making the music work as best they can. This is a long way from the aspirations of some of the hard-line practitioners of Early Music thirty years ago. For them, the authority for what they did was the evidence for the way it was done in the past. For their modern successors (in some cases the same musicians, thirty years older) the very idea of authority is hazy. The Early Music movement had thrown out the established guardians of traditional performing practices, and replaced them with the hard evidence of the past. Now that everyone agrees the evidence is not so hard as some people thought, the idea that we can have an authoritative knowledge of the past has been put firmly in its place. But what has replaced it? Certainly not any clear idea of authority, beyond that of taste and pragmatism. It is as if the past and present have ended up providing musicians with a menu of possibilities, from which they can pick and choose at will.

Some of the thinking involved in the choice is muddled and produces performances that lack clear purpose, but some of it is inspired and produces wonderful results by any standard. It is also subject to the forces of pragmatism and the market. The modern Period Sound, with its straight, silver strings and old-style wind instruments, has been spectacularly successful. If there is Handel or Vivaldi coming out of loudspeakers in a hotel lobby anywhere in the world, it is now as likely to be played by a period group as by a conventional one. And the style has become so globalised that, as in conventional music-making, it is almost impossible to tell apart period instrument groups from Britain, Holland, Japan or the USA.

One of the prices paid for modern globalisation and modern polish that afflicts the period-instrument scene is a tendency to fall back on standardised forms of expression, mannerisms that musicians can understand quickly. Michael Morrow was already complaining about this in the 1970s: 'In recent years the emergence of the old-music virtuoso has done much to encourage the manufacture of counterfeit performing styles. One finds performer after performer adopting the same mannerisms, mannerisms based on no known historical practice, but merely in imitation of a hero's personal idiosyncracies.'[31] In particular, over the years the familiar swelling and sighing of the *messa di voce*, and the scampering of fast passages, have created a *lingua franca* of period expression. Both of these habits began with a basis of good scholarship, but their habitual use in all circumstances in Baroque music has become a cliché. The fact that everyone does it makes it easy to take any musicians from different countries of the world and get them to play together with little rehearsal. But it has levelled Baroque music down to a tiresome common denominator. And one of the few things we know for certain about performance in the eighteenth century and earlier is that there were few if any common denominators: musicians in different towns and countries had different instruments, different pitches, different styles.

The very best players of period instruments today are those who have techniques as good as those of the conventional performers, rise above the generalised clichés of period expression, and think things out for themselves. Some of the leading players work in both period and conventional fields, and carry over experience from one to the other. There is certainly compromise, but there is also fruitful cross-fertilisation of ideas. A good example is the violinist Erich Höbarth, who leads both the Quatuor Mosaïques, a highly admired period-instrument quartet, and the Vienna Sextet, which plays on conventional instruments. Höbarth also leads the Concentus Musicus of Vienna. The difference in sound and style between the period-style Quatuor Mosaïques and the 'modern' Vienna Sextet is not very great. Both groups are excellent, but in the way they play Mozart, for example, the Quartet sounds quite close to a conventional ensemble, while the Sextet has elements of period influence. The vibrato of the Quartet is slightly more restrained than in a modern group, but virtually all long notes have it, and the style of phrasing, detailed care over nuances, the placing of accents and shaping of phrases, are all very modern in style. Only a slight stringiness to the tone, the gently 'etched' articulation of the old-style bows, and a slightly different sonority and balance distinguish them from a modern-instrument ensemble. The Sextet is, for a conventional group, quite restrained in its use of vibrato, so that at times its members sound almost as if they are playing period instruments.

In conversation Erich Höbarth says that the two things that make the greatest difference between period and modern playing are the pitch and the strings. The lower pitch for period performance changes the resonance of the instrument, partly because of the pitch-change itself, partly because of the reduction in tension. The use of all-gut strings also reduces the tension. And with a gut E-string, it is impossible to play with an aggressive style: a steel E-string will withstand a forceful attack, but a gut string will not respond, and the sound breaks up. So it is what gut makes impossible, as well as what it allows, that contributes to the difference in style. But in any case, Höbarth prefers to play with a gut E-string most of the time, even in the modern-instrument Sextet. He likes the greater sense of physical contact with the gut string.

Steven Isserlis finds the solidity of a gut string under the hand satisfying, compared with which the modern steel and covered strings almost 'disappear'.

But his main reason for preferring gut to steel is the sound: 'It is not that one cannot do much with the sound [of steel strings] – on the contrary, one can do a lot; but one cannot do nothing to it. The player has to make the sound come alive by various means – vibrato, portato, etc.; whereas with gut, the sound is alive to start with, and therefore one can play as purely as one likes, without adding anything – the sound will be engaging.'[32] This difference in physical sensation between steel and gut must partly account for the difference in the sound of shifting between many old and modern recordings. Even a rapid and discreet shift carried out by Arnold Rosé or Adolf Busch has a characteristic sound of a whistling glide that is virtually inaudible in conventional modern playing. And the gentler attack required when using gut also helps to account for some of the differences of articulation between the old and the new. The Chicago Symphony Orchestra under Solti in the 1970s had a cutting edge that would have been impossible in Rosé's pre-war Vienna Philharmonic. In the Vienna recordings one hears not cutting, but tugging.

Erich Höbarth agrees that there are, for him, no clear-cut distinctions between period and conventional playing. For many years he has played on the same violin in both the Quatuor Mosaïques and the Vienna Sextet, whether he is playing Mozart or Brahms, though with different bows. For Baroque music he borrows a different instrument. He has a beautiful violin, which he chose partly because of its fairly light construction, which makes it suitable for period performance. He admits that there is little difference in style between the way he plays the Schubert Quintet on period violin with the Quatuor Mosaïques, or on modern violin with the Vienna Sextet. And he stresses that there is no question of performing 'as it was' in the time of Mozart or Schubert. The players simply equip themselves with a convenient approximation to the instruments that the composer had in mind, and use their musical intelligence.

In this respect, attitudes have not only retreated from the literalism of a few years ago, but actually moved back closer to the early twentieth-century approach to 'Old Music'. The 1936 review of the Busch Chamber Players quoted earlier described them as playing the Brandenburg Concertos 'under conditions reproducing those of Bach's own day with a fidelity profound as to the spirit if not exact in antiquarian accuracy'. Though ideas of 'fidelity as to spirit' are never static, the emphasis of the best modern musicians on spirit rather than 'antiquarian accuracy' is not far removed from much of the thinking of the early twentieth century. Earlier in this chapter Landowska's statement of principle was quoted: 'At no time in the course of my work have I ever tried to reproduce exactly what the old masters did. Instead, I study, I scrutinize, I love, and I recreate.' In the 1970s it was usual to smile at that statement as an old-fashioned and romantic attitude to period performance. But the smile has now faded, and has been replaced by a nod of recognition.

Into the melting-pot

The relationship between period and conventional performance has reached an interesting stage. Just at the moment when the limits of historical accuracy have become accepted, the influence of the period movement has become all-pervading. Nicholas Kenyon, former editor of *Early Music* and former Controller of BBC Radio 3, discussed this in the Royal Philharmonic Society's 2001 Lecture, 'Tradition isn't what it used to be'.[33] He began by recalling an 'electrifying' performance of Beethoven's Seventh Symphony played by the Berlin Philharmonic Orchestra conducted by Bernard Haitink, at a Promenade Concert in 2000: 'It was an absolute model of what an up-to-date modern Beethoven performance could be, a performance that had absorbed some of the best insights of the period-instrument movement while remaining resolutely crafted out of the sound of the Berlin Philharmonic, achieving miracles of textural clarity.' He then quotes a number of performers and scholars to demonstrate that the gung-ho belief that period performers are actually reconstructing 'authentic' past performances is by now well and truly dead. He concludes:

> So what is happening now? It looks as if two very contrasted movements from opposite ends of the spectrum may lead in the same direction. On the one hand, you have the early music movement rushing, as fast as its little *messa di voce* legs will take it, away from the idea that there was a single historical style to which everyone had to conform. But on the other hand, there has been the extraordinary spectacle of our most traditional musical institutions wanting desperately to get up to speed with what is going on and to use the insights of the early music movement to rejuvenate themselves . . . . The fact is that the best conductors, the Abbados and the Haitinks, have come to terms with changes in taste and changes in performance styles. They relish it, and even those who don't admit it have been influenced by it. Great performers know the imperative to change . . . . András Schiff and Alfred Brendel would own the influence of period pianos, even though they don't want to play them in public . . . . The musical melting pot is now a fact, like it or not . . . . the walls are down in a big way, the principal guest conductor of the Orchestra of the Age of Enlightenment is becoming music director of the Berlin Philharmonic [Simon Rattle] and the first guest conductor he will invite is William Christie. What next?

Musicians are, to varying degrees, always responsive to important trends. Period style is only the latest trend to influence musicians, though a particularly powerful one, and it has had the advantage of CDs and broadcasting for its dissemination. Ironically, aspects of it mean that musicians are being encouraged to undo some of the most recent changes which preceded the period movement:

the spread of continuous vibrato, and the general increase in power. It may well be that the orchestras of Vienna and Berlin, influenced by conductors with period connections, will end up sounding more like they did before World War II, and therefore closer to their 'traditional' style than they became in the late twentieth century. But if this does happen, the result will be a sanitised version of the old style, made suitable for modern requirements. There can be no real stepping back.

Similarly, the styles of period soloists move on rather than back, as evidence derived from historical documents is balanced against the prevailing taste of the performer's own day. There are, for example, specific issues to do with rhythmic freedom. Recordings of harpsichordists and other period performers show that the kinds of rhythmic freedom that are allowed in Baroque music have changed greatly over the last hundred years. Modern scholarship has revealed more about the performing practice of the seventeenth and eighteenth centuries, and performers have responded to that evidence. But far greater than changes resulting from research are the changes resulting from the general stylistic context within which period performers work. At the time that Violet Gordon Woodhouse recorded Bach's Italian Concerto in 1927, the piano-playing with which she was surrounded (and was herself brought up) was full of dislocated rubato, arpeggiation and detailed flexibility of rhythm. Her harpsichord-playing is like that too. The kinds of flexibility in modern harpsichord-playing – Koopman, Leonhardt, Kenneth Gilbert – are more in line with modern piano-playing. Though arpeggiation is part of the histori- cally derived harpsichord style of today, harpsichordists' rubato consists more of smoothly accomplished accelerations and slowings than of the more detailed rhythmic irregularities of Woodhouse's day. Tenuti are approached and left with deliberation, not with the suddenness of the early twentieth century. There is less detailed irregularity, less impulsiveness. Like a pianist's perfor- mance of Rachmaninoff or Chopin, a harpsichordist's performance of Bach or Couperin has become generally more deliberate and considered, more smoothed-out in expression.

Tradition versus Chinese Whispers

In a strange way, despite the recordings of the last hundred years, we are at the end of an oral tradition. Until the last thirty years or so, the prime way of learning music at the highest level was to encounter representatives of a symbol or tradition of living performance – old men and women who were 'carrying the torch' from their own teachers and their teachers' teachers. Recordings preserve some of the evidence of what was being handed down, from pupils of Liszt, Chopin, Leschetizky, Joachim. In the best examples it was an ethos, an approach, an understanding of what music means, and how to release that meaning, that were being passed on.

Christopher Small, in his book *Musicking*, has a vivid illustration of the complexity surrounding inherited tradition:

> In the little Catalan town where I live, the procession of the town's patron saint every August can move me to tears of joy, not because of the ostensibly Christian connotations of the event (it is in any case at least as much pagan as Christian) but because it affirms, explores and celebrates a centuries-old community's sense of itself and of its social order. It is not, however, a nostalgic celebration of a past order but a thoroughly contemporary affirmation of the community's present-day relationships rooted in its sense of its own history. That sense of its own history does not have to be the history that the history books relate; as long as the history is believed, or half-believed, or even wished to be true, the ritual retains its power. I dare say that if one traced the history of this little town's allegedly ancient Festa Major procession, much of it would prove to be of quite recent origin, but that does not matter as long as one believes the story.[34]

This makes a telling comparison with Leon Botstein's story about the student who had learned how to play a Chopin Ballade from his famous teacher. Botstein is talking about teaching, Small about ritual, but they are each taking an example of tradition handed down from generation to generation, and drawing opposite conclusions from it. Small says it does not matter whether it is historically true: it is the belief and the present-day power of the tradition that matters. Botstein says that the handing on of traditional teaching is just Chinese Whispers (or 'Telephone') and cannot be trusted. This brings us to the crux of the matter: what can we trust, and what can we not? What is the purpose of handing on tradition, and what is the purpose of scholarly reconstruction? What is achievable by either means?

In 1916, Dolmetsch expressed something approaching despair at the task of understanding historical style. Chapter 1 of his book, 'Expression', ends with a long quote from Johann Joachim Quantz's famous treatise on flute-playing published in 1752, *Versuch einer Anweisung die Flöte traversiere zu spielen*, including the following paragraph:

> Page 110: 'Another indication of the dominant passion in a piece is the word to be found at the beginning. It may be: *Allegro, Allegro non tanto, Allegro assai, Allegro molto, Moderato, Presto, Allegretto, Andante, Andantino, Arioso, Cantabile, Spiritoso, Affettuoso, Grave, Adagio, Adagio assai, Lento, Mesto,* &c. All these words, unless they be used thoughtlessly, severally demand a particular expression. And besides, as was said before, each piece of the character described above being capable of expressing a mixture of thoughts – pathetic,

caressing, gay, sublime, – or light, you must at each bar, so to speak, adopt another passion, and be sad, gay, serious, &c., as these changes are absolutely necessary in music. Whoever can acquire this perfection will not fail to gain the applause of his auditors, and his expression will always prove touching. But it must not be thought that these fine distinctions can be acquired in a short time. We cannot even hope to find them in young people, who are usually too quick and impatient for that. We grow into them gradually as feeling and judgement ripen.'

On this passage, Dolmetsch sadly remarks, 'All this is so clear and logical that comments would be superfluous. We cannot help feeling somewhat discouraged, however, for if it was so difficult to find the proper expression of music when its style was familiar to all, and good models were available, what studies and meditations shall we have to go through to achieve even a measure of success, we who not only have no examples to follow, but are hampered by modern training and the prejudices of our time!'[35]

Recordings enable us to step back a hundred years in time, as Dolmetsch could not. Does this ability make the process of change clearer, or hamper us further in our search for historical styles? And in any case, what are we looking for? If recordings demonstrate that literal reconstruction of the past is impossible, and yet we mistrust traditional teaching, what are we trying to do? Does a century of recorded performances have anything useful to offer us, or does it just demonstrate the folly of trying to leap the years?

CHAPTER EIGHT

Listening Back: Lessons from the Twentieth Century

For the first time in history, we have a vast archive of recorded performances stretching back over a century. We can hear how very different music-making was in the early twentieth century compared with now, and we can find in the recordings everything from broad trends to tiny details. 'Everything' is an exaggeration: there is a lot that is not preserved on records. The musicians themselves are missing and we do not see the expressions on their faces, how they move around the instruments, or their physical responses to the music and to each other. Though there are films of musicians from the first half of the twentieth century, when we listen to a sound recording we have to imagine what they looked like as they played. The sounds of the musicians have been isolated from everything else. And even the sounds are limited. On early recordings the frequency range is very restricted, and we cannot really judge the volume or balance, particularly of a large orchestra. We cannot be sure how the performance on the recording might differ from what was done in the concert hall the day before, or the following year, or with a different audience. Although we, the listeners, are their audience, the musicians can never be aware of us or respond to us as they do to an audience in a concert. A recording is something incomplete, and fixed. And it also removes the element of risk. In the early days musicians still had to play continuously for a few minutes, but they were often able to repeat a side again and again, and choose the best take. When tape-recording was introduced the best sections could be edited together. In the concert hall there is one chance only, nothing can be undone, and musicians and audiences have to take what comes and make the best of it.

But what does survive on the recordings is enough to fill whole libraries of books. The fact that it has not yet done so shows how recently the world has woken up to the potential of the recording archive. It is only in the last ten years that scholars have started to study recordings in significant numbers, and sound archives have started to become accessible for research. The questions to ask at this stage are, therefore, basic. How has performance changed over the last hundred years? Is it helpful to know that? What does such knowledge tell us about the development of modern styles and practices? How do we use this information? What has the existence of recording done to us? Have the effects been good or bad? Where do we go from here?

Trends of the century

The basic trends of the twentieth century are clearly preserved on recordings, and can easily be summarised. The most basic trend of all was a process of tidying up performance: ensemble became more tightly disciplined; pianists played chords more strictly together, and abandoned the old practice of dislocating melody from accompaniment; the interpretation of note-values became more literal, and the nature of rubato changed, becoming more regular and even. Acceleration of tempo was more tightly controlled, and the tempo range within a movement tended to narrow; the use of portamento became more discreet and more selective; bowing styles became more powerful and assertive; vibrato became more prominent and more continuous, both on strings and on most woodwind (and there was a broadly similar trend among singers); different schools and national styles became less distinct. In the second half of the century the Early Music movement, previously a fringe activity, became one of the driving forces of change, with its use of period instruments and appeal to historical scholarship. The movement began as a challenge to conventional performing styles, but towards the end of the century it started to cross-fertilise with orthodox playing.

To put these trends the opposite way round, a century ago ensemble was looser, pianists arpeggiated and dislocated, there was much overdotting, hurrying of short notes, accelerating and portamento, but vibrato was often very restrained, and bowing styles broad and gentle. There were great differences of style between schools and countries. These fundamental shifts in style and practice over the twentieth century applied, in different ways, to every aspect of music-making, at least in the classical field. While jazz players and singers happily developed old-fashioned dislocated rubato to new heights, classical musicians of all kinds moved firmly in the opposite direction. Similarly, while portamento has, in the jazz field, been developed on clarinet and saxophone, in classical music its use has been discouraged, or at least much refined, even on stringed instruments.

These are some of the changes that are audible on recordings. But they did not take place in a vacuum. They went hand in hand with broader changes, and with a shift in the relationship between musicians and audiences. In the days before recording, a performance occurred once only. Because of its unrepeatability, the performing styles of the day had as their main raison d'être the need to put the music over to an audience who might not hear it again. The accurate rendering of the text came second in priority. Although this is still true of the best modern playing, the priorities have shifted noticeably, so that a level of accuracy and clarity that did not exist a hundred years ago is now taken for granted world-wide. This has been encouraged by the pervasive influence of recordings themselves. The ability to examine and correct one's own playing has led to an unprecedented level of self-awareness and an attention to minute detail that was never possible before. And because of the wide availability of recordings, there has been a general globalisation of styles, standards and expectations.

Modernity of the period movement

Modern period playing is subject to much the same pressures to be neat and tidy, and to avoid old-fashioned sloppiness of any kind. There are, admittedly, particular areas in which period playing has reversed the trends of the twentieth century. These include power, bowing styles, and vibrato. Old bows playing on gut strings, narrow-bore brass instruments (even though the trumpets are compromise instruments), and general restraint in the use of vibrato on wind and strings, and to some extent among voices, these features of period performance have genuinely cut across the broader trends of the late twentieth century. But the fundamental ethos of period performance has far more in common with conventional modern music-making than with the past. This has been stated by a number of writers, and comparison with early recordings proves the point. One only has to sample three different performances of the same work – a conventional modern performance, a period modern performance, and a performance from the early twentieth century – and ask the question, 'Which is the odd one out?'

Take, for example, the opening of Mozart's Piano Concerto in G major K.453, played by Alfred Brendel with the Academy of St Martin-in-the-Fields conducted by Neville Marriner (1978), Malcolm Bilson (on fortepiano) with the English Baroque Soloists conducted by John Eliot Gardiner (1985), and Edwin Fischer with his Chamber Orchestra (1937). The tempi of the two modern recordings are about the same ($\downarrow$ = 140 before the first piano entry). Although Bilson's tempo drops slightly towards the end of his first entry, and then recovers (the result of editing?), both of the modern recordings give the general impression that everything is firmly under control, and that all the details are clearly in place. The sounds of the pianos are quite distinct, of course, and the period strings of the English Baroque Soloists are lighter and stringier than those of the Academy of St Martin-in-the-Fields. But the contrast between these two performances and Fischer's is much more striking.

Fischer and his orchestra seem to come from another world entirely. The tempo is much faster than that of the modern recordings ($\mathstrut = 160$ before the first piano entry), and it is less firmly controlled. Whenever there are continuous semiquavers (sixteenth notes), there is a tendency to rush. The short notes of dotted rhythms, and other semiquaver groups, are lighter and quicker than in the modern versions, giving a more casual, less emphatic, impression. These are all features that are familiar from many recordings of the 1920s and 1930s. It was the style of the time. The two modern recordings are also in the style of their time. Although one is a conventional performance, the other a period performance, with all the background of scholarship that implies, their similarities are much more striking than their differences if they are contrasted with Fischer's performance.

Similarly, Melvyn Tan's (very good) recordings of Beethoven sonatas are firmly rooted in modern style, and have none of the old-fashioned flexibility or volatility of Schnabel, just as Norrington's, Gardiner's and Brüggen's recordings of the symphonies have none of the freedoms of Furtwängler, Richard Strauss or even the comparatively straightforward Weingartner.

Period recordings of J. S. Bach are as much modern as period. Take any recent recording of a harpsichordist playing the slow movement of the Italian Concerto, and put it side by side with any modern pianist, and Violet Gordon Woodhouse's recording of 1927. The modern performances have freedoms, but within the confines of present-day taste. Woodhouse is shockingly mercurial, both in her tempo and in her old-fashioned use of tenuti and rhythmic dislocation.

This sort of comparison becomes particularly striking if the old recording has some historical connections of its own. Early twentieth-century pianists who studied with pupils of Chopin have in common the old-fashioned approach to rubato and loose synchronisation between melody and bass. No modern pianist plays like that, even when playing on a piano of Chopin's day. Emanuel Ax (1997) plays Chopin's F minor Piano Concerto on an 1851 Erard piano. It sounds beautiful, and Ax's playing is refined and expressive. But it is entirely modern playing, indistinguishable in its essential style from any other recording of the concerto from the last thirty years. It has absolutely none of the old-fashioned freedoms of Cortot or Marguerite Long in this work, let alone Rosenthal or Koczalski (neither of whom recorded the Second Concerto).

The implications of this are fundamental. Recordings show, in great detail, how modern style developed from that of the early twentieth century. It also seems clear that much of the change away from the freedoms of the past towards modern ideas of clean and tidy performance was encouraged by recordings themselves, with their steady influence on both performers and audiences. This development is therefore not just the result of another century like any other in the long history of music, but something new. There is no reason to suppose that our modern ideas of 'a clean and finished execution', as Stravinsky put it, have ever existed previously in the history of music. There is no reason to think that they were the fashion in the times of J. S. Bach, Mozart, Beethoven or Chopin. And yet even period performance, on 'original' instruments, cannot escape from this requirement of modern taste and expectation. In this absolutely basic aspect of music-making, a gulf, and it seems an unbridgeable one, separates us from the real past, as opposed to the imagined past of the period-instrument movement.

The receding past

One thing that has changed is that we now have to look further back into the past to find players who sound old-fashioned. Comparatively little has changed in performing styles since the 1950s (putting aside the period-instrument movement). In the fifty years before that, the entire musical world had undergone massive change.

Bernard Greenhouse, cellist of the Beaux Arts Trio, recalled 'having been moved by a Mischa Elman performance of the Brahms Violin Concerto. He was terribly impressed, he says, by the glissandi, the expressive interludes, the vibrato – but it would sound incompetent today. His present-day students would laugh.'[1] That was reported in 1985. Elman was born in 1902, and, like his contemporary Heifetz, was a pupil of Auer. He was one of the generation whose style was transitional between the old nineteenth-century approaches and what we now think of as modern playing.

Several musicians who took part in the wartime concerts at the National Gallery in London in the 1940s were survivors from an earlier musical world. The violinist May Harrison (sister of Beatrice the cellist) was one who, to judge from Howard Ferguson's description of her playing, would not now be tolerated on the concert platform:

> I knew her very well, and used to go to her flat in Chelsea and have dinner with her. And afterwards I'd say, 'May, do let's play a sonata.' And it was most interesting, because, suppose she chose a Brahms sonata, you'd get the feeling – her playing wasn't always in tune, and it wasn't always on the spot – but it was a marvellous conception of the work. You know, you felt that at the beginning she knew what the end was going to be and how she was going to get there. And it was always immensely enjoyable to play with her. I think her concerts – I don't think she gave many at the Gallery – but I think it would have been more for the sake of that sort of vision of music, rather than any technical qualities. And the same would happen with a pianist like Adela Verne, who used to come on in her carpet slippers because she had bunions.

She was a marvellous player. She used to play Schumann, she'd actually studied with Madame Schumann, and she played Schumann splendidly.[2]

Would we find Verne's Schumann splendid now? John Amis, who used to assist at the National Gallery concerts, remembers: 'Adela Verne was, or seemed, very old indeed, and her recitals were mostly sketchy and wayward, but occasionally the heavens opened and we had five or ten minutes of playing from another and grander world.'[3] Would ten minutes in a two-hour recital be enough for today's audiences and critics?

Arnold Rosé, veteran quartet player and leader of the Vienna Philharmonic Orchestra, was also in London during the 1940s together with his cellist Friedrich Buxbaum. They played at the National Gallery Concerts in piano trios with Myra Hess, and in string quartets with Walter Price and Ernest Tomlinson. According to Howard Ferguson, Rosé's playing was more secure than that of May Harrison or Adela Verne, and reviews of their concerts in *The Times* are extremely respectful: 'The special interest of the occasion was Brahms's B major trio, in which just over 50 years ago Professor Rosé played the violin with Brahms himself at the piano, when the first performance of the revised version was given. Professor Rosé's grasp of the great classical tradition of chamber music playing does not depend, however, on such an adventitious circumstance, however interesting and happy it is that there should be this personal link with this particular work. Beethoven's early C minor trio was played with the same command of the traditional style . . . a most satisfying experience.'[4] 'His interpretation of Brahms has an authority beyond that which most others can claim . . . . Young players should take every opportunity of hearing such mature performances as these.'[5] This enthusiasm was not confined to performances of Brahms: 'Mr. Rosé is the last of the great stylists, and to hear him lead a Mozart quartet is a lesson in the interpretation of the classics not to be missed.'[6]

One young musician who did take the opportunity to hear Rosé playing chamber music at the National Gallery was the violinist Yfrah Neaman. His reaction to this 'mature' and 'classical' playing demonstrates vividly the gulf between generations of musicians that existed in the 1940s, which he, as a string-player, felt more acutely than pianist Howard Ferguson:

This is a terrible thing to admit, but you can't belong to the age which is not your age. And when you are very young, and you hear somebody who was supreme, particularly in musicianship, but physically – in producing a sound, and intonation – could no longer control everything so well (he was nearly in his eighties, and eighties in 1942 or so was quite different from the eighties today), I would say to myself, 'Where is this wonderful playing, where is that great artistry?' Because I wasn't mature enough to see *behind* the physical blemishes, and to understand the – how shall I put it? –

intensity, the intellectual depth of what he was doing. And a *dry* sound, which one felt was over-dry, not dry in the *service* of something.

This contrasted with Neaman's response to the Busch Quartet, whose complete cycle of Beethoven quartets he attended in London after the war:

Adolf Busch in 1946 was also no longer in the prime of his physical mastery, and there may have been little scratches here or there, or maybe a few notes out of tune. But somehow it still was playing that you didn't need to be an archaeologist to admire, you could just sit and listen, and say, 'Well this is so . . . the power of the insight is so great that it bypasses everything.' You couldn't quite say that with Arnold Rosé. Adolf Busch played a lot of *senza vibrato* – and so do I, and I encourage others, particularly in Beethoven quartets, to play with this extraordinarily other-worldly sound. Busch could put it across, so that you were deeply moved. But with Rosé it seemed to be a little bit, 'Well, we just don't use vibrato. You shouldn't.' It was quite a different thing. So I have to confess, and I apologise to him profusely, that I couldn't quite get on that wave-length.'[7]

In February 1934, another veteran from an earlier age appeared in London. Moriz Rosenthal, then aged seventy-one, played Chopin's Concerto in E minor with Beecham and the London Philharmonic Orchestra, and gave two recitals at the Wigmore Hall. Critics were divided in their opinion of his playing. Richard Capell in the *Daily Telegraph* wrote, 'All would-be Chopin-players should have been there to hear. This veteran's art is richer in sheer charm than is that of any of the other great virtuosi. He is too urbane to preach or harangue. He plays to please, but – his nature and style being formed by the traditions and culture of a great civilisation – to please nobly!'[8]

There were similarly enthusiastic reports in *The Times* and the *Morning Post*. But 'McN' in the *Musical Times* reacted quite differently: 'Moriz Rosenthal stepped out of the Middle Ages to play Chopin's E minor Pianoforte Concerto, and used it to display a philosophy of comeliness that is out of fashion nowadays and worthy of neither more nor less respect for that reason. Mr. Rosenthal commanded the situation with his modest and compelling personality, even to the extent of making a Philharmonic audience sit up and take notice when he played his Fantasia on Viennese Waltzes.'[9]

The range of reaction to Rosenthal's Wigmore Hall recitals was even more extreme. Reporting on his second recital, the critic of *The Times* described him as belonging 'to the authentic tradition of such masters as Chopin, Schumann, and Liszt' and praised in particular the 'luminous colours' of Schumann's Fantasie. In the *Musical Times* 'G.C.' wrote of the same recital, 'Moriz Rosenthal's second recital at Wigmore Hall was unhappy. . . . The Schumann "Fantasie" . . . was played without fervour or imagination, and with an almost grotesque exaggeration of every vulgarity pianists are likely to commit. Were Rosenthal writing a book instead of playing the pianoforte the critics would say to him, "Begin again – and concentrate." For it is difficult to believe that Rosenthal understands the music he is playing . . . he has his virtuosity no longer, and his lack of musicianship is therefore laid bare. . . . For long stretches in the Schumann "Fantasie" Rosenthal indulged in whimsical disorder.'[10]

There were similar extremes in reports of Rosenthal's American concerts. Abram Chasins heard him twice in the 1930s, and wrote that the sight of the 'unhappy and bewildered veteran being sadistically pushed out onto the platform was the most pathetic thing I have ever seen. Not a trace was left of his distinction. Having heard from everyone of Rosenthal's wizardry, of his daring exploits in his prime, I am deeply and frequently haunted by the vision of him as a lost, helpless and terrified man.'[11] But the North American tours on which Chasins heard Rosenthal were widely reported as triumphs. When he played at New York Town Hall in November and December 1936 he was described by the *New York World-Telegram* as a 'master distiller of piano tone'. According to the *New York Times*, 'His is the commanding style of the past; there are not many artists left who play with such boldness of outline and flair for grandeur . . . . Modern pianists may be more meticulous about details but Mr. Rosenthal's aim is to set forth the essential romantic spirit of the work.'

The generation gap that Greenhouse identified in Elman's playing applies even more to Rosé and Rosenthal, who were born in the 1860s, thirty years before Elman. Already by the 1930s and 1940s they represented the styles of the past, not the present, and the reaction of those who heard them play at that time provides a vivid illustration of changing fashion. Whether they were entranced or repelled, those who described them in the 1930s and 1940s were describing the same thing: their impression of musicians whose playing represented an earlier age and was not like that of today. Their habits and style were still treasured by some, and rejected by others, but it is clear from recordings just what those habits were. In the case of Rosenthal the recordings provide enough evidence for us to be able to imagine just what writers reacted to so strongly. For Chopin's E minor Concerto, we have not only the commercial recording made by Rosenthal in 1930–1 (and reviewed enthusiastically in the *Gramophone* in May 1931 and October 1938), but also a radio broadcast of the slow movement, part of a seventy-fifth birthday tribute broadcast by NBC in 1937. The live recording of the movement is a little slower than the studio recording (and has its orchestral introduction, which was cut for the 78 rpm record). Both performances are full of the characteristic rubato of his generation, in which the melody frequently parts company from the bass. But what is most striking about both performances, and particularly the closely-miked radio broadcast, is the ancient freedom which Rosenthal brings to the simple accompanying quavers of the opening theme. He plays them with an uneven, rocking rhythm, which is so exaggerated in the first two bars as to make the music sound as if it is written in $\frac{12}{8}$, not $\frac{4}{4}$.

Recordings of Arnold Rosé were made several years before his appearances at the National Gallery. In 1927 the Rosé Quartet recorded Beethoven's Quartets Opus 18 No. 4, 'The Harp' Opus 74, and Opus 131. The restrained use of vibrato, which Neaman found 'dry' in the early 1940s, is clearly audible on the recordings. But it is quite possible that Rosé's control of intonation had declined in the years since the recordings were made, and that by the time Neaman (and the *Times* critic) heard him, greater allowance had to be made for his old age.

Despite this caution, it is difficult to imagine any player who could have provoked such wildly contrasted reactions at the end of the twentieth century or the beginning of the twenty-first. There were musicians in their seventies and eighties still playing regular concerts in the year 2000, but none of them seemed to the audiences and critics of the time as if they had 'stepped out of the Middle Ages'. Alfred Brendel in 2002 was the same age as Moriz Rosenthal in 1934, yet nobody thought of him as anything other than a modern pianist. No doubt this is partly because seventy is not 'old' in the way it was in the early twentieth century. But it is mostly because styles have shifted much less in the most recent half-century than they did in the half-century before that. The process of change has slowed down.

What does this mean? Is it a new phenomenon, or is it a return to the slow pace of the distant past, before recordings existed? Then, change was slow because people were not constantly bombarded by information and new (or old) ways of doing things. Musicians were brought up to play in a certain way, and matured slowly over the years. Their experience of other artists was, by modern standards, sparse. If they had the opportunity to hear one of the great musicians, it could be a revelation that might radically change the way they wanted to play. But they might wait years to hear someone of the calibre of Joachim or Ysaÿe. Now, in the early twenty-first century, change is once again slow, not because we lack information but because we have had as much as we can take. The changes accomplished over the period of recordings – the cleaning up, the accuracy, the clarity, the rhythmic control – have gone as far as they can go. And since everyone hears everyone else all the time, in the pseudo-perfect guise of their recording personae, these new standards are maintained. The only major change in the performance of classical music since 1960 has been the 'period' phenomenon. And, as we have seen, period musicians too have to a large extent moulded themselves to conform to modern expectation.

Musicians of the past judged by their recordings

One important limitation of recordings is that some musicians do not respond well to the recording process. There are those who are very nervous in the recording studio. There are those who need an audience. There are some who make records when they are too old (or, these days, too young).

One example of a musician who is not well represented by his recordings is Paderewski. Fred Gaisberg of the Gramophone Company, who made the first recordings of the pianist at his home in Switzerland, wrote, 'Paderewski, from the first, diffidently consented to record and never completely reconciled himself to the ordeal. He always doubted whether a machine could capture his art. Today, knowing better what Paderewski was and the limitations of the gramophone, I am inclined to agree with him. His art involved such broad and unrestrained dynamics – the faintest *pianissimo* crashing into a great mass of tone. In other words, he painted on a vast canvas, and the gramophone could only reproduce a miniature of his mighty masterwork.'[12] But more must have been missing than the dynamic range of Paderewski's playing. His financial success as a concert pianist was greater than that of any other pianist up to that time. He had a commanding stage presence, later enhanced by his fame as a politician and Polish patriot. Not surprisingly, none of that is conveyed by the recordings. In addition, Paderewski was already fifty-one when he made his first recordings in 1911, and in his late seventies when he made his last records. Therefore, he never made records in his prime. The same is true of Vladimir de Pachmann. When Pachmann played Chopin's B minor Sonata in London in 1911, his playing was 'a reminder of what it had been in past years'.[13] In other words, he was already well past his best.

According to Claudio Arrau, Schnabel too was past his prime by the time he made records:

> He was a really uncompromising interpreter, and a great player – but not really on record; on record you don't get the complete thing. He was not old when he started making records, but already he was past his peak when he recorded Beethoven. People don't realise that when he came to England and America he was already nervous, and had suffered a lot from stage fright. His technique wasn't quite controlled any more. But I heard him many, many times in Germany, before Hitler, and in those days he was technically flawless. Never a wrong note, technically clean; he had wonderful fingers. Even on records, of course, the slow movements are wonderful. But in the fast movements he starts rushing and so on, which he never did before.[14]

Can we trust this memory? Was Schnabel really that perfect and controlled in concert, or was it partly that elements of uncontrol and inaccuracy stand out under the cold scrutiny of a recording?

Stephen Kovacevich gives Paderewski, Toscanini and Szell as examples of musicians who cannot be wholly judged by their recordings:

> Paderewski, from what I can gather from people who heard him, was magic in the concert hall. He's not magic on records. But this has certainly to do with his personality, and something probably of the quality of his sound. So

I don't think one knows much about Paderewski – it was really a concert
that he gave, from what I gather. In the same way that, I'm sure, much as
we love some of Toscanini's records, people who heard him in person say
that that was ten times more incredible. I know from my own listening
experience that Szell's recordings are, I think, about as interesting to listen to
as if a Mercedes could play; but his concerts, the ones that I heard, were
electrifying. I heard him do Beethoven's Seventh with the New York
Philharmonic, and it was simply incredible. And then I bought the recording
with the Cleveland, which of course is excellent, but it's not the same at all.[15]

Myra Hess was another pianist who rarely came over at her best on
recordings. According to Howard Ferguson, her recordings rarely sound like
her: 'She was terrified of a microphone. Much the best recording that she
made is of the Beethoven E major Sonata Opus 109. That sounds more like
her playing than anything else – apart from tiny little things like the Scarlatti G
major Sonata: that's very like her, because that has the humour and lightness
that was so much a part of her playing, which in most of her records doesn't
come out at all.'[16] Hess herself hated the process of recording, and hated most
of the results, while admitting that Opus 109 and Schumann's *Carnaval* were
'not too bad'.[17] For a musician of such a temperament, there was clearly no
substitute for being there in the concert hall, communicating to an audience,
when remarkable and unrepeatable things could happen.

An example of the sort of 'event' that Hess was capable of creating in
concert was described in 1946 by pianist Bruce Hungerford, then a graduate
student at the Juilliard School.[18] Hess was in America and 'had been hailed by
everyone from Rosina Lhévinne and Olga Samaroff and Ernest Hutcheson,
down to the basest music critic, as the greatest pianist at present in the country'.
This astonished him because he had heard some of her records, which he
thought 'pretty dull and lifeless, not to say pedantic'. But then he had the
opportunity to hear her playing Beethoven's C minor Piano Concerto with
Toscanini and the NBC Orchestra. He described not only the beauty of her
playing, but also the effect she had on Toscanini. The concert had begun with
Beethoven's *Coriolan* Overture, 'played as if on a rivetting machine'. The first
orchestral tutti of the concerto was 'wonderful', Hess's first entry 'a little
nervous', but she got into her stride and then 'The whole first movement was
played just as I would ever want to hear it'. The slow movement was 'superb',
comparable only to Schnabel in its depth of feeling. 'It was marvellous to hear
in this slow movement how she cast a spell over Toscanini, who generally
rushes slow movements. Myra played the movement so slowly and reverently
and Toscanini actually seemed to be mesmerized by the hushed atmosphere she
created and he did his part so beautifully; in fact, I think it is one of the most
soul-searching performances I have heard from him (who is generally so

unyielding).' Overall, 'you felt here, for once in an American performance, that the whole orchestra and soloist were playing for sheer love of the music'.

A limitation of recording, then, is that some musicians need the occasion, the circumstances, the audience, and the interaction with other musicians in concert, to communicate their best, and Hess was undoubtedly one of them.

Sense of identity

The beginning of the twenty-first century is a time when, in many ways, people have lost their sense of certainty, and of the reasons for doing things. Politics, religion, international relations, financial markets, social structures, education, the arts, are all subject to this loss of stability and purpose. At the same time the speed of modern communications has resulted in globalisation. Perhaps it is not surprising that the performance of music should also be in the state it is. We have more music available than ever before, standards are generally higher than ever before, and yet it is not at all clear where the performance of classical music goes from here.

The phenomenal success of the period-instrument movement has settled into an orthodoxy of performing style. Turn on the radio in the middle of a period performance of eighteenth-century music, and, just as in conventional performance, the chances are that it will be impossible to know where the group comes from. And yet, despite this world-wide understanding of the current style, few musicians make claims to historical authenticity. The instruments are called 'original', and the musicians have learned to play in a manner that loosely relates to historical instructions. But the results are acknowledged as being our modern attempt, rather than the real thing.

Despite this acknowledgement of the limitations of period performance, the fact that it has achieved such success over the last forty years has had a serious impact on conventional music-making and teaching. Many conventional conductors, pianists and string players have been influenced by the period movement in more or less subtle ways, and the position of traditional teachers has been affected. Meanwhile, recorded performances stretch back over more than a hundred years and CDs reach to every corner of the globe. We can hear how the finest performers of our own generation play, and those of our parents', grandparents' and great-grandparents' generations. We can hear how styles and standards of music-making were quite different in the early twentieth century, and we can hear how modern styles evolved.

How do we make coherent sense of this? On what authority do we play the way we play? How much attention should we be paying to these various strands of thinking? The existence of recordings has made us highly self-aware and self-examining, but we are bombarded by a potentially bewildering array of contradictory advice and examples. Where, in all this, is our own sense of who we are? In the previous chapter Michael Morrow was quoted, lamenting the reliance on available clichés among performers in the Early Music field. He concludes, 'I'm afraid I rarely listen to gramophone records of old music, my own or anyone else's. For me, recordings that give pleasure are those of musicians performing with confidence in a style they were born to.'[19]

The BBC music producer Bill Lloyd writes:[20]

> The plethora of recordings simply makes it impossible for young artists now to avoid being swamped by influences which don't 'belong' to them emotionally or socially. In fact they don't have any human connection at all. I've recently been working with the pianist and teacher Ruth Nye, whose life and music-making have been absolutely moulded by the mentorship of Claudio Arrau. Not just by the example of his peerless playing or his 70 years' experience of the 'European' tradition, but also by the warmth, complexity and even ambiguity of having him as a teacher, and, latterly, friend. With all his faults, the books on his shelf, the roses in his garden that he dared not prune, his taste for lobster and horses and even, dare I say, his vulnerability in the face of homosexual opportunities. None of this richness can be got from a CD. So you can't know how much of themselves artists put into their playing unless you really know them and the world from which they come. I truly believe that most young players don't even realise that this kind of integral expression is possible as they flit from performance to performance, teacher to teacher, trying to extract the most tasty ingredients from each.

These observations contain something important about the role of teachers. The debate about whether teachers really carry a tradition, or whether there is a strong element of Chinese Whispers about the process, leaves out what continues to be most important about the best teachers. Despite the challenge to the authority of traditional teaching in the late twentieth century, there were still teachers who commanded immense respect, and to whom the best young musicians flocked. One of them was Sandor Végh, who presided over the International Chamber Music Seminars at Prussia Cove in Cornwall. Végh was one of the last string players alive who had been taught by Hubay. Hubay's teacher had been Joachim, and Hubay had played with Brahms. This, of course, impressed Végh's students, but that was not why they came to him, year after year. They came because he was a man of special insights into the art of rendering the meaning of music clear. He himself insisted that he was upholding a European tradition. This was not based narrowly on his pedigree that linked him back to Brahms, but on having been brought up with an understanding of the rhetoric of performance which allows music to 'speak', rather than to pass by in an undifferentiated flow (the importance of this approach was also stressed by Leschetizky, Schoenberg and others). Susan Tomes, who was herself taught by Végh, and played for his masterclasses, writes, 'Végh used to say that the European way of using tone and timing to shape phrases was vital to giving European art music its true voice. He complained that the influence of America was wiping it out, and that soon all string players would be playing with American-style constant vibrato, and with a big tone that projected to the back of the concert hall, regardless of whether such a tone suited the music. He called it "showing off" the music to the audience, not "giving" it to them. And he said we must understand and digest the European way, giving the music the rise and fall of natural speech and song patterns, or the art would be lost.'[21]

Végh would work away with young musicians at a particular way of playing a particular phrase in a Brahms sonata until it was 'right'. The purpose, however, was not to inflict a single interpretation on them, but to develop their understanding of how the language and the rhetoric of the music works. Students went away with a deepened understanding of the musical language of Brahms and Beethoven and Bartók, and how to make its meaning clear to the audience.

If the importance of a good teacher is to do with insight more than pedigree, the same is true of performers. Who taught Casals or Rostropovich or Fournier or Feuermann is of great interest to historians of musical performance, but not of much significance to audiences. As with Végh, their playing carries some of the characteristics of the different schools and traditions in which they were brought up, but what is ultimately of value is what they have made of all these influences by their own powers of insight and expression, and what they therefore have to offer to us, and to tell us about the music.

The impact of recordings

Where does the existence of a century of recordings fit into all this? What good or bad have they done to us, and how can we make best use of them?

One thing that many musicians agree is that recordings have a stultifying effect if they are used as a substitute for deep thought about matters of interpretation. Pianist Stephen Hough almost never listens to modern recordings of pianists, and deplores the excessive reliance on them by students: 'I'm convinced that those students who listen to ten different Chopin 1st Ballade CDs as they learn the piece are narrowing their horizons rather than broadening them. To digest 10 options means that you deny yourself 10,000.'[22] This echoes the thinking of Clifford Curzon forty years earlier. Asked what he thought about the influence of modern recordings, he replied: 'Well, it's good and it's bad. It's a bad influence on young artists, because they all listen to records day and night. And anybody can copy anything, really. You don't have to be really gifted. And I find that records are becoming a copy of a copy of a copy. Somebody said to me the other day, "In the end there'll only be one record of each work" . . . . It's unfortunately varying less and less, because everybody hears everybody all the time.'[23]

The general globalisation of performance through recordings is a mixed blessing. On the one hand, standards across the world have risen to an extraordinary extent over the last fifty years. On the other hand, there is great pressure for musicians who wish to succeed in the international market to model themselves on the international standard. This has two main effects. It limits the development of individual imagination, and it drives out local traditions. Nobody wants to be successful only locally, and therefore local traditions gradually become eroded. There are still some limited differences between performance traditions across the world: Russian brass- and string-playing still have a certain earthy vigour which is characteristic, though perhaps it has only survived as long as it has because of the comparative isolation of Russian musicians until late in the twentieth century. In general, the differences between players and orchestras across the world are slight, and many recordings sound much the same as each other.

One of the dangers of this constant diet of the almost identical is staleness. And this applies both to musicians and to audiences, to the music itself as well as to its performance. The world-wide availability of CDs means that perfectly honed performances of any piece of music can be played at any time by anyone who has access to the equipment. It has become like the availability of asparagus and tomatoes all the year round. There was a time when, to eat asparagus in England, you had to wait for the short season. It was a rare treat, to be looked forward to. Now you can buy asparagus at any time of the year, imported from abroad when it is out of season here. And often it is not as much of a treat as one was hoping, because it does not taste of much. Similarly, we no longer have to wait to hear a piece of music, like Ethel Smyth waiting to hear the latest Brahms symphony at the Leipzig Gewandhaus. So it is more and more difficult for anything to come as a surprise. Stravinsky commented wryly on the effects of overexposure when he wrote in 1962, '*Petrushka*, like *The Firebird* and *Le Sacre du Printemps*, has already survived a half-century of destructive popularity, and if it does not sound as fresh today as, for example, Schoenberg's *Five Pieces for Orchestra* and Webern's six, the reason is partly that the Viennese pieces have been protected by fifty years of neglect.'[24]

In both food and music, there has been a limited reaction against the predictable perfection of modern products. People have begun to tire of the constantly available tomato, perfect and regular in appearance, but almost tasteless. So a market has developed for tomatoes 'on the vine' – more expensive, and with more taste. But these are still remarkably perfect fruit compared with the much more variable and irregular shapes and flavours of tomatoes forty years ago. Similarly, there has developed a market for so-called 'live' recordings. This has partly been driven by economics, it obviously being cheaper to issue a recording of a concert than to book separate recording sessions. But it also represents a response to a feeling that the highly edited studio recordings have, in many cases, become a little predictable and dull. As with tomatoes, there are limits to the current state of this trend. Just as tomatoes on the vine are still expected to be perfect, so 'live' recordings cannot have mistakes in them. Most recordings of concerts are corrected with editing, either from combining more than one concert, or by engaging the musicians for a 'patching' session. To shift the metaphor slightly, we seem to want our cake and to eat it: we want the excitement of the live event without any uncertainties.

Constant Lambert, in his classic 1934 book *Music Ho! A Study of Music in Decline*, wrote about 'The Appalling Popularity of Music'. His main target was the radio (or rather 'wireless') and the way it had made music available through loudspeakers:

> It is to be noticed that the more people use the wireless the less they listen to it. . . . The people, and they are legion, who play bridge to the accompaniment of a loud speaker, cannot be put off their game even by *The Amazing Mandarin* of Béla Bartók. Were the Last Trump to be suddenly broadcast from Daventry by special permission of Sir John Reith – and I can think of no event more gratifying to the stern-minded governors of the BBC – it is doubtful whether it would interfere with the cry of 'No Trumps' from the card table. . . . It would not matter so much were the music bad music, but, as the BBC can boast with some satisfaction, most of it is good. We board buses to the strains of Beethoven and drink our beer to the accompaniment of Bach. And yet we pride ourselves on the popular appreciation of these masters.[25]

Much has changed since Lambert wrote those words seventy years ago. CDs have added to the general availability of music, and the music issuing from loudspeakers is more often pop music than classical. But Lambert's basic point is even more telling today than it was seventy years ago.

It was partly the excessive availability of the classical repertoire on CD and radio that enabled the Early Music movement to take off so spectacularly in the 1970s. It was not that the music-loving audience necessarily knew all the classical repertoire and was bored by it, but the general sound of Mozart and Beethoven and Brahms was so familiar at a casual level that the public was ready for some new stimulus. The word 'wallpaper' is often used to describe the use of music as background, and it was as if people were ready to change the old, too-familiar wallpaper in their living-rooms. The vigorous, fresh colours of Early Music were just what was required to wake up jaded senses.

A similar basic process surely applies to musicians too. The reason that the period movement moved on from Bach to Haydn, Beethoven, Brahms and beyond, was not just an upsurge in interest in historical time-travelling and the availability of scholars. It was a sense that the standard way of doing things had become too familiar. Karl Richter's Bach, Klemperer's Beethoven and Karajan's Brahms were all very well, but a new angle could surely be found on this repertoire. The irony is that now the period approach has become so accepted, it too is sounding tired. The sighing and scurrying of the standard modern period performance of Vivaldi or Purcell begins to pall. So what next? And do we still have it in us, as musicians or audiences, to be surprised?

Losing the element of surprise

To be surprised or even shocked by a performance is an important ability, but it is increasingly difficult to preserve in a world saturated by music. Even the basic impact of music is under threat, because of the qualities of modern recording and reproduction. The volume of an orchestra from a seat in the concert hall is less than what is available from loudspeakers in a living room, or through headphones, or in the modern cinema with its lush and overwhelming impact. Listening to a string quartet or a solo piano in a large hall involves the audience in a process of focusing into the sound, because it is so much more distant than it is on a recording at home. Add to that the inescapable onslaught of high-volume commercialised pop music, and it is hardly surprising if classical musicians sometimes feel they are struggling to be heard.

Similarly, to be surprised by the performance itself is more difficult than it used to be. In the early years of Musica Reservata, one of the most striking sounds was the voice of Jantina Noorman, singing medieval and Renaissance music with a vocal delivery completely unfamiliar in the West, sometimes raucous, sometimes soft and cooing, but always without a trace of conventional vibrato or polite shaping of phrases. It was a delivery to match the sound of shawms and crumhorns, and it was thrillingly unfamiliar. Somewhat similar styles of delivery were attempted by later groups, but nothing has repeated the shock of Noorman's pioneering sound. And, of course, it is impossible to recapture the original impact by listening to her recordings now. They are still impressive, but they are familiar, and therefore cannot any longer convey the edge of stimulating discomfort that she produced at the time.

One of the inevitable effects of preserving performance on record is that any element of strangeness or surprise will necessarily diminish with familiarity. For musicians and audiences who want to get to know new and difficult repertoire this can be a good thing. But for older classical music and the revisiting of old ways of playing it, familiarity breeds, if not contempt, certainly a blunting of reaction and a spirit of polite acceptance.

The recordings of Moriz Rosenthal, who caused such extreme reactions in his audiences in the 1930s, have lost their power to shock. The sound of such old-fashioned playing is becoming familiar because of the market in historical recordings. We recognise it as the style of that generation, and accept it for what it is. Thirty years ago, a recording of Joachim playing a Brahms Hungarian Dance, if played to an audience, used to make them laugh. It was a completely unfamiliar and, from the perspective of the 1970s, ludicrous manner of playing, and it was impossible to imagine that this was the great violinist for whom Brahms wrote his Violin Concerto. Now his recordings are the subject of academic study, and if they are played to a group of students they tend to elicit respectful silence. This is partly because the idea of playing the violin with almost no vibrato is now commonplace, even if not in Brahms. But it is mostly because we have heard everything, and nothing sounds strange any more.

There is, too, an element of nostalgia. There is naturally something touching about listening to the recordings of a long-dead, great musician, whose ideas of playing the piano seem so charmingly ramshackle, or whose way of sliding on the violin is so unashamed. The surface noise helps too: it is like an old sepia photograph of a gentleman with whiskers, wearing a top hat, and it carries the same aura of a glimpse into a vanished world.

After all the glowing testimonials of CD booklets, it is rare, and curiously refreshing, to come across a wholeheartedly hostile reaction to a historical recording. When a volume of recordings by pupils of Clara Schumann was issued in the 1980s, Samuel Lipman wondered what all the fuss was about. While a few enthusiasts such as Jerrold Northrop Moore were praising Fanny Davies and Adelina de Lara to the skies, as the bearers of the hallowed tradition of Clara Schumann, Lipman wrote, '. . . when the records are carefully and dispassionately listened to, it must be said that they contain no riches, but rather something humdrum and on occasion unrefined, insensitive, and even grossly in error . . . everything in these Davies performances, whether inspired by the immortal Clara Schumann or not, is just dull, dull, dull . . . de Lara sounds not like a great pianist, but like a teacher doggedly demonstrating for students how the pieces should go.'[26]

The playing of the early twentieth century is so different from our own that it surely ought to sound strange to us. Perhaps it is a good thing that we should be able to listen to the playing of our great-great-grandparents' generation and take it in our stride. But perhaps it is more complex, and less positive, than that. If those old ways of playing no longer sound strange, have we not lost a sense of passing generations? Perhaps this is another indication that we have lost our nerve, and that we no longer have a clear sense of our own judgement about how music should be played.

One of the characteristics of a recording is that it preserves the sound without being a memory. If the recording is of something that we do also remember, then listening to the recording is as likely to surprise as to confirm the memory. If there were anyone still alive who actually remembered hearing Joachim play, the sound of his playing, so long after his death, would undoubtedly come as a shock compared with the memory of the great man in person.

An old recording is an actual copy of a piece of the past, though a limited and distorted one. What one hears on the recording is what actually happened – even though heard from a strange perspective, recorded in unusual circumstances, and in latter years not even recorded all at once. And it remains essentially unchanged over the years while everything and everyone around it changes, evolves, grows up, learns through experience, and dies. In real life, a memory is much more precious than a recording. The voice of a much-loved grandfather, played back thirty years after his death, is as likely to disturb as to comfort. Did he really sound like that? Somehow one had remembered his voice as deeper, and without that suggestion of a Scottish intonation. But if you play the recording again and again, you get used to it, and it replaces the original memory. You can no longer recall how your grandfather sounded to you as a child. You can only remember how he sounds now, even though he is long dead. That is more of a loss than a gain.

Musical memories are like that too. The most vivid memories are of events, not of recordings (though hearing a recording for the first time can itself be an event). The one Toscanini concert you attended; the breathtaking encore Clifford Curzon played at the end of a nervous and inaccurate recital; the intimate moment when Joe Pass, unannounced, walked out and accompanied Ella Fitzgerald on guitar in the middle of a concert; the first time David Munrow assembled a Renaissance band; Carlos Kleiber conducting the opening of Verdi's *Otello*, and making the chorus at Covent Garden sing ten times louder than they had ever sung in their lives. It is possible to have a recording of each of these events. But listening to it has the effect of subverting your memory, not preserving it. You know what it *sounds* like now, but you can no longer remember what it *was* like then, when you lived through it as a complete and unrepeatable experience. Recordings of events one was not at, and of musicians one never heard, do not have that way of destroying specific memory. But they nevertheless erode reactions as they become familiar. The records of Joachim, shockingly bald and swoopy at first hearing, become tamed by familiarity.

But there are good things about the existence of old recordings. The most obvious is that they preserve, for people who never heard them, the performances of musicians of exceptional insight: Cortot, Schnabel, Busch, Casals, Toscanini, Furtwängler, Rachmaninoff, Elgar, and many others. When we become disillusioned with modern recordings, all we have to do is put on the Busch Quartet playing late Beethoven, or Casals playing Bach, to hear the sound of musicians who, despite their masterly technical command, were uninterested in the smooth perfection of today, and were anxious only to make the music 'speak'.

In a more general way, recordings preserve old ways of doing things. However familiar we become with them, and however dulled our responses, they will always be there to show us that the styles and practices of musical performance are in constant flux, in a way that is not entirely controllable or predictable. We can hear how our modern habits and styles evolved from those of the past. And we can be reminded that the way we do things now is only the latest step on the way to future styles. Recordings themselves, with their promotion of self-examination, homogenisation and globalisation, have slowed down that process of change. But as long as there are musicians alive to play music, they will always have new thoughts about how to do it, and things will move on. No doubt, in a hundred years our generation too will sound old-fashioned.

On what authority do we perform?

Young musicians today are bombarded with so many different kinds of evidence – traditional teaching, period playing, old and new recordings – that they could be forgiven for being thoroughly confused. But it is no good stepping out onto the concert platform with a set of possible questions. Musicians need answers, and a sense of certainty.

So on what authority should we now base our performing styles and habits? One answer might be to say that there is no authority left. We cannot rely on historical evidence, we cannot trust tradition or the teachers who claim to be preserving it. Recordings show that everything changes, and that there is no going back. So the way we do things is just the way we do things. There is now such a general consensus about the sort of playing that sounds comfortable, and such a high standard among musicians, that not much thought is needed to achieve a plausible result. Groups of musicians from around the world, whether on period or conventional instruments, can sit down together and quickly get the job done. On the other hand, if someone does come along with an idea, there is no authority to stop them trying it. The menu of possibilities, from current period and conventional practice, from new and old scholarship, and from a hundred years of recordings, is vast. We can pick what we like, as long as we make it sound neat and tidy and sell it in an attractive package.

That is a somewhat dismal picture to paint, and very unfair to the best musicians, but a lot of modern music-making does sound rather like that. It is either smoothly predictable, particularly in orchestral playing, or shows evidence of a new idea being tried out. The results are sometimes successful, but often routine, or, in the case of a new idea, unripe or even half-baked. One could argue that much the same applied a hundred years ago. The world was different, but most musicians had their routine ways of doing things. When someone with a powerful personality came along with a new idea, it would gradually catch on. Casals encouraged cellists to avoid the traditional swooping, and most of them followed eventually, and in the end out-cleaned him. Kreisler spread the gospel of continuous vibrato, and the world responded and developed the idea further. The late twentieth-century period-instrument movement spread the contrary gospel of less vibrato, and the world has been responding to that. What is the difference? At the highest level of music-making there is no difference. The finest musicians of the mid-twentieth century took the new ways of playing and made them their own. The finest musicians of today have taken some of the ideas of the period movement and have enhanced the vigour and subtlety of their playing with them.

What matters is the quality and maturity of thought that goes into the use of any aspect of style or interpretation. And one of the things that recordings prove is that, in all generations, any ingredient of style can go to make great or mediocre music-making. Music can be freer or more constant in tempo, stricter or more informal in ensemble, purer or more vibrant, cleaner or swoopier. It is a question of how these practices are used. In recordings old and new there are many performances which give the impression that the goal of the musicians has been no more than to make a decent job of playing in the style of the time. The great musicians of any period also have to work, to a large extent, within the conventions of their day. But for them, the tastes and styles of the time are only tools. The same applies to new ideas. A conductor may be able to switch an orchestra's vibrato off, or try out a composer's metronome marking that was thought impossible, or introduce some unfashionable portamento. Often the impression is that these things are being done for the sake of variety, or because the conductor is bored or wishes to attract attention. It is much rarer to feel that these novelties are there to serve the music. One's reaction is usually 'Goodness, can that be how it goes?' With the greatest music-making, however, the reaction is 'Of course, that is what the composer meant'.

A good analogy for the kind of maturity needed in music-making is the compost heap. As any gardener knows, you can use almost any organic material to make good compost. But choosing the ingredients is only a start. If, having assembled a heap of material, you come back a week later, it will look much the same. It takes a long time to produce anything useful, and it needs a certain amount of air and moisture (but not too much) to generate heat and to break the material down properly. If the conditions are right, in a few months' time what were separately identifiable ingredients have become a rich, light humus, in which new plants will grow. They in their turn will yield material for new compost, which will enable new growth to take place, and so on from generation to generation.

Similarly, the best music-making can be made up of any ingredients that are lying around. It really doesn't matter how much one's study of the composer's score is informed by teachers, or historical evidence, or recordings old or new.

But assembling the ingredients is only the start. What is required is a maturing process, so that what emerges at the end is not just a regurgitation of the separate ingredients that went in, but a transformation into our own thoughts, capable of enriching new music-making. This is the difference between the best musicians and the others. The highest level of musician lives in the same world as the mediocre, and has the same range of ingredients to choose from. But great music-making transcends the limitations of the styles of the day, even though it is formed from them.

One of the heartening things about old recordings is that the qualities that we value in the greatest musicians – in particular, the sense that the meaning of the music is being revealed in performance – are still communicable from another age. Joachim's recordings are too dim, and he was probably too old, for us to get much impression of the qualities that his contemporaries described. But once we get on to the 1920s and 1930s, with Cortot, Casals and the rest, the penetrating insights of their playing shine through, even though the way they played is not the way we would play today.

How can this rich archive of recordings help musicians and music-lovers of the twenty-first century? The knowledge that things used to be so different has the danger that it might add to the layers of confusion in a young musician. On the other hand, it is also potentially liberating. Modern performance has become more predictable and more standardised than ever before. But if someone claims, 'this is the way it should be done', we know, from the evidence of recordings, that great musicians of the past have thought differently. The most striking manifestation of this is the greater freedom of performers on early recordings, in the interpretation of note-values, rhythms, ensemble and tempi, compared with the more literal approach that is now orthodox. The knowledge that these old freedoms used to be the norm, among composers as well as performers, should encourage modern musicians to strike out against the modern trend, particularly when the emphasis on smooth perfection inevitably tends towards uniform dullness.

But an even more important lesson from the archive is that nothing much is achieved without mature reflection and development. The great musicians of the past were not just clever people looking around for good ideas. And they certainly did not spend their time wondering what style they should play in. They were people of musical breadth, insight and patience, to whom the music and their way of playing it 'belonged'. And they demonstrate that, in the end, authority is not something you pick up, ready-made, from the sources around you, but something you have to create for yourself.

Notes

Introduction

1. R. M. Philip, 'Some Changes in Style of Orchestral Playing, 1920–1950, as Shown by Gramophone Records', Ph.D. Dissertation, University of Cambridge, 1974.

1 Life before Recordings

1. Most recently in Timothy Day's *A Century of Recorded Music: Listening to Musical History* (New Haven and London, 2000).
2. Max Graf, *Legend of a Musical City* (New York, 1945; reprinted, 1969), p. 67.
3. Artur Schnabel, *My Life and Music* (London, 1961; reissued with *Reflections on Music*, 1970), pp. 41, 63.
4. *The Memoirs of Ethel Smyth*, abridged and introduced by Ronald Crichton (Harmondsworth, 1987), p. 69.
5. Ibid., p. 92.
6. Sir Dan Godfrey, *Memories and Music: Thirty-Five Years of Conducting* (London, 1924), p. 41.
7. Charlotte Haldane, *Music, My Love!* (London, 1936), pp. 17–19.
8. George S. Bozarth, 'The Brahms-Keller Correspondence', *American Brahms Society Newsletter,* vol. xiv, no. 1, Spring 1996, p. 7.
9. Philip Brett, 'Britten, Benjamin', *The New Grove Dictionary of Music and Musicians*, 2nd ed. (London, 2001), vol. 4, p. 373.
10. *The Memoirs of Ethel Smyth*, abridged and introduced by Ronald Crichton (Harmondsworth, 1987), p. 73.
11. John H. Mueller, *The American Symphony Orchestra: A Social History of Musical Taste* (Bloomington, 1951; London, 1958), p. 23.
12. E. M. Forster, 'From the Audience', in *National Gallery Concerts* (London, 1944), pp. 6–7.
13. Florence May, *The Life of Johannes Brahms* (London, 1905; 2nd rev. ed., c.1948), vol. 2, p. 531.
14. *Musical Times*, quoted in Arthur Jacobs, *Henry J. Wood: Maker of the Proms* (London, 1994), p. 89.
15. Ibid., p. 144.
16. *Letters from and to Joseph Joachim*, selected and trans. Nora Bickley (London, 1914), p. 350.

17. Reported by Theodor Pfeiffer in *Studien bei Hans von Bülow* (1894), quoted in *The Piano Master Classes of Hans von Bülow: Two Participants' Accounts*, trans. and ed. Richard Louis Zimdars (Bloomington, 1993), p. 44.

18. Vienna, 14 Jan. 1879, Brahms to E. von Herzogenberg, *Briefwechsel*, vol. 4, quoted in Florence May, *The Life of Johannes Brahms*, vol. 2, p. 540.

19. Michael Kennedy, *Adrian Boult* (London, 1987), p. 94.

20. Max Kalbeck, ed., *Johannes Brahms im Briefwechsel mit Heinrich und Elisabet von Herzogenberg* (Berlin, 1907), footnote on p. 145.

21. Vienna, [?20] Jan. 1886. *Johannes Brahms in Briefwechsel mit Joseph Joachim*, ed. Andreas Moser (Berlin, 1912), p. 220. Quoted in Hans Gál, *Johannes Brahms: His Work and Personality* (London, 1963), p. 66, originally published as *Johannes Brahms: Werk und Persönlichkeit* (Frankfurt am Main, 1961).

22. Cyril Ehrlich, *The Music Profession in Britain since the Eighteenth Century: A Social History* (Oxford, 1985), pp. 194–211.

23. Sir Dan Godfrey, *Memories and Music: Thirty-Five Years of Conducting* (London, 1924), pp. 234–5.

24. Alfred Stanley Deahl (1901–96) was interviewed by his daughter, Dr Paula James, on 9 July 1994.

25. 'Elgar as a Conductor', Part 2. Lecture to the Elgar Society, 6 October 1975, published in *Elgar Society Journal*, vol. 8, no. 2, May 1993, pp. 554–6.

26. *Musical Times*, vol. 26, no. 512, Oct. 1895, pp. 744–5.

27. *Musical Times*, April 1894, p. 239.

28. *Musical Times*, April 1899, p. 245.

29. *Musical Times*, July 1900, p. 478.

30. *Musical Times*, Aug. 1900, p. 537.

31. 8 March 1905 to 'Mr Fano', an agent, from Harvey Sachs, *The Letters of Arturo Toscanini* (London, 2002), p. 72.

32. *Musical Times*, June 1894, p. 389.

33. *Musical Times*, Oct. 1899, p. 653.

34. *Musical Times*, Oct. 1895, p. 741.

35. Godfrey, *Memories and Music*, p. 241.

36. H. Saxe Wyndham, *Augustus Manns and the Saturday Concerts* (London, 1909), p. 130.

37. *Musical Times*, May 1896, p. 314.

38. Carl Flesch, *Memoirs* (London, 1957), pp. 72, 76.

39. *Musical Times*, Dec. 1897, p. 838.

40. Natalie Bauer-Lechner, *Erinnerungen an Gustav Mahler* (Leipzig–Vienna–Zurich, 1923), p. 99.

41. *Corriere della sera*, 27 Dec. 1922, quoted in George R. Marek, *Toscanini* (London, 1976), p. 129.

42. To Ferdinand Hiller, Oct. 1888, from Styra Avins, *Johannes Brahms: Life and Letters* (Oxford, 1997), p. 581.

43. Felix Weingartner, *Buffets and Rewards: A Musician's Reminiscences* (London, 1937), p. 66.

44. Eduard Hanslick, *Music Criticisms, 1846–99*, trans. and ed. Henry Pleasants (London, 1951; rev. ed., Harmondsworth, 1963), pp. 234–5.

45. Willi Schuh, *Richard Strauss: A Chronicle of the Early Years, 1864–1898*, trans. Mary Whittall (Cambridge, 1982), originally published as *Richard Strauss: Jugend und frühe Meisterjahre, Lebenschronik, 1864–1898* (Zürich and Freiburg, 1976), p. 79, from R. Strauss, 'Erinnerungen an Hans von Bülow', *Betrachtungen und Erinnerungen', 2nd ed. (Zürich, 1957), p. 183.

46. *Musical Times*, 1 March 1882, of a Beethoven concert in Leipzig.

47. John H. Mueller, *The American Symphony Orchestra: A Social History of Musical Taste*

(Bloomington, 1951; London, 1958), pp. 73–4, 78–80.

48. Carl Flesch, *Memoirs*, p. 148.
49. Quoted in *The New Grove Dictionary of Music and Musicians*, 2nd ed. (London, 2001), vol. 13, p. 245.
50. *Neue Freie Presse*, quoted in *Musical Times*, Aug. 1897, p. 525.
51. *Musical Times*, May 1899, p. 306.
52. Louis P. Lochner, *Fritz Kreisler* (London, 1951), p. 86.
53. Dennis Rooney, 'Instinctive Partnership: Franz Rupp Reminisces about Playing with Fritz Kreisler', *Strad*, vol. 98, no. 1161 (Jan. 1987), p. 31.
54. Joseph MacLeod, *The Sisters d'Aranyi* (London, 1969), p. 264.
55. Quoted in Robert Craft, 'The Furtwängler Enigma', *New York Review of Books*, 7 Oct. 1993, vol. 40, no. 16, p. 14.
56. *Thank you, Jeeves* (London, 1934; reprinted, 1999), pp. ix–x.

2 The Experience of Recording

1. Roland Gelatt, *The Fabulous Phonograph* (London, 1955; 2nd ed., 1977), p. 114. James Methuen-Campbell, *Chopin Playing from the Composer to the Present Day* (London, 1981), pp. 76–7.
2. Larry Sitsky, *Busoni and the Piano* (New York, 1986), p. 328.
3. Brian Bell, notes for CD transfer, BSO Classics 171002.
4. See Claude Graveley Arnold, *The Orchestra on Record, 1896–1926: An Encyclopedia of Orchestral Recordings made by the Acoustical Process* (Westport, CT, and London, 1997).
5. Nuccio Fiorda, *Arte beghe e bizze di Toscanini* (Rome, 1969), quoted by Harvey Sachs in his note for the CD reissue of Toscanini's acoustic recordings: *RCA Toscanini Collection*, vol. 71, GD 60315. Nuccio Fiorda was on the coaching staff of La Scala, and sometimes played as an extra percussionist in the orchestra.
6. Details of this recording session and its preparations are given in Jerrold Northrop Moore, *Elgar on Record: The Composer and the Gramophone* (Oxford, 1974), pp. 19–21.
7. Sitsky, *Busoni and the Piano*, p. 328.
8. *Gramophone*, Feb. 1924, p. 183.
9. See Cyril Ehrlich, *The Piano: A History* (London, 1976; rev. ed., 1990), pp. 133–7.
10. 'The Piano Roll: Recording or Artefact?', BBC Radio 3, 10 Feb. 1979.
11. Sitsky, *Busoni and the Piano*, p. 326.
12. Jerrold Northrop Moore, *Elgar on Record*, p. 47.
13. Moore, ibid., pp. 133–4.
14. Henry-Louis de la Grange, *Gustav Mahler*, vol. 2 (Oxford, 1995), p. 769.
15. Eric Wetherell, *Albert Sammons Violinist: The Life of 'Our Albert'* (London, 1998), p. 78.
16. *Gramophone*, Feb. 1924, p. 183.
17. Letter from Boult to Edward Johnson, 14 Dec. 1971.
18. See details in Robert Philip, *Early Recordings and Musical Style* (Cambridge, 1992), p. 29.
19. Letter from Stokowski to Edward Johnson, 15 Dec. 1971.
20. De la Grange, *Gustav Mahler*, vol. 2, p. 818. Other aspects of Mengelberg's and Walter's recordings of the 'Adagietto' are discussed in chapter 5.
21. Louis P. Lochner, *Fritz Kreisler* (London, 1951), p. 265. Rachmaninoff confirmed this difference of approach between Kreisler and himself. See Barrie Martyn, *Rachmaninoff: Composer, Pianist, Conductor* (Aldershot, 1990), p. 442.
22. Interview in *American Music Lover*, 1938.
23. Moore, *Elgar on Record*, pp. 59–62.
24. A. J. and K. Swan, 'Rachmaninoff: Personal Reminiscences', *Musical Quarterly*, vol. 30 (1944), p. 11.
25. John Griffiths, *Nimbus: Technology Serving the Arts* (London, 1995).

26. Griffiths, *Nimbus*, p. 36.
27. Griffiths, *Nimbus*, pp. 138–46.
28. Griffiths, *Nimbus*, p. 144.
29. Griffiths, *Nimbus*, p. 181.
30. Elisabeth Schwarzkopf, *On and Off the Record* (London, 1982); John Culshaw, *Ring Resounding: The Recording in Stereo of Der Ring des Nibelungen* (London, 1967), and *Putting the Record Straight* (London, 1982). The changing role of the producer, from Gaisberg to Culshaw, is usefully summarised by Timothy Day in *A Century of Recorded Music: Listening to Musical History* (New Haven and London, 2000), pp. 38–46.
31. This description is taken from a paper, 'The Recording Process – From the Performers' Point of View', delivered at a symposium, Record Time, Jerusalem Music Centre, May 1998. The full text appears in Susan Tomes's book, *Beyond the Notes: Journeys with Chamber Music* (Woodbridge, 2004), pp. 140–50.
32. 11 Dec. 1983, transmitted on BBC Radio 3, 29 Feb. 1984.
33. 'A Winter's Journey', *Guardian*, 1 March 2002. The full text appears in Susan Tomes, *Beyond the Notes*, pp. 155–9.
34. Interview with the author, 18 Aug. 2001. The full text was published as part of Open University course A870, *The Postgraduate Foundation Module in Music* (2003), Offprints, pp. 42–8.
35. 'George Szell talks to Alan Blyth', *Gramophone*, vol. 47, no. 555 (August 1969), p. 262.
36. Christopher Bishop, 'Recording with Sir Adrian Boult', *Gramophone*, vol. 51, no. 611 (April 1974), p. 1843.
37. 'The Inner Sleeve', vol. 72C3/4, accompanying Charles Rosen's LP set, The Late Beethoven Sonatas, CBS M3X30938, issued 1973.
38. Interview with John Amis, BBC recording, LP30756, 24 April 1967.

3 Ensemble and Freedom: Orchestras

1. Adam Carse, *Orchestral Conducting* (London, 1929), pp. 27–32.
2. Letter from Strauss's agent, Alfred Schulz-Curtius, to Francesco Berger, 13 Dec. 1898. From Raymond Holden, 'Richard Strauss and the Philharmonic Society, London', *Richard Strauss Blätter* (International Richard Strauss-Gesellschaft), Dec. 2000, vol. 44, p. 130.
3. J. T. Carrodus, *How to Study the Violin* (London, 1895), p. 41.
4. Charles Reid, *John Barbirolli* (London, 1971), pp. 53, 93.
5. Artur Schnabel, *My Life and Music* (London, 1961; reissued, 1970, with *Reflections on Music*), p. 41.
6. *Musical Times*, March 1908, p. 163.
7. Charles Reid, *John Barbirolli*, p. 24.
8. *Selected Letters, 1911–14*, ed. Karl Dreyfus, 1985, p. 79, quoted in Arthur Jacobs, *Henry J. Wood: Maker of the Proms* (London, 1994), p. 40.
9. Arthur Jacobs, *Henry J. Wood*, p. 213.
10. BBC recording, 8 Sept. 1936, CD reissue on Symposium 1150.
11. 5 October 1924, Jerrold Northrop Moore, *Edward Elgar: The Windflower Letters. Letters to Alice Caroline Stuart Wortley and her Family* (Oxford, 1989), p. 295.
12. Frank Howes, *Full Orchestra* (London, 1942), p. 158, quoted in Jacobs, *Henry J. Wood*, p. 412.
13. *National Music and Other Essays*, 1963, pp. 267–8, quoted in Jacobs, *Henry J. Wood*, p. 412.
14. Arthur Jacobs, *Henry J. Wood*, p. 412.
15. *Gramophone*, Sept. 1929 p. 160. 'K.K.' was W. R. Anderson.
16. Michael Kennedy, *Adrian Boult* (London, 1987), p. 79.

17. Adrian Cedric Boult, *My Own Trumpet* (London, 1973), p. 97.
18. W. J. Turner, 'Our Royal Schools of Music', *Musical Meanderings* (London, 1928), pp. 95–6.
19. Cyril Ehrlich, *The Music Profession in Britain since the Eighteenth Century: A Social History* (Oxford, 1985), pp. 209–11.
20. *An Autobiography* (New York, 1936), pp. 148–9.
21. *An Autobiography*, p. 150. Stravinsky wrongly names Ansermet as the Paris Symphony Orchestra's conductor.
22. Natalie Bauer-Lechner, *Recollections of Gustav Mahler* (Vienna, 1923; Eng. trans., London, 1980), pp. 89, 99–100.
23. Bauer-Lechner, ibid., p. 13.
24. Ibid., pp. 120–1, 125.
25. Carl Flesch, *Memoirs* (London, 1957), pp. 50–1.
26. Article in *Gramophone*, Sept. 1944; extract reprinted in *International Classical Record Collector* (*ICRC*), Spring 1996, p. 26.
27. Flesch, *Memoirs*, pp. 281–2.
28. Horatio Parker in the *Boston Transcript*, 1907, quoted in notes for CD reissue 'The first recordings of the Boston Symphony Orchestra', BSO Classics 171002.
29. 1 Feb. 1924, Robert Craft, ed., *Stravinsky: Selected Correspondence* (London, 1982), vol. 2, p. 65.
30. *The Times*, 2 June 1930, p. 12.
31. H. Saxe Wyndham, *Augustus Manns and the Saturday Concerts* (London, 1909), p. 131.
32. 'Elgar as a conductor', Part II. Lecture to the Elgar Society, 6 October 1975, published in *Elgar Society Journal*, vol. 8, no. 2, May 1993, pp. 554–6.
33. Alan Jefferson, *Sir Thomas Beecham: A Centenary Tribute* (London, 1979), p. 88.
34. In Sheffield a score of this symphony exists, with a note that it was used for the preparation of that edition. The note is dated 30 Oct. 1940.
35. Letter from Brahms to Ferdinand Hiller, Oct. 1888, in Styra Avins, *Johannes Brahms: Life and Letters* (Oxford, 1997), p. 581.
36. Eduard Hanslick, *Music Criticisms, 1846–99*, trans. and ed. Henry Pleasants (London, 1951; rev. ed., Harmondsworth, 1963), p. 234.
37. Erwin Mittag, *The Vienna Philharmonic*, trans. J. R. L. Orange and G. Morice (Vienna, 1950), pp. 32–3.
38. Felix Weingartner, *Buffets and Rewards: A Musician's Reminiscences* (London, 1937), p. 168.
39. Christopher Fifield, *True Artist and True Friend: A Biography of Hans Richter* (Oxford, 1993), p. 148.
40. Richard Heuberger, *Erinnerungen an Johannes Brahms (Tagebuchnotizen aus den Jahren 1875 bis 1897)*, ed. Kurt Hofmann (Tutzing, 1971), p. 133.
41. Arnold Schoenberg, 'Gustav Mahler', 'Stil und Gedanke', *Gesammelte Schriften*, I, ed. Ivan Vojtěch (Frankfurt, 1976), pp. 7ff., quoted in Henry-Louis de la Grange, *Gustav Mahler*, vol. 3 (Oxford, 1999), p. 372.
42. Robert Baldock, *Pablo Casals* (London, 1992), pp. 118–24.
43. Adrian C. Boult, 'Casals as Conductor', *Music & Letters*, vol. 4 (1923), pp. 149–52.
44. Carl Flesch, *Memoirs*, pp. 228–9.
45. Robert Craft, ed., *Stravinsky: Selected Correspondence* (London, 1982), vol. 1, p. 191.
46. Adrian C. Boult, 'Arthur Nikisch', *Music & Letters*, vol. 3 (1922), pp. 119–21.
47. Adrian C. Boult, 'Nikisch and Method in Rehearsal', *Music Review*, 11 (1950), pp. 122–5.
48. Letter to Ada Mainardi, 8 June 1935. *The Letters of Arturo Toscanini*, compiled, edited and translated by Harvey Sachs (London, 2002), p. 188.
49. Hugo Burghauser, chairman of the Vienna Philharmonic Orchestra, interviewed in B. H. Haggin, *The Toscanini Musicians Knew* (2nd ed., New York, 1980), p. 154.

50. Letter to Ada Mainardi, 23 Oct. 1933, *The Letters of Arturo Toscanini*, p. 156.
51. Leopold Stokowski, *Music For All of Us* (New York, 1943), p. 195.
52. Reported in Adrian C. Boult, 'Nikisch and Method in Rehearsal', pp. 122–5.
53. *Guardian*, 16 Feb. 2002, p. 24.
54. Michael Kennedy, *Adrian Boult* (London, 1987), pp. 85–6.
55. BBC Radio 3, 'Artist in Focus', in conversation with Humphrey Burton, 9 Aug. 2002.
56. See Clive Gillison and Jonathan Vaughan, 'The Life of an Orchestral Musician', *The Cambridge Companion to the Orchestra* (Cambridge, 2003), p. 198.
57. E. A. Baughan in *Monthly Musical Record*, quoted in Arthur Jacobs, *Henry J. Wood: Maker of the Proms* (London, 1994), p. 64.
58. Paul Bechert, *Musical Times*, Aug. 1930, p. 750.
59. Letter to Rex Palmer at the Gramophone Company, 23 March 1933, in Jerrold Northrop Moore, *Elgar on Record* (Oxford, 1974), p. 195.
60. Craft, ed., *Stravinsky: Selected Correspondence*, vol. 3, p. 258.
61. Interview with the author, 1994.
62. Nancy Toff, *The Flute Book* (London, 1985), p. 101.
63. Conducted by Cristian Mandeal (recorded 1995), Arte Nova 74321 34051 2.
64. Conducted by Myer Fredman (recorded 1994), Naxos 8.553001.
65. Robert Philip, *Early Recordings and Musical Style* (Cambridge, 1992), pp. 179–204).

4 Ensemble and Freedom: Chamber Groups and Pianists

1. Barrie Martyn, *Rachmaninoff: Composer, Pianist, Conductor* (Aldershot, 1990), p. 443.
2. The portamenti in this performance, and some of those which follow, are shown in music examples in Robert Philip, *Early Recordings and Musical Style* (Cambridge, 1992), pp. 156ff.
3. For the history of rubato, see Richard Hudson, *Stolen Time: The History of Tempo Rubato* (Oxford, 1994), and Clive Brown, *Classical and Romantic Performing Practice, 1750–1900* (Oxford, 1999), pp. 375–414.
4. *Memoirs* (London, 1957), p. 79, quoted in L. Ginsburg, *Ysaÿe* (Moscow, 1959; English translation, Neptune City, N.J., 1980), p. 301.
5. 'Eugène Ysaÿe: Quelques notes et souvenirs', *Revue musicale*, 188 (1939), pp. 30–1.
6. Ysaÿe's recordings of Vieuxtemps's Rondino and Wagner's 'Prize Song' are analysed in Robert Philip, *Early Recordings and Musical Style*, pp. 66, 156.
7. *My Life of Music* (London, 1938), p. 128.
8. This passage is shown as a music example in Robert Philip, *Early Recordings and Musical Style*, p. 169.
9. Laurence Dreyfus caused a stir in Early Music circles in 1992 by comparing the Flonzaley's recording of Mozart's D minor String Quartet with modern recordings, both period and conventional, and preferring the Flonzaley. See 'Mozart as early music: a Romantic antidote', *Early Music*, vol. 20, no. 2 (1992), pp. 297–309. The publication of this paper coincided with that of my discussion of this recording in *Early Recordings and Musical Style*, pp. 67–9, 82.
10. Carl Flesch, *Memoirs* (London, 1957), pp. 181–2.
11. Richard Strauss, letter of 13 Jan. 1884 to Thuille, quoted in Willi Schuh, *Richard Strauss: A Chronicle of the Early Years, 1864–1898*, trans. Mary Whittall (Cambridge, 1982), originally published as *Richard Strauss: Jugend und frühe Meisterjahre, Lebenschronik, 1864–1898* (Zürich and Freiburg, 1976), p. 67.
12. J. A. Fuller-Maitland, *Joseph Joachim* (London and New York, 1905), pp. 29–30.
13. Margaret Campbell, *The Great Cellists* (London, 1988), p. 137.
14. Review of a Monday Popular Concert in *Musical Times*, vol. 12, no. 288, 1 Feb. 1867, p. 472.

15. *Musical Times*, May 1898, p. 315.
16. *Szigeti on the Violin* (London, 1969), p. 174.
17. J. Levin, 'Adolf Busch', *Die Musik*, vol. 18, no. 10 (July 1926), p. 746.
18. Albert E. Kahn, *Joys and Sorrows* (Chichester, 1970), p. 116, quoted in Margaret Campbell, *The Great Cellists*, p. 137.
19. Roger Nichols, 'The Poet of the Piano', on Cortot, BBC Radio 3, 6 April 1993. Tape No. T41317.
20. The repertoire of the Cortot/Thibaud/Casals Trio, and the number of times they performed each work, are listed in the notes by Jean Loubier accompanying the CD reissue of their recordings on EMI Références CHS7 64057–2.
21. Robert Baldock, *Pablo Casals* (London, 1992), p. 69.
22. Artur Weschler-Vered, *Jascha Heifetz* (London, 1986), pp. 109–10, quoted in Harvey Sachs, *Arthur Rubinstein* (London, 1996), p. 276.
23. Arthur Rubinstein, *My Many Years* (New York, 1980), p. 494, quoted in Sachs, *Arthur Rubinstein*, p. 276.
24. Letter of 18 Nov. 1941. Rubinstein Archives, quoted in Sachs, *Arthur Rubinstein*, p. 277. On the relationship between Feuermann and Heifetz see Annette Morreau, *Emanuel Feuermann* (New Haven and London, 2002), pp. 219–20, 238–42.
25. Nicholas Delbanco, *The Beaux Arts Trio* (London, 1985), p. 174.
26. Ibid, p. 150.
27. Review of CD of Beethoven Piano Trios Opus 70, *Guardian*, 24 Jan. 2003, Review, p. 19.
28. J. J. Eigeldinger, *Chopin vu par ses élèves* (Neuchâtel, 1970). English trans., *Chopin: Pianist and Teacher as Seen by his Pupils* (Cambridge, 1988), p. 49.
29. *Stolen Time*, pp. 329–40.
30. *Piano Questions Answered* (London, 1909), reprinted with *Piano Playing* (New York, 1976), p. 100.
31. Gwendolyn Mason, the harpist on this recording, who was still teaching at Trinity College of Music in the 1960s, used to tell pupils that Ravel had indeed conducted the work, though 'in a somewhat superficial manner' (reported by Peter Copeland, *Historic Record*, vol. 24, July 1992, p. 36).
32. Personnel: 1932 Foveau (cornet), Godeau (clarinet), Dhérin (bassoon), Delbos (trombone); 1954: Robert Nagel (trumpet), David Oppenheim (clarinet), Loren Glickman (bassoon), Erwin L. Price (trombone).
33. Interview with Bernard Keeffe. BBC recording LP 29683, 4 Aug. 1965.

5 Questions of Authority: the Composer

1. From notes by Allan Evans, 1993, issued with Pearl GEMM CD 9012.
2. From notes by Jean-Charles Hoffelé, 1997, issued with Dante LYS 287.
3. *Elgar on Record* (Oxford, 1974).
4. Jerrold Northrop Moore, *Elgar and his Publishers: Letters of a Creative Life* (Oxford, 1987), p. 490.
5. *Musical Times*, vol. 67 (1926), p. 550, and *The Times* (27 April 1926), p. 14.
6. Jerrold Northrop Moore, *Elgar and his Publishers*, p. 454.
7. Jerrold Northrop Moore, *Elgar on Record*, p. 194.
8. According to Ivor Newton, who played the piano for the rehearsal, Elgar's famous declaration that he was 'off to the races' occurred after they had played through the complete concerto and discussed it, not after a mere thirty bars as Menuhin claimed in later life. See Ivor Newton, *At the Piano* (London, 1966), pp. 185–7.
9. Basil Maine, *Elgar: His Life and Work* (London, 1933), vol. 1, p. 264.
10. *Musical Times*, vol. 67 (1926), p. 550.

11. Letter to Edward Johnson, 14 Dec. 1971.
12. 6 July 1928, Moore, *Elgar on Record*, p. 84.
13. *Musical Times*, July 1935, p. 647.
14. *An Autobiography* (New York, 1936; reprinted, 1962), p. 34.
15. See my discussion of his revisions to *Petrushka*, and the differences between his recordings, in *Early Recordings and Musical Style*, pp. 31–3.
16. *An Autobiography*, pp. 150–2.
17. Peter Hill compares these two recordings, and many others, in *Stravinsky: The Rite of Spring* (Cambridge, 2000), pp. 118–39.
18. *An Autobiography*, p. 167.
19. Igor Stravinsky and Robert Craft, *Themes and Conclusions* (London, 1972), p. 139.
20. *An Autobiography*, p. 157.
21. Igor Stravinsky and Robert Craft, *Dialogues and a Diary* (New York, 1963; London, 1968), p. 89.
22. Maria Michailova (soprano), orchestra (recorded in St Petersburg, 1906–7), in 'Singers of Imperial Russia', vol. 5, part 1. Pearl GEMM CDS 9111(2).
23. BBC LP 26667, 17 Nov. 1960. Also LP 27475, where Wellesz talks to Deryck Cooke, 1962.
24. Oskar Fried, 'Erinnerungen an Mahler', *Musikblätter des Anbruch*, vol. 1, no. 1, quoted in Kurt Blaukopf, *Mahler: A Documentary Study* (London, 1976), p. 240; Henry-Louis de la Grange, *Gustav Mahler*, vol. 3, *Vienna: Triumph and Disillusion* (Oxford, 1999), p. 260.
25. *Mahler's Unknown Letters*, ed. Herta Blaukopf (London, 1986), p. 50. She adds in a footnote that Mahler's note was 'rendered partially inapplicable in the light of subsequent revisions'.
26. Blaukopf, ibid., p. 53.
27. De la Grange, *Gustav Mahler*, vol. 3, p. 262.
28. BBC LP 36246, interviewed by Peter Heyworth. Also printed in *Conversations with Klemperer*, ed. Peter Heyworth (London, 1973; revised ed., 1985), pp. 29–30.
29. Letter to Alma, 22 May 1908?, in Alma Mahler, *Gustav Mahler: Memories and Letters*, trans. Basil Creighton, ed. Donald Mitchell and Knud Martner (4th ed., London, 1990), p. 305, originally published as *Gustav Mahler: Erinnerungen und Briefe* (Amsterdam, 1940).
30. Heyworth, *Conversations*, p. 38.
31. Peter Heyworth, *Otto Klemperer: His Life and Times*, vol. 1, *1885–1933* (Cambridge, 1983), p. 155.
32. De la Grange, *Gustav Mahler*, vol. 2, pp. 379–80.
33. De la Grange, *Gustav Mahler*, vol. 3, p. 790.
34. De la Grange, vol. 3, p. 26.
35. See *The Mahler Companion*, ed. Donald Mitchell and Andrew Nicholson (Oxford, 1999), p. 329; Henry-Louis de la Grange, *Gustav Mahler*, vol. 3, pp. 38–9; and Alma Mahler, *Gustav Mahler: Memories and Letters*, p. 73.
36. 'Bij de sterfdag van Gustav Mahler', article in *Algemeen Handelsblad*, 18 May 1926, quoted in Mitchell and Nicholson, *The Mahler Companion*, p. 327.
37. *The Mahler Companion*, p. 331.
38. Eduard Reeser, *Gustav Mahler und Holland: Briefe* (Vienna, 1980), p. 27, quoted in *Mahler: His Life, Work and World*, compiled and edited by Kurt Blaukopf and Herta Blaukopf (London, 1991), p. 224.
39. Notes to CD Deutsche Harmonia Mundi 05472 77374–2, recorded 1995.
40. 'Making a Stand against Sterility', *New York Times*, 2 Feb. 1997.
41. Letter to Alma, in Alma Mahler, *Gustav Mahler: Memories and Letters*, p. 249.
42. Ibid., p. 273.
43. 1 Oct. 1909, Alma Mahler, *Gustav Mahler: Memories and Letters*, p. 308.

44. Henry-Louis de la Grange, *Gustav Mahler*, vol. 3, p. 34.

45. Most recently in James H. North, 'Mengelberg and Mahler', *International Classical Record Collector*, Spring 1998, vol. 3, no. 12, p. 11.

46. De la Grange, *Gustav Mahler*, vol. 2, p. 391.

47. *At the Piano with Debussy* (1960; English trans., London, 1972).

48. Marguerite Long, *At the Piano with Fauré*, trans. Olive Senior-Ellis (London, 1981), p. 102.

49. Review of the première of the G major Piano Concerto in 1932, quoted in Arbie Orenstein, *Ravel: Man and Musician* (New York and London, 1975), p. 103.

50. Gordon Bryan, a pianist who heard Ravel play in London in 1928 and 1929. Roger Nichols, *Ravel Remembered* (London, 1987), p. 91, from Norman Demuth, *Ravel* (London, 1947), p. 175.

51. Ernesto Halffter, pupil of de Falla. Interview with Mildred Clary, France-Culture, 1983. Roger Nichols, *Ravel Remembered*, p. 92, quoting Marcel Marnat, *Maurice Ravel* (Paris, 1986).

52. Welte-Mignon roll, recorded 1913. Reissue: EMI 2C 153–12845.

53. Welte-Mignon. Reissued on Teldec 8.43931.

54. Reissued on LP: Telefunken GMA 79.

55. Reissued in The Condon Collection: Bellaphon 690.07.005.

56. Edward Lockspeiser, *Debussy: His Life and Mind* (London, 1962), vol. 2, p. 35.

57. Marguerite Long, *At the Piano with Fauré* (Paris, 1963; English trans., London, 1981), p. 67.

58. 31 July 1907, J. Barrie Jones, *Gabriel Fauré: A Life in Letters* (London, 1988), p. 127.

59. Cecilia Dunoyer, *Marguerite Long: A Life in French Music, 1874–1966* (Bloomington, 1993), pp. 39–40.

60. *At the Piano with Fauré*, p. 111.

61. Cecilia Dunoyer, *Marguerite Long: A Life in French Music*, p. 25.

62. *At the Piano with Fauré*, p. 65.

63. *At the Piano with Fauré*, p. 91.

64. Recorded 1994 in *Gabriel Fauré, The Complete Music for Piano*, Hyperion CDA 66911/4.

65. *Revue musicale* (April 1932), p. 320, quoted in Arbie Orenstein, *Ravel: Man and Musician*, p. 102.

66. *At the Piano with Ravel* (Paris, 1971; English trans., London, 1973), p. 16.

67. For example, Pearl GEMM CD 9927.

68. Jean Touzelet, 'Interprétations historiques', in Arbie Orenstein, *Maurice Ravel: Lettres, Écrits, Entretiens* (Paris, 1989), p. 411.

69. *At the Piano with Ravel*, p. 16.

70. Orenstein, *Maurice Ravel: Lettres, Écrits, Entretiens*, p. 188.

71. *Gramophone*, Sept. 1927.

72. Orenstein, *Maurice Ravel: Lettres, Écrits, Entretiens*, p. 413.

73. Hamish Milne, *Bartók: His Life and Times* (Tunbridge Wells, 1982), p. 67.

74. *The Observer*, 26 March 1922, quoted in Malcolm Gillies, 'Bartók in Britain: 1922', *Music & Letters*, vol. 63 (1982), p. 222.

75. Joseph Szigeti, *With Strings Attached* (London, 1949), p. 128.

76. Paul Griffiths, *Bartók* (London, 1984), p. 113.

77. Quoted ibid., p. 112, from notes by László Somfai accompanying the collected recordings of Bartók, Hungaroton LPX 12326-33.

78. H. H. Stuckenschmidt, *Arnold Schoenberg* (London, 1959), pp. 78–9.

79. Transcription from booklet accompanying CD reissue, Archiphon ARC–103/4.

80. *Style and Idea*, ed. Leonard Stein (English trans., London, 1975; 2nd ed., 1985), pp. 345–7.

81. 'For a Treatise on Performance' (1923 or 1924), *Style and Idea*, p. 319.

82. Ibid., p. 342.
83. 'Today's Manner of Performing Classical Music', ibid., p. 320.
84. At a day of research papers organised by Sheffield University Music Department, *Music and Recording: A Century of Change*, The British Library, 24 March 2001.
85. E-mail to the author, 26 June 2003.
86. Interview with Fiona Richards for Open University course AA302, *From Composition to Performance: Musicians at Work* (1998), CD 8 Track 6.
87. From conversation with the author.
88. At the Guildhall School of Music and Drama, London, 6 Feb. 2002.
89. Report in the Hamburg *Correspondent* of a concert by the Hamburg Philharmonic Orchestra conducted by Brahms, Dec. 1884. Florence May, *The Life of Brahms* (2 vols, London, 1905; 2nd rev. ed., 1948), vol. 2, p. 576.
90. Ivor Newton, *At the Piano* (London, 1966), p. 186.

6 Questions of Authority: Schools of Playing

1. John Steane's *The Grand Tradition: Seventy Years of Singing on Record* (London, 1974) provides the best introduction to the subject.
2. BBC recording LP 29683, 4 Aug. 1965.
3. See Robert Philip, *Early Recordings and Musical Style* (Cambridge, 1992), pp. 51–3.
4. *Music Criticisms, 1846–99*, ed. Henry Pleasants (rev. ed., Harmondsworth, 1963), p. 237.
5. Chopin's advice quoted in A. F. Christiani, *The Principles of Expression in Pianoforte Playing* (New York, 1885; rev. ed., 1974), pp. 299–303.
6. *Moura: Her Autobiography* (London, 1991), p. 47.
7. In an interview with Dan Zerdin in 'The ideal pianist', BBC Radio 4, Aug. 1972, quoted in Bryan Crimp, *Solo: The Biography of Solomon* (Hexham, Northumberland, 1994), p. 105.
8. *Piano Playing* (London, 1909; reprinted with *Piano Questions Answered*, New York, 1976), p. 59.
9. Gregor Benko, 'Hofmann, Josef', *The New Grove Dictionary of Music and Musicians* (London, 1980), vol. 8, p. 634; Abram Chasins, *Speaking of Pianists* (New York, 1958), p. 19; Harold C. Schonberg, *The Great Pianists* (London, 1974), pp. 356–7.
10. *Piano Questions Answered*, p. 25.
11. Arthur Rubinstein, *My Young Years* (New York, 1973), and *My Many Years* (New York, 1980). For a more impartial analysis of Rubinstein's life and upbringing, see Harvey Sachs, *Arthur Rubinstein* (London, 1996).
12. Carl Flesch, *Die Kunst des Violinspiels* (Berlin, 1923–8), English trans. by F. H. Martens as *The Art of Violin Playing* (New York, 1924–30), vol. 1, p. 52.
13. Joseph Joachim and Andreas Moser, *Violinschule* (Berlin, 1905), vol. 2, p. 94.
14. The subject of nineteenth-century bowing and articulation is explored at length in Clive Brown, *Classical and Romantic Performing Practice, 1750–1900* (Oxford, 1999).
15. Charles Van den Borren, 'Ysaÿe', in A. Eaglefield-Hull (ed.), *A Dictionary of Modern Music and Musicians* (London, 1924), p. 539.
16. *The Art of Violin Playing*, vol. 1, p. 40.
17. Ibid.
18. Louis P. Lochner, *Fritz Kreisler* (London, 1951), p. 19.
19. *Violin Playing as I Teach It* (New York, 1921; reprinted, 1960, 1980), p. 83.
20. *Szigeti on the Violin* (London, 1969), p. 172. Szigeti refers to Auer's *Graded Course of Violin Playing* (New York, 1926).
21. *Violin Playing as I Teach It*, p. 22.
22. *Szigeti on the Violin*, p. 172.

23. See Eric Wetherell, *Albert Sammons Violinist: The Life of 'Our Albert'* (London, 1998), pp. 9–17.

24. J. Corredor, *Conversations with Casals* (London, 1956), p. 24; Alfredo Piatti, *Méthode de Violoncelle* (London, 1878), p. 3.

25. E. Feuermann, ''Cello Playing: A Contemporary Revolution', *Violoncello Society Newsletter* (Spring 1972), p. 2, quoted in E. Cowling, *The Cello* (London, 1975), p. 172.

26. Joachim Stutschewsky, *Das Violoncellspiel/The Art of Playing the Violoncello* (Mainz, 1932–7), vol. 3, pp. 114–15, 117.

27. *Style and Idea*, p. 357.

28. *The Art of Quartet Playing: The Guarneri Quartet in Conversation with David Blum* (London, 1986), pp. 102–3.

29. Margaret Campbell, *The Great Cellists* (London, 1988), p. 118.

30. Interview with the author, 10 Jan. 1995.

31. Nicholas Delbanco, *The Beaux Arts Trio* (London, 1985), p. 52.

32. Robert Philip, *Early Recordings and Musical Style*, pp. 109–39.

33. Paul Taffanel and Philippe Gaubert, *Méthode complète de la flûte* (Paris, 1923), p. 186, quoted in Nancy Toff, *The Flute Book* (London, 1985), p. 111.

34. Paul Taffanel and Louis Fleury, 'Flûte', in A. Lavignac (ed.), *Encyclopédie de la musique et dictionnaire du Conservatoire* (Paris, 1921–31), 2ème partie, vol. 3, p. 1523.

35. *Woodwind Magazine*, vol. 7 (1950), p. 4.

36. 'Expression Unconfined', *Musical Quarterly*, vol. 30 (1944), p. 193, quoted in Nancy Toff, *The Flute Book* (London, 1985), p. 107.

37. 'The training of musicians', *Musical Quarterly*, vol. 84, no. 3, Fall 2000, pp. 330–1.

7 Questions of Authority: the Archaeological Approach

1. *Gramophone*, vol. 7, no. 77 (Oct. 1929), pp. 185–6.

2. 'K.K.', in *Gramophone*, vol. 7, no. 76 (Sept. 1929), p. 159.

3. See Margaret Campbell, *Dolmetsch: The Man and his Work* (London and Seattle, 1975), pp. 232–3.

4. Arnold Dolmetsch, 'Home Music', *The Consort*, no. 1 (Oct. 1929), p. 12.

5. George Bernard Shaw, *Music in London, 1890–94* (London, 1932), vol. 3, p. 258.

6. *Musical Times*, vol. 63, no. 951 (May 1922), pp. 344–5.

7. *The Interpretation of the Music of the XVII and XVIII Centuries* (London, 1915; rev. ed., 1946), p. 284.

8. The details of Woodhouse's rubato in the slow movement of the Italian Concerto are shown in Robert Philip, *Early Recordings and Musical Style* (Cambridge, 1992), p. 60.

9. Denise Restout, ed., *Landowska on Music* (New York, 1965), p. 355.

10. Steuart Wilson, 'The English Singers', *Recorded Sound* (1965), p. 375.

11. 'M.M.S.', in *Musical Times*, vol. 76, no. 1113 (Nov. 1935), p. 1031.

12. *Musical Times*, vol. 77, no. 1125 (Nov. 1936), pp. 1035–6.

13. See Harry Haskell, *The Early Music Revival: A History* (London, 1988), and Nicholas Kenyon, ed., *Authenticity and Early Music* (Oxford, 1988).

14. In interview with Andrew McGregor, CD Review, BBC Radio 3, Saturday 28 Oct. 2000.

15. The reconstruction of medieval music in the twentieth century, and its changing fashions, are discussed in Daniel Leech-Wilkinson, *The Modern Invention of Medieval Music* (Cambridge, 2002).

16. 'Bach gegen seine Liebhaber verteidigt', collected in T. Adorno, *Prismen* (Berlin, 1955), English trans. *Prisms* (London, 1967; reprinted, 1981). Quoted in Harry Haskell, *The Early Music Revival*, p. 179.

17. Richard Taruskin, 'Resisting the Ninth', *Nineteenth-Century Music*, vol. 12, no. 3

(1988–9), pp. 241–56, reprinted in *Text and Act* (Oxford and New York, 1995), p. 260.

18. 'Early music defended against its devotees: a theory of historical performance in the twentieth century', *Musical Quarterly*, vol. 69 (1983), pp. 297–322.

19. Quoted in Dominic Gill, ed., *The Book of the Violin* (Oxford, 1984), p. 154.

20. 'A new species of instrument: the vented trumpet in context', *Historic Brass Journal*, vol. 10 (1998), p. 1, quoted by Colin Lawson in *The Cambridge Companion to the Orchestra* (Cambridge, 2003), pp. 164–5.

21. *Early Music News*, no. 174 (May 1993), p. 1.

22. 'Harnoncourt: The future of music's past', *Classic CD*, Feb. 1993, p. 17; Roger Norrington, in *Early Music News*, no. 170 (Jan. 1993), p. 1.

23. Contribution to 'The Limits of Authenticity', *Early Music*, vol. 12 (Feb. 1984), pp. 3–12, reprinted in *Text and Act* (Oxford, 1995), pp. 67–82; 'The modern sound of early music', *New York Times*, 29 July 1990, reprinted in *Text and Act*, pp. 164–72.

24. Michael Morrow, 'Musical performance and authenticity', *Early Music*, vol. 6 (1978), pp. 233–46.

25. Farquharson Cousins, *On Playing the Horn* (2nd ed., Chapel-en-le-Frith, 1992), p. 17.

26. 'Bad vibrations', article in the *New York Times*, reprinted in *The Guardian*, 1 March 2003, Review, p. 16.

27. 'Historical performance, metronome marks and tempo in Beethoven's symphonies', *Early Music*, vol. 19 (1992), p. 248.

28. Andrew Green, 'Unashamed Romantics' (interview with John Boyden), *Classical Music*, no. 446 (8 Feb. 1992), p. 19.

29. Saul Seminar given by Charles Mackerras at the British Library, 13 March 2001.

30. John Boyden, 'The New Queen's Hall Orchestra: A personal point of view', in the programme for a concert at Fairfield Hall, Croydon, 2 Dec. 1993.

31. Michael Morrow, 'Musical performance and authenticity', pp. 233–46.

32. Steven Isserlis, 'In Gut We Trust', published on the website of his agent, Harrison Parrott, and in abbreviated form in their newsletter, Spring 2003. The description of steel 'disappearing' is from a conversation with the author.

33. Barbican Centre, London, 24 Feb. 2001. These quotations are taken from the edited text printed by the Royal Philharmonic Society.

34. Christopher Small, *Musicking* (Hanover, 1998), p. 94.

35. Dolmetsch, 1946 ed., pp. 25–6.

8 Listening Back: Lessons from the Twentieth Century

1. Nicholas Delbanco, *The Beaux Arts Trio* (London, 1985), p. 203.

2. Interview with the author, Nov. 1994.

3. John Amis, *Amiscellany* (London, 1985), p. 82.

4. *The Times*, 7 Nov. 1940.

5. *The Times*, 24 June 1941.

6. *The Times*, 24 Dec. 1941.

7. Interview with the author, 10 Jan. 1995.

8. Quoted in Bryan Crimp, *'Dear Mr Rosenthal . . .' 'Dear Mr Gaisberg . . .': An account of the making of Moriz Rosenthal's HMV recordings compiled from the correspondence of the pianist and his record producer, Fred Gaisberg* (Horsham, 1987), p. 17.

9. *Musical Times*, March 1934, p. 263.

10. 'G.C.', in *Musical Times*, March 1934, p. 264.

11. Bryan Crimp, *'Dear Mr Rosenthal . . .'*, p. 4, quoting Abram Chasins, *Speaking of Pianists* (New York, 1961).

12. F. W. Gaisberg, *Music on Record* (London, 1946), p. 174.

13. *Musical Times*, March 1911, vol. 52, p. 189.

14. Interview with the author, 1975.
15. Interview with the author, 1977.
16. Interview with the author, Nov. 1994.
17. BBC archive recording LP 27878, Hess interviewed by John Amis, 1962.
18. This description is taken from letters to his mother, quoted in 'Hess–Hungerford Correspondence', ed. Thomas M. Stanback III, *International Piano Archive at Maryland Newsletter*, no. 5 (Fall 1993), p. 10.
19. Michael Morrow, 'Musical performance and authenticity', *Early Music*, vol. 6 (1978), pp. 233–46.
20. E-mail correspondence, 17 Sept. 2002.
21. 'The visionary thing', *The Guardian*, 17 Sept. 2002, G2, p. 15. A longer description of Végh as a teacher is included in Susan Tomes, *Beyond the Notes: Journeys with Chamber Music* (Woodbridge, 2004), pp. 125–31.
22. E-mail correspondence, 8 Sept. 2001.
23. Interview with Bernard Keeffe, BBC recording LP 29683, 4 Aug. 1965.
24. Igor Stravinsky and Robert Craft, *Expositions and Developments* (London, 1962), p. 137.
25. Constant Lambert, *Music Ho! A Study of Music in Decline* (London, 1934), pp. 200–1.
26. Samuel Lipman, 'The pupils of Clara Schumann and the uses of tradition', *The New Criterion*, Sept. 1986, pp. 60–6.

Index

Abbado, Claudio 227
Academy of Ancient Music 214
Academy of St Martin in the Fields
  recordings
    Mozart, Piano Concerto in G, K453
      (Brendel/Marriner) 233
Adorno, Theodor
  on Bach performance 215
agogic accents *see* tenuti
d'Albert, Eugen 185
Alexanian, Diran 195, 196
Alexis Vlassoff Choir
  recordings
    Stravinsky, *Symphony of Psalms*
      (Stravinsky) 152
Alwyn, William 15, 78, 86–7
Amadeus Quartet 127
  vibrato 133
Amis, John 236
Amsterdam Concertgebouw Orchestra
    see Concertgebouw Orchestra
Ančerl, Karel
  recordings
    Dvořák, Symphony No. 9
      ('New World') 48
Ansermet, Ernest 43, 93
Anthologie Sonore, l' 205, 210
Aranyi, Jelly d' 23
Argerich, Martha 132
Arrau, Claudio
  Bill Lloyd on 243
  changing style 132
  on Schnabel 240
  recordings

Beethoven, Piano Sonata in E flat,
    Opus 31 No. 3 132
  Schumann, Piano Concerto 132
Ashkenazy, Vladimir
  recordings
    Rachmaninoff, Rhapsody on a Theme
      of Paganini 173
audiences
  demand encores 10–11
  effect of recording on 4, 245–50
  E. M. Forster on 9–10
  relationship with performers 10–12
  Schnabel on 5
Auer, Leopold
  and the 'Russian' violin school 191–5
  on vibrato 194
  pupils 193–4, 235
  recordings
    Tchaikovsky, *Souvenir d'un lieu cher*,
      'Mélodie' 194
Austen, Jane 7
'authenticity' and period instruments
      204–30, 233–5
Ax, Emanuel
  recordings
    Chopin, Piano Concerto No. 2 in
      F minor 234

Babbitt, Milton 180
Bach, Johann Sebastian
  Adorno on Bach performance 215
  Concerto for Two Violins 23
  Goldberg Variations 208
  Fantasia in C minor, BWV906 209

Italian Concerto 208, 228, 234
Nun freut euch, arr. Busoni 189
Orchestral Suite No. 3 in D 83
Partita in B flat 207
Backhaus, Wilhelm
changing style 132
recordings
Beethoven, Piano Sonata in C minor,
Opus 13 ('Pathétique') 132
Baillot, Pierre 193
Baldock, Robert 126
Barbirolli, John
Barbirolli Chamber Orchestra 69–70,
148
Elgar on 148
recordings
Brahms, Violin Concerto (Kreisler)
40
Elgar, 'Enigma' Variations 148
Elgar, Introduction and Allegro 70,
148
Elgar, Symphony No. 1 148
Barclay, Robert 217
Barenboim, Daniel 93
Barrère, Georges
pupils 200
vibrato 199–200
Barth, Karl Heinrich 191
Bartók, Bela 7, 140
Amazing Mandarin 246
as pianist 132, 173–5
Klemperer on 174
Scholes on 174
tempi and metronome markings 174
recordings
Bartók, *Allegro barbaro* 173
Bartók, *Mikrokosmos* 174
Scarlatti, Sonata in G, Kk 427 173
Baumann, Hermann 220–1
Bayreuth Festival 18
Bazelaire, Paul
recordings
Saint–Saëns, Sonata for Cello and
Piano No. 1 in C minor 111
BBC 6, 52–3, 66–7, 246
BBC Symphony Orchestra 49, 65, 68,
84, 94
Alfred Einstein on 69
Elgar on 90

founding 69, 70
Promenade Concerts 66–7
recordings
Berlioz, *Roman Carnival* (Boult) 69
Elgar, *Cockaigne* (Elgar) 90
Bean, Hugh 194
Beaux Arts Trio 127
Beecham, Thomas 13, 59, 68, 69, 71, 200
marking of parts 78–81
recordings
Berlioz, *Roman Carnival* 69
Debussy, *Prélude à l'Après-midi d'un
faune* 200
Delius, *Irmelin*, Prelude 98–9
Mendelssohn, *Midsummer Night's
Dream*, Scherzo 65, 76
(as pianist) Delius, songs (Labette)
131
Beethoven, Ludwig van
Fidelio, Overture 73
Grosse Fuge 79–80
King Stephen Overture 60
Piano Concerto No. 3 in C minor 111,
241
Piano Concerto No. 5 in E flat
('Emperor') 11
Piano Sonatas 184
Piano Sonata in C, Opus 2 No. 3
185
Piano Sonata in E flat, Opus 7 40
Piano Sonata in C minor, Opus 13
('Pathéthique') 132
Piano Sonata in E flat, Opus 31 No. 3
132
Piano Sonata in B flat, Opus 106
('Hammerklavier') 40, 43
Piano Sonata in A flat, Opus 110 132
Piano Trios, Opus 1 126
Piano Trio in C minor, Opus 1 No. 3
236
Piano Trio in B flat, Opus 97
('Archduke') 126
Rondino in E flat, WoO 25 30
Sonata for Violin and Piano in A,
Opus 47 ('Kreutzer') 110
Sonata for Violin and Piano in G,
Opus 96 105–8
String Quartet in G, Opus 18 No. 2
120–1

String Quartet in C minor, Opus 18
        No. 4   239
String Quartet in F, Opus 59 No. 1
        118–19
String Quartet in E flat, Opus 94
        ('Harp')   239
String Quartet in B flat, Opus 130   124
String Quartet in C sharp minor,
        Opus 131   115–17, 124
String Quartet in A minor, Opus 132
        40
Symphonies   218–19
Symphony No. 3 ('Eroica')   67, 73, 78
Symphony No. 5   28, 65, 73, 77, 83
Symphony No. 6   40
Symphony No. 7   76, 84, 227
Symphony No. 9   48, 215
Variations in C minor, WoO 80   189
Violin Concerto   21, 221
Beinum, Eduard van   75
Bell, Joshua   221
Bérart, Jean   125
Berg, Alban
Violin Concerto   174
Berlin Hochschule für Musik   202
Berlin Philharmonic Orchestra   73, 227
compared with Vienna PO   75
performs *Don Quixote* with Strauss   64
Simon Rattle on   86
Stravinsky on   91
tours with Furtwängler   21
woodwind style   96–7, 201
recordings
        J. S. Bach, Brandenburg Concerto
                No. 3 (Furtwängler)   73
        Beethoven, *Fidelio*, Overture (Kopsch)
                73
        Beethoven, Symphony No. 3
                ('Eroica') (Pfitzner)   73
        Beethoven, Symphony No. 5
                (Nikisch) 28, (Furtwängler) 73
        Brahms, Symphony No. 3
                (Furtwängler)   100
        Stravinsky, *Jeu de Cartes* (Stravinsky)
                91, 152
        Stravinsky, *Rite of Spring* (Karajan)
                153
        Tchaikovsky, Symphony No. 5
                (Mengelberg)   100–1

Berlin State Opera Orchestra (Berlin
        Staatskapelle)
recordings
        Beethoven, Symphony No. 5 (Strauss)
                73
        Mahler, Symphony No. 2
                ('Resurrection') (Fried)   28,
                154–5
        Mozart, *Marriage of Figaro*, Overture
                (L.Blech)   73
        R. Strauss, *Don Juan* (Strauss)   73
Berlioz, Hector
Monteux on Colonne's memories of
        141–2
Roman Carnival   69
Romeo and Juliet   66, 72
Symphonie fantastique   40, 72–3, 92–3,
        141
Trojans, 'Royal Hunt and Storm'   66
Bernstein, Leonard
recordings
        Mahler, Symphony No. 2
                ('Resurrection')   155
        Stravinsky, *Rite of Spring*   61
Best, Martin   46
Betti, Adolfo   *see* Flonzaley Quartet
Bie, Oskar   157
Bilson, Malcolm
recordings
        Mozart, Piano Concerto in G, K453
                233
Birmingham Festival   8
Blagrove, Henry   124
Blech, Harry   91
Blech, Leo
recordings
        Mozart, *Marriage of Figaro*, Overture
                73
Blumenfeld, Felix   189
Bohemian Quartet   21, 192
Flesch on   122–3
portamento   114, 118
vibrato   133
recordings
        Dvořák, String Quartet in F
                ('American')   118, 120
        Smetana, String Quartet No. 1 in
                E minor ('From my Life')   118
Bonavia, Ferrucio   34

Boston Symphony Orchestra 75–6, 77, 90
  financing 19
  founding 9
  Monteux on 76
  portamento 102
  woodwind 94–5
  recordings
    Rachmaninoff, *Isle of the Dead*
      (Koussevitzky) 77
    Sibelius, Symphony No. 2
      (Koussevitzky) 77
    Tchaikovsky, Symphony No. 4
      (Muck) 76
    Tchaikovsky, Symphony No. 6
      ('Pathétique') (Koussevitzky) 77
    Wagner, *Lohengrin*, Act 3, Prelude
      (Muck) 28
Botstein, Leon 202, 229
Boulanger, Nadia 205
  recordings
    Monteverdi, madrigals 211
Boulez, Pierre
  recordings
    Stravinsky, *Rite of Spring* 153
Boult, Adrian 68
  Alfred Einstein on 69
  on BBC Symphony Orchestra 70
  on Ethel Smyth 11
  on London Symphony Orchestra 68
  on Nikisch 28
  on 'patching' 60
  on Talich and Czech Philharmonic
    Orchestra 86
  on 78 rpm time limit 38
  recordings
    Berlioz, *Roman Carnival* 69
    Elgar, 'Enigma' Variations 148
    Elgar, Symphony No. 1 148
    Elgar, Symphony No. 2 148
    Elgar, Violin Concerto (Menuhin)
      147
Bournemouth Municipal Orchestra 17
Boyden, John 222–3
Brahms, Johannes
  as pianist and conductor 181
  cylinder recording of 140
  on applause 11
  on Bülow and Meiningen Orchestra
    19, 163

  on Hans Richter 82
  on tempo changes 11–12
  piano-duet arrangements 7
  Clarinet Quintet 40, 41–2
  German Requiem 191
  Hungarian Dances 46
  Piano Trio in B 236
  String Quartet in A minor 30, 40
  Symphony No. 1 82
  Symphony No. 2 10, 76, 101–2
  Symphony No. 3 99–100
  Variations on a Theme by Haydn 76,
    84, 95
  Violin Concerto 11, 46, 66–7, 248
Brain, Dennis 71, 221
Brainin, Norbert 133
brass
  French 72–3, 96
  effect of globalisation 95–6
  period instruments 216, 217, 220–1
  Russian 95–6, 245
Brassart, Johannes 210
Brett, Philip 7
British Broadcasting Corporation *see* BBC
British Museum 206
British National Opera Company 64
Britten, Benjamin 140
  Saint Nicholas 7
  Variations on a Theme of Frank Bridge
    70
  recordings
    Schubert, *Schöne Müllerin* (Pears)
      61
Brooke, Gwydion 94
Brown, Clive 222
Brüggen, Frans 213, 224
  recordings
    Beethoven, Symphonies 234
Budapest Quartet (led by Hauser) 192
  portamento 114, 133
  vibrato 133
  recordings
    Beethoven, String Quartet in F,
      Opus 59 No. 1 118, 119
    Beethoven, String Quartet in B flat,
      Opus 130 133
Budapest Quartet (led by Roisman)
  portamento 113
  vibrato 133–4

recordings
  Beethoven, String Quartet in B flat,
    Opus 130 133
  Brahms, String Quartet in B flat 40
  Mozart, String Quartet in F, K590
    121–2
Bülow, Hans von 8, 11, 219
  Brahms on 19, 163
  rehearsal and discipline 19, 79–80
  rubato and flexible tempo 11, 20
Burne-Jones, Edward 206
Busch, Adolf 211–3
  on recording Brahms, Clarinet Quintet
    41–2
Busch Chamber Players 211–13
  recordings
    J. S. Bach, Brandenburg Concertos
      212
    J. S. Bach, Orchestral Suites
      212–13
    Handel, Concerti Grossi, Opus 6
      212–13
Busch Quartet
  portamento 115–17
  Yfrah Neaman on 237
  recordings
    Beethoven, String Quartets 249
    Beethoven, String Quartet in C,
      Opus 59 No. 3 122
    Beethoven, String Quartet in C sharp
      minor, Opus 131 115–17
    Beethoven, String Quartet in
      A minor, Opus 132 40
    Brahms, Clarinet Quintet (Kell)
      40–2
    Schubert, String Quartet in G, D887
      122
Busoni, Ferruccio 190
  on the experience of recording 27
  piano rolls 34
Busscher, Henri de 94
Buxbaum, Friedrich 236
  see also Rosé Quartet

Cage, John 180
Calvet Quartet
  recordings
    Beethoven, String Quartet in C sharp
      minor, Opus 131 117

Ravel, Introduction and Allegro 37,
    134
Camden, Archie 94
Cape, Safford
  recordings with Pro Musica Antiqua
    210
Capell, Richard 237
Capet Quartet 192
  portamento 114, 115–17
  vibrato 133
  recordings
    Beethoven, String Quartet in C sharp
      minor, Opus 131 115–17
Carrodus, John 64
Carse, Adam 63–4
Caruso, Enrico 50
Casals, Pablo
  as cellist 195–6, 197, 251
    Feuermann on 195
    Greenhouse on 197
    on bowing technique 195
    Schoenberg on 176, 195
  recordings
    J. S. Bach, Suites for
      Unaccompanied Cello 249
    Chopin, Nocturne in E flat, Opus 9
      No. 2 196
    Dvořák, Cello Concerto 40, 176
    Elgar, Cello Concerto 196
  as conductor of Casals Orchestra of
    Barcelona 79, 82–3
    Boult on 82–3
  recordings
    Beethoven, Symphony No. 4 83
  see also Cortot–Thibaud–Casals Trio
Cavalli, Francesco 214
CBS 45
Celibidache, Sergiu 85
Chailly, Riccardo
  recordings
    Tchaikovsky, Symphony No. 5 96
Chasins, Abram 238
Cherkassky, Shura 46
Chicago Symphony Orchestra 9, 226
Chilingirian, Levon
  and Chiligirian Quartet 128
Chopin, Fryderyk 7
  pupils and grand-pupils 129–31, 186–7
  rubato 129

Ballade No. 1 in G minor 129–31
Ballade No. 4 in F minor 188
Barcarolle 132
Berceuse 186
Etude in G flat ('Black Keys') 27
Mazurka in E minor, Opus 41 No. 2
189
Mazurka in C sharp minor, Opus 63
No. 3 185
Nocturne in E flat, Opus 9 No. 2 186,
(arr. cello) 196
Nocturnes, Opus 15 27
Nocturne in F, Opus 15 No. 1 185
Piano Concerto No. 1 in E minor 237,
238
Piano Concerto No. 2 in F minor 132,
234
Piano Sonata No. 3 in B minor 43, 187
Polonaise No. 2 in E flat minor 188
Polonaise No. 3 in A 186
Preludes 187
Scherzo No. 2 in B flat minor 186
Scherzo No. 3 in C sharp minor 132
Waltz in D flat, Opus 64 No. 1
('Minute') 186, (arr. Hofmann)
188
Christie, William 227
Cincinnati Symphony Orchestra 9
cinema
musicians employed in 13, 14, 71
clavichord
made by Arnold Dolmetsch 206, 208
played by Arnold Dolmetsch 206–7
Clements, Andrew 127
Cleveland Orchestra
rehearsal 84
recordings 45, 89, 201
Beethoven, *King Stephen* Overture
(Szell) 60
Beethoven, Symphony No. 7 (Szell)
241
Brahms, Variations on a Theme by
Haydn (Szell) 95
Coates, Albert 68
recordings
Beethoven, Symphony No. 3
('Eroica') 90
Borodin, *Prince Igor*, Overture 90
Stravinsky, *Petrushka* 40

Cohen, Harriet 190
recordings
Elgar, Piano Quintet 190
Cohen, Isidore 127
Collegium Aureum 213
Colonne, Edouard
Monteux on 141–2
Colonne Orchestra
recordings
Berlioz, *Romeo and Juliet* (Pierné) 72
Berlioz, *Symphonie fantastique* (Pierné)
92
Columbia History of Music 204, 207
Columbia Symphony Orchestra
recordings
Stravinsky, *Firebird* (Stravinsky) 150
Stravinsky, *Rite of Spring* (Stravinsky)
150
composers
recordings by, or associated with
140–182
Concentus Musicus of Vienna 213, 225
Concertgebouw Orchestra of Amsterdam
21
brass style 75, 96
ensemble 75, 90
portamento 100–1, 160–2
Mahler conducts 158–63
rehearsal 83
Slowik on 160
recordings
Mahler, Symphony No. 4
(Mengelberg) 160, 163
Mahler, Symphony No. 5, Adagietto
(Mengelberg) 160–2
Tchaikovsky, *Romeo and Juliet*
(Mengelberg) 75
Tchaikovsky, Symphony No. 5
(Chailly) 96
Tchaikovsky, Symphony No. 5
(Mengelberg) 75
concerts
audience's experience of 9–11
compared with studio recordings 47–9,
249
encores 10–11
importance of before recordings 4ff
conductor
'period' conductors 218–19

rehearsal technique   78–86
rise of the virtuoso   20–1
Consort of Musicke   213
Cooper, Joseph   38
Copland, Aaron   140
Coppola, Piero
  recordings
    Schumann, Symphony No. 3   90
Cortot, Alfred   132, 188, 190, 191
  as conductor   191
  Fauré on   166–7
  recordings
    Chopin, Ballades   40
    Chopin, Piano Concerto No. 2 in
      F minor   234
    Chopin, Piano Sonata No. 3 in
      B minor   187
    Chopin, Preludes   187
    Fauré, Sonata No. 1 in A for Violin
      and Piano (Thibaud)   168
    Ravel, Concerto for Piano, Left Hand
      170
    Ravel, *Jeux d'eau*   170
    Ravel, *Gaspard de la nuit,* 'Ondine'
      170
    Ravel, *Sonatine*   170
    Schumann, *Carnaval*   187
    Schumann, Piano Concerto   187
Cortot–Thibaud–Casals Trio   125–6, 127
  Ravel on   170
  recordings
    Beethoven, Piano Trio in B flat,
      Opus 97 ('Archduke')   126
    Schubert, Piano Trio in B flat, D898
      40, 126
Costa, Michael
  marking of parts   78
  orchestral discipline   17–18, 20
Couperin, François   205, 208, 209
  'Couperin Society' recordings   209
  L'Oiseau-Lyre edition   209
  Concerts royaux   210
Couperin, Louis   205
Covent Garden   *see* Royal Opera House
Cowen, Frederic   143
Craft, Robert
  recordings
    Stravinsky, *Rite of Spring*   153
Craxton, Harold   190

Cropper, Peter   128
Crystal Palace Concerts   8
Cuénod, Hugues
  recordings
    Monteverdi, madrigals (Boulanger)
      211
Culshaw, John   50
Curzon, Clifford   185, 190, 249
  on Schnabel   138, 184, 185
  on impact of recordings   244–5
cutting
  Busoni on   29
  Elgar, *Violin Concerto*   29
  works for recordings   27, 29–30
  works in concert   30, 67
Czech Philharmonic Orchestra   40
  Boult on   86
  recordings
    Dvořák, Symphony No. 9 ('New
      World') (Ančerl)   48
    Smetana, *Ma Vlást* (Talich)   86
Czech Quartet   *see* Bohemian Quartet

Damrosch, Walter   20, 68, 76
  recordings
    Brahms, Symphony No. 2   76
    Ravel, *Mother Goose*   76
Danco, Suzanne
  recordings
    Mozart, *Marriage of Figaro,*
      'Non so più'   112
Dart, Thurston   216
Davies, Fanny   187, 248
  rubato   131, 188
  recordings
    Schumann, *Kinderszenen*   188
    Schumann, Piano Concerto   188
Davis, Colin
  recordings
    Berlioz, *Symphonie fantastique*   93
Deahl, Alfred   13–15, 86–7
Debussy, Claude   140
  as conductor   10, 65
  as pianist   164
  Marguerite Long on   164
  Estampes   165
  Images for orchestra, 'Gigues'   83
  Images for piano   165
    'Poissons d'or'   165

L'Isle joyeuse 165
La Mer 64, 65
Nocturnes, 'Fêtes' 10, 72, 77
Prélude à l'Après-midi d'un faune 65
piano rolls 164–5
  Children's Corner, 'Dr Gradus ad
    Parnassum' 165
  Estampes, 'Soirée dans Grenade' 165,
    166
  Preludes, 'La cathédrale engloutie'
    164–5
recordings
  Ariettes oubliées (Garden) 164
  Pelléas et Mélisande, extracts (Garden)
    164
Decombes, Emile 187
Defauw, Désiré 164
Delecluse, Ulysse 134
Delius, Frederick
  Cello Concerto 64
  Irmelin, Prelude 98–9
Derenne, Paul
recordings
  Monteverdi, madrigals (Boulanger)
    211
Desormière, Roger
recordings
  de Lalande, *Musique pour les soupers du
    Roi* 210, 211
Diémer, Louis 191
Dolmetsch Family 204–6, 216, 220
  Compton Mackenzie on 205
recordings
  Dowland, Norcome, Weelkes, viol
    consorts 205–6
Dolmetsch, Arnold 204, 208, 229–30
  harpsichord by 208
  G. B. Shaw on clavichord by 206
  *Interpretation of the Music of the XVII
    and XVIII Centuries* 207,
    229–30
  on discovery of old music and
    instruments 206
  on J. J. Quantz 230
  on tempo rubato 208
  patrons 206
recordings
  J. S. Bach, 48 Preludes and Fugues
    206–7

J. S. Bach, Chromatic Fantasia and
  Fugue 207
Dolmetsch, Carl 204, 207
Dolmetsch, Cécile 204
recordings
  Dowland, 'Awake sweet love' 206
Dolmetsch, Rudolph 204
recordings 207
Domus 50–2
recordings
  Fauré, Piano Quartets 51–2
Donizetti, Gaetano
  Don Pasquale, Overture 29
Donohoe, Peter 132
D'Oyle Carte Opera Company 14
Draper, Haydn
recordings
  Ravel, Introduction and Allegro
    134–5, 172
Dreyfus, Laurence 216
Dufay, Guillaume 210
Dushkin, Samuel 194
Dusinberre, Edward 128
Dutoit, Charles
recordings
  Ravel, Piano Concerto in G
    (Thibaudet) 169
Dvořák, Antonin
  on Hans Richter 82
  Cello Concerto 40, 176
  Slavonic Rhapsody No. 3 82
  String Quartet in F ('American') 120
  Symphony No. 8 40
  Symphony No. 9 ('New World') 48
Dyer, Louise 205

Early Music
  influence on conventional performance
    227–30
  in late 20th century 213–26
  period instruments and 'historically
    aware' performance 204–30
  pioneers 204–13
  popularity of 214, 246
Early Music Consort of London 204, 213,
    214
Ecole de Musique Ancienne 205
Ecole Normale 205
Edinburgh Festival 45, 131

Edison, Thomas Alva 25
editing *see under* recording
Ehrlich, Cyril 13
Eigeldinger, Jean–Jacques 128–9
Elgar, Edward 50, 90, 140
    as pianist 131
    Boult on his conducting 147–8
    concerts 147–8
    on Barbirolli 148
    on BBC Symphony Orchestra 145
    on Henry Wood 67
    on Leon Goossens 146
    on London Symphony Orchestra 145
    on performance instructions 181
    tempi in his recordings 29, 142–9
    Cello Concerto 196
    'Enigma' Variations 149
    Introduction and Allegro 70, 148
    Piano Quintet 190
    Symphony No. 1 42, 143, 148
    recordings
        Cello Concerto (Harrison) 147
        Cockaigne 65, 90
        cuts in 29
        Froissart 146
        'Enigma' Variations 42, 65, 66, 98,
            142–5, 223
        Improvisations (piano) 131
        Nursery Suite 36
        portamento in 145
        Sea Pictures 36
        Violin Concerto (Hall) 29, 146,
            (Menuhin) 29, 36, 146–8
Elman, Mischa 194, 235
EMI 71
Enesco, Georges
    Rumanian Rhapsody 83
English Baroque Soloists 213–4
    recordings
        Mozart, Piano Concerto in G, K453
            (Bilson/Gardiner) 233
English Concert 214
English Singers
    recordings of madrigals 210–11
ensemble
    in orchestras 63–103
    in chamber groups 104–39

Fachiri, Adela 23, 192

recordings
    Beethoven, Sonata in G for Violin and
        Piano, Opus 96 105–8
Farmer, Adrian 46, 58, 218
Farrar, Geraldine 39
Fauré, Gabriel
    Marguerite Long on 164, 166–8
    metronome markings 167–8
    on Cortot 166–7
    piano rolls 164–5
        Barcarolle No. 1 in A minor 165
        Impromptu No. 2 in F minor 167
        Nocturne No. 4 in E flat 168
        Piano Quartets 51–2
        Pièces brèves 165
        Sonata No. 1 in A for Violin and Piano
            168
Fellowes, E. H. 204
    recordings with St George's Singers
        210
Ferguson, Howard 9
    on Adela Verne 235
    on May Harrison 235
    Piano Sonata 190
Ferrier, Kathleen
    recordings
        Mahler, *Kindertotenlieder* 220
        Schumann, *Frauenliebe und –leben*
            131
Feuermann, Emanuel
    David Soyer on his portamento 196
    Rubinstein on 126
    recordings
        piano trios with Heifetz and
            Rubinstein 126
        Chopin, Nocturne in E flat, Opus 9
            No. 2 196
Fischer, Edwin 190, 214
    recordings
        Mozart, Piano Concerto in G, K453
            233
Fitzgerald, Ella 249
Flagler, Henry Harkness 19–20
Flesch, Carl
    on American orchestras 75
    on Arnold Rosé 74
    on Bohemian Quartet 122–3
    on bow holds 191–2
    on Joachim Quartet 122

on Kreisler's vibrato 193
on Lamoureux 18
on Mengelberg 83
on Nikisch 20
on Ysaÿe 110
pupils 171, 197
Fleury, Louis 198
Flonzaley Quartet
portamento 114–15, 121
vibrato 133, 193
recordings
Beethoven, String Quartet in G,
Opus 18 No. 2 120–1
Haydn, String Quartet in D, Opus 64
No. 5 ('Lark') 121
Mozart, String Quartet in D minor,
K421 121
Schubert, String Quartet in G, D887
122
Florestan Trio 50, 52–4, 56, 127, 179
recordings
Schubert, Piano Trio No. 2 in E flat,
D929 53–4
Schumann, Piano Trio No. 1 in
D minor 53
Fontana, Julian 203
Forster, E. M.
on National Gallery Concerts 9–10
Fournier, Pierre 201
Freitas-Branco, Pedro de
recordings
Ravel, Piano Concerto in G
(M. Long) 163
French Radio National Orchestra
(Orchestre National de France)
recordings
Stravinsky, *Rite of Spring* (Boulez)
153
Fried, Oskar
relationship with Mahler 154–6
recordings
Mahler, Symphony No. 2 28, 154–5
Tchaikovsky, Symphony No. 6
('Pathétique') 65
Friedheim, Arthur
recordings
Liszt, *Hungarian Rhapsody* No. 2 186
Friedländer, Max 156
Friedman, Ignacy

rubato 131, 184
recordings
Chopin, Nocturne in E flat, Opus 55
No. 2 184
Friedmann, Samuel
recordings
Tchaikovsky, Symphony No. 5 96
Furtwängler, Wilhelm 20, 21, 68, 213,
234
on American orchestras 23–4
recordings 73
J. S. Bach, Brandenburg Concerto
No. 3 73
Beethoven, Symphony No. 5 73
Brahms, Symphony No. 3 100

Gaisberg, Fred 27, 36, 49–50, 75
on Paderewski 240
Galimir Quartet
recordings
Ravel, String Quartet 171–2
Galli-Curci, Amelita
recordings
Mozart, *Marriage of Figaro*,
'Non so più' 112
Galway, James 97
Garden, Mary
recordings
Debussy, *Pelléas et Mélisande*, extracts
(Debussy) 164
Ariettes oubliées (Debussy) 164
Gardiner, John Eliot 160, 213, 218–9,
224
recordings
Beethoven, *Missa solemnis* 220
Beethoven, Symphonies 218–9,
234
Berlioz, *Symphonie fantastique* 92–3,
220
Mozart, Piano Concerto in G, K453
(Bilson) 233
Gaubert, Philippe
as conductor
recordings
Debussy, *Nocturnes* 72
as flautist 94, 172, 198, 199
Méthode complète de flûte (with Taffanel)
198, 199
recordings 199

'Georges Enescu' Bucharest Philharmonic
        Orchestra
    recordings
        Brahms, Symphony No. 2 (Mandeal)
            96
Gesellschaft der Musikfreunde, Vienna   8
Gewandhaus Orchestra   *see* Leipzig
        Gewandhaus Orchestra
Gilbert, Geoffrey   94, 200
    recordings
        Debussy, *Prélude à l'Après-midi d'un
            faune* (LPO/Beecham)   200
Gilbert, Kenneth   228
Gilbert and Sullivan operettas   14
Gillet, Georges   95
Gluck, Christoff Willibald
    Orfeo ed Eurydice, 'Dance of the blessed
        spirits' ('Mélodie')   184
Glyndebourne Opera
    recordings
        Mozart, *Marriage of Figaro* (F. Busch)
            122
Godfrey, Dan   6, 13, 17
Goehr, Alexander   179
Goehr, Walter   40
Goldberg, Szymon   75
Goossens, Eugene
    recordings
        Stravinsky, *Petrushka*   29
Goossens, Leon   94, 200
    Elgar on   146
Gould, Glenn   60, 216
Gounod, Charles
    Faust, Waltz arr. Liszt   27, 29
    Romeo and Juliet   64
Graf, Max   5
Grainger, Percy   66
    recordings
        Chopin, Piano Sonata No. 3 in
            B minor   43, 187
Gramophone   28, 30, 37, 68, 170, 205, 206,
        238
Gramophone Company   49, 71
Grange, Henry-Louis de la   36, 38, 156
Greef, Arthur de   185
    recordings
        Grieg, Piano Concerto   97
Greenberg, Noah   204, 213
    recordings

Play of Daniel   214
Greene, Harry Plunket   138
Greenhouse, Bernard
    in Beaux Arts Trio   127
    on Casals   197
    on Elman   235
Grieg, Edvard   141
    Piano Concerto   97–8
    Sonata No. 3 in C minor for Violin and
            Piano   105, 109
Griffiths, Paul   174
Grove, George   17–18
Grumiaux, Arthur   125, 201
Grümmer, Paul   197

Haitink, Bernard   38, 227
Halban, Desi
    recordings
        Mahler, Symphony No. 4 (Walter)
            36
Haldane, Charlotte   6
Hall, Marie   194
    recordings
        Elgar, Violin Concerto   29
Hallé, Charles   8
Hallé Orchestra   8, 94
    recordings
        Berlioz, *Romeo and Juliet*, 'Queen Mab'
            Scherzo (Harty)   66
        Berlioz, *Trojans*, 'Royal Hunt and
            Storm' (Harty)   66
        Elgar, 'Enigma' Variations (Harty)   66
Hambourg, Mark
    rubato   131, 184
    recordings
        Beethoven, Piano Sonata in C,
            Opus 2 No. 3   185
        Glück, *Orfeo ed Eurydice*, 'Mélodie'   184
Handel, George Frideric
    Concerti Grossi Opus 6   212–13
    harpsichord music   17
    Messiah   208
Handel Festival, Crystal Palace   8, 17
Hanover Band
    recordings
        Beethoven, Symphonies   46, 218
Hanslick, Eduard
    on Bülow and Meiningen Orchestra
            19, 79–80

on Rosenthal 186
Harnoncourt, Nikolaus 213, 224
   on 'authenticity' 219
   recordings
      Beethoven, *Missa solemnis* 220
harpsichord
   by Dolmetsch 207
   by Pleyel for Landowska 208–9
   developments in late 20th century
      215–16
   played by Violet Gordon Woodhouse
      207–8
   used by Adolf Busch 212
Harrison, Beatrice
   recordings
      Elgar, Cello Concerto (Elgar) 147
Harrison, May 235
Harty, Hamilton 66, 69
   recordings
      Berlioz, *Romeo and Juliet*, 'Queen Mab'
         Scherzo 66
      Berlioz, *Trojans*, 'Royal Hunt and
         Storm' 66
      Elgar, 'Enigma' Variations 66
      Haydn, Symphony No. 95 69
Haskell, Harry 214
Haskil, Clara 190
Hauser, Emil *see* Budapest Quartet
Haydn, Franz Josef 7
   String Quartet in D, Opus 64 No. 5
      ('Lark') 121
   Symphony No. 95 69
   Symphony No. 101 ('Clock') 78
Heifetz, Jascha 23, 100, 125, 201
   bowing and vibrato 193
   Rubinstein on 126
   recordings
      Piano trios with Feuermann and
         Rubinstein 126
      Piano trios with Piatigorsky and
         Rubinstein 126–7
Hempel, Frieda
   recordings
      Mozart, *Magic Flute*, 'Zum Leiden'
         112
Henschel, George 8
Hess, Myra 190, 241–2
   National Gallery Concerts 9, 236
   recordings 241

Beethoven, Piano Sonata in E,
   Opus 109 241
Ferguson, Piano Sonata 190
Scarlatti, Sonata in G, Kk14 241
Schumann, *Carnaval* 39–41, 241
Schumann, Piano Concerto 40–1
Heyworth, Peter 156
Higginson, Henry L. 19
Hill, Peter
   on Messiaen 178
   recordings
      Messiaen, *Vingt regards sur l'enfant Jésus*
         178
Hindemith, Paul 141
Hitler, Adolf 74, 240
Höbarth, Erich 128
   on period and conventional playing
      225–6
Hofmann, Josef 129, 188–9
   on Anton Rubinstein 188
   recordings
      Chopin, Ballade No. 4 in F minor
         188
      Chopin, Polonaise No. 2 in E flat
         minor 188
      Chopin, Waltz in D flat, Opus 64
         No. 1 ('Minute'), arr. Hofmann
         188
      Schubert, *Moment musical* in F minor,
         arr. Godowsky 188
Hogwood, Christopher 214, 224
Horowitz, Vladimir 49, 59, 189
   recordings 214
      J. S. Bach, *Nun freut euch*, arr. Busoni
         189
      Beethoven, Variations in C minor,
         WoO 80 189
      Chopin, Mazurka in E minor,
         Opus 41 No. 2 189
      Scarlatti, Sonata in B minor, Kk87
         189
      Schumann, *Arabesque* 189
Hough, Stephen 173
Howes, Frank 67
Hubay, Jenő 243
Huberman, Bronislaw 23
Hudson, Richard 129
Hutcheson, Ernest 241
Hyperion Records 50, 51–2

International Quartet
  recordings
    Ravel, String Quartet   170–1
Isserlis, Steven   125
  on gut strings   225–6

Jacobs, Arthur   68
Jaeger, A. J.   143, 144, 145
Jaques–Dalcroze, Emile
  on Ysaÿe's rubato   110
jazz
  performance compared with classical
    180, 232
Joachim, Joseph   123, 191, 206
  agogic accents   105, 123
  and the 'German School'   191–12, 202
  as conductor   10, 11, 12
  as violinist   11, 21, 23, 125, 243, 248
  on vibrato   192
  pupils   192
  recordings
    Joachim, Romance in C   192
Joachim Quartet   21, 122–4
  Flesch on   122
  Fuller-Maitland on   123
  Klemperer on   123
  membership   124
  Richard Strauss on   123
Johnson, Edward   38

Kalbeck, Max   11
Karajan, Herbert von   21, 247
  recordings
    Stravinsky, *Rite of Spring*   153
Katin, Peter   190
Keener, Andrew   50–60
Kell, Reginald   94
  recordings
    Brahms, Clarinet Quintet   40–2
Keller, Hans   217
Keller, Robert   7
Kempe, Rudolf   84
Kempff, Wilhelm   191
  changing style   132
  recordings
    Beethoven, Piano Sonata in A flat,
      Opus 110   132
Kennedy, Daisy   66
Kenyon, Nicholas   227

Kincaid, William   200
Kirkpatrick, Ralph   216
Kleiber, Carlos   85, 249
Kleiber, Erich
  recordings
    Mozart, *Marriage of Figaro*   112
Klemperer, Otto   247
  on Bartók   174
  on Joachim Quartet   124
  relationship with Mahler   154,
    156–7
  recordings
    Beethoven, Symphony No. 9   48
    Mahler, Symphony No. 2   155, 157
Klengel, Julius   195, 196
  pupils   197
  William Pleeth on   197
Klingler, Karl   192
Koch, Lothar   201
Koczalski, Raoul
  rubato   129–31, 186–7, 234
  recordings
    Chopin, Ballade No. 1 in G minor
      129–31, 187
    Chopin, Scherzo No. 2 in B flat
      minor   186
Kodály, Zoltan   7, 141
Kolisch Quartet
  Schoenberg on   175
  recordings
    Schoenberg, String Quartets   175
    Schubert, String Quartet in G, D887
      122
Kolisch, Rudolf   194
  recordings
    Schoenberg, *Pierrot Lunaire*
      (Schoenberg)   175
Koopman, Ton   228
Kopsch, Julius
  recordings
    Beethoven, *Fidelio*, Overture   73
Koussevitzky, Serge
  recordings   90, 213
    Rachmaninoff, *Isle of the Dead*   77
    Sibelius, Symphony No. 2   77
    Tchaikovsky, Symphony No. 6
      ('Pathétique')   77
Kovacevich (formerly Bishop), Stephen
    190, 240–1

Krauss, Clemens
  recordings
    Brahms, Symphony No. 3 99–100
    Mozart, *Marriage of Figaro*, Overture
      73
Kreisler, Fritz 23, 74, 100, 146, 193, 202,
    251
  attitude to recording 39
  reluctance to rehearse 22
  vibrato 193
  recordings
    Beethoven, Sonata in G for Violin and
      Piano, Opus 96 105, 109
    Brahms, Violin Concerto 40
    Grieg, Sonata No. 3 in C minor for
      Violin and Piano 39, 105
    Schubert, 'Ave Maria' (McCormack)
      109–10
    Schubert, Sonata in A for Violin and
      Piano 39, 41, 109
Kubelik, Jan 194
Kurtág, György 179
Kurz, Selma
  recordings
    Mozart, *Magic Flute*, 'Zum Leiden'
      112

Labette, Dora
  recordings
    Delius, songs 131
Lalande, Michel-Richard de 205, 209
  Musique pour les soupers du Roi 210
Lambert, Constant 246
Lamond, Frederic
  rubato 131, 186
  recordings 185
    Beethoven, Piano Sonata in C minor,
      Opus 13 ('Pathétique') 185
    Brahms, Capriccio in B minor,
      Opus 76 No. 2 186
Lamoureux, Charles 20, 89
  Flesch on 18
Lamoureux Orchestra 18
Landowska, Wanda 204–5, 208–9,
    211
  on 'authenticity' 208–9, 226
  recordings 209, 214
    J. S.Bach, Fantasia in C minor,
      BWV 906 209

'Couperin Society' 209
  Scarlatti, Sonatas 214
Lara, Adelina de 188, 248
Laskine, Lily 37, 134
Leeds Festival 8, 15
  Sullivan conducts *Messiah* at 17
Legge, Walter 50, 55, 71
Léhar, Franz 141
Leipzig Gewandhaus Orchestra 5–6,
    245
  Ethel Smyth on 8
  Nikisch's rehearsals 83
Léner Quartet 30
  portamento 112–14
  vibrato 133
  recordings
    Mozart, String Quartet in G, K387
      112–14
Leningrad (St Petersburg) Philharmonic
    Orchestra
  brass style 95–6
  recordings
    Tchaikovsky, Symphony No. 5
      (Mravinsky) 96
Leoncavallo, Ruggiero 141
Leonhardt, Gustav 213, 215, 216, 228
Leppard, Raymond 214
Leschetizky, Theodor 129, 244
  pupils 184–5
  rubato 185
  piano rolls 34
    Chopin, Nocturne in D flat, Opus 27
      No. 2 185
Lester, Richard *see* Florestan Trio
Lévy, Lazare 190
Lhévinne, Josef 189
  piano rolls compared with recordings
    33–4
  recordings
    Liszt, Transcendental Studies No. 3,
      La campanella 34
    Schumann arr. Liszt, *Frühlingsnacht*
      189
    Johann Strauss II arr. Schulz-Evler,
      Blue Danube 33, 189
Lhévinne, Rosina 241
Ligeti, György 179
Lindsay Quartet (The Lindsays) 128
Lipman, Samuel 248

Liszt, Franz   27, 32, 129
  pupils   185–6, 202
  Concert Studies, No. 4, 'La Leggierezza'
    185
  Frühlingsnacht (from Schumann)   189
  Hungarian Fantasy   66
  Soirées de Vienne, No. 6 (from Schubert)
    186
  Transcendental Studies, No. 3, *La
    campanella* (from Paganini)   34
Lloyd, Bill   243
London
  concerts   8,9,10
  National Gallery Concerts   9–10, 235–6
  orchestral standards   15–18, 63–71
  Promenade Concerts   15, 17, 66–8
London Classical Players   214
London Philharmonic Orchestra   40, 68,
    90, 145
  Alfred Einstein on   69
  Elgar on   90
  rehearsal and marking of parts   79–81
  portamento   98–9
  woodwind   94, 200
  recordings
    Berlioz, *Roman Carnival* (Beecham)
      69
    Delius, *Irmelin*, Prelude (Beecham)
      98–9
London Symphony Orchestra   15, 40
  Alfred Einstein on   69
  Elgar on   145
  recordings
    Berlioz, *Symphonie fantastique*
      (C. Davis)   93
    Elgar, Violin Concerto
      (Menuhin/Elgar)   146–8
    Haydn, Symphony No. 95 (Harty)
      69
    Mendelssohn, *Midsummer Night's
      Dream*, Scherzo (Beecham)   65,
      76
    Stravinsky, *Rite of Spring* (Bernstein)
      61
London Wind Players   91
Long, Kathleen   132, 190
Long, Marguerite   187
  on Debussy   164
  Ravel on   168–9

  relationship with Fauré   164, 166–8
  rubato   111
  recordings
    Beethoven, Piano Concerto No. 3 in
      C minor   111
    Chopin, Piano Concerto No. 2 in
      F minor   234
    Fauré, Impromptu No. 2 in F minor
      167
    Fauré, Nocturne No. 4 in E flat   168
    Ravel, Piano Concerto in G   169–70
Longy, Georges   75
Loriod, Yvonne
  recordings
    Messiaen, *Vingt regards sur l'enfant Jésus*
      178
Ludlow, John   222–3
Lupu, Radu   132
Lympany, Moura   187–8, 190
  on Mathilde Verne   187–8
  recordings
    Schumann, Piano Concerto   188

McCabe, John   179
McClure, John   61
McCormack, John
  recordings
    Schubert, 'Ave Maria'   109–10
Mackenzie, Alexander   16
Mackenzie, Compton   148
  on Dolmetsch family   205
Mackerras, Charles   214, 224
  on orchestral portamento   223
  recordings
    Elgar, 'Enigma' Variations   145
Mahler, Alma   154, 158
Mahler, Gustav
  as conductor   18, 20, 74, 82, 153–63
  Klemperer on   157
  metronome markings   154–5
  on Mengelberg   158, 162–3
  on Mottl   158
  on Nikisch   155–6
  on Weingartner   158
  piano rolls   141
    Mahler, Symphony No. 4, finale
      153, 163
    Mahler, Symphony No. 5, first
      movement   153

rehearsals 79, 82, 155, 156, 159, 162
relationship with Fried 154–6
relationship with Klemperer 156–7
relationship with Mengelberg 83,
 158–63
relationship with Walter 157–8, 163
Schoenberg on 82
Wellesz on 154
Das Lied von der Erde 35–6, 75, 158,
 160
Symphony No. 2 ('Resurrection') 28,
 74, 154–7
Symphony No. 3 156–7
Symphony No. 4 36, 153, 158, 160,
 162, 163
Symphony No. 5 153, 155–6, 158,
 Adagietto 38, 99, 160–2
Symphony No. 6 86, 162
Symphony No. 7 159
Symphony No. 8 ('Symphony of a
 Thousand') 157, 162–3
Symphony No. 9 35–6, 75, 158, 160
Maier, Franzjosef 213
Maine, Basil 146–7
Malcolm, George 216
Malsch, William 94
Mangeot, André 170–1
Manns, Augustus 8
 on Michael Costa 78
Marriner, Neville
 recordings
 Mozart, Piano Concerto in G, K453
 (Brendel) 233
Marwood, Anthony *see* Florestan Trio
Mascagni, Pietro 141
Massart, Joseph 193
Matthay, Tobias 190
Matthews, Denis 190
Megane, Leila 36
Meiningen Court Orchestra 8, 9, 19
Mendelssohn, Felix
 Midsummer Night's Dream, Scherzo 65,
 76, 77
 Violin Concerto 55
Mengelberg, Willem 20, 68, 90, 96
 Flesch on 83
 portamento 100–1, 160–2
 rehearsal 75, 79, 83, 159, 160–3
 relationship with Mahler 83, 158–63

Slowik on 160
Stravinsky on 83
recordings
 Mahler, Symphony No. 4 160, 163
 Mahler, Symphony No. 5, Adagietto
 38, 160–2
 Tchaikovsky, *Romeo and Juliet* 75
 Tchaikovsky, Symphony No. 5 75,
 100–1
 Wagner, *Flying Dutchman*, Overture
 76
Menuhin, Yehudi 125
recordings
 Elgar, Violin Concerto (Elgar) 29,
 36, 146–8, (Boult) 147
Mercury Records 44
messa di voce 224, 227
Messiaen, Olivier 141
 Peter Hill on 178
 Vingt regards sur l'enfant Jésus 178
Mewton–Wood, Noel 190
Meyerbeer, Giacomo
 L'Africaine 82
Michalowski, Alexander
 recordings
 Chopin, Polonaise No. 3 in A 186
 Chopin, Waltz in D flat, Opus 64
 No. 1 ('Minute') 186
Mikuli, Karol 186–7, 203
Milhaud, Darius 141
Milstein, Nathan 194
Moiseiwitsch, Benno
 rubato 131, 184
 recordings
 Rachmaninoff, Prelude in B minor,
 Opus 32 No. 10 184
 Weber, *Perpetuum Mobile* 185
Molique, Bernhard 195
Monteux, Pierre 72
 on Berlioz and Colonne 141–2
 on Boston SO 76
 recordings
 Berlioz, *Symphonie fantastique* 40,
 72–3, 92–3, 141–2
 Stravinsky, *Rite of Spring* 72, 151
Monteverdi, Claudio
 madrigals
 'Chiome d'oro' 211
 'Hor ch'el ciel e la terra' 211

'Lasciatemi morire'   211
operas   214
Montréal, Orchestre Symphonique de
     recordings
     Ravel, Piano Concerto in G
          (Thibaudet/Dutoit)   169
Moore, Jerrold Northrop   36, 42, 248
Mordkovitch, Elena and Lydia
     recordings
     Grieg, Sonata No. 3 in C minor for
          Violin and Piano   109
Morel, Mystil   210
Morris, Gareth   71
Morris, William   206
Morrow, Michael   204, 213, 214, 216–7,
     247
     on 'authenticity'   219, 224
Moscow State Orchestra
     recordings
     Stravinsky, *Rite of Spring* (Craft)   153
Moscow Symphony Orchestra
     recordings
     Stravinsky, *Petrushka* (Stravinsky)   153
Mottl, Felix   16
     Mahler on   158
Moyse, Marcel   93, 96, 152
     on Paul Taffanel   198–9
     on vibrato   198–9
     recordings   72
     Debussy, *Prélude à l'Après-midi d'un
          faune* (Straram)   199
     Ravel, Introduction and Allegro
          134, 172
Mozart, Wolfgang Amadeus
     'Exsultate, jubilate'   67
     Magic Flute, 'Zum Leiden'   112
     Marriage of Figaro   122
          Overture   73
          'Non so più'   112
          'Voi che sapete'   111–12
     operas   214
     Piano Concerto in G, K453   233–4
     Sinfonia Concertante for Violin and
          Viola   57
     String Quartet in G, K387   112–14
     String Quartet in D minor, K421   121
     String Quartet in F, K590   121–2
     Symphony No. 35 ('Haffner')   78
     Symphony No. 40   79–81

Symphony No. 41 ('Jupiter')   40
Mravinsky, Evgeny
     recordings
     Tchaikovsky, Symphony No. 5   96
Muck, Karl
     recordings
     Tchaikovsky, Symphony No. 4   76
     Wagner, *Lohengrin*, Act 3, Prelude   28
Munrow, David   204, 213, 249
Murchie, Robert   15
     recordings
     Ravel, Introduction and Allegro
          (Ravel)   134–5, 172
Musica Reservata   204, 213, 214, 216–17,
     247
music-making, amateur   4–8, 63, 206

National Gallery Concerts, London   9–10,
     235–6
NBC Symphony Orchestra   49, 77, 89, 90
     recordings
     Beethoven, Piano Concerto No. 3
          (Rubinstein/Toscanini)   111
     Beethoven, Symphony No. 3
          ('Eroica') (Toscanini)   78
     Haydn, Symphony No. 101 ('Clock')
          (Toscanini)   78
     Mendelssohn, *Midsummer Night's
          Dream*, Scherzo (Toscanini)   77
     Mozart, Symphony No. 35 ('Haffner')
          (Toscanini)   75
     Paganini, *Moto Perpetuo* (Toscanini)
          78
Neaman, Yfrah
     on Busch Quartet   237
     on Arnold Rosé   236–7
     on Max Rostal and Jacques Thibaud
          197
Neel, Boyd and Boyd Neel Orchestra
          69–70, 211
     recordings
     Britten, Variations on a Theme of
          Frank Bridge   70
     Elgar, Introduction and Allegro   70
     Vaughan Williams, Fantasia on a
          Theme by Thomas Tallis   70
Newman, Alfred   175
Newman, Ernest   147
     as pianist   131

New Queen's Hall Orchestra (early 20th century) *see* Queen's Hall Orchestra
New Queen's Hall Orchestra (founded 1992) 222–4
New Symphony Orchestra (= Royal Albert Hall Orchestra) 147
New York Philharmonic Orchestra (to 1928) 9
  recordings
    Mendelssohn, *Midsummer Night's Dream*, Scherzo (Toscanini) 76
    Wagner, *Flying Dutchman*, Overture (Mengelberg) 76
    see also New York, Philharmonic Symphony Orchestra of (from 1928)
New York, Philharmonic Symphony Orchestra of 21, 49, 68, 76–7, 84, 89, 102
  compared with Vienna PO 89
  visits London 77
  recordings
    Beethoven, Symphony No. 5 (Toscanini) 76
    Beethoven, Symphony No. 7 (Toscanini) 76
    Brahms, Variations on a Theme by Haydn (Toscanini) 76, 95
    Haydn, Symphony No. 101 ('Clock') (Toscanini) 68
    Mahler, Symphony No. 2 ('Resurrection') (Walter) 155
    Mendelssohn, *Midsummer Night's Dream*, Scherzo (Toscanini) 76–7
    Mozart, Symphony No. 35 ('Haffner') (Toscanini) 89
    Stravinsky, *Rite of Spring* (Stravinsky) 150
    Verdi, *Traviata*, Preludes (Toscanini) 89
New York Pro Musica 204, 213
  recordings
    Play of Daniel 214
New York Symphony Orchestra 9, 20, 68, 76
  recordings
    Brahms, Symphony No. 2 (Damrosch) 76

Ravel, *Mother Goose* (Damrosch) 76
New Zealand Symphony Orchestra
  recordings
    Delius, *Brigg Fair* (Fredman) 96
Nichols, Roger 125
Nikisch, Arthur 219
  Boult on 83
  Elgar on his 'Eroica' 67
  Flesch and Tchaikovsky on 20
  Mahler on 155–6
  rehearsal 79, 83
  recordings
    Beethoven, Symphony No. 5 28
Nimbus Records 44, 60, 45–6, 218
Noorman, Jantina 247
Norrington, Roger 160, 214, 221–2, 224
  and orchestral vibrato 221–2
  on 'authenticity' 219
  recordings
    Beethoven, Symphony No. 9 215
    Berlioz, *Symphonie fantastique* 220
    Brahms, Symphonies 219
Nye, Ruth 243

Oberlin, Russell 204
Obrecht, Jacob 210
Oiseau-Lyre, Editions de l' 205, 209–10
Oiseau-Lyre, Orchestre de l'
  recordings
    de Lalande, *Musique pour les soupers du Roi* (Desormière) 210
Oistrakh, David 201
orchestra
  and the rise of the conductor 20–1
  and recording techniques 44–5
  ensemble and standards 12–20, 48–9, 63–103
  in America 9, 19–20, 75–8
  in Britain 8, 13–18, 63–71
  in continental Europe 8, 18–19, 71–5
  in pre-electric recordings 21, 27–9
  impact of electrical recordings 34–5
  period-instrument 216–24
  see also brass, portamento, rehearsal, strings, woodwind
Orchestra of the Age of Enlightenment 227
Orchestre Révolutionnaire et Romantique
  recordings (Gardiner)

Beethoven,
    Symphonies   218–19
    Berlioz, *Symphonie fantastique*
        (Gardiner)   92–3
Ormandy, Eugene   101
Oubradous, Fernand
    recordings
        F. Couperin, *Concerts royaux*   210

Pachmann, Vladimir de   240
    rubato   128, 129, 131
Paderewski, Ignacy   27, 185, 209, 240
    Gaisberg on   240
    Kovacevich on   240–1
    rubato   128, 129, 131
    recordings
        Chopin, Mazurka in C sharp minor,
            Opus 63 No. 3   185
        Chopin, Nocturne in F, Opus 15
            No. 1   185
        Liszt, Concert Studies, No. 4
            ('La Leggierezza')   185
Paganini, Niccolò   193
    Moto Perpetuo   78
Paris, Orchestre de   93
Paris Conservatoire   198
Paris Conservatoire Orchestra
    horn vibrato   96
    recordings
        Berlioz, *Symphonie fantastique* (Walter)
            93
        Debussy, *Nocturnes*, 'Fêtes' (Gaubert)
            72
        Schumann, Symphony No. 3
            (Coppola)   90
Paris Symphony Orchestra   40
    Stravinsky on   72
    recordings
        Berlioz, *Symphonie fantastique*
            (Monteux)   72–3, 92–3
        Stravinsky, *Rite of Spring* (Monteux)
            72
Parrott, Andrew   214
Pass, Joe   249
Patti, Adelina
    rubato and portamento   111
    recordings
        Mozart, *Marriage of Figaro*,
            'Voi che sapete'   111–12

Pears, Peter
    on recording Schubert, *Schöne Müllerin*
        61
period instruments and performance
        204–30, 233–5
Perlman, Itzhak   125
Pfitzner, Hans
    recordings
        Beethoven, Symphony No. 3
            ('Eroica')   73
Philadelphia Orchestra   9, 21, 38, 40–1,
        77
    portamento   101–2
    rehearsal and discipline   84, 90
    woodwind   94–5, 200
    recordings
        Brahms, Symphony No. 2
            (Stokowski)   101–2
        Debussy, *Nocturnes*, 'Fêtes' (Stokowski)
            77
        Rachmaninofff, *Isle of the Dead*
            (Rachmaninoff)   77
        Rachmaninoff, Piano Concerto No. 2
            (Rachmaninoff/Stokowski)   38
        Rimsky-Korsakov, *Sheherazade*
            (Stokowski)   77
        Weber, *Invitation to the Dance*
            (Stokowski)   77
Philharmonia Orchestra   71
    recordings
        Beethoven, Symphony No. 9
            (Klemperer)   48
Philharmonic Society, London   8, 16, 64
Philip, Robert
    Early Recordings and Musical Style   97,
        198
Philipp, Isidor
    recordings
        Saint-Saëns, Sonata No. 1 in C minor
            for Cello and Piano   111
pianists
    rubato and 'ensemble'   128–32
    schools   183–91
piano rolls   30–34
    Ampico   31, 33–4
    Debussy's   164–5
    Duo-Art   31, 34
    Fauré's   164–5
    Leschetizky's   34, 185

Player Piano Group 32
  Rachmaninoff's 33
  Ravel's 164–5
  Welte-Mignon 31, 34
Piatigorsky, Gregor 197
  recordings
    piano trios with Heifetz and
      Rubinstein 126–7
Piatti, Alfredo 124, 195, 196
Pierné, Gabriel
  recordings
    Berlioz, *Romeo and Juliet* 72
    Berlioz, *Symphonie fantastique* 92,
      141–2
Pinnock, Trevor 214
Pitt, Percy 28
Pleeth, William 197
Pletnev, Mikhail 132
  recordings
    Tchaikovsky, Symphony No. 5 96
Pleyel harpsichords
  for Landowska 208, 209, 216
Ponsonby, Robert 84
Pople, Anthony 178
portamento
  chamber music 105, 109–10, 112–124
    Bohemian Quartet 118, 120
    Budapest Quartet 118, 121
    Busch Quartet 115–17
    Capet Quartet 114, 115–17
    Flonzaley Quartet 121
    Léner Quartet 112–114
    Rosé Quartet 114–17, 175
  in Elgar 145
  in Mahler 160–2
  orchestral 72, 97–103
    BBC SO 145
    Berlin PO 100, 101
    Boston SO 102
    Concertgebouw Orchestra 75,
      100–1, 160–2
    London PO 98–9, 145
    New Queen's Hall Orchestra
      222–3
    New York PSO 102
    Philadelphia Orchestra 101–2
    Royal Albert Hall Orchestra 97–8,
      101, 145
    Vienna PO 99–100, 160–2

cellists 195–6
  Casals 195–6
  Feuermann 196
  W. H. Squire 196
singers 109–12, 210
  Hempel 112
  McCormack 109–10
  Patti 111
violinists
  Joachim 123
  Kreisler 109–10
  Ysaÿe 111
Pougnet, Jean 57
Poulenc, Francis
  as pianist 132, 141
  on Viñes 166
Pressler, Menahem 127
Price, Walter 236
Prokofieff, Sergey 141
Promenade Concerts, London 15, 17,
  66–8
Pro Musica Antiqua of Brussels
  recordings
    Dufay, Obrecht, Brassart (Cape) 210
Prunières, Henry 168
Prussia Cove, International Chamber Music
    Seminars at 243
Puccini, Giacomo
  on standards in Italy 18
  on Toscanini 19
  Madam Butterfly 64
  Manon Lescaut 18
Pugno, Raoul 27
Puyana, Rafael 209

Quantz, Johann Joachim 229–30
Quatuor Mosaïques 128, 225, 226
Queen's Hall Orchestra 8, 15, 17, 18, 64,
  65, 94
  at Promenade Concerts 65–6
  Debussy on 65
  standards 65
  recordings
    Elgar, Violin Concerto
      (Sammons/Wood) 36–7, 65

Rachmaninoff, Sergey 23, 132, 141, 189
  attitude to recording 39, 43
  platform manner 22

Prelude in B minor,
    Opus 32 No. 10   184
rubato   33, 105, 131, 172–3, 182
tempi   173
recordings
  take numbers   39–41
  Chopin, Piano Sonata No. 2 in
    B flat minor   39, 41
  Grieg, Sonata No. 3 in C minor for
    Violin and Piano (Kreisler)   105,
    109
  Mendelssohn, *Song without Words*
    Opus 67, No. 4 ('Spinning
    Song')   39, 41
  Rachmaninoff, *Isle of the Dead*   41, 77
  Rachmaninoff, 'Lilacs'   33
  Rachmaninoff, Piano Concerto No. 2
    38, 39, 40, 172, 173
  Rachmaninoff, Prelude in C sharp
    minor, Opus 3 No. 2   41
  Rachmaninoff, Prelude in G minor,
    Opus 23 No. 5   173
  Rachmaninoff, Rhapsody on a Theme
    of Paganini   41, 172–3
  Schubert, Sonata in A for Violin and
    Piano (Kreisler)   105, 109
RAF Orchestra   71
Rameau, Jean Philippe   205, 208
Randegger, Alberto   17
Rattle, Simon   86, 227
  recordings
    Elgar, 'Enigma' Variations   144–5
    Mahler, Symphony No. 2
    ('Resurrection')   155
Ravel, Maurice
  as conductor   164
  as pianist   164
  metronome markings   169, 170
  on Cortot–Thibaud–Casals Trio   170
  on interpretation   169
  on Marguerite Long   168–9
  on Ricardo Viñes   165
  Boléro   165
  Concerto for Piano, Left Hand   170
  Daphnis and Chloé   15
  Gaspard de la nuit   165, 170
  Jeux d'eau   165, 170
  Menuet antique   165
  Miroirs   165, 'Oiseaux tristes' 165

Mother Goose   76
Piano Concerto in G   168–70
Piano Trio   164
Shéhérazade   170
String Quartet   170–2
Tombeau de Couperin   168–9
piano rolls   141, 164–5
  Sonatine   165
recordings
  Boléro   165–6
  Introduction and Allegro   37, 134,
    172
recording
  cutting works for   27, 29–30
  'direct cut'   45, 46
  editing   42–9, 53–62, 218, 246
  electrical   34–42
  experience of   26–62
  influence on audiences   4, 245–50
  influence on musicians   4, 24–5, 26–62,
    201–2, 234–5, 239–43, 244–7,
    250–2
  LP and CD   42–62
  microphones and recording techniques
    44–5, 51
  pre-electric (acoustic)   26–30
  producers   49–61
  side lengths of 78 rpm   34–8
  studio and live recording   47–9, 54, 55
  take numbers of 78 rpm   38–42
  unavailability before 20th century   4–25
Reed, W. H.   36
rehearsal
  and ensemble in chamber groups
    104–28, 133–9
  conductors' methods   78–86
  Joachim   21
  Kreisler   22
  orchestras
    deputy system   15, 64, 68, 71–2, 74
    England   13–18, 63–103
    Italy   18–19
    Lamoureux   18
    Meiningen   19
    Vienna   18, 74
Richter, Hans   8, 10, 20, 149
  Brahms on   82
  Dvořák on   82
  Elgar on   67

rehearsal and discipline 80–2
  Weingartner on 82
Ries, Louis 124
Rimsky-Korsakov, Nikolay
  Sheherazade 77
Roberts, Bernard 46
Roisman, Josef *see* Budapest Quartet
Ronald, Landon 28
  on Toscanini's Elgar 149
  recordings
    Brahms, Symphony No. 2 101
    Grieg, Piano Concerto (de Greef) 97
    Mendelssohn, *Midsummer Night's
      Dream*, Scherzo 65, 76
    Mozart, *Marriage of Figaro*,
      'Voi che sapete' (Patti) 111–12
Röntgen, Engelbert 5
Rooley, Anthony 213
Rosé, Arnold 23, 192
  leader of Vienna PO and Court Opera
      Orchestra 74–5, 161, 226
  vibrato 74, 236–7
Rosé Quartet
  in London 236–7, 238
  Neaman on 236–7
  portamento 114–17, 175
  relationship with Brahms 236
  relationship with Schoenberg 175
  recordings
    Beethoven, String Quartet in C
      minor, Opus 18 No. 4 239
    Beethoven, String Quartet in E flat,
      Opus 94 ('Harp') 239
    Beethoven, String Quartet in C sharp
      minor, Opus 131 115–17
Rosenthal, Moriz 185, 186, 237–9,
      247–8
  Fantasia on Viennese Waltzes 237
  Hanslick on 186
  reviews in 1930s 237–8
  rubato 128, 131, 186, 234
  recordings
    Chopin, Berceuse 186
    Chopin, Nocturne in E flat, Opus 9
      No. 2 186
    Chopin, Piano Concerto No. 1 in
      E minor 238
    Liszt, *Soirées de Vienne*, No. 6 186
Rostal, Max 197

Rostropovich, Mstislav 201
Roy, René le 200
Royal Academy of Music 70–1
Royal Albert Hall Orchestra
  Elgar on 90
  portamento 97–9, 101, 103
  recordings
    Brahms, Symphony No. 2 (Ronald)
      101
    Elgar, Cello Concerto
      (Harrison/Elgar) 147
    Elgar, *Cockaigne* (Elgar) 65, 90
    Elgar, 'Enigma' Variations (Elgar) 65,
      98, 142–5, 223
    Grieg, Piano Concerto
      (de Greef/Ronald) 97–8
    Mendelssohn, *Midsummer Night's Dream*,
      Scherzo (Ronald) 65, 76
    Stravinsky, *Petrushka* (Goossens) 29
Royal College of Music 70–1, 206
Royal Opera House, Covent Garden
      15,16, 17, 64, 249
Royal Philharmonic Orchestra (early 20th
      century)
  recordings
    Beethoven, Symphony No. 5
      (Weingartner) 65
    Tchaikovsky, Symphony No. 6
      (Pathétique) (Fried) 65
Royal Philharmonic Orchestra (founded
      1946) 71, 223
  marking of parts 79–91
  recordings
    Delius, *Irmelin*, Prelude (Beecham)
      98–9
Rozhdestvensky, Gennadi 84
rubato *see* tempo rubato
Rubinstein, Anton 129
  Josef Hofmann on 188
  pupils and influence 188–9, 202
Rubinstein, Arthur 191
  changing style 132
  rubato 111
  recordings
    Beethoven, Piano Concerto No. 3 in
      C minor 111
    Chopin, Barcarolle 132
    Chopin, Piano Concerto No. 2 in
      F minor 132

Chopin, Scherzo No. 3 in
C sharp minor   132
piano trios with Heifetz and
Feuermann   126
piano trios with Heifetz and
Piatigorsky   126–7
Rumchiysky, Simon   190
Rupp, Franz
on Kreisler   22
recordings
Beethoven, Sonata in G, Opus 96, for
Violin and Piano (Kreisler)   105
Russian National Orchestra
recordings
Tchaikovsky, Symphony No. 5
(Pletnev)   96
Russian Philharmonic Orchestra
recordings
Tchaikovsky, Symphony No. 5
(Friedmann)   96

Sachs, Curt
L'Anthologie sonore   205, 210
as conductor   210, 211
Two Thousand Years of Music   205
St George's Singers
recordings
madrigals (Fellowes)   210
St Petersburg Philharmonic Orchestra
see Leningrad PO
Saint-Saëns, Camille   141
on pianists' rubato   128
Rouet d'Omphale   83
Sonata No. 1 in C minor for Cello and
Piano   111
Salzburg Camerata   221
Samaroff, Olga   241
Sammons, Albert   65, 146, 194–5
recordings
Elgar, Violin Concerto   13, 36–7,
146
Sarasate, Pablo   23
Sauer, Emil von   185
recordings
Liszt, Piano Concerto No. 1   186
Scala, La (Milan)
Tours with Toscanini   21
Verdi's *Falstaff* at   16–17
recordings of orchestra

Donizetti, *Don Pasquale*, Overture
(Toscanini)   29
Scarlatti, Domenico
Sonatas   208, 209
Sonata in G, Kk 14   241
Sonata in B minor, Kk 87   189
Sonata in G, Kk 427   173
Scharrer, Irene   190
Schiff, András   125, 132, 174, 227
Schnabel, Artur   31, 111, 132, 137, 241
Arrau on   240
Beethoven Piano Sonatas, edition   137
Curzon on   184
on amateurs and professionals   5
on audiences   5
on deputy system   64
tempi   184
recordings
Beethoven, Piano Concerto No. 3 in
C minor   111
Beethoven, Piano Sonatas   137–8,
184
Beethoven, Piano Sonata in E flat,
Opus 7   40
Beethoven, Piano Sonata in B flat,
Opus 106 ('Hammerklavier')
40, 43, 184
Schneiderhan, Wolfgang   194
Schoenberg, Arnold
on Hollywood, Kolisch and Rosé
Quartets   175
on Mahler's rehearsals   82
on performance   175–7, 244
Five Pieces for Orchestra   245
String Quartets   175
Verklärte Nacht   175
recordings
Pierrot Lunaire   175
Schola Cantorum Basiliensis   204, 213
Scholes, Percy
On Bartók   174
Columbia History of Music   204
Schubert, Franz
'Ave Maria'   109
Piano Trio No. 1 in B flat, D898   40,
126
Piano Trio No. 2 in E flat, D929
53–4,126
Piano Sonatas   57

String Quartet in G, D887 122
String Quintet in C, D956 226
Schöne Müllerin 61
Winterreise, 'Der Leiermann' 138
Schumann, Clara 129
pupils 187–8, 202, 248
Schumann, Elisabeth
recordings
Mozart, 'Exsultate, jubilate' 67
Wagner, *Die Meistersinger*, Quintet 122
Schumann, Robert 7
Arabesque 189
Carnaval 40
Fantasie in C 237–8
Frauenliebe und -leben 131
Frühlingsnacht, arr. Liszt 189
Kinderszenen 188
Piano Concerto 40, 132, 187–8
Piano Trio No. 1 in D minor 53
Symphony No. 3 90
Symphony No. 4 158
Schwarzkopf, Elisabeth 50
Ševčík, Otakar
pupils 194
Shaw, George Bernard 207
on Dolmetsch's clavichord 206
Sheffield Festival 8
Shore, Bernard 67
Shostakovich, Dimitri 141
Shumsky, Oscar 46
Sibelius, Jan
Symphony No. 7 69
Slowik, Kenneth
recordings
Mahler, Symphony No. 5, Adagietto
160–1
Small, Christopher 229
Smetana, Bedřich
Ma Vlást 86
String Quartet No. 1 in E minor 118
Smithsonian Chamber Players
recordings
Mahler, Symphony No. 5, Adagietto
(Slowik) 160–1
Smyth, Ethel
on music–making in Leipzig 5–6, 8,
245
on maintaining tempo 11
Mass in D 11

Soldat-Roeger, Maria 192
Solomon 188, 190
on Mathilde Verne 188, 190
Solti, Georg
recordings 226
Mahler, Symphony No. 5, Adagietto
38
Wagner *Ring des Nibelungen* 43
Southampton
musical life in 13–14
Soyer, David 196
Squire, William H
recordings
Elgar, Cello Concerto 196
Standage, Simon 214
standards of performance
chamber ensembles 104–128,
133–139
effect of recording on 25, 42–62
orchestras 63–103
period instruments 216–19
pianists 128–132
woodwind 91–2
see also rehearsal
Stern, Isaac
recordings
Schubert, String Quintet in C, D956
125
Still, Ray 201
Stockhausen, Karlheinz 180
Stokowski, Leopold 21, 213
rehearsal and discipline 84, 90
recordings
Brahms, Symphony No. 2 101–2
Debussy, *Nocturnes*, 'Fêtes' 77
Rachmaninoff, Piano Concerto No. 2
(Rachmaninoff) 38
Rimsky-Korsakov, *Sheherazade* 77
Weber, *Invitation to the Dance* 77
Stott, Kathryn
recordings
Fauré, Impromptu No. 2 in F minor
167
Fauré, Nocturne No. 4 in E flat 168
Straram Orchestra 151
recordings
Debussy, *Prélude à l'Après-midi d'un
faune* (Straram) 199
Stravinsky, *Firebird* (Stravinsky) 150

Stravinsky, *Rite of Spring* (Stravinsky)
40, 72, 150
Straus, Volker   127
Strauss, Johann II
Blue Danube, arr. Schulz-Evler   33
Strauss, Richard
conducts *Don Quixote*   64
conducts Suite, Opus 4 with Meiningen
Orchestra   19
Ein Heldenleben   83
Oboe Concerto   88
on Joachim Quartet   123
recordings
Beethoven, Symphony No. 5   73
Strauss, *Don Juan*   73
Stravinsky, Igor   7, 141
Autobiography   150–1, 152
Baiser de la fée   71
Firebird   245
on deputy system in Paris   71–2
on his recordings   150–1, 152
on interpreters and performance   149,
152
on orchestras   153
on popularity of his works   245
Petrushka   28–9, 40, 245
Rite of Spring   72, 76, 245
works for pianola   30
recordings
Firebird   150
Jeu de Cartes   91, 152
Petrushka   40, 150, 153
Rite of Spring   40, 72, 150, 151
Soldier's Tale   93, 135, 150, 152
Symphony of Psalms   151–2
Streep, Meryl   54, 55, 59
string-playing, schools of
violin   191–5
cello   195–9
string quartets   112–124
Stroh violin   27–8
Stutschewsky, Joachim   195
Suggia, Guilhermina   197
Suisse Romande Orchestra   43, 93
Sullivan, Arthur   17
Supervia, Conchita
recordings
Mozart, *Marriage of Figaro*,
'Non so più'   112

Szell, George
on recordings   60
rehearsals   79, 84
Kovacevich on   241
recordings
Beethoven, *King Stephen* Overture
60
Brahms, Variations on a Theme by
Haydn   95
Dvořák, Cello Concerto (Casals)   40
Szeryng, Henryk   125
Szigeti, Joseph
on Auer's bow-hold   194
on Bartók's timings   174

Tabuteau, Marcel   95, 200
Taffanel, Paul
and the French flute school   94, 134,
172, 198–201
conducts *Meistersinger*   18
Fleury on   198
Méthode complète de flûte (with Gaubert)
198, 199
Moyse on   198–9
on vibrato   198
Tak, Max   159
Takács Quartet   128
Talich, Václav
Boult on   86
recordings
Dvořák, Symphony No. 8   40
Smetana, *Ma Vlást*   86
Tan, Melvyn
recordings
Beethoven, Piano Sonatas   234
Taruskin, Richard
on Mahler (Slowik, Walter, Mengelberg)
160
on Norrington's Beethoven   215
'The modern sound of early music'   219
Tausig, Carl   186
Taverner Choir and Consort   214
Tchaikovsky, Peter Ilyich
Eugene Onegin   153
Piano Concerto No. 1   189
Romeo and Juliet   75
Symphony No. 5   75, 96, 100–1
Symphony No. 6 ('Pathétique')   16, 65,
77, 96

tempo
  and the 78 rpm side limit   35–8
  Bartók   73–4
  Elgar   142–9
  Fauré   167–8
  flexible   11–12, 73, 105–8, 118–21
  Mahler   154
  Ravel   169–71
  Stravinsky   150
tempo rubato   11–12, 228
  Bazelaire and Philipp   111
  Bartók   173–4
  Bohemian Quartet   118
  Debussy   165
  Dolmetsch on   208
  Elgar   144
  Fauré   165
  Flonzaley Quartet   121
  in ensemble   110–12
  jazz   180
  Joachim   123
  Koczalski   129–30
  pianists   128–132, 184–191, 202
  piano rolls   32
  Rachmaninoff   105, 109, 172–3
  Rosenthal   238
  singers   111–12, 138
  V. G. Woodhouse   208
  Viñes   166
  Ysaÿe   110–11
tenuti
  Bohemian Quartet   118
  Flonzaley Quartet   121
  Joachim   123
  Rachmaninoff   105, 109, 172–3
  Tovey   105–8
Terry, Richard   204
Thibaud, Jacques
  Neaman on   197
  recordings
    Fauré, Sonata No. 1 in A for Violin
      and Piano (Cortot)   168
  see also Cortot–Thibaud–Casals Trio
Thibaudet, Jean-Yves
  recordings
    Ravel, Piano Concerto in G   169
Tippett, Michael   141
Tomes, Susan   50–4
  see also   Domus, Florestan Trio

Tomlinson, Ernest   236
Toscanini, Arturo   20, 21, 35, 49, 149,
      154, 241–2, 249
  disagreement with Ravel   165
  ensemble and discipline   87, 89, 90
  Kovachevich on   241
  on *Götterdämmerung* at Covent Garden
      16
  on Nikisch   28
  Puccini on   19
  rehearsals   79, 84
  Vaughan Williams on   68
  recordings
    Beethoven, Piano Concerto No. 3
      (Rubinstein)   111
    Beethoven, Symphony No. 3
      ('Eroica')   78
    Beethoven, Symphony No. 5   77
    Beethoven, Symphony No. 6   40
    Beethoven, Symphony No. 7   76
    Brahms, Variations on a Theme by
      Haydn   76, 95
    Donizetti, *Don Pasquale*, Overture
      29
    Elgar, 'Enigma' Variations   149
    Haydn, Symphony No. 101 ('Clock')
      78
    Mendelssohn, *Midsummer Night's
      Dream*, Scherzo   76
    Mozart, Symphony No. 35 ('Haffner')
      78, 89
    Paganini, *Moto Perpetuo*   78
    pre-electric   29
    Tchaikovsky, Piano Concerto No. 1
      (Horowitz)   189
Tovey, Donald
  recordings
    Beethoven, Sonata in G, Opus 96, for
      Violin and Piano (Fachiri)
105–8
Trenet, Charles   211
trumpet
  the modern 'Baroque'   217
Tureck, Rosalyn   216
Turner, W. J.   70–1

Uchida, Mitsuko   132

Vaughan Williams, Ralph   141

Fantasia on a Theme by Thomas Tallis
    70
  on The Proms   67–8
  Symphony No. 2 ('London')   17
Végh, Sandor   221
  teaching   243–4
  Végh Quartet   127
Verdi, Giuseppe
  Aida   64, 157
  Falstaff   16
  Otello   249
Verne, Adela   235–6
Verne, Mathilde   187–8
vibrato
  brass   95–6, 153
  Schoenberg on   176
  singers   138, 152, 210
  strings   74–5, 117–22, 133–4, 138, 146,
      153, 171, 175–6, 191–7, 221–2,
      225–6
  woodwind   93–5, 96–7, 134–5, 152,
      153, 172
Vienna   5, 10
Vienna Court Opera (Hofoper)
  Mahler at   18, 74, 157, 161
  Richter at   82
  Walter at   157
  shortage of rehearsal   18
Vienna Philharmonic Orchestra   8, 23, 24,
      40, 49, 74–5, 90
  compared with Chicago SO   226
  compared with New York PSO   89
  ensemble   75
  portamento   99–100, 160–2
  vibrato   94, 201, 221
  recordings
    Brahms, Symphony No. 3 (Krauss,
        Walter)   99–100
    Mahler, *Das Lied von der Erde* (Walter)
        35–6, 75, 158, 160
    Mahler, Symphony No. 2
        ('Resurrection') (Walter)
        154–5
    Mahler, Symphony No. 4 (Walter)
        163
    Mahler, Symphony No. 5, Adagietto
        (Walter)   99, 160–2
    Mahler, Symphony No. 9 (Walter)
        35–6, 75, 158, 160

Mozart, *Marriage of Figaro*, Overture
    (Krauss)   73
Wagner, *Ring des Nibelungen* (Solti)
    43
Vienna Sextet   225, 226
Vieuxtemps, Henri
  Rondino for Violin and Piano, Opus 32
      No. 2   110
  vibrato   193
Villa-Lobos, Heitor   141
Viñes, Ricardo
  disagrees with Ravel about tempo   165
  Poulenc on   166
  works dedicated to 165
  works premiered by   165
  recordings
    Debussy, *Estampes*, 'Soirée dans
        Grenade'   166
    Debussy, *Images*, 'Poissons d'or'   166
Vuillermoz, Emile   164

Wagner, Richard
  Flying Dutchman, Overture   76
  Lohengrin, Preludes   14, 28
  Meistersinger   18, 74, 82, 122, Overture
      69, 'Prize Song' 110–1
  Parsifal   191
  Tannhäuser, Venusberg Music   17
Walter, Bruno
  relationship with Mahler   154, 157–8,
      163
  recordings   49, 90, 160
    Brahms, Symphony No. 3   99–100
    Mahler, *Das Lied von der Erde*   35–6,
        75, 158, 160
    Mahler, Symphony No. 2
        ('Resurrection')   154–5
    Mahler, Symphony No. 4   36, 163
    Mahler, Symphony No. 5, Adagietto
        38, 99, 160–2
    Mahler, Symphony No. 9   35–6, 75,
        158, 160
    Mozart, Symphony No. 41   40
    (as pianist) Schumann, *Frauenliebe und
        -leben* (Ferrier)   131
Wand, Günter   84–5
Weber, Carl Maria von
  Invitation to the Dance   77
  Perpetuum mobile   185

Webern, Anton
  Six Pieces for Orchestra 145
Weingartner, Felix
  Mahler on 158
  on Bülow and Meiningen Orchestra 19
  recordings 234
    Beethoven, Symphony No. 5 65
Wellesz, Egon 154
Wenzinger, August 204, 213
Weschler–Vered, Artur 126
Wetherell, Eric 36–7
Wieniawski, Henryk
  vibrato 193
Wilde, David 32
Wilson, Steuart 210
Wodehouse, P. G. 24–5
Wood, Henry 10–11, 16, 213, 222
  bans deputising 15, 65
  Barbirolli on 66
  compared with Lamoureux 89
  Elgar on 67
  Grainger on 66
  marking of parts 78
  orchestral discipline 17–18, 20, 65,
    66–8
  Promenade Concerts 66–8
  recordings
    Elgar, Violin Concerto (Sammons)
      36–7, 65
    Vaughan Williams, Symphony No. 2
      ('London') 17

Woodhouse, George 134
Woodhouse, Violet Gordon 204,
    207–8
  rubato 208, 278
  recordings
    J. S. Bach, Italian Concerto 208,
      228, 234
woodwind 91–5, 198–201
  American 94–5, 200
  British 93–4, 134–5, 201
  Czech 201
  French 72, 91–3, 134–5, 198–201
  in Berlin and Vienna 94, 201
  period instruments 216
Woolrich, John
  Ulysses Awakes 178

Yeats, W. B. 206
Ysaÿe, Eugène 23, 125, 146
  and the 'Franco–Belgian' school 191–5,
    202
  bowing 193
  Flesch on 193
  rubato 110–11
  portamento 111
  vibrato 193
  Wood on 111
  Ysaÿe Quartet 124

Zimbalist, Efrem 23, 194
Zukerman, Pinchas 125